Mark Herkenrath (Ed. for the World Society Foundation)

The Regional and Local Shaping of World Society

World Society Studies

A series edited by

the World Society Foundation,
Zurich

www.worldsociety.ch

Volume 2007/II

LIT

Mark Herkenrath
(Ed. for the World Society Foundation)

The Regional and Local Shaping of World Society

LIT

Umschlag: zwoelf Karlsruhe

Bibliographic information published by the Deutsche Nationalbibliothek
The Deutsche Nationalbibliothek lists this publication in the Deutsche
Nationalbibliografie; detailed bibliographic data are available in the Internet at
http://dnb.d-nb.de.

ISBN 978-3-03735-166-6 (Schweiz)
ISBN 978-3-8258-0534-0 (Deutschland)

A catalogue record for this book is available from the British Library

© LIT VERLAG GmbH & Co. KG Wien,
Zweigniederlassung Zürich 2007
Dufourstr. 31
CH-8008 Zürich
Tel. +41 (0) 44-251 75 05
Fax +41 (0) 44-251 75 06
e-Mail: zuerich@lit-verlag.ch
http://www.lit-verlag.ch

LIT VERLAG Dr. W. Hopf
Berlin 2007
Auslieferung/Verlagskontakt:
Fresnostr. 2
D-48159 Münster
Tel. +49 (0)251–62 03 20
Fax +49 (0)251–23 19 72
e-Mail: lit@lit-verlag.de
http://www.lit-verlag.de

Distributed in the UK by: Global Book Marketing, 99B Wallis Rd, London, E9 5LN
Phone: +44 (0) 20 8533 5800 – Fax: +44 (0) 1600 775 663
http://www.centralbooks.co.uk/acatalog/search.html

Distributed in North America by:

Transaction Publishers
New Brunswick (U.S.A.) and London (U.K.)

Transaction Publishers
Rutgers University
35 Berrue Circle
Piscataway, NJ 08854

Phone: +1 (732) 445 - 2280
Fax: + 1 (732) 445 - 3138
for orders (U. S. only):
toll free (888) 999 - 6778
e-mail:
orders@transactionspub.com

Contents

The Regional and Local Shaping of World Society: An Introduction 1
Mark Herkenrath

How 'Global' is Economic Globalization? 17
Rafael Reuveny and William R. Thompson

Globalization, Regionalism, and the Organization of Transnational Collective Action within World Regions, 1980-2000 47
Dawn Wiest and Jackie Smith

Economic Glocalizing, Regional Embedding, and State Scaling 79
A Comparative Analysis of the Pearl River Delta and the Yangtze River Delta in China
Xiangming Chen

East Asia: Structure and Formation of a World Region 111
Patrick Ziltener

Islam in the World System 151
Amir Sheikhzadegan

Northeast Asian Competition for Russian Far East Natural Resources 177
Possibilities of Russo-Chinese Geo-economic Integration
John Gulick

The Chad-Cameroon Pipeline Project and the Making of World Society in Central Africa 205
Yves Alexandre Chouala

The Resilience of Cultural Diversity 235
Reinventing Local Identity in Ireland as the "Gesamt" Creation of Enterprise, State and Civil Society
Martha C.E. Van Der Bly

Contributors 269

Acknowledgements
Three contributions to this volume (Herkenrath; Reuveny and Thompson; Wiest and Smith) were published, with different titles, in the April 2007 issue of the International Journal of Comparative Sociology (a special issue on "The Local and Regional Dynamics of Global Social Change", edited by Mark Herkenrath). The editor and the publisher would like to thank Sage Inc., London, and Jeffrey Kentor (Editor) for their permission to include these articles in the present volume.

Mark Herkenrath wishes to thank all the contributors to this volume for what has been a wonderful and inspiring cooperation.

The Regional and Local Shaping of World Society
An Introduction

Mark Herkenrath

The "end of geography" and the "tyranny of territoriality"

Over the past two and a half decades, advances in communication technologies and the ever lower costs of international transport have brought about dramatic social changes worldwide. Most notably, there has been an enormous increase in the volume and speed of transnational flows of goods, information, and to a lesser extent, people. According to Giddens, a consequence of this increase has been the growing importance of "action at a distance" (Giddens 1990). People all over the world are increasingly enmeshed in far-reaching networks of transnational social ties and affected by decisions made in places which are geographically ever more remote. Observers thus describe this process as the continuing compression of time and space (Harvey 1989; Mittelman 1996, 1999), the decoupling of social and spatial distance, and even the "end of geography" (cf. Hettne 1999a: xx; MacLeod 2001: 804).

As The New York Times columnist Thomas Friedman puts it (in an interview with Daniel H. Pink, Wired Magazine, May 2005, www.wired.com/wired/archive/13.05/friedman.html),

> "... the world is becoming flat. Several technological and political forces have converged, and that has produced a global, Web-enabled playing field that allows for multiple forms of collaboration without regard to geography or distance–or soon, even language. ... This is Globalization 3.0. In Globalization 1.0, which began around 1492, the world went from size large to size medium. In Globalization 2.0, the era that introduced us to multinational companies, it went from size medium to size small. And then around 2000 came Globalization 3.0, in which the world went from being small to tiny. There's a difference between being able to make long distance phone calls cheaper on the Internet and walking around Riyadh with a PDA where you can have all of Google in your pocket. It's a difference in degree that's so enormous it becomes a difference in kind."

What catchphrases such as the "end of geography" and the "flattening of the word" fail to reflect, however, is that technological progress is always embedded in pre-existing social relations characterized by disparities in power and income. While new technologies promote global social change, the production and distribution of these technologies are shaped by economic demand and, hence, the unequal distribution of global income. Global income inequality, in turn, has been on the rise over the past decades (World Bank 2000: 3). As a consequence, the extent to which technological advances have contributed to the shrinking of perceived distances between geographic places shows substantial regional variation. Although there exists a dense network of long-distance communications and transport media connecting ever more remote places, current discussions of the "digital divide" and related issues make it clear that in several macroregions the degree of transnational connectedness is low and that many places in the hinterlands of these regions remain difficult to reach. Notions of a "small world" (cf. Urry 2004) becoming increasingly smaller and of the people of this world growing ever more interconnected may be valid with regard to the industrialized nations of the global North; they do not hold to the same degree for the people of the global South. To the extent that access to new technologies is structured by old inequalities, these technologies contribute not only to global social change but also to the reproduction of pre-existing, spatially structured income and power disparities.

Notions about the world growing smaller and geography becoming irrelevant, then, tend to overlook the fact that access to "global" communications and transport is the almost exclusive domain of the global North and small elites in the global South. A short look at the absolute and relative costs of a round-trip flight ticket between Lagos (Nigeria) and London (UK) may help to illustrate this. Tellingly, real prices for passenger flights from Lagos to London are already higher than real prices for the same flight in the opposite direction, from London to Lagos. A round trip from Lagos to London costs approximately 960 US$ (www.britishairways.com; quote from October 12, 2006, for November 9-20, 2006), whereas a round trip from London to Lagos costs only 870 US$ (ibid.), almost 100 US$ less. Yet the true difference lies not in absolute prices, but in the relative prices of long-distance traveling as measured in terms of average income and purchasing power. In Nigeria, the price of a round trip from Lagos to London amounts to 170% of the annual (!) per capita income, which according to the World Bank's World Development Indicators for the year 2005 was as low as 560 US$ (web.worldbank.org). In the United Kingdom, the price for a round-trip flight from London to Lagos amounts to a mere 2% of the annual per capita income. Hence, in the subjective perspective of an English traveler, the distance to Lagos is far "shorter" than the same distance is in the perspective of a Nigerian (potential) traveler. For the inhabitants of the global North, the "end of geography" may indeed be coming closer; in Nigeria and other countries in the global South, home to more than 80% of the world's population (United Nations Development Programme: URL), most citizens are still plagued by what could be called the "tyranny of territoriality." To conceive of globalization as a process of time-space compression does not do sufficient justice to the complexity of the issue. What has happened, instead, is a partial de-configuration and complex re-configuration of the territorial aspects of social life. Among other changes, to the extent that real access to global communications and transport systems is dependent on one's socio-economic position in an increasingly unequal world society, the subjective importance of spatial relations has become more divergent.

In view of the phenomena outlined above, the articles in this volume examine the territorial aspects of contemporary globalization processes and, in particular, the dialectical relation between globalization, localization, and regionalization. The authors investigate the extent to which the various dimensions of globalization are spatially structured and how different local configurations of global processes bring about different outcomes. It is probably no exaggeration to claim that the contributions to this volume should be seen as the precursors of a fourth wave of globalization studies, which will focus on the spatial, and in particular the regional, dynamics of global social change. As Bruff (2005) notes, a first wave of globalization studies emphasized the economic aspects of contemporary globalization processes, whereas a second wave of studies explored political aspects and the issue of global governance. In a third wave of studies, the principal focus lay on cultural aspects and particularly on the diverse subjective interpretations and perceptions of globalization at the local level. The present contributions to what is emerging as a fourth wave of globalization studies build on the insights of the previous waves, insofar as they conceive of globalization as a multidimensional (economic, political and cultural) process involving both "objective" structural changes and locally variable "subjective" perceptions. In addition to this, the present studies emphasize the important role played by spatial relations and socially constructed boundaries, with which the processes of global social change are bound to interact.

The spatial structure of trade and investment globalization

Ironically, the "end of geography" thesis is problematic not only with regard to the obvious spatial structure of transnational communications systems and long-distance passenger transport, but also with regard to international trade and foreign direct investment (FDI) flows. Although trade and FDI tend to be seen as the most dynamic elements, perhaps the driving forces, of economic globalization, they are not as "global" as the term globalization suggests. FDI flows, for instance, occur primarily between the Triad of the European Union, the United States of America, and Japan. Over the past two decades, 75-85% of total world FDI flows originated in this Triad, which also accounted for 60-70% of total world FDI inflows. In 2005, the EU alone accounted for almost half of global inward and outward flows (UNCTAD 2006: 6, Table I.1, and Annex table B.1). China received 7.9% of total world FDI inflows, but only 1.5% of total world FDI outflows originated in this country (UNCTAD 2006: Annex table B.1, own calculations). In investment globalization, it seems, geography matters. (For data on the notable concentration of trade on the Triad and China, see World Trade Organization: URL).

Given the high concentration of global FDI flows within the Triad, it is no surprise that developing countries play only a minor role in the allocation of these FDI flows. Although their share has been on the rise over the past decades, starting from an average of 20% in 1978-80, developing countries still received only 36% of total world FDI inflows in 2005 (UNCTAD 2006: 3). Moreover, the performance of different countries and regional groups was notably uneven, as Brazil, China, Hong Kong, Mexico and Singapore–which had been the five largest host developing economies for several years before–accounted for 48% of total flows to developing countries (UNCTAD 2006: 5). The share of African countries fell, in turn, "from 10% of total inflows to developing countries in 1978-1980 to around 5% in 1998-2000" (UNCTAD 2006: 6)–even though in the past few years FDI flows to Africa seem to have grown again. As the United Nations Conference on Trade and Development puts it in its World Investment Report 2006, Africa "continues to exhibit weaknesses that constrain its ability to attract quality FDI of the kind that would generate broader beneficial effects in its economies" (UNCTAD 2006: 40).

In view of these figures, macroregions such as Sub-Saharan Africa are often seen as marginalized from economic globalization. However, the notion of these regions being excluded from economic globalization is both partly valid and partly invalid, depending on whether one views the issue from outside these countries or from within these countries. From the outsider perspective taken by, say, investors in the global North, FDI flows to Sub-Saharan Africa and other poor regions are almost negligible. But, from the perspective of the recipient countries themselves when seen in relation to the comparatively small size of these countries' formal economies, their FDI inflows and inward stocks turn out to be decisively influential. In Nigeria, for instance, the ratio of the country's FDI inward stock in 2005 to its GDP amounted to a noteworthy 35% (Chad: 71%; Cambodia: 45%), whereas the same ratio was only 13% in the U.S. and 2% in Japan (UNCTAD 2006: Annex table B3). Depending on the point of view, then, Nigeria and other developing countries can be seen as more strongly "globalized" than the U.S. and other high-income countries, since the relative importance of foreign-owned firms within these countries' internal markets is more pronounced. The main difference between the two groups is that in the case of developing countries, integration into the world economy has been more passive than in the case of high-income countries, as the latter are not only penetrated by FDI inward flows (and stocks) but simultaneously serve as home countries for companies investing abroad.

In summary, it is important to note that the processes of economic, political and cultural globalization take different forms in different areas. The various manifestations of contemporary globalization are less "global" and less homogeneous than is often assumed, but vary across regions in both intensity and character. Global forces encounter and interact with pre-existing local conditions, thus producing different reactions and consequences in different places. FDI flows, to use the same example once again, contribute positively to economic growth when foreign investors have to submit to certain regulations and legal standards (for a discussion of growth and development-oriented FDI policies such as local-content clauses and export requirements, see Herkenrath 2003; cf. also Herkenrath and Bornschier 2003) but reduce growth when such regulations are absent. In other words, when interacting with local and regional contexts, global forces are transformed; and to the extent that local reactions retroact on the global forces that initiate them, global social change becomes increasingly complex. In many instances, however, and particularly in the least developed countries, individual citizens, communities, and even countries lack the economic and political clout to have substantial impact on the course of global social change–unless they co-operate with each other and build up collective power.

The New Regionalism

Research has shown that individual citizens and communities conceive of globalization not only as an opportunity and positive challenge, but also as a threat. According to the World Bank's webpage introducing the World Development Report 1999/2000, increasing global interrelations and dependencies are often seen as transferring power and influence from local actors to "global players" such as transnational corporations and inter-governmental organizations. Hence, "improved communications, transportation and falling trade barriers are not only making the world smaller they are also fueling the desire and providing the means for local communities to shape their own future" (URL: http://econ.worldbank.org/wdr/). As a response to this desire for self-determination, new forms of decentralized local governance, which increasingly include direct citizen participation and deliberative practices, seem to be on the rise: "National governments are increasingly sharing responsibilities and revenues with subnational levels of government that are closer to the people affected by policy decisions, ... thereby raising levels of participation in decisionmaking and ... giving people more of a chance to shape the context of their own lives. By decentralizing government so that more decisions are made at subnational levels, closer to the voters, localization nourishes responsive and efficient governance" (World Bank 1999: 4-5).

The consequences of this new participatory localism are ambivalent. On the one hand it can be argued that the decentralization of political decisionmaking and the strengthening of participatory deliberations will contribute to the empowerment of the citizens involved. Individual citizens receive access to politically relevant information and acquire new skills. They learn, for instance, how to express themselves in public discussions and vis-à-vis the media and how to forge coalitions and compromises with like-minded partners. Skeptics, on the other hand, emphasize that, "when poorly designed, decentralization can result in overburdened local governments without the resources or the capacity to fulfill their basic responsibilities of providing local infrastructure and services. It can also threaten macroeconomic stability if local governments, borrowing heavily and spending unwisely, need to be bailed out by the national government" (Wolfensohn 1999: iii). What is more, decentralization and local participation can also be seen as "placebo politics" with symbolic, rather than real effects. While truly important political decisions are made elsewhere, often within the framework of intergovernmental organizations or in the headquarters of transnational corporations, new forms of local governance may lull citizens into receiving the overly optimistic impression that their interests and ideas actually make a difference.

Yet globalization has contributed not only to new forms of localism but also to what numerous authors call the "New Regionalism" (e.g., Hettne, Inotati, and Sunkel 1999; Hettne 1999a, 1999b; Mittelman 1999; MacLeod 2001). An increasing number of communities and states realize they lack the resources and capabilities to cope with global transformations on the local and the national level. Accordingly, more and more states and subnational entities seek to establish new forms of transnational (and translocal) regional co-operation. For the proponents of the New Regionalism approach it is clear that, "[f]ollowing its decline in theory and practice in the 1970s, regionalism both revived and changed dramatically in the 1980s, and has gained strength in the 1990s" (Mittelman 1999: 25). They argue that since the mid-1980s "there has been a new trend towards regionalism in all parts of the world" (Hettne 1999a: xvii)–that is, a trend towards "a multidimensional form of integration which includes economic, political, social and cultural aspects and thus goes far beyond the goal of creating region-based free trade regimes or security alliances" (Hettne 1999a: xvi).

The principal carriers of the new regionalism are what Hettne (1999a) calls "peripheral regions", which show somewhat different characteristics and motivations for co-operation than "core regions." While the latter "are politically stable and economically dynamic and organize for the sake of being better able to control the world," peripheral regions are "politically more turbulent and economically more stagnant; consequently they organize in order to arrest a process of marginalization, at the same time as their regional arrangements are fragile and ineffective" (Hettne 1999a: xvii). In many peripheral regions, regional co-operation is defensive, in that it aims at shielding the region from the negative consequences of external dependence. Regionalism helps to put in practice what Mittelman (1999) has termed the "developmental integration model." This model "stresses the need for close political co-operation at the outset of the integration process. Not only does it assign priority to the co-ordination of production and the improvement of infrastructure, but it also calls for a higher degree of state intervention than does the market model as well as redistributive measures such as transfer taxes or compensatory schemes administered by regional funds or specialized banks. ... A counter-weight to economic liberalism, it seeks to redress external dependence, especially through the regulation of foreign investment. ... [D]evelopment integration is a multilevel approach engulfing production, infrastructure, finance, and trade" (Mittelman 1999: 32-33).

Regarding peripheral regions and their development integration model, it is important to note that regionalism in the 1980s and the 1990s differs substantially from the earlier, autocentric regionalism, which called for global de-linking and collective self-reliance (Mittelman 1999:27). The current trend marks a "second wave" of regionalism, or indeed a "new regionalism", which according to Hettne (1999a: xviii) is different from the first wave in several ways: "Some notable differences between 'old' and 'new' regionalism are ... that current processes of regionalization are more from 'below' and 'within' than before, and that not only economic, but also ecological and security imperatives push countries and communities towards co-operation within new types of regionalist frameworks. The actors behind regionalist projects are no longer states only, but a large number of different types of institutions, organizations and movements. Furthermore, today's regionalism is extroverted rather than introverted, which reflects the deeper interdependence of today's global economy."

The regions so created are diverse with regard to both the institutional level on which they operate and their degree of internal homogeneity and cohesion. As Russett (1996: URL) reminds us, the term "region" is a rather vague one: "It is typically defined with some geographical reference, often to a continent or part of a continent. But such geographic references may be very imprecise, and laden with economic, cultural or political distinctions. ... ... Physical, political, economic and cultural definitions of regions rarely delineate the same boundaries." The proponents of the New Regionalism perspective have thus been "been programmatically open-minded as far as definitions are concerned" (Hettne 1999a: xv, original emphasis), even though most would agree that regions are territorially based sub-systems of the world system with higher levels of internal homogeneity (in at least one dimension of social life) and a denser web of social interactions than the system as a whole. What is clear is that we can distinguish at least three types of region: international regions ("macroregions" in Mittelman's terminology) involving several states; transnational regions ("subregions") transcending national boundaries but including only select (border) areas, not entire states; and subnational regions ("microregions") operating within the borders of a single sovereign state (cf. Mittelman 1999: 28). These three types of region then show different degrees of integration and organized co-operation in different dimensions of social life–among others, culture, economic policies, security, division of labor, and political regimes.

Regionalism and globalization: new research questions

The new wave of regionalism has given rise to questions of critical sociological importance. One of the most crucial questions, for instance, is what it takes for peripheral regions to produce economic growth, overcome their vulnerability to external shocks, and bring about sustained human development. For a region to cope successfully with the challenges of global transformations, which dimensions of social life need to be integrated the most? According to MacLeod (2001), research has shown regions to exhibit the greatest economic performance when economic co-operation meets intra-regional co-operation among civil society actors. He contends "that a major source of a region's competitive advantage is embedded in the operation of its ... civil society ... This relates to a series of historically cultivated socio-institutional infrastructures like networks, norms, conventions, trust-based (often face-to-face) interactions and horizontal relations of reciprocity, which are seen to enhance the benefits of investments in physical and human capital ..." (MacLeod 2001: 805-806). The question that follows, then, is how one can foster co-operation and integration among the civil societies of regions involving various states and different cultures.

For those interested in changes at the global level, the new regionalism also gives rise to the question of how this trend will affect the various dimensions of globalization. For instance, there is considerable controversy among economists on whether regional free trade areas such as NAFTA should be seen as stumbling blocks or stepping stones on the road to global trade and investment integration: while one school of thought contends "that by helping national economies to become more competitive in the world market, regional integration will lead to multilateral co-operation on a global scale and thus reduce conflict," the other sees regionalism as "ultimately promoting conflicts among exclusionary groups centred on the leading economies" (Mittelman 1999: 29). Likewise, scholars of world society theory should ask to what extent the cultural dimension of regionalism, the formation of regional collective identities, may contribute to or inhibit the development of cosmopolitan attitudes and individual identification with humankind as a whole. What does it mean, for example, that the organizers of the III People's Summit of the Americas (the countersummit against the OAS Summit of the Americas in Mar del Plata, November 2005) recycled the slogan of the World Social Forum, "Another World Is Possible!", converting it into "Another America Is Possible!"? Do (Latin) American social movement activists no longer care about the world as whole? Or do they feel the most effective way for them to contribute to global social change is by strengthening their impact on the regional level?

What is clear is that globalization and regionalism, though constituting two analytically distinct phenomena, go together. The question of whether the world is currently witnessing a process of regionalization rather than a process of globalization creates a false dichotomy. As Mittelman (1999: 25) puts it, "political and economic units are fully capable of walking on two legs"–that is, the two processes take place simultaneously and interact with one another. It is, thus, possible to think of regionalism as both a stumbling block and a stepping stone on the road to further global integration. For Hettne (1999a) it is clear that the two processes are mutually shaping each other in a complex, dialectical way. "The two processes are articulated within the same larger process of global structural transformation, the outcome of which depends on a dialectical rather than linear development. The latter cannot therefore be readily extrapolated or easily foreseen. ... Regions are emerging phenomena, ambiguously forming part of and driving, but also reacting against and modifying the process of globalization" (Hettne 1999a: xxi). Growing regional co-operation between states and communities helps to mitigate the negative effects of unfettered global competition, but to the extent that it creates new political and economic blocs opposing each other, it also transposes conflict to another level. Simultaneously, regionalism may help overcome narrow-minded nationalisms and push civil society in the direction of a transnational, and ultimately, universal consciousness. The true question, then, is under which conditions and in what configurations do which effects prevail?

Overview

The contributions in this volume examine the questions addressed in the present introduction from different vantage points. Rafael Reuveny and William R. Thompson, for instance, analyze the uneven distribution of trade globalization in the long-term macroperspective of world-systemic leadership cycles, whereas Xiangming Chen examines the effects of the most recent wave of investment and trade globalization by adopting the microperspective of two regions in China. In fact, the articles in this volume not only adopt different methodological approaches, but also focus on different types of regions. Dawn Wiest and Jackie Smith, for example, examine how social movement organizations are affected by institutionalized political co-operation in international regions such as the European Union, while John Gulick's study analyzes the internal and external dynamics of a single transnational border region, the Russian Far East and China's Northwest. Given the diversity of its contributions, this volume can thus be seen as reflective of the challenging, yet profoundly inspiring, complexity of the regional and local dynamics of global change.

Is globalization a truly global process? The first article in this volume, *Rafael Reuveny* and *William R. Thompson's* "The Limits of Economic Globalization: Still Another North-South Cleavage?", demonstrates that economic globalization proceeds unevenly in different zones of the world system. According to Reuveny and Thompson, the deepening of transnational economic integration is a path-dependent process that affects different areas differently: "Economic globalization is an old process of increasing pre-existing levels of integration between different units and zones of economic activity. Simply because we refer to it as globalization does not make it so." To substantiate this claim, the authors examine the long-term development of one of the most important dimensions of economic globalization, openness to exports, and explore differences in this development across the global North and the global South. The results in the first part of the analysis show that in the period from the 1880s to the present there have been three long waves of trade globalization, which correspond to the long-wave chronology discussed in the literature on the long cycles of world-systemic leadership. In addition, it becomes clear that trade globalization in this period has been virtually monopolized by countries in the global North. Although there has been a slight long-term increase in the global South's overall export openness, trade globalization has been significantly more pronounced in the North. Regression analyses in the second part of the paper demonstrate that changes in the level of trade globalization can be explained by changes in world economic growth and systemic leadership. However, as systemic leadership and economic growth are mainly focused in the global North, the correspondence between these systemic variables and trade globalization is far less evident in the global South than in the North. As Reuveny and Thompson (in this volume) put it, there are "two globalization dynamics, and still another North-South cleavage."

While Reuveny and Thompson examine differences between the global North and the global South, two "metaphorical regions" with no territorial basis, nor any institutionalized forms of political cooperation, *Dawn Wiest* and *Jackie Smith's* study takes as its point of departure the rising number and significance of regional-level intergovernmental bodies such as the EU, ASEAN, and NAFTA. Wiest and Smith show that regional institution-building helps to explain the recent growth of transnational social movement organizations (TSMOs), as well as variation in citizens' TSMO participation across countries. While research in the tradition of the Political Opportunities Model has demonstrated global governance bodies such as the United Nations, the International Monetary Fund, and the World Bank to have contributed to the formation and growth of TSMOs in general, Wiest and Smith show that regional intergovernmental institutions promote the formation of regional TSMOs. Not only do the policies of regional intergovernmental bodies give rise to the same grievances across different countries, but the meetings of these bodies also provide a forum (however insignificant) for input by moderate civil society organizations and serve as crystallization points for the countersummits of those excluded from this forum. In fact, Wiest and Smith find that both regional and global institutional contexts are predictive of citizens' participation in regional TSMOs. Moreover, their analysis uncovers how qualitatively different forms of regionalism translate into significantly different levels of regional TSMO formation. They find that, "In Europe, where the regional institutional structure is more elaborated than elsewhere in the world, the number of regional TSMOs in which citizens participated greatly outpaced that found elsewhere."

Xiangming Chen's article makes a forceful point to the effect that the local consequences of globalization cannot be understood without taking into account what he calls the "crucial middle" role of regions. As regions bridge and integrate global, national, and local economies, Chen argues, "regional dynamics are capable of mediating or restructuring global-local economic relations in varied ways to either facilitate or hinder the course of local economic growth and industrial upgrading" (Chen, in this volume). To illustrate this point, Chen analyzes the recent economic developments in two regions in China, the Pearl River Delta (PRD) and the Yangtze River Delta (YRD). His analysis shows that while the cities and towns in these two deltas have not created any institutionalized regional governance bodies, they are embedded in regional production networks with a clearly visible intra-regional division of labor. The spectacular growth of some of the cities and towns in the PRD and

YRD would not have been possible had it not been for their proximity to and ties with global-regional hubs such as Hong Kong and Shanghai, respectively, and second-tier cities such as Shenzhen and Suzhou. However, the problem in both regions is that second-tier cities have become heavily dependent on foreign investment and, while labor shortages lead to rising wages, there is a widespread fear that foreign firms will relocate to lower-cost cities in other parts of China. Moreover, fierce intra-regional competition among bottom-tier manufacturing towns has forced these towns to specialize in low-skill and wage-squeezing production, which they seem "locked in" to now.

Patrick Ziltener's contribution again focuses on East Asia, the region that includes several of the most rapidly industrializing and fastest growing economies in the world. Analyzing the historical formation and structure of East Asia as a world region, Ziltener makes it clear that any meaningful explanation of East Asia's current economic success must take into account the historical interplay of world-systemic forces and specific regional responses. East Asian societies, Ziltener demonstrates, draw on a strong tradition of comparatively high levels of socio-political differentiation, which had a substantial influence on the nature and outcomes of their encounters with colonialism. Moreover, most East Asian societies show comparatively high levels of socio-cultural homogeneity and have been successful post-colonial state builders. And yet, differences among East Asian societies in terms of precisely these characteristics complicate the process of regional political integration.

The subject of *Amir Sheikhzadegan's* contribution, a historical analysis of the role of Islam in the world system, could hardly be more timely or better focused to address a major issue in contemporary world politcs. Several years after the terrorist attacks on the World Trade Center in New York City, Islam in its many variants and facets—peaceful, radical, contemplative, fundamentalist, philosophical—still makes for a number one topic in the mass media. Unlike daily news coverage and op-eds linking Islam with fundamentalism and contemporary transnational terrorism, however, Sheikhzadegan reviews the history of Islam since its very beginning. focussing on the complex interplay between global trends and local responses in the Islamic world. It is only in the last part of the article that Sheikhzadegan deals with Islamist fundamentalism, which he interprets as a response to both the political lapses of U.S. hegemony and the shortfalls of allegedly pro-Western governments in the Islamic world itself. While many states in the Islamic world fail to convert oil revenues into sustained economic growth and seem unable to meet the basic needs of the masses, fundamentalist organizations provide social safety nets and welfare programs.

John Gulick's contribution examines the geopolitics and political economy of energy cooperation between Russia and China as they have played out in recent years. Explicitly framing the issue in a setting where the interstate relations of the late Cold War years have been left behind but the mechanisms of the US's informal empire still loom large, he simultaneously investigates the local, regional, and global dimensions of a particularly significant oil pipeline project in Northeast Asia. This project is dissected from several angles: its foundation in the scramble for valuable natural resources that accompanied the collapse of the transcontinental Soviet state in the Russian Far East (RFE), its possibility rooted in the fossil fuel dependence of mature and rapidly industrializing East Asian economies, and its prospect further nurtured by a developing Russo-Chinese strategic partnership but also frustrated by Russian fears of demographic decline and economic weakness in the Far East. Gulick is interested not only in why China ultimately gains the upper hand–if ever so tentatively and slightly–over Japan in the routing and the construction of the pipeline; he is also preoccupied with exploring the possible ramifications of Russo-Chinese energy cooperation on the vastest canvas possible. He argues that the recent direction of US foreign policy has necessitated the strengthening of Russo-Chinese strategic collaboration and this in turn has made honoring energy cooperation commitments all the more crucial. Weakening elite resistance in the RFE to cross-border ties with Northeast China has also helped energy cooperation along. If this sort of "geo-economic integration" acquires momentum, fed by but autonomous from pipeline politics, then the multipolar world which Moscow and Beijing celebrate will come one step closer to actualization, Gulick contends.

While Gulick analyzes the geo-strategic interests vested in a pipeline in the Russian Far East, *Yves-Alexandre Chouala* deals with the local political and cultural effects of the World Bank sponsored pipeline in Chad and Cameroon. Chouala's contribution makes it clear that this multi-million foreign-financed project fostered the emulation of (Western) world cultural standards and practices, thus leading to a stronger integration of Chad and Cameroon into world society. However, the pipeline seems to have failed to contribute to environmentally sustainable economic growth and social development. Rather, Chouala argues, the pipeline increased preexisting inequalities and political cleavages, strongly contributing to anomic tendencies.

Finally, *Martha C.E. Van Der Bly* examines the cultural consequences of globalization and, to a lesser degree, European regionalization from the perspective of a small town in Ireland. The town she investigates, Leixlip, is not just any town, however, just as Ireland is not just any country. Rather, Leixlip hosts the subsidiaries of several multinational corporations–among others, Intel's biggest production facility outside the U.S.–and is, thus, the town with the greatest FDI stock in the whole country. Ireland, in turn, according to several indices is the world's single most globalized country. For Van Der Bly, this raises the question of how Leixlip's penetration by foreign firms has affected local culture. Has local culture been replaced by the elements of an ever more homogeneous world culture, or has the interaction between the two cultures been more complex? To answer this question, Van Der Bly takes her readers on a tour through the town, analyzes sign posts, deciphers the symbolic content of tourist brochures and investment guides, and conducts numerous interviews with key informants such as teachers and historians. The results show that the presence of foreign firms in Leixlip has indeed brought about substantial changes; however, an important element of these changes has been the stronger emphasis on local identity formation through the creative (re-)construction of local history and language. A bilingual signboard indicates that the people of Leixlip also speak Irish, while another board presents the town as the original home of Guinness, the producer of Ireland's world-famous stout (which is no longer Irish-owned but part of a global company headquartered in London). Interestingly, though, the initiators of this new emphasis on Leixlip's "Irishness" are diverse. The renaissance of the Irish language can be credited, at least partly, to the efforts of local school teachers, but the signboard introducing Leixlip as the birthplace of Guinness has been sponsored by the Guinness company as part of its global expansion. As Van Der Bly (in this volume) puts it, "Guinness needed to become as Irish as possible in order to expand globally and needed an Irish home: Leixlip." Leixlip's globalized-localized identity can thus be seen as an assemblage of various cultural influences, as a "gesamt-creation" (Van Der Bly, in this volume) by civil society, foreign firms, and the state.

Taken together, the contributions in this volume are somewhat heterogeneous, but their diversity simply reflects the multi-dimensional and fragmented character of the global transformations this volume addresses. The articles demonstrate that the process of globalization is but one aspect of current global transformations, as economic, political and cultural globalization trends are accompanied by processes of local decentralization and by increased regionalism. These can be seen as responses to increased globalization, but they also retroact (in regionally variable forms and intensities) on globalization. While Reuveny and Thompson's study shows that allegedly global processes show uneven spatial patterns, the contributions by Van Der Bly, by Chouala, by Ziltener, and by Sheikhzadegan make clear that global forces interact with different pre-existing conditions in different local contexts. The contributions by Chen, by Gulick and by Dawn and Wiest demonstrate in turn that local responses to external challenges can only be seen as embedded in and mediated by regional dynamics.

References

Bruff, Ian. 2005. "Making Sense of the Globalisation Debate when Engaging in Political Economy Analysis." *British Journal of Politics and International Relations* 7: 261-280.
Giddens, Anthony (1990): *The Consequences of Modernity*. Stanford: Stanford University Press.
Harvey, David. 1989. *The Condition of Postmodernity*. Oxford: Blackwell.
Herkenrath, Mark. 2003. *Transnationale Konzerne im Weltsystem. Globale Unternehmen, nationale Wirtschaftspolitik und das Problem nachholender Entwicklung*. Wiesbaden: Westdeutscher Verlag.
Herkenrath, Mark, and Volker Bornschier. 2003. "Transnational Corporations in World Development. Still the Same Harmful Effects in an Increasingly Globalized World Economy?" *Journal of World Systems Research* 9 (1): 105-139.
Hettne, Björn. 1999a. "The New Regionalism: A Prologue." Pp. xv-xxix in *Globalism and the New Regionalism*, edited by Hettne, Björn, András Inotai, and Osvaldo Sunkel. London: Macmillan, and New York, NY: St. Martin's Press.
Hettne, Björn. 1999b. "Globalization and the New Regionalism: The Second Great Transformation." Pp. 1-24 in *Globalism and the New Regionalism*, edited by Hettne, Björn, András Inotai, and Osvaldo Sunkel. London: Macmillan, and New York, NY: St. Martin's Press.
Hettne, Björn, András Inotai, and Osvaldo Sunkel (eds.). 1999. *Globalism and the New Regionalism*. London: Macmillan, and New York, NY: St. Martin's Press.
MacLeod, Gordon. 2001. "New Regionalism Reconsidered: Globalization and the Remaking of Political Economic Space." *International Journal of Urban and Regional Research* 25 (4): 804-829.
Mittelman, James H. 1996. "The Dynamics of Globalization." Pp. 1-19 in *Globalization: Critical Reflections*, edited by Mittelman, James H. Boulder, CO: Lynne Rienner.
Mittelman, James. 1999. "Rethinking the 'New Regionalism' in the Context of Globalization." Pp. 25-53 in *Globalism and the New Regionalism*, edited by Hettne, Björn, András Inotai, and Osvaldo Sunkel. London: Macmillan, and New York, NY: St. Martin's Press.
Russett, Bruce. 1996. "Global or Regional: What Can International Organizations Do?" in *Globalism and Regionalism: Selected Papers Delivered at the United Nations University Global Seminar ,96 Shonan Session*, edited by Tanaka, Toshiro, and Takashi Inoguchi. On-line publication by the United Nations University Press. URL: http://www.unu.edu/unupress/globalism.html (accessed November 5, 2006).
United Nations Conference on Trade and Development (UNCTAD). 2006. *World Investment Report 2006. FDI from Developing and Transition Economies: Implications for Development*. New York, NY, and Geneva: United Nations.
United Nations Conference on Trade and Development (UNCTAD). NN. "Foreign Direct Investment." Programme on Investment, Technology and Enterprise Development Website. URL: http://www.unctad.org/Templates/StartPage.asp?intItemID=2527 (accessed on November 5, 2006).
United Nations Development Programme. 2005. Human Development Report 2005 On-line Data. URL: http://hdr.undp.org/statistics/data (accessed on November 5, 2006).

Urry, John. 2004. "Small Worlds and the New 'Social Physics.'" *Global Networks* 4 (2): 109-130.
Wolfensohn, James. 1999. "Foreword." Pp. iii-iv in *World Development Report 1999/2000: Entering the 21st Century*, edited by The World Bank. New York, NY: Oxford University Press.
World Bank. 1999. *World Development Report 1999/2000: Entering the 21st Century.* New York, NY: Oxford University Press.
World Bank. 2000. *World Development Report 2000/2001: Attacking Poverty.* New York, NY: Oxford University Press.
World Bank. NN. World Development Report 1999/2000 Website. URL: http://econ.worldbank.org/wdr/ (accessed on November 5, 2006).
World Trade Organization. 2005. WTO Statistics Database On-line. http://stat.wto.org (accessed on November 5, 2006).

1
How 'Global' is Economic Globalization?

Rafael Reuveny and William R. Thompson

Economic globalization has loomed, at least for some, as the world system's next crisis carrier. Globalization is said to accelerate economic growth rates, compel closer economic interactions throughout the globe, and trample on the distinctiveness of local cultures and sovereignty. While we accept the existence of economic globalization, our question in this paper is whether globalization, or at least one important dimension of it, is truly a "global" process. A number of cleavages that have characterized the global North and South in the past appear to be growing more acute. Globalization, predicated on a motor of global economic growth, should be expected to be less than universal if the pulsations and effects of global economic growth are less than universal across the global South and North. That being the case, our theory anticipates that that one aspect of economic globalization, conceptualized here as economic openness to exports, and measured by the ratio of export value to economic output, will be more discernible in the global North, than in the global South. Moreover, trade globalization in the North, should be positively affected by a rise in world economic growth and systemic leadership, whereas trade globalization in the South should be driven largely by Southern autonomous inertia and periodic economic crises. The empirical results largely support our theoretical expectations.

Hard on the heels of putting the Cold War bogeyman to rest, economic globalization has loomed, at least for some, as the world system's next crisis carrier. Globalization creates winners and losers and tramples on the distinctiveness of local cultures and sovereignties. For others, though, globalization compels closer economic interactions throughout the globe, carrying technological progress and economic integration to all parts of the planet and accelerating economic growth. Let the market do its job and the poor will catch up to the rich via trade-driven growth. The cleavages separating global North and South–developed and less developed countries, respectively–will disintegrate and the world will be a better and Pareto-optimal, happier place.

While we certainly accept the existence of economic globalization processes, our question in this paper is whether all aspects of it are truly "global" processes. In other words, are all dimensions of economic globalization experienced in the same intensity by the global North, or industrialized countries, and the global South, or the developing countries? There are a number of cleavages that have characterized the global North and South in the past and present. They appear to be growing more acute–rather than less so. Economic globalization, in general, predicated on a motor of global economic growth, should be expected to be less than universal if the pulsations and effects of global economic growth are less than universal across the global North and global South. Indeed, to the extent that economic growth and integration are monopolized by the North, North-South cleavages are likely to be only accentuated–not attenuated–by economic globalization.

In this paper, we anticipate that in the long run most of the important dimensions of economic globalization will be significantly more discernible in the global North than in the global South. By long run, we mean time periods encompassing more than one hundred years. The theoretical analysis builds on, and extends, the leadership long-cycle approach to global international political economy to deal with processes of Northern and Southern economic globalization. We remain consistent in our expectation that systemic leadership and long waves of economic growth are drivers of systemic phenomena such as economic globalization. However, we now develop a stronger historical case for the expectation that the impacts of economic growth stimuli should be felt unevenly due to stratified, path dependencies that are entrenched in the modern history of economic growth. Systemic leadership, long waves of economic growth, and economic globalization are expected to be mainly focused in the global North and much less so in the global South, thereby further accentuating the cleavages between North and South and intensifying global inequalities. We test this theory empirically, using statistical analysis.

To model statistically the behavior of Northern and Southern economic globalization, a number of design issues need to be resolved. First, we need to distinguish between Northern and Southern countries, which is done using a method discussed later. Second, economic globalization is a multidimensional concept, involving international movements of goods and services (trade), physical capital (foreign direct investments), financial capital (portfolio investments) and, less so, labor (migration). We focus solely on trade since data on investments, especially in terms of specific Southern investments, are not available for the long time periods that we need to examine. Since we are narrowing our empirical examination, the usual reservations about not claiming that our results address all facets of economic globalization should prevail.

Second, how should one best measure trade globalization? We utilize series on exports measured in constant prices, since data on imports are also not available for our long period. Export globalization is defined conventionally by the ratio of export value to gross domestic product (GDP). Third, the nature of our problem demands data that are highly comparable across time and space. The bulk of these data, therefore, come from Angus Maddison (1995).

The empirical analysis consists of two parts: visual and statistical. Visual analysis suggests that export openness in the global system is almost a monopoly of the North. Southern export openness over time does not resemble a completely flat line but, compared to the results for the North, there is considerably little variance demonstrated since 1870. We then utilize our theory in developing a statistical model for Northern export openness. The independent variables are world economic growth rate and level of systemic leadership. Control variables are Northern export openness inertia, level of Northern democracy, and level of Northern conflict (militarized disputes involving a Northern state at least on one side of a dyad, and civil wars that take place inside the North). The Southern model is specified similarly. Southern export openness is regressed on systemic leadership, world economic growth, Southern trade openness inertia, Southern democracy, Southern conflict, and a measure of Southern debt crisis.

In the empirical test, our variables capture much of the variance in Northern export openness. The effects of system leadership, world economic growth, Northern export openness inertia, and Northern democracy on Northern export openness are found to be positive and statistically significant. The effect of Northern conflict on Northern openness is mixed. We then turn to the South. We find that world economic growth, and the levels of Southern democracy and Southern conflict are not statistically significant determinants of Southern export openness. Systemic leadership has a weak positive effect on Southern export openness. Southern export openness is primarily determined by inertia (its value in the previous period) and Southern debt crises. The effect of Southern export inertia on Southern export openness is positive. The effect of debt crises on Southern export openness is negative in the short run, and positive in the longer run.

In sum, the trade export dimension of globalization is proceeding very unevenly across the planet. The implications for Southern development are not attractive. It is frequently argued that economic globalization, particularly international trade, is the engine of economic growth. While a small number of countries in Asia may have capitalized on the economic growth-promoting influence of focusing their national production on exports, the global South, as a whole, does not appear to be following this path. Thus, contrary to the market optimists, we should not expect that economic globalization will reduce the contemporary growing income gap between the rich global North and the much poorer global South. It seems more likely that economic globalization will expand the gap. How that will affect the argument that globalization will eliminate all national differences and local traditions is less clear. But if globalization is less than global, one would think that the juggernaut interpretation of globalization as a destroyer of all local traditions and culture is also likely to be exaggerated.

The remainder of this paper is organized as follows. The next two sections present an overview of the leadership-long cycle perspective on global international political economy, and extend it to deal with Northern and Southern economic openness to export. Section four presents our research design and describes our data and indicators. This is followed by a section discussing our empirical results. We conclude the paper with a summary and discussion of the broader implications of our findings.

The leadership-long cycle perspective

The leadership-long cycle perspective observes that historically, systemic leadership and world economic growth have followed consistently a twin-peaked wave pattern, each wave lasting roughly 50 years.[1] During the first–ascent– wave, one country rises to leadership in the world system. During the second– catchup–wave, the leader is established but then begins a relative decline as competitors emerge. In upswing phases of each wave, leadership and growth are expanding. In downswing phases of each wave, they are contracting or growing more slowly. In the ascent wave, political relationships among the most powerful states are destabilized by uneven growth. In the downswing phase of the ascent wave, a global competition follows the destabilization, which historically (between 1494 and 1945 in any event) involved global combat between coalitions led by the leader and by a challenger. One state emerges as the principal winner thanks in large part to its lead in technological innovation. This state is denoted as the system leader. However, leadership is a dynamic force. A catchup wave follows in which the competition of the leader with new challengers builds up. The leader gradually loses its economic and political edge, and a new ascent wave is initiated with the next system leader emerging.

A number of generalizations related to this interpretation have been developed and tested empirically elsewhere.[2] For instance, the key to global ascent is the successful monopolization of radical innovations in leading sectors of commerce and industry.[3] The introduction of leading sectors leads to the growth of the pioneering lead economy and, in turn, the growth of the lead economy stimulates world growth. The monopoly profits finance the buildup of the leader's global reach military forces critical for maintaining its global economic and security concerns. At its peak, the system leader maintains a commanding lead in global reach power. Then, as its economic centrality dissipates, so too does its lead in global reach military capabilities. World economic growth and shifting concentrations in radical innovation eventually reduce the economic lead of the pioneer. Even so, only some economies are able to converge on the leader's position of affluence and technological sophistication.

One primary feature of this process is its discontinuous nature. Economic growth and radical innovations have been manifested as long waves that decay when the innovational novelties lose their ability to accelerate growth. As old innovations become routine components of the world economy, new spurts in economic growth hinge on the advent of the next cluster of radical technological change. A second strong feature, therefore, are alternating periods of fast growth (stimulated by new technology) and slow growth (brought on by the routinization of now old technology). To the extent that new technology is slow to emerge or encounters various infrastructure inadequacies, or political restrictions on change, slow or negative economic growth (world economic depression) is likely to persist until at least some of these barriers are overcome.

Several extensions of the leadership-long cycle perspective to deal with various North-South-related socioeconomic and political phenomena have been pursued recently in the literature. These extensions have centered on issues such as North-South income inequality, recurring Southern debt crises, and North-South violent conflict.[4] For each of these phenomena, a theoretical and empirical case has been made that they are strongly influenced by global structures and processes, which predicated ultimately on the nature of technological change and the consequent political-economic hierarchy outlined in the above discussion.

Basic expectations about export globalization

In this section, we combine leadership long cycle principles with some selected observations made by economic historians about what might be called the 19th and 20th century channels of world economic growth and trade. We retain the assertion of the leadership-long cycle perspective that systemic leadership and the long waves of discontinuous economic growth, for which system leaders are primarily responsible, drive long-term fluctuations in world economic activity. Economic innovation in the lead economy of the system leader creates technological spurts that drive long waves of economic growth and fund systemic leadership foundations and capabilities. Yet economic growth and trade never operate on a level playing field. Some parts of the world economy are always favored over other parts, and we need to build this fact of life into our models of growth and trade.

From our perspective, economic growth and trade are especially dependent on the intermittent surges in technological change introduced by the system's lead economy. As a consequence, new products and industries emerge in discontinuous fashion. So, too, do new ways of distributing commodities faster and cheaper. Radical innovations and lowered transaction costs do not simply fall from the sky; they are introduced and developed primarily by system leaders. In the 17th century, it was the Dutch. The 18th and 19th centuries were dominated by British technological change. In the 20th and perhaps the 21st centuries, the U.S. economy has served as the principal pioneer of changes in the way people produce and exchange goods.

Surges in globalization, therefore, are fueled by waves of long-term growth stimuli emanating primarily from the system leader's economy. These spikes in economic growth drive economic growth and lowered transaction costs in the system leader's economy that, in turn, drive growth and lowered transaction costs in the rest of the world. In order to obtain the new products, some reductions in barriers to trade will ensue. Technological diffusion will enhance the ability of some other economies to produce the new products and these expanded competencies will also encourage lowered trade barriers. In the process, the system leader also serves as a principal source of investment and finance, thereby providing further encouragement for positive growth spirals.

Order in long distance commerce is another contribution traceable to system leaders. Technological growth and predominance in leading sectors of commerce and industry give the system leader an added incentive to develop specialized capabilities of global reach. Trade routes must be kept open and made relatively secure from interference and piracy. For this reason a concentration in economic technological innovation tends to be accompanied by a concentration in global reach capabilities that historically have been predominately naval given the maritime medium favored by long distance trade throughout much of the past five centuries. Not only does the system leader have a strong incentive to develop such power, it also has the wherewithal–thanks to the rents from technological leadership–to fund it.

Globalization is thus stimulated fundamentally by a package of technological change, lowered transaction costs (including costs pertaining to security), lowered trade barriers, expanded investment, and economic growth diffusion all of which are attributable to some great extent to the economic and political-military actions of system leaders. If the source of these changes is highly concentrated, it should come as no surprise that the impacts of the changes are apt to be less than universal. Some parts of the world are likely to benefit more while others benefit less, depending on various factors such as resource endowment, location, and receptivity to technological diffusion.

If we continue with the assertions that technological innovation is critical to modern economic growth, discontinuous in time, and initially concentrated in space, we find, according to leadership long cycle theory, that Britain in the 19th century and the United States in the 20th century have been the most favored locations in the world economy and the lead economies of the past two centuries. But what about the rest of the world? Is it reasonable to argue that all other parts of the world economy had equal chances to either produce their own leader or to catch up to the technological leaders? We think not.

Maddison (1995), following the lead of Adam Smith (1776), argues that from an 1820 perspective, a combination of various criteria (per capita income, resource endowment, population, and institutional/societal characteristics likely to influence economic performance) would have yielded the following regional hierarchy of zones within the world economy that were most likely to do well in the future [where 1 stands for most likely and 7 stands for least likely]: (1) Western Europe (including Britain); (2) Western offshoots (e.g., Canada, the United States, Australia, New Zealand); (3) Southern Europe; (4) eastern Europe (including Russia); (5) Latin America; (6) Asia; and (7) Africa. To a considerable extent, we argue, as does O'Brien (2006) that their prospects were also affected by the degree to which they were to become integrated to the world economy through migration, investment, and trade.

The first two zones (western Europe and its offshoots) performed best in terms of growth and trade in the 19th and 20th centuries. Southern Europe, for the most part, began to catch up with western Europe in the second half of the 20th century. Eastern Europe has had mixed success thanks in part to an extended period of unsuccessful experimentation with highly centralized economic production decisions and deliberate efforts to reduce the degree of integration with western Europe. The last three zones, Latin America, Asia, and Africa, have also experienced considerably mixed outcomes ranging from the remarkable catching up by Japan, and other Asian tigers (realized and still emerging), respectively, to the stagnation and worse fate of a number of African economies. Overall, however, the point is that the 1820 regional hierarchy has by and large been maintained into the 21st century.[5]

Why might this be the case? Part of the answer is that the western European and offshoots zones have so far retained world technological leadership. Diffusion from, and imitation of, the British and U.S. industrialization leads were most likely to occur within these two zones because of the criteria suggested by Maddison (essentially relative affluence and facilitative environments for economic growth and trade). As a consequence, Belgium, France, Germany, and the United States were among the first places to follow the British industrial lead in the first half of the 19th century. Moreover, 19th and 20th century flows of skilled labor and investment demonstrated a bias in moving from western Europe to its offshoots. O'Brien (2006) adds that the external security costs of the offshoots were augmented in a major way by the 19th century services of the British navy. Later, in the second half of the 20th century, western Europe was the region that was the most successful in converging on the U.S. lead in per capita income. This convergence can also be attributed non-controversially in part to the external security subsidies provided by U.S. military capabilities after 1945 (see, for instance, Gilpin, 1975, among many others).

At the other end of the regional hierarchy, different stories characterized specific locales within the heterogenous "Third World" of Asia, Latin America, and Africa. Yet, for a long time, there were also some common denominators in terms of relatively high population growth, subsistence-oriented economic production, marked income inequalities, and institutions that were less than conducive to economic growth. To a great extent, these three zones have also specialized in exporting undiversified primary products to the more technologically advanced zones, and, to a lesser extent, importing their manufactured goods. Nor has it helped that a number of the "first world's" technological innovations have created manufactured substitutes for many of the "third world's" raw materials. The fact that much of the 19th-20th century pool of movable investment capital and skilled labor migrated elsewhere is another negative contribution to Southern economic growth.

The "in-between" zones of southern and eastern Europe enjoyed or suffered different fates that may even out in the long run but in the intermediate run has led to a more rapid integration of southern and western Europe. Some parts of eastern Europe probably will emulate this convergence while other parts will do so much more slowly, if at all. Nevertheless, our current concern is not with forecasting possible outcomes within or between Maddison's seven zones.

We suggest instead that the regional hierarchy can be simplified further into two macro-zones. Western Europe and the western offshoots are the core of a global North that has been augmented by adherents from southern and eastern Europe, as well as by a small number of Asian states. Latin America, Asia, and Africa historically have constituted the core of a global South, incorporating as well, at various times, parts of eastern and southern Europe. Neither macro-zone assignment guarantees permanent success or failure in economic growth and trade. Nor is membership in one zone a terminal categorization. It is conceivable that Northern states can become Southern and certainly the opposite type of status mobility exists. But the prospects for economic growth and trade, along with other imaginable outcomes, have been in the 19th and 20th centuries and will probably continue to be more benign in the global North than in the global South.

Economic globalization is an old process of increased interaction and integration between and among populations located initially within Afro-Eurasia and, much later, incorporating the Americas and Australia. Interaction and integration does not proceed inexorably or continuously. Instead, interaction and integration, along with technological innovation and economic growth, pulsate or come in accelerated spurts. But if the world economy is composed of zones with much different prospects for generating economic growth and trade, it is reasonable to expect that a) contemporary globalization will proceed unevenly and that b) Northern participation in contemporary globalization processes should outpace Southern participation. Technological development, led by the world system's lead economy, with implications for the emergence of new products, new ways of production, and faster, less expensive transportation modes, should be more intensely registered within the North than within the South. Northern economies are better prepared to accommodate successive changes in best practices. They are also more inclined to both create products for export that reflect their advanced technology and to trade with other similar advanced economies that can afford and absorb their exports. The contemporary globalization of trade should thus proceed with a marked intra-Northern bias and be driven by waves of economic growth and leadership generated by the system leader.

One empirical question is just how marked that bias is. Is it moderate or extremely strong? If the bifurcation of growth and trade prospects into two zones is quite pronounced, as we think it is and has been for some time, we should expect to find that the unevenness of globalization propensities is also quite strong. It may even be that the often-discussed threat to indigenous cultures and traditions emanating from globalization pressures may prove to be less worrisome since the Southern participation in contemporary trade globalization is simply too limited.

But we need to examine the underlying empirical questions before we jump to possible conclusions—just how biased, if at all, are contemporary trade globalization processes? Are they virtually monopolized by a vibrant North? Or, are we exaggerating the bi-zonal division of the world economy and the expectation of much different trade globalization propensities? Moreover, our assertion that the system leader's edge in technological growth and global reach capabilities, coupled with discontinuous long waves of growth stemming from technological spurts, are important drivers of globalization also needs empirical assessment.

Empirical research design

The units of analysis in our interpretation are North and South. For the empirical test then, we need to assign countries to Northern and Southern groups. In aggregating variables for both groups, we will focus on differences between the groups and assume that the differences within each of the groups are not sufficient to undermine the rationale for our comparison. Threats to validity posed by this approach are discussed toward the end of this section. But first we must discuss the empirical model, and then attend to several design issues. The dependent variables are the levels of globalization attained by each bloc. The core right hand side variables are world economic growth and systemic leadership.

Empirical data and model

North and South Classification: There is no convention for North-South classification. Some studies base their identifications of countries as Northern and Southern on the timing and extent of industrialization, but leave the criteria implicit (e.g., Rostow, 1979; Freeman and Perez, 1988; McCormick, 1988). Other studies classify countries as Northern or Southern on the basis of shorter periods of time, often mixing economic and military capabilities (Arrighi and Drangel, 1986; Kick, 1987; Kentor, 2000).

We classify countries as Northern or Southern based on level of economic development, but with a systemic twist. A country is classified as Southern if its real gross domestic product (GDP) per capita is equal to or less than 25 percent of the highest real GDP per capita in the system; otherwise, it is classified as Northern (Reuveny and Thompson, 2002, 2003, 2004a). Economic development, in this view, is a process of catching up, or at least closing significantly the gap, with the technological frontier established by the system leader. Our use of GDP per capita does not mean that economic development is simply a matter of attaining some level of income. We use it because it is simple and comes close to working without intervention. Constructing indexes on the national "modernity" of technology would constitute an ambitious project in its own right.

While our North-South classification method is not perfect, we need a threshold that is not static. Using a single absolute threshold, as suggested, for example, by Kuznets (1972) or Passe-Smith (1998), will not work for long historical series. Our experimentation with higher thresholds (for example, 33 percent, 50 percent) restricted the North to a few Western European states and a few of its offshoots. The 25 percent threshold permits more non-Western European/non-North American states to join the North beginning in the 1920s. If forced to choose between a conservative and liberal North-South threshold, we prefer to err on the liberal side. Table 1 presents the resulting coding beginning in 1870.[6]

Table 1 conforms to clues provided in the economic history literature. The order of leaving the South and joining the North implied by Table 1 seems

Table 1. North-South countries classifications

North		South	
United Kingdom	Japan (after 1894)	Argentina	Philippines
United States	Finland (after 1919)	Brazil	Taiwan (to 1976)
Belgium	Poland (after 1929)	Chile	Thailand
Netherlands	Russia (after 1931)	Colombia	China
Switzerland	Greece (after 1956)	Mexico	India
Denmark	Portugal (after 1957)	Peru	Burma
Austria	Taiwan (after 1977)	Venezuela	Indonesia
France	South Korea (after 1983)	Turkey	Pakistan
Sweden		Japan (to 1893)	Bangladesh
Canada		Finland (to 1918)	Ethiopia
Australia		Poland (to 1928)	Egypt
New Zealand		Russia (to 1930)	Morocco
Ireland		Bulgaria	Nigeria
Czechoslovakia		Yugoslavia	Zaire
Hungary		Rumania	Ivory Coast
Norway		Greece (to 1955)	Kenya
Spain		Portugal (to 1956)	Tanzania
Italy		South Korea (to 1982)	

Note: Maddison (1995) provides economic data for these states prior to their independence, wherever that is applicable. Thus, these states are considered as Northern or Southern from 1870 on unless their series begin later than 1870 due to missing data, or as otherwise indicated due to movement from the South to the North.

intuitively satisfying: The Western European countries leave the South and enter the North before Australia, New Zealand, and Japan. Some southeast European countries enter the North before the Asian countries. Our South also includes many of the overtly less developed countries (LDCs), such as Kenya and India.[7] Overall, we find this list to be less than perfect but possessing considerable face validity.[8]

Economic Globalization: Our dependent variable, economic globalization, is a multifaceted concept that involves trade, foreign direct investment, portfolio investment, and movement of factors of production across countries (physical capital, and much less so labor). The empirical analysis of our expectations require long time series. For almost all countries, data on foreign direct investments and portfolio investments are only available for recent decades. Fortunately, trade data are more readily available for many countries over long periods of time. While our argument pertains to all aspects of economic globalization, we focus here on the more operationalizable activity of trade globalization.

Our indicator of trade globalization is constructed utilizing time series data on export values. The export indicator is defined by the ratio of total export value of the North or the South to the world, expressed in constant dollars, to total gross domestic product (GDP) of the North or South, expressed in constant dollars from the same base year. Our focus on exports is partly motivated by the fact that import data are not available for long periods. It should also be recalled that any export also is someone else's import. Some countries import-export balances are highly imbalanced, to be sure, but we expect these national asymmetries to even out in the aggregates with which we are working.

Initially, we attempted to create national export series for each of the countries in our Northern and Southern samples.[9] This approach proved to be fruitless, especially for the Southern states, because of the lack of early data and the usual difficulties encountered in meshing extant information in multiple currencies, with and without various controls for price fluctuations. Our default strategy consisted of first calculating for each country in our sample the proportion of world trade as reported in Banks (1971), and updated via various volumes of the U.N. Statistical Yearbook. We then aggregated this information into Southern and Northern proportions of world trade. Maddison (1995:239) reports a series on the value of world exports in constant 1990 dollars for 1870, 1881-1913, 1924-1938, and 1950-1992. After interpolating straight forwardly for the missing years, we then converted the world export figures into Southern and Northern exports for each year between 1870 and 1992, based on our classification of countries to North and South, discussed above.[10] These numbers were then divided by the respective GDP aggregations for the South and North developed in earlier studies (Reuveny and Thompson, 2002, 2003, 2004a) to create macro-trade openness indices (exports/gdp).

In as much as Maddison's data tend to stop short of the 21st century, there is some possibility that stopping our analysis in 1992 will distort the evidence for fairly recent Southern globalization. When appropriate, we will introduce an independent measurement of export globalization that encompasses the 1983-2003 era as a check on the possibility of distortion. These data will not be fully comparable with Maddison's data, which are based on different constant price assumptions, but they allow us to assess whether they suggest similar or dissimilar tendencies to what we are observing towards the end of the 1870-1992 series.

World economic growth: Our first independent variable, world economic growth, is measured by aggregating national data. Time series for world economic growth inevitably require construction. Therefore, these data may exhibit bias toward data that are readily available in a comparable format. Annual real GDP data, expressed in 1990 dollars, for 17 major countries since 1870, come from Maddison (1992).[11] The national GDP data are aggregated to represent the world's real GDP. Yearly growth rates are then computed from the world's GDP series.

Systemic leadership: Our second core independent variable, systemic leadership, is measured by the leader's share of global reach capabilities, approximated by concentration of naval forces. Coming from Modelski and Thompson (1988), this measure has been used in both the leadership long-cycle research program and outside of it.[12] It is predicated on the extent to which capabilities are concentrated in one state. In 1870-1992, it is computed based on naval expenditures, first class battleships, dreadnought class battleships, aircraft carriers, nuclear attack submarines, and nuclear ballistic missiles, for Britain, France, Germany, Japan, Russia/USSR, and the United States. Maritime or naval power and the power to project coercion over long distances were largely synonymous in much of the post-1494 era. More recently, other dimensions of global reach have been developed that rely less on naval platforms (air power, satellites, cruise missiles), but often these too require naval support.

There also are economic forms of systemic leadership, manifested in economic predominance. Reuveny and Thompson (1999, 2004b) show there is a close relationship between economic leadership and global reach capability. In terms of the newer dimensions of global reach, we suspect that the preponderant profile established by a naval lead also reflects leads in other coercive components, with the possible exception of land forces.[13]

In any event, in 1870-1945, the system leader role was played by Britain (less so after World War I). Britain, however, was in relative decline from at least 1870 on. From 1946 to 1992 (the end of our data) the system leader role was performed by the US. The time series for systemic leadership is thus generated by splicing the global reach capability share data of Britain with that of the US in 1946.

While we view systemic leadership and world economic growth as the principal drivers of economic globalization, other forces, no doubt, also influence this phenomenon. We need a modeling platform suggesting control variables. Unfortunately, the literature has not suggested a model of macro-zonal (North-South) trade with the world. Existing trade models either deal with bilateral trade or with comparative advantage. We employ insights from related studies as well as analytical intuition in identifying four possible controls for our purpose: democracy, conflict, macro-zonal trade openness inertia, and debt default.

Democracy: Several studies suggest that democracies trade more with other democracies than with autocracies (e.g., Dixon and Moon, 1993; Morrow et al., 1998). This is attributed to higher intra-democratic trust levels in comparison to democratic-autocratic trust levels. It is reasonable to expect that political freedom in a country will promote economic freedom in that country, which also should include more international trade overall. These considerations lead us to expect that trade flows of the macro-zone with the world should rise as the aggregate level of democracy in the macro-zone rises.

Northern and Southern democracy levels are measured based on Polity III data (Jaggers and Gurr, 1995). This data set records a 10-point index that measures democratic characteristics of national regimes since the early 19th century, and a 10-point index that measures autocratic characteristics. Because many governments have both democratic and autocratic characteristics, we measure the level of democracy as the difference between the two indices (see, e.g., Oneal and Russett, 1999; Londregan and Poole, 1996; Mansfield and Snyder, 1995). This procedure generates a yearly national index ranging between -10 (most autocratic regime) and +10 (most democratic regime regime). We aggregate these national indices across the North and across the South. Since, these indices represent countries with different populations, in aggregating them we use a weighted average, where yearly weights are given by the ratio of national population to the total Northern and Southern population, respectively.

Conflict: Some analyses anticipate that bilateral trade will decline as conflict between trade partners increases (e.g., Pollins, 1989; Gowa, 1994; Reuveny, 2001). As tensions rise, importers may worry that they will not be able to obtain exports at all, or on a timely manner. They may also be concerned about payments. Traders may worry that governments will restrict trade by imposing various sanctions on the activities of adversaries. Hence, Northern (Southern) conflict may diminish trading tendencies and thereby negatively influence Northern (Southern) trade openness. Zonal trade with the world, however, may not necessarily decline in the face of increased conflict. Other countries may enjoy more demand for their products as trade is diverted to them from hostile parties, or as demand for their products rises due to the war efforts of others. If the zonal trade is not greatly diminished, we may also see no general effect of conflict on the macro-zone's openness to trade.

Northern and Southern military conflict data come from the dyadic Militarized Interstate Dispute (MIDs) data set, covering the years 1816 to 1992.[14] It is possible to differentiate MIDs in terms of a verbal threat to use force, limited use of force, and war. But, it is not clear that a limited use of military force is necessarily more conflictual than a strong verbal threat to use force. Further, wars are relatively rare events. Consequently, as is done in other studies, we employ all MIDs in a year. We assume that years with more MIDs are more conflictual than other years. The occurrences of MIDs are aggregated for Northern conflict–conflict between a Northern country and any county in the system, Southern or Northern, and for Southern conflict–conflict between a Southern country and any country in the system. At each point in time, this sum is normalized by the number of dyads that can be formed in the international system.

Trade Openness Inertia: Movements in trade openness may be slow. Consider a rise in trade openness. In this case, tastes need to change, opposition to trade needs to be overcome, production needs to be reoriented, and so forth. Social structures affecting trade openness such as cultural differences among countries, or ownership of production factors also may change slowly. We therefore anticipate that trade openness will exhibit inertia. In empirical work, inertia is modeled customarily by incorporating the lag of the dependent variable as a control. This force is applicable in both North and South, but may be more pronounced in the South. The South generally only gradually attained independence from colonial powers, an initial prerequisite for re-orienting the local economy from metropole to the world.

Debt Default: When agents fail to service or pay back debts they are in default. Debt default can affect exports in two ways. In the short run, the defaulting unit may exhibit a decline in exports, particularly when imported production inputs are in short supply due to the crisis. As the crisis deepens, the economy, including the exporting center, may decline (Reuveny and Thompson, 2004b). In the longer run, however, it is possible that the crisis may raise openness as nations try to obtain foreign currency from export in order to pay their debts. In addition, if the default is particularly damaging to the domestic economy. If GDP declines more than exports decline, openness, which is the ratio of export to GDP, may rise.

Annual Southern debt default data, based on Suter's (1992) series, come from Reuveny and Thompson (2004). These data provide the number of countries in a state of debt-default (i.e., do not service their debt in terms of making interest payments or paying the principle due), or undergoing debt rescheduling (postponing payment deadlines and renegotiating terms and amounts). The debt-default series ends in 1985 and the rescheduling series begins in 1956. Between 1956 and 1985, Reuveny and Thompson average the two series and use this average as our measure. Hence, our dependent variable measures the aggregated level of Southern debt problems.[15] The debt time series accounts for changes in the size of the international system by normalizing the number of Southern countries exhibiting debt problems by a count of the number of states in the system, in any given year.

Model: With all the variables in the model defined, we can now state the following model for each of our two units of analysis, North and South:

(1) EXPOPEN = f (SYSLEAD, WGROWTH, CONFLICT, DEMOCRACY, INERTIA, DEBTDEF).

In this model, export openness of a region (EXPOPEN) depends on six variables: systemic leadership (SYSLEAD), World economic growth (WGROWTH), level of conflict that involves countries in the region (CONFLICT), level of democracy in the region (DEMOCRACY), export openness inertia (INERTIA)–a lagged value of EXPOPEN, and the level of debt default in the region–failure to service debt on time or pay due principle–(DEBTDEF). Given that debt defaults did not occur often in the North, DEBTDEF is only included in the Southern model.

Model design issues

Given our model, we need to consider several design issues. First, some of the right hand side variables could be affected by export openness. A decline in openness could promote a debt crisis as foreign reserves are depleted. A rise in openness could promote democracy, as economic freedom can promote political freedom. To the extent that trade is an engine of growth, world economic growth could be affected. Trade could have a pacifying effect on conflict. On the other hand, leadership is not likely to be directly affected by export openness. In our leadership-long cycle perspective, systemic leadership is a function of the performance of the system leader in leading economic sectors.

In general, if a statistical model ignores reciprocal relationships between variables, the results will likely be biased. At the same time, fully accounting for all possible reciprocal effects can obviously turn into a monumental task. In addition, the size of the simultaneity bias in practice may be small. While most empirical studies, in fact, ignore reciprocal effects, some models deal with simultaneity by lagging the independent variables (e.g., Muller and Seligson, 1994, Oneal and Russett, 1999; Li and Reuveny, 2003). The rationale for this method is that the current value of a variable cannot affect the past value of another variable. We will use this method for world economic growth, democracy, conflict and debt default. For systemic leadership, we do not employ this method because our theoretical perspective does not attribute a causal factor to trade openness in bringing about leadership.

The effects of many socio-political-economic forces develop relatively slowly, or adjust dynamically (Greene, 1997). Dynamic adjustment is commonly modeled by employing lags of variables–distributed lags. This approach assumes that the past levels of the explanatory forces can affect the dependent variable. Our method of dealing with simultaneity employs the first lag of explanatory variables (except for leadership). This itself is dynamic adjustment with a lag length of one. In general, the adjustment lag lengths may be longer than one, and may vary across variables.

World economic growth and democracy may take more than one period to influence trade openness. Current values of leadership could affect openness, but current openness may also incorporate previous leadership effects. However, when all is said and done, our argument (similar to most dynamic interpretations in social science) does not specify the number of lags for the empirical analysis. "The appropriate length of lag is rarely, if ever, known, so one must undertake a specification search" (Greene, 1997: 786). As is done in many studies, we chose the lag structure from a systematic search. Our search will provide many results, from which we chose the best specification in terms of goodness of fit, levels of significance, and signs of effects compared with theoretical expectations.[16]

Our primary empirical model will be the one specified for Northern openness. We expect weaker effects of our leadership long-cycle variables in the South, and perhaps no effect at all. Therefore, we will look for the lag structure found to fit the Northern model, and then employ the same specification as a baseline in testing whether our findings hold for Southern openness.

It is tempting to translate distributed lags into substantive terms. In distributed lag models, however, one looks for lags first as a check on causality–if x influences y, x should antecede y as a matter of data fitting. As noted, our theory does not tell us what sorts of lags to anticipate. Moreover, we rarely have enough observations to examine long lags of, say, generational length. Thus one should be reticent to attribute considerable significance to the lag length. The question is not so much whether we can isolate lagged effects precisely in terms of time between impact and maximum effect. Rather, do we find significant relationships, and do the signs of the effects agree with the theoretical predictions?

When models include distributed lags, the interpretation of results can be complicated. The signs and significance levels of lags for the same variables may vary. As many studies do, we will report results from both individual coefficients and sums of lag coefficients for each variable (Greene, 1997). These sums have the same interpretation as individual coefficients, but give the overall effect of a shock with a duration of its lag length in a right hand side variable on the dependent variable.

In addition to our variables, a number of structural variables that could affect export openness (e.g., structure of contracts, institutional qualities, internal power distribution) are absent. Structural variables typically change slowly and their effects are manifested by export openness inertia, which, as noted, is typically modeled by including a lagged dependent variable. Hence, in addition to the theoretical notion of openness inertia, the lagged dependent variable captures effects of potentially missing structural variables. As noted by Burkhart and Lewis-Beck (1994) and others, this method makes it more difficult for spurious effects to be reported. It also makes it harder to find significant results (Li and Reuveny, 2003). Hence, our modeling approach can be said to be conservative.

Given the time series nature of our data, we need to consider the possibility of serial correlation. With serial correlation, estimated coefficients are not biased, but their standard errors are biased. The inclusion of the lagged dependent variable on the right hand side is expected to alleviate problems associated with serial correlation (Beck and Katz, 1995). Nevertheless, we also will estimate robust standard errors, as suggested by Newey and West (1987). In concordance with Morrow et al. (1998) and Oneal and Russett (1999), we use a one-tailed t-test for coefficients whose sign is theoretically expected, and two-tailed t-tests otherwise. Hence, for world economic growth, leadership, inertia, democracy, and debt default we employ a one-tailed t test, and for conflict we employ a two-tailed t test.[17]

As will be shown in Figure 1, in our 1870-1992 sample, trade openness exhibited three sub-dynamics: 1870-early 1920s, early 1920s-1945, and 1945-1992. After 1945, the leadership data are based on US values; before 1946, they are based on British values. Since our theory is expected to work in the long run, we use the full sample. But it is desirable to employ samples that combine US and Britain leadership data, as well as use portions of the sample for robustness checks. It is also clear that a sample that is too short will exhibit only part of the dynamics, leading to spurious results. These considerations suggest using three samples: 1870-1992, 1870-1945, and 1919-1992.

Finally, Equation (1) assumes that trade openness processes can be profitably aggregated into Northern and Southern processes. The reader may recall that our theory predicts different behaviors for North and South. If we are correct, we would expect to see significant effects for the North, and much less so for the South. But one may argue that changes in Northern national openness are brought about by unique national factors. We think this threat is unlikely to be so serious as to completely undermine our approach for the North. If Northern trade openness has the clear dynamic shown in Figure 1, then different countries in the region are probably reacting to common stimuli. For our purpose, it does not really matter if there are elements associated with some cases and not with others, as long as there are common factors across cases. The possibility that Northern openness is traced primarily to idiosyncratic national factors is relegated to the statistical error term in any case, and should work against us in the test. If this threat is large, our model should not find empirical support.

Southern openness is expected to be less responsive to leadership and world economic growth. Again, it is possible that some Southern countries will be positively affected by growth and leadership, absorb radical innovations emanating from the lead economy, break the shackles of underdevelopment, and forge ahead in export openness. This possibility certainly exists but it is not expected to be the general case. If most of the South does not adhere to this assumption, our findings should not support our expectations.

Empirical results

We first inspect plots of our variables. Since our raw data are noisy, they are difficult to read when plotted. To improve our ability to visually read them, we average the data over decades. Figure 1 presents a decadal look at Northern and Southern openness. From 1870 to the early 1920s, the two series did not change much. Since then, Northern openness declined up to the 1940s, and has risen since then. In the same period, the Southern series continued to hover around openness ratios of about 4-5 percent. It is also possible to discern long waves in the series. The first wave in Northern openness peaks in the 1880s, and the second, or an extension of the first, in the 1920s. A third wave rides a rising trend, beginning in the mid 1940s and peaking in the 1960s. The Southern openness waves are considerably less pronounced than the Northern openness waves. The first wave peaks in the 1910s, the second in the 1940s, and the third in the 1970s. The timing of the openness waves, particularly the Northern series, generally correspond to the long wave-chronology discussed in the leadership-long cycle studies, as shown in Figure 2.

Figure 2 presents the decade averages for systemic leadership and world economic growth. Forty to fifty-year "long waves" are observable for world economic growth. World economic growth peaks are evident in the 1880s, 1920s, and 1960s.[18] Systemic leadership peaks are evident in the 1880s and in the 1950s. The 1950s peak is expected by the leadership-long cycle perspective. The 1880s peak for the British leadership is not the largest one in the 19th century. A larger peak in the British leadership data occurred shortly after the Napoleonic Wars (Thompson, 1988), with a similar timing to the US case after World War II. Thanks to the victory in war, exhaustion of opponents, war-induced military edge, and the economic platform provided by the system's leading economy, systemic leadership is strongest immediately after the conclusion of the global war that essentially installs leaders in a trial by combat.

Figures 1 and 2 suggest that on average Northern openness increases when world economic growth and systemic leadership are high, and vice versa. On the other hand, the correspondence between the rise and fall in Southern openness and the two systemic variables is much less evident. In general, it seems that the ups and downs in leadership and worl economic growth do not have much effect on Southern openness, which continues to hover around 4-5 percent throughout the sample. These observations generally support our theoretical interpretation, which expects two globalization dynamics, and still another North-South cleavage. Yet, these figures do not pinpoint how our

Figure 1. Openness, decade average

variables relate to each other statistically. To discern these effects, we turn to the regression analyses. These analyses are conducted using the raw, original data (not the averaged data presented in Figures 1 and 2).

The grid search looking for the lag lengths that fit the data best suggests using the first and second lags for world economic growth, the current value for systemic leadership, and the first lag for Northern democracy and Northern conflict. Table 2 presents the estimation results for the North.[19] Columns 1 and 2 present results for the full, 1870-1992 sample. The model's goodness of fit, based on the R-square measure, is 0.96, which is high. The effect of each of the five right hand side variables, except Northern conflict, on the level of Northern openness is statistically significant. This result is consistent with the interpretation according to which intense conflict in the North, as witnessed in two world wars, tends to be offset by increased, war-related production by Maddison's "western offshoots" that were distant from the combat zones. The effect of Northern openness inertia on Northern openness is positive; the effect of Northern democracy is positive, the effect of world economic growth is positive, and the effect of systemic leadership on Northern openness is positive. All of these results, including the one for Northern conflict, conform to our theoretical expectations.

In columns 3-6 of Table 2, we present estimation results from the 1870-1945 and 1919-1992 periods, as called for in our research design. The R-square in the 1870-1945 period is 0.92, and in the 1919-1992 period it is 0.96, both of

Figure 2. Independent variables, decade average

which are high. The signs and significance of all the five variables in the two additional samples conform with the results in the full sample. The statistical results presented from the full sample then are robust.

Table 3 presents the estimation results for the South. Columns 1-2 again present results for the full, 1870-1992 sample. The model's goodness of fit, based on the R-square measure, is 0.82, which is also fairly high. The effects of Southern openness inertia and Southern debt defaults are statistically significant. The sign of the effect of Southern openness inertia on Southern openness is positive, as expected. The effect of Southern debt default on Southern openness is negative in the short run, and positive in the longer run, also as expected. None of the effects of the other variables in the model are statistically significant. In particular, Southern openness does not appear to be responding to changes in world economic growth and systemic leadership.

In columns 3-6 of Table 2, we report results for the 1870-1945 and 1919-1992 periods. The R-square in the 1870-1945 period is 0.84, and in the 1919-1992 period it is 0.7, both of which are strong, albeit weaker than the corresponding results for the North. The signs and significance levels in the 1870-1945 sample are almost identical to those reported for the full sample.

Table 2. Estimation results for the North

Variables	Coefficients 1870-1992	Sums of Coefficients	Coefficients 1870-1945	Sums of Coefficients	Coefficients 1919-1992	Sums of Coefficients
Northern Openness$_{t-1}$	1.0081***		0.5089***		1.0164***	
Northern Democracy$_{t-1}$	0.0005*		0.0031***		0.0006**	
Northern Conflict$_{t-1}$	0.0095		0.0271**		0.0447	
World Economic Growth$_{t-1}$	0.0071	0.0355***	0.0005	0.0302*	-0.0069	0.0314**
World Economic Growth$_{t-2}$	0.0284**		0.0297*		0.0383**	
Systemic Leadership$_t$	0.0050***		0.0199***		0.0059**	

Note: *** denotes statistical significance at 1% level; ** at 5%; and * at 10%.

Unlike the full sample, however, the effect of world economic growth is significant, as in the North, suggesting that large changes in growth (see Figure 2) do affect Southern trade openness. The effect of debt default on Southern openness resembles the one in the full period, but it is not significant at conventional levels.[20]

The results in the 1919-1992 period resemble the results from the full sample, except that now the positive effect of systemic leadership is statistically significant, as in the North. This result suggest that large changes in leadership, which characterize this period, are able to affect Southern economic openness. In sum, as in the North, the results presented from the full sample for the South are robust. Yet we come away from the Southern analysis with the strong impression that systemic influences are less easy to generalize about than in the North.

Finally, another possible threat to the validity of our analysis is the design decision to focus on series that end in 1992. Is it possible that we are missing a Southern trade globalization explosion that is discernible empirically only after 1992? To check this possibility, we constructed shorter Southern and Northern, aggregated exports/gdp series for the 1983-2003 period.[21] The outcome is shown in figure 3. The Southern exports/gdp ratio is .058 in 1983 and remains more or less at the same level a decade later in 1992 (.059). By 2003, however, the trade openness ratio has increased to .094–something on the order of a 62 percent increase between 1983 and 2003. Thus, it may seem that ending an analysis in 1992 biases the outcome somewhat by missing some significant post-1992 activity.[22]

Lest we be too hasty to criticize our own research design, however, the Southern outcome needs to be compared to the Northern outcome. In 1983,

Table 3. Estimation results for the South

Variables	Coefficients 1870-1992	Sums of Coefficients	Coefficients 1870-1945	Sums of Coefficients	Coefficients 1919-1992	Sums of Coefficients
Southern Openness$_{t-1}$	0.8397***		0.8239***		0.0679***	
Southern Democracy$_{t-1}$	0.00002		0.00002		-0.0004	
Southern Conflict$_{t-1}$	0.02936		0.0223		0.0443	
World Economic Growth$_{t-1}$	-0.0069	-0.0107	0.0143*	0.0253**	-0.0057	-0.0099
World Economic Growth$_{t-2}$	0.0038		0.0011		-0.0042	
Systemic Leadership$_t$	0.0004		-0.0064		0.0052*	
Debt Default$_{t-1}$	-0.0057**	-0.0013	-0.0057	-0.0012	-0.0290**	0.0032
Debt Default$_{t-2}$	0.0044**		0.0045		0.0322**	

Note: *** denotes statistical significance at 1% level; ** at 5%; and * at 10%.

the Northern aggregated ratio stood at .162. By 2002, the Northern exports/GDP ratio had expanded to .267. Thus, in terms of percentage increases, the Southern and Northern series increase roughly on the same order: 62 percent for the South and 65 percent for the North. But the gap between the Southern and Northern positions in 1983 is .104. By 2003, this gap had expanded to .173–a roughly 66 percent increase in the size of the North-South trade globalization gap. So, it turns out that stopping our data analysis in 1992 is not as much of a threat to the validity of the analysis as it might otherwise appear. If our data series extended from 1870 into the early 2000s, as opposed to 1992, we probably would have found even stronger evidence for a widening North-South trade globalization gap.[23]

Conclusion

This paper studies a dimension of the extent of economic globalization in the global North and South over a long period of time. Economic globalization is measured here solely in terms of trade openness. Our leadership-long cycle theoretical perspective expects that world economic growth and systemic leadership will promote Northern economic openness but will have a much smaller effect on Southern export openness. Our empirical analysis, which employed a statistical modeling approach, supports our theory. Our results are found to be robust across sub periods in our sample.

Figure 3. Updating the globalization gap

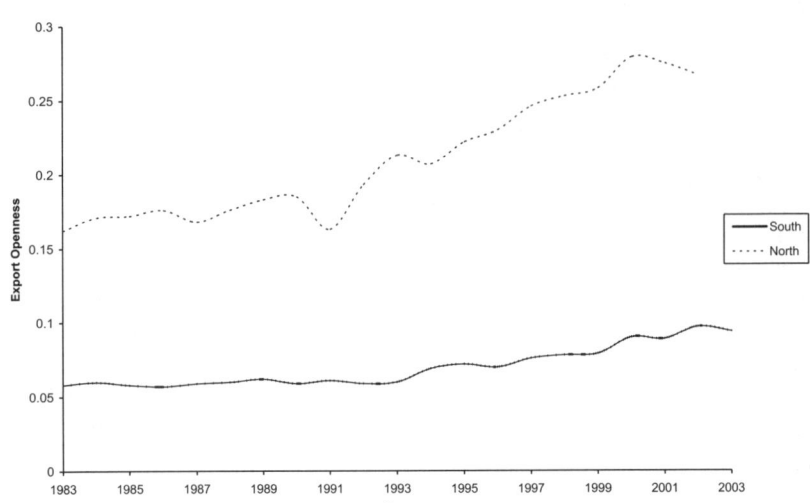

Economic globalization is an old process of increasing pre-existing levels of integration between different units and zones of economic activity. Simply because we refer to it as globalization does not make it so. Or, alternatively, if we make globalization synonymous with increasing economic integration and interaction somewhere, we cannot assume that all actors are equally affected. We are not the first authors to suggest that contemporary globalization is an uneven process.[24] We may be the first to identify, theoretically and empirically, globalization drivers that appear to work more strongly in the North than they do in the South.

Because trade globalization works more strongly in the North than it does in the South, we should expect it to make the gap between North and South worse rather than better. A global North that is more integrated to the world economy should experience higher levels of economic development over time than a global South that is less integrated to the world economy. The gap between North and South standards of living, then, is expected to grow. North-South economic convergence, which is predicted by neoclassical economic growth theory, is not expected to occur from our theoretical perspective any time soon, nor do our empirical results suggest that it occurs in the real world.[25]

While there will always be a few national exceptions to these generalizations, it follows that one cannot rely exclusively on market processes to even out the economic growth playing field. That field is already highly stratified into zones in which the chances for growth and trade have been and continue to be, with some major exceptions, grossly unequal. Economic globalization does not appear to be breaking down these historical stratifications. Rather, it is economic globalization that tends to be channeled by these past grooves of strong and weak growth. The national units that are already integrated to the world economy become more integrated to the world economy; the less well-connected often stay that way. So far, only a very small number of states have managed to break out of the low-growth ruts of the world system. The implications of this grim outcome for world political stability are stark. To the extent that poverty and underdevelopment facilitate continuing conflict between North and South, we may expect to see more of these phenomena in the future, not less. To be sure, substantial quality of life improvements that are not captured by our focus on export openness have been registered in the South. But, we ask whether these improvements should be expected to compensate for relatively slower improvements in many Southern economies? Or, is it possible that more mouths to feed and people to employ without widely distributed economic growth may contribute even more to future instability?

Notes

[1] Given its scope, we cannot review fully the leadership-long cycle literature. For expositions (without attention to Northern and Southern globalization) see Modelski and Thompson (1996) and Thompson (2000).
[2] See, e.g., Modelski (1987, 1996), Thompson (1988, 2000), Rasler and Thompson (1994), Modelski and Thompson (1988, 1996), and Reuveny and Thompson (1999, 2000, 2001, 2004b).
[3] Examples of these radical innovations include mechanized textile looms, steam engines, electrification, automobiles, jet engines, and computers.
[4] On North-South military conflict, see Reuveny and Thompson (2002). On North-South income inequality, see Reuveny and Thompson (2003), and on Southern debt crisis and default, see Reuveny and Thompson (2004a).
[5] The major exception to the stickiness of the regional hierarchy is the heterogenous Asian region.
[6] We include Middle Eastern oil producers and South-American states in the South. While some of these states qualify in recent years as Northern in terms of our indicator, they lag in ability to absorb innovation. Some countries have capitalized on oil production. A few South American states are not pure raw material providers, but are still grappling with absorbing earlier innovations, while the North is now mastering information technology.
[7] A dependence on the standardized GDP data provided by Maddison (1995) precludes more extensive LDC coverage for series going back to 1870.
[8] Note that our evaluation does not hinge on economies qualifying in specific years but whether they move from one category to another roughly (as in the Soviet Union moving into the North between the two world wars or Taiwan and South Korea doing so in the late 1970s or early 1980s) about when one might expect some change in status.
[9] Another early approach that had to be abandoned was to take the globalization series developed by Chase-Dunn, Kawano, and Brewer (2000) and decompose it into Northern and Southern information. Unfortunately, we found that this measure is highly dependent on largely Northern data well into the 20th century and, therefore, could not serve our

present purposes. Nonetheless, we are indebted to Christopher Chase-Dunn for the opportunity of examining the raw data used to construct that series.

[10] Obviously, the interpolation for the missing war years would be less desirable if one of our primary questions was the impacts of World Wars I and II on exports. However, this is not one of our principle questions in this analysis.

[11] The countries are: Australia, Austria, Belgium, Canada, Denmark, Finland, France, Germany, Italy, Japan, Netherlands, New Zealand, Norway, Sweden, Switzerland, UK and US. Japan's data begin in 1885, and Switzerland's data in 1899.

[12] See, e.g., Modelski and Thompson (1988), Thompson (1988), McKeown (1991), Boswell and Sweat (1991), Rasler and Thompson (1994), Reuveny and Thompson (1999, 2004a, 2004b).

[13] Historically, system leaders have not excelled in developing armies. The current system leader is proving to be an exception to this generalization.

[14] The MID data (version 2.1) are taken from Zeev Maoz (http://www.spirit.tau.ac.il/~zeevmaoz).

[15] Whether a country defaulted or was allowed to reschedule its debt is not relevant for our purpose, as we control for debt problems, and not for their type.

[16] Many studies employ this approach, including Stern et al (1976), Geraci and Preow (1982), Campbell and Mankiw (1987), Rasler and Thompson (1994), Reuveny (2001), and Reuveny and Thompson (1999, 2001, 2002, 2004a, 2004b).

[17] Significance levels of one, five, and ten percent are used.

[18] We view the 1880s and 1920s as parts of the same long wave that is disrupted by World War I.

[19] We used the statistical package Regression Analysis Time of Time Series (RATS) (Doan, 2000). We guard against the possibility of serial correlation by estimating the model from the method of Newey and West (1987), which generates robust standard errors.

[20] The difference in the result for debt seems to reflect both the large changes of world economic growth, which leave less of the small variance in Southern openness to be explained by the debt variable, and the smaller sample.

[21] The data come from a World Bank source at http://devdata.worldbank.org/dataonline. We used exports of goods and services and GDP enumerated in constant 1995 US dollars. We were able to obtain data for very similar samples to those constructed using Maddison's data. The Southern group encompasses Argentina, Bangladesh, Bolivia, Brazil, Bulgaria, Chile, China, Colombia, Congo/Zaire, Cote d'Ivoire, Egypt, Ethiopia, India, Indonesia, Kenya, Mexico, Morocco, Nigeria, Pakistan, Peru, Romania, Tanzania, Thailand, Turkey, and Venezuela. The Northern group includes Austria, Australia, Belgium, Canada, Czechoslovakia/Czech Republic, Denmark, Finland, France, Germany, Greece, Hungary, Ireland, Italy, Japan, South Korea, the Netherlands, New Zealand, Norway, Poland, Portugal, Russia, Spain, Sweden, Switzerland, the United Kingdom, and the United States.

[22] Some of this change definitely can be attributed to China. Removing China from the Southern group reduces the 1983 ratio from .058 to .055. The 2003 ratio would be reduced from .094 to .089. Still, the changes are not exactly overwhelming.

[23] A related validity threat potentially emanates from our approach to categorizing North and South. We allow Southern and Northern actors to move from one category to the other while some analysts would prefer that we define the South in fixed 1870 terms. While we do not find this latter approach very appealing, we (Reuveny and Thompson, 2003) have examined North-South gap data utilizing it without finding substantively different results from an analysis using our "flexible" North-South approach. What may be most important about our North-South categorization approach is that it would be highly vulnerable to misinterpretation if there was a fair amount of movement between the two categories. This has not been the case historically. With the exception of Russia (after 1992), no Northern state has moved into the South and few Southern states have moved into the

North. Within our sample, only Japan, Taiwan, and South Korea have made the transition in the many states outside of Europe and the western offshoots. Perhaps equally telling is that the size of the South measured in terms of population has expanded greatly in absolute terms but has stayed about the same proportionally. In 1870, our Southern sample had a population of about 712 million people (or 76.1% of the total). In 2000, the Southern sample encompassed 3961 million people (or 75.6% of the total). It seems safe to conclude that we are not artificially shrinking the South to obtain desired results. Over the last 130 years, it continues to capture some three-fourths of the world's population.

[24] See, among others, Hirst and Thompson (1999).
[25] This statement does not say that standards of living in the South have not improved. Clearly, they have but so have Northern standards of living. Our point is that the difference between Northern and Southern standards of living is not necessarily improving. Alternatively put, Northern standards of living are improving faster than are Southern standards of living.

References

Arrighi, Giovanni and Jessica Drangel. 1986. "The Stratification of the World-Economy: An Exploration of the Semiperipheral Zone." *Review* 10 (1): 9-74.
Banks, Arthur. 1971. *Cross-Polity Time Series Data*. Cambridge, MA.: MIT Press.
Beck, Nathaniel and Jonathan. N. Katz. 1995. 'What to Do (and Not to Do) With Time-Series Cross-Section Data', *American Political Science Review* 89 (3): 634-47.
Boswell, Terry and Michael Sweat. 1991. "Hegemony, Long Waves, and Major Wars: A Time Series Analysis of System Dynamics, 1496-1967." *International Studies Quarterly* 35 (2): 123-49.
Burkhart, Ross E. and Michael Lewis-Beck. 1994. "Comparative Democracy: The Economic Development Thesis." *American Political Science Review* 88 (4): 903-910.
Campbell, John Y. and Gregory Mankiw. 1987. "Are Output Fluctuations Transitory?" The *Quarterly Journal of Economics* 102 (4): 857-880.
Chase-Dunn, Christopher, Yukio Kawano, and Benjamin Brewer. 2000. "Trade Globalization Since 1795: Waves of Integration in the World-System." *American Sociological Review* 65 (1): 77-95.
Dixon, William J. and Bruce E. Moon. 1993. "Political Similarity and American Foreign Trade Patterns." *Political Research Quarterly* 46 (1): 5-25.
Doan, Thomas A. 2000. *Regression Analysis Time Series (RATS)*. Evanston, IL: Estima.
Freeman, Christopher and Carlota Perez. 1988. "Structural Crises of Adjustment: Business Cycles and Investment Behavior." Pp. 38-66 in *Technical Change and Economic Theory*, edited by Dosi, Giovanni Christopher Freeman, R. Nelson, Gerlad Silverberg, and L. Soete. London: Pinter.
Geraci, Vincent J. and Wilfred Preow. 1982. "An Empirical Demand and Supply Model of Bilateral Trade." *The Review of Economics and Statistics* 64 (3): 432-661.
Gilpin, Robert. 1975. *U.S. Power and the Multinational Corporation*. New York: Basic Books.
Gowa, Joan 1994. *Allies, Adversaries, and International Trade*. Princeton, NJ: Princeton University Press.

Greene, William H. 1997. *Econometric Analysis*. New York: Macmillian.
Hirst, Paul and Grahame Thompson. 1999. *Globalization in Question*. Cambridge: Polity
Jaggers, Keith and Ted Robert Gurr. 1995. "Tracking Democracy's Third Wave With the Polity III Data." *Journal of Peace Research* 32 (4): 469-483.
Kentor, Jeffrey. 2000. *Capital and Coercion: The Economic and Military Processes That Have Shaped the World Economy, 1800-1990*. New York: Garland.
Kick, Edward. 1987 "World System Structure, National Development and the Prospects for a Socialist World Order." Pp. 127-155 in *America's Changing Role in the World-System* edited by Boswell Terry and Albert Bergesen. New York: Praeger.
Kuznets, Simon, S. 1972. *Postwar Economic Growth*. Cambridge, MA: Harvard University Press.
Li, Quan. and Rafael. Reuveny. 2003. "Economic Globalization and Democracy: An Empirical Analysis." *British Journal of Political Science* 31 (1): 29-54.
Londregan, J. B. and K. T. Poole. 1996. "Does High Income Promote Democracy?" *World Politics* 49 (1): 1-30.
Maddison, Angus M. 1992. *Dynamic Forces in Capitalist Development: A Long-run Comparative View*. New York: Oxford University Press.
Maddison, Angus M. 1995. *Monitoring the World Economy, 1820-1992*. Paris: OECD.
Mansfield, Edward and Jack Snyder. 1995. "Democratization and the Danger of War." *International Security* 20 (1): 5-38.
McCormick, James, B. 1988. *The World Economy*. Totowa, NJ: Barnes and Noble.
McKeown, Timothy. 1991. "A Liberal Trade Order? The Long-Run Pattern of Imports to the Advanced Capitalist States." *International Studies Quarterly* 35 (2): 151-72.
Modelski, George. 1987. *Long Cycles in World Politics*. London: Macmillan.
Modelski, George. 1996. "Evolutionary Paradigm for Global Politics." *International Studies Quarterly* 40 (3): 321-342.
Modelski, George and William R. Thompson. 1988. *Sea Power in Global Politics, 1494-1993*. London: Macmillian.
Modelski, George and William R. Thompson. 1996. *Leading Sectors and World Power: The Coevolution of Global Economics and Politics*. Columbia: University of South Carolina Press.
Morrow, James., Randolph. D. Siverson and C. Tabares. 1998. "The Political Determinants of International Trade: The Major Powers 1907-1990." *American Political Science Review* 92 (3): 649-661.
Muller, Edward. N. and Mitchell A. Seligson. 1994. "Civic Culture and Democracy: The Question of Causal Relationship." *American Political Science Review* 88 (3): 635-652.
Newey, W. and K. West. 1987. "A Simple Positive Semi-Definite, Heteroscedasticity and Autocorrelation Consistent Covariance Matrix." *Econometrica* 55: (4) 703-708.
O'Brien, Patrick K. 2006. "Colonies in a Globalizing Economy, 1815-1948." In *Globalization and Global History*, edited by Barry K. Gills and William R. Thompson. London: Routledge.

Oneal, John and Bruce Russett. 1999. "Assessing the Liberal Peace with Alternative Specifications: Trade Still Reduces Conflict." *Journal of Peace Research* 36 (4): 423-442.
Passe-Smith, John T. 1998. "The Persistence of the Gap Between Rich and Poor Countries: Taking Stock of World Economic Growth, 1960-1993." Pp. 27-40 in *Development and Underdevelopment: The Political Economy of Global Inequality*, edited by Mitchell. A. Seligson & John. T. Passe-Smith. Boulder, CO: Lynne Rienner.
Pollins, B. M.. 1989. "Does Trade Still Follow the Flag?" *American Political Science Review* 83 (2): 465-480.
Rasler, Karen and William R. Thompson. 1994. *The Great Powers and Global Struggle: 1490-1990*. Lexington: University Press of Kentucky.
Reuveny, Rafael. 2001. "Bilateral Import, Export, and Conflict/Cooperation Simultaneity," *International Studies Quarterly* 45 (1): 131-158.
Reuveny, Rafael and William R. Thompson. 1999. "Economic Innovation, Systemic Leadership, and Military Preparation for War: The U.S. Case." *Journal of Conflict Resolution* 43 (5): 570-595.
Reuveny, Rafael and William R. Thompson. 2001. "Leading Sectors, Lead Economies and Economic Growth." *Review of International Political Economy* 8 (4): 689-719.
Reuveny, Rafael and William R. Thompson. 2002. "World Economic Growth, Northern Antagonism, and North-South Conflict." *Journal of Conflict Resolution* 46 (4): 484-515.
Reuveny, Rafael and William R. Thompson. 2003. "Exploring the North-South Gap." *Japanese Journal of Political Science* 4 (1): 77-102.
Reuveny, Rafael and William R. Thompson. 2004a. "World Economic Growth, Systemic Leadership and Southern Debt Crises." *Journal of Peace Research*, 41 (1): 5-24.
Reuveny, Rafael and William R. Thompson. 2004b. *Growth, Trade and Systemic Leadership*. Ann Arbor: University of Michigan Press.
Rostow, Walt W. 1979. *The World Economy: History and Prospect*. Austin: University of Texas Press.
Smith, Adam 1776[1937]. *An Inquiry into the Nature and Causes of the Wealth of Nations*, edited by Edwin Cannan. New York: The Modern Library.
Stern, Robert M., Jonathan Francis, and Bruce Schumacher. 1976. *Price Elasticities in International Trade: An Annotated Bibliography*. London: Macmillan.
Suter, Christian., 1992. *Debt Cycles in the World-Economy: Foreign Loans, Financial Crises, and Debt Settlements, 1820-1990*. Boulder, CO: Westview.
Thompson, William R. 1988. *On Global War: Historical-Structural Approaches to World Politics*. Columbia, SC: University of South Carolina Press.
Thompson, William R. 1996. "Democracy and Peace: Putting the Cart Before the Horse?" *International Organization* 50 (1): 141-74.
Thompson, William R. 2000. *The Emergence of the Global Political Economy*. London: UCL Press/ Routledge.
United Nations (multiple volumes) *Statistical Yearbook*. New York: United Nations.
Wolf, Martin. 2004. *Why Globalization Works*. New Haven, CT: Yale University Press.

2
Globalization, Regionalism, and the Organization of Transnational Collective Action within World Regions, 1980-2000

Dawn Wiest and Jackie Smith

Since the late 1980s, governments have focused intensely on formalizing political and economic relationships within regions. There has also been a concurrent rise in transnational, regional level organizing among social movement activists globally, suggesting the regionalization of "global civil society." However, opportunities for participation in transnational associations vary widely across countries. In this paper, we examine the influence of international (both global and regional) institutional contexts, citizen participation in international society, and national level factors on varying levels of participation in regional transnational social movement organizations (TSMOs). We use negative binomial regression to examine relationships among these factors at three time points: 1980, 1990, and 2000. We find that in the early time period, citizen network connections to international society facilitated the formation of and participation in regionally organized TSMOs. Over time, however, regional and global institutional contexts were more predictive of participation in regional TSMOs than were international network ties. Our analysis also uncovered how qualitatively different forms of regionalism translated into significantly different levels of TSMO regionalization. In Europe, where the regional institutional structure is more elaborated than elsewhere in the world, the number of regional TSMOs in which citizens participated greatly outpaced that found elsewhere. Irrespective of international, institutional factors, however, state-level features remained crucial to explaining the development of regional TSMO sectors and the variable levels of participation in them. Citizens in states with restrictions on political rights and civil liberties had significantly lower participation in these organizations in 1990 and 2000. Even so, over time, citizens in states with more ties to global and regional multilateral processes found more ways to overcome this disadvantage and strengthen their participation in regional, transnational civil society.

In recent years especially, analysts and observers of global politics have documented the central role that transnational associations play in developing civil society relations across borders (Boli and Thomas 1999; Sikkink and Smith 2002; Wapner 1995).[1] Moreover, there is a reciprocal relationship between intergovernmental institutions and civil society actors. Global institutions provide focal points and opportunities for transnational citizen mobilization, and citizen-led advocacy campaigns have, in turn, shaped the evolution of global institutions (Anand 1999; Chatfield 1997; Friedman, Clark, and Hochstetler 2005; Moghadam 2000; Smith Forthcoming). As citizens' groups have become more active in global arenas, analysts have sought to better understand how global variations in access to resources and organizing opportunities affect participation in what many see as a globalizing civil society. Who participates in transnational organizations? And how are these associations organized in relation to the inter-state political arena?

While we know that the population of transnational associations has grown tremendously in recent decades, we know little else about changes in the ways people have combined across national borders to promote a variety of activities. We also know very little about how changes in the global political context affect transnational associations. In this paper we explore patterns of transnational organizing among groups formed for the explicit purpose of promoting social change, groups we call transnational social movement organizations or TSMOs. Data from the Yearbook of International Organizations show that, since the mid-1980s, a larger percentage of transnational social change organizations were organized along regional lines—a pattern that mirrors developments in intergovernmental arenas (e.g. Coleman and Underhill 1998; Fawcett and Hurrell 1995; Mansfield and Reinhardt 2003; Sidaway 2002; Taylor 2003). Two different explanations might account for this organizational pattern. One interpretation is that the regionalization of transnational organizing results from the failures of prior organizing efforts to overcome major cleavages that divide the world's regions. In other words, civil society remains polarized along the lines of tension that continue to divide governments and inhibit more effective international cooperation. Another interpretation is that regionalization reflects activists' efforts to take advantage of institutional openings to maximize their influence in supra-national political arenas.

Smith's earlier analysis (2005) of the ties between regionally organized transnational social movement organizations and other non-governmental organizations found support for the latter argument, that regionalization corresponds to institutional opportunities. A significantly greater proportion of regional TSMOs based in the global north than in the south maintained ties either predominately or exclusively with other regional nongovernmental organizations. But, regional TSMOs based in the global south maintained significantly more cross-regional ties than their northern counterparts. This latter finding suggests that polarization between the world's regions is not driving the patterns of regional organizing we find here. If polarization was at work, we would expect activists in the global south to be more focused on regional ties, given their relative disadvantage in global settings. Instead, these groups were far more globally oriented than their northern counterparts.

In a subsequent analysis (Wiest and Smith 2006), we found further support for the argument that institutional contexts are the principal drivers of regionalization among TSMOs. Our analysis showed that regional TSMOs based in the south were more likely to maintain ties to global intergovernmental organizations (IGOs), and they were less likely to report ties only to regional IGOs than their northern counterparts (see figure 1).[2]

Figure 1. Regional TSMO ties to IGOs, year 2000

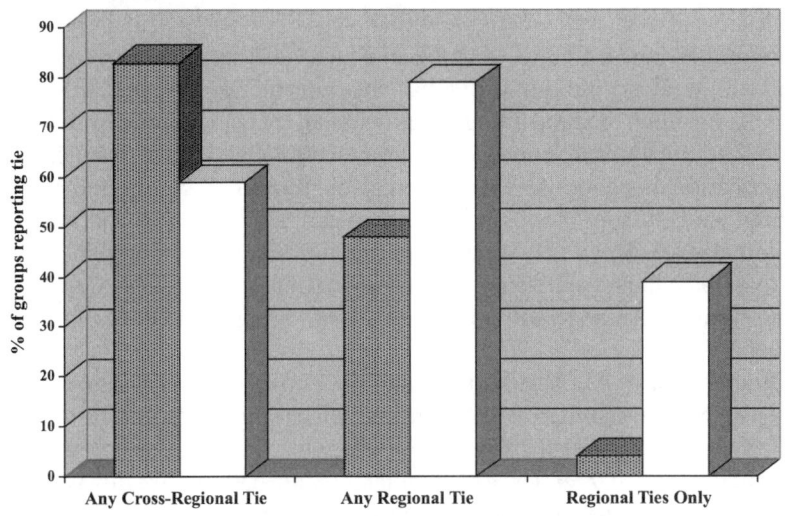

Source: Yearbook of International Organizations; Southern N=52; Northern N=99

This evidence not only supports an institutional explanation for why transnational SMOs have been more likely to organize along regional lines, but it also shows that forces shaping the development of a more regionally organized TSMO sector differ between regions. In the north, for instance, the institutions of the European Union are highly developed, exhibiting strong sectoral differentiation as well as varied mechanisms for the participation of civil society groups. Although not nearly as developed as in Europe, regional level institution-building in the global south has accelerated in recent years, particularly during the 1990s. Regional bodies such as the African Union, ASEAN, and Mercosur are playing increasingly important roles in global, regional, and national political and economic arenas. Influenced by global democratic norms, they are also creating openings (however small) for the input of civil society in regional-level policy making. To what extent can regional institution building explain the growth of regional TSMO sectors, as well as variation across countries with regard to participation in regional TSMOs? What other factors might explain a rising tendency for TSMOs to be organized within regions?

To address these questions, we examine the relationship between government participation in regional-level institutions and citizen participation in regional TSMOs. In a recent paper, Smith and Wiest (2005) showed that government linkages to the world polity via participation in intergovernmental organizations (IGOs) and ratification of human rights treaties had a strong, significant influence on citizen participation in TSMOs. Moreover, that research showed that government participation in IGOs was particularly important for understanding TSMO participation among citizens in poor countries. States with weak positions in the global economic hierarchy seek to overcome their weaknesses by joining intergovernmental organizations, and by doing so, they create the 'internal conditions' that facilitate civil society participation in transnational coalitions and movement organizations. Smith and Wiest's research lends further empirical support to case studies of transnational activism that have shown that state ties to the international system play important roles in facilitating citizen participation in transnational social movement coalitions and networks (Ball 2000; Brysk 1993; Khagram 2004; Lewis 2002; Tarrow 2005).

Other research has also shown that the consolidation of international norms such as human rights over time has fueled the expansion of transnational civil society (Tsutsui 2004; Tsutsui and Wotipka 2004). Moreover, while domestic factors such as level of democracy and national wealth were the main predictors of participation in non-governmental transnational human rights organizations in the 1970s, by the 1980s, such factors were overshadowed in importance by the facilitative effect of linkages to global civil society generally (Tsutsui and Wotipka 2004). We build upon this earlier research to consider national-level characteristics that might explain why people from different countries are more or less active in regional TSMOs. In particular, we explore the relative importance of a country's internal characteristics and its embeddedness in international contexts for understanding patterns of citizen participation in regional TSMOs. We also consider whether and how factors shaping regional networks have changed over time. Data from 1980, 1990 and 2000 are used to explore shifts in the patterns of regional organizing over this important period for the expansion of transnational civil society.

National and international influences on transnational association

Contemporary states are embedded in an increasingly dense network of transnational relations. As they ratify new treaties, expand the agenda of the United

Nations, and increase the volume of transnational interactions in economic and other sectors, they create new possibilities as well as constraints on future actions. This embeddedness of the state within a broader context of relations has important implications for how we understand other transnational processes. For instance, the rise of inter-governmental organizations to address problems that transcend geographic borders requires that citizens seeking to influence policies on many issues must also organize to engage inter-governmental political arenas. Expanding transnational relationships between governments as well as other social actors (such as transnational corporations or civil society actors) affect the demands on governments and their range of policy choices (Meyer; Meyer, Boli, Thomas, and Ramirez 1997; Sassen 1998). Violating international agreements can cost governments in terms of their ability to achieve foreign policy objectives and their capacity to manage problems emerging from global interdependence (Friedman, Clark and Hochstetler 2005).

Research on social movements shows that national political contexts have important influences on whether and how people engage in politics (see, e.g., McAdam, McCarthy, and Zald 1996; Tarrow 1996). A government's tolerance of a wide range of public associations, its overall respect for civil and political rights, and the extent to which it allows political competition among diverse parties all affect the possibilities for social movement mobilization. And although these regime characteristics may be shaped by a nation's relationships to the broader global system, all transnational relationships are filtered through this domestic context (Lewis 2002; Tarrow 2001). Thus, in attempting to understand why the citizens of different nations are more or less likely to be active in regionally organized transnational social movement organizations, we must account for the character of national regimes.

National contexts also shape possibilities for transnational mobilization by defining the access citizens have to the resources needed for political action. Key resources include financing for voluntary associations and skills relevant for political organizing work. Past research shows that citizens from countries with higher levels of income and more widespread access to education, particularly at advanced levels, will be more likely than those without such resources to be involved in political organizing both within their own countries and transnationally (Smith and Wiest 2005; cf. McCarthy and Zald 1977).

Even as factors internal to states shape people's access to resources and their space for political organizing, global level processes increasingly influence these domestic contexts. For instance, the expansion of international human rights norms and the growth of mechanisms for monitoring states' compliance with these norms enhance pressures on states to democratize their practices, and it limits their range of possible responses to internal dissent (Sassen 1998). Institutional practices at the global level have led states to adopt similar practices and organizational structures, a process known as isomorphism (Giugni 2002; Meyer et al. 1997). The growing scale and frequency of trans-border exchanges facilitates the diffusion of ideas and models for action across national boundaries, further blurring the boundaries between domestic and international politics. Thus, explaining changes in the ways people engage in politics requires sensitivity to a nation's relationships to other states and supra-national institutions.

International agreements addressing trans-border problems by their nature seek to enhance international transparency. In the course of doing so, they tend to extend authority to non-state actors that can help verify or disprove states' claims, thereby fostering greater openness in transnational politics. This expands openings for groups that have access to information and expertise relevant to the issues addressed by a given treaty regime. Thus, an expansion of environmental treaties creates new sources of leverage for local groups providing information on states' environmental performances as well as for those with scientific expertise. International human rights bodies help to legitimize and certify human rights advocacy groups. More generally, the expansion of international forums for transnational problem solving enhances the space for new forms of claims making in these areas (Tilly 2004). We expect that variation in the extent to which a country is enmeshed in multilateral processes will help explain some of the variation in levels of citizen participation in regional TSMOs.

Global multilateral processes have facilitated the expansion of regional political spaces in which non-state actors can organize transnational collective action. The interplay of state capacities within the world system and global institutional dynamics shaped the emergence of the regional system that characterizes the world order today. As newly independent states joined the United Nations in the 1960s and 70s, and as they sought to enhance their political and economic footing vis-à-vis the "Great Powers," they consolidated their interests by forming regional blocs. In this way, the early expressions of regional cooperation that blossomed within the context of the United Nations system was a reflection of and a response to global shifts in power relations associated with the end of WWII, the growing East-West conflict, and the dissolution of the colonial empires. The United Nations responded to regional strategies by granting recognition and support to such initiatives, thus encouraging states to formalize these regional relationships. For example, as the number of African states with membership in the United Nations grew, African diplomats began to turn their attention away from regional cooperation with Asia and toward formal cooperation and integration within Africa through the formation of the Organization of African Unity. Efforts such as these were supported by the

United Nations Charter, which includes explicit provisions for the formation of functional regional organizations through Articles 51, 52, and 53.

The United Nations plays another direct role in consolidating regional relationships through its regional bodies. The UN Economic Commissions (UN-EC), for example, aim to directly facilitate regional cooperation in economic development and in related areas, such as environmental protection. The Commissions are essential features of the architecture of regional cooperation and play an integral role in bolstering governments' ability to adequately address important transborder issues within the region.[3] For example, the United Nations Economic Commission for Africa (ECA) contributed extensively to development projects in Africa beginning in the 1960s, including the sponsorship of a regional leadership-training institute in Dakar, Senegal. Moreover, the ECA worked closely with the OAU to establish the African Development Bank. In Europe, the "Environment for Europe" program takes place under the auspices of the UN-ECE. This program strengthens efforts to coordinate environmental protection and sustainable development projects across the continent.

The embeddedness of regional institutions within global institutional processes becomes clear when we also consider the legal instruments of regional integration and cooperation. For example, elaborate regional human rights systems exist within Europe, the Americas, and Africa. These systems are viewed as complements to and modifications of the global system of rights (Ouguergouz 2003). Although their enforcement capacities differ dramatically, the regional systems provide the legal language with which individuals, NGOs, and social movements can challenge the practices of states. Moreover, the compatibility between regional and global rights systems facilitates the linking of domestic, regional, and global networks organized around rights regimes.

These international factors are likely to be most relevant for patterns of transnational social movement organization when a country has direct ties to regional and global institutions—including both intergovernmental organizations (IGOs) and treaties. In addition, the extent to which a country is embedded in the world polity is also indicated by non-governmental cross-border connections, including citizen links to international non-governmental organizations (INGOs) of all kinds. Given this understanding of institutional evolution, we expect the international factors we mention to have stronger effects over time. This is because structured, routine participation in the world polity, through governments' memberships in global and regional organizations and treaties, helps "socialize" states into the norms of international society (Finnemore 1996; Riemann 2002). Risse and his colleagues (1999) refer to this as the "norms spiral," whereby a state moves from denying accusations of violations and refusing to recognize international jurisdiction to making tactical and legal concessions to eventual compliance with norms (see also Clark 2003). Evidence from other studies also suggests that transnational, or world cultural processes are becoming more influential over time. For instance, longitudinal studies by Ramirez and his colleagues and by Tsutsui and Wotipka found stronger world cultural effects on the adoption of women's suffrage and on participation in international human rights NGOs, respectively, in more recent years than they found in earlier years (Ramirez, Soysal and Shanahan 1997; Tsutsui and Wotipka 2003). Thus, while effects of a country's ties to regional and global institutions are likely to be minimal in the first time period we examine, we expect them to be stronger in the latter period. Moreover, given the ways global institutions have sought to encourage regional association, we would expect to find that over time the correspondence between ties to global and regional institutions increases.

Despite overall increases in global-level integration, our data show that countries vary tremendously in how extensively they are involved in a variety of transnational exchanges at governmental and societal levels. In particular, important differences remain between different regions of the world. Whereas European countries have long been on a path towards more extensive regional cooperation, the rest of the world lags behind. Regionalism in North America and in the global south is not nearly as consolidated as it is in Europe. We expect this varying density of regional integration among governments to shape patterns of mobilization by TSMOs. Indeed, a comparison of the number of TSMOs organized solely within Europe and the number organized elsewhere shows that European TSMOs account for half of all regional TSMOs active in 2000 and nearly 80% of all TSMOs organized within the global north (see Figure 2).

This evidence about variation between different world regions provides strong support for our argument that supra-national institutions play central roles in shaping patterns of transnational citizen organizing. But thus far we have only looked at broad geographic categories of north and south or geographic region. We have not yet looked for differences across national-level boundaries. This study will further test the effects of regional- and global-level institutional processes on transnational associations by introducing country-level data to our analysis.

Data and methods

Data for this study were drawn from three editions of the Yearbook of International Associations. The editions chosen were 1980/81, 1990/91, and 2000/01 to correspond with the emergent trend of regionalization within the

Figure 2. Northern and Southern TSMOs–proportional share of population, year 2000

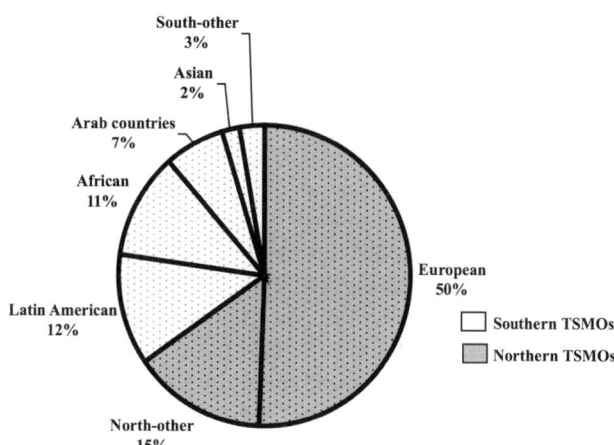

Source: Yearbook of International Organizations; Southern N=52; Northern N=99

population of TSMOs and to also reflect important shifts in the regional infrastructure of the world polity. While regional concentrations of trade and political cooperation (as well as other forms of intra-regional exchange) have been common throughout modern history, the extent to which these concentrations have been formalized into regional agreements increased since the late 1980s (Coleman and Underhill 1998; Sidaway 2002). With regard to economic agreements, for instance, of the 76 regional economic agreements existing in 1996, half originated in the 1990s (Sidaway 2002). Moreover, during this time, older organizations, such as the Association of Southeast Asian Nations (ASEAN) and the Organization of African Unity (OAU), acquired new responsibilities that had never before been formalized.

Dependent variable

From each Yearbook, the research team selected international non-governmental organizations[4] that were mobilized to promote explicit social or political change goals using non-violent tactics. Coders recorded evidence about the organization's goals and activities, founding, organizational structure, ties to IGOs and other INGOs, and the geographic scope of membership. The resulting dataset included TSMOs organized around such issues as human rights, peace, labor, economic justice, environmental protection, world government, and women's rights.

From these organizational data we next created a country-level dataset that included the raw counts of regionally organized TSMOs that reported having members in the country. This raw count is our dependent variable. We included countries where state leaders were eligible to participate in regional IGOs and to ratify regional treaties in 2000. Countries from the following four regions are included in our analysis: Africa, the Americas, Southeast Asia, and Europe.[5] The countries included in analysis are listed in Appendix 1.

Independent variables

Economic resources: Our measure of economic resources is GDP per capita in constant U.S. dollars. We collected data on this variable for each of the three time points from the World Bank's Human Development Indicators electronic data file. Because the distributions are heavily right-skewed, we converted each distribution using a log 10 transformation before entering the variables into our regression models. Like all of our independent variables except treaty ratification, GDP per capita is lagged 5 years.

Political and Civil Rights: We collected data on the availability of political resources for mobilization from the Freedom House dataset of world country ratings on political rights and civil liberties. In that dataset, countries are assigned a rating for both political rights and civil liberties on two scales ranging from 1 to 7, with 1 representing a high degree of freedom present and 7 representing a low level of freedom. We converted the two scales to make them more intuitive, with 1 representing low freedom and 7 representing high freedom. We then took the average of the two scales to create our final variable.

Ties to international civil society: This measure is the raw count of all international non-governmental organizations (INGOs) active in each country minus the number of regional TSMOs. The data were collected from the Yearbook of International Organizations for the three time points. The distributions are heavily right skewed, and we transformed them using a log 10 transformation.

State participation in IGOs: These data were also collected from the three editions of the Yearbook. The Yearbook includes separate counts for regional IGO memberships, and we used these counts to construct our regional IGO variables. The variable for global IGO participation was created by subtracting the number of regional IGOs in which a country had membership from the total number of IGO memberships for a given year.

United Nations Core Multilateral Treaty Ratification: Data on multilateral treaties were collected from the United Nations report on world commitment to the rule of law in international relations. Prepared for the September, 2005 Millennium Summit, the report lists each of the core multilateral treaties and includes the date that a state became party to each treaty. We selected all treaties that were open to ratification before the year 2000 and for each country we recorded the year of ratification. We then calculated the total number of core treaties ratified by the countries before each year of analysis.

Regional treaties: Data on regional treaty ratification were collected from the websites of the Organization of American States, the African Union, ASEAN, and the European Union. The European Union had several categories of treaty ratification, and we selected the category that included treaties open to all European countries, irrespective of EU status. As with core multilateral treaties, we selected all treaties that were open to ratification before the year 2000 and we recorded the year of ratification for each country. We then calculated the total number of regional treaties ratified by the countries before each year of analysis.[6] The distributions, however, were heavily right-skewed. We thus transformed the variable using a log 10 transformation.

Analytic method

Because we aim to examine institutional effects on the regional TSMO sector as a whole, our method compares the population of TSMOs at each time point rather than across distinct founding-year cohorts. Thus, each time point includes TSMOs that were active prior to that year and TSMOs that were founded around that year. This method of selection helps us to control for any systematic error related to the lag time between organizational founding and inclusion in the Yearbook. By bringing all regional TSMOs into the analysis rather than a selection of groups identified in the earliest period that remained active in 2000/01, our models better capture the effects of our independent measures on the changing population of regional TSMOs.

Our dependent variable is a right skewed, discrete count of organizational memberships. A model that relaxes the assumptions of OLS regression and includes a parameter that accounts for unmeasured variance is therefore required. We use a generalized version of the Poisson model–negative binomial regression estimated by maximum likelihood (see, e.g. Hammond and Holly1998; Agresti 1996). Negative binomial regression allows for the excess variability (overdispersion) that characterizes event counts (King 1989). Our models take on the following negative binomial form:

$$P(y_i \mid \alpha, \lambda_i) = \frac{\Gamma(\alpha + \lambda_i)}{\Gamma(\alpha)\Gamma(y_i + 1)} (\frac{\alpha}{\lambda_i + \alpha})^\alpha (\frac{\lambda_i}{\lambda_i + \alpha})^{y_i}$$

An overdispersion parameter, $\sigma 2$, is included in the models. The value of the parameter represents the factor by which the variance of λi exceeds its expectation. When $\sigma 2$ approaches 1, the negative binomial model is the same as Poisson. A significant overdispersion parameter translates into a rejection of the null hypothesis that $\lambda i = 1$.

Results

Table 1 shows that the average number of regional TSMOs with membership in any of the countries increased steadily from 1980 to 2000. While in 1980 the average was 6, in 2000 it was 24. Further, this table reveals that some countries had a very large increase in memberships, as the maximum number of TSMOs active within countries nearly doubled from 1980 to 1990 (33 to 63) and did double from 1990 to 2000 (63 to 121). Because we expect that the European context was the most conducive to the formation of regional TSMOs throughout the period under analysis, we compared European and non-European countries. Among European countries, the average number of TSMO memberships more than quadrupled between 1980 and 2000, from 14 to 59. Growth among non-European countries was also evident, but while the overall average tripled during this time period (from 4 to 12), it remained far lower than that for Europe average.

Another important difference between Europe and other regions is the change from 1980 to 2000 in the maximum number of regional TSMOs. While the maximum number of regional TSMOs active in non-European countries doubled between 1980 and 1990 (from 10 to 20), it increased by only 1 from 1990 to 2000. The rise in the maximum number of TSMOs evident in the overall population during the 1990s was wholly accounted for by changes in the European sector. There, the maximum number of regional TSMOs doubled between 1980 and 1990, and doubled again between 1990 and 2000. So far our findings provide preliminary support for our contention that regional institutional contexts have important consequences for the development of transnational social movement sectors within them.

We now turn to our multivariate models to assess the relative importance of domestic and international factors in explaining the variation found across countries over the three time periods. The first column of table 2 shows the results for the effects of our control variables on regional TSMO memberships in 1980. Countries with higher per capita GDP and those where political rights and civil liberties were protected had significantly more regional TSMOs active within their borders. Controlling for resources and rights, European countries also had significantly higher participation in regional TSMOs. The findings here point to the importance of both domestic factors and distinct regional contexts for facilitating the development of regional TSMO sectors.

Our second model for 1980 includes the effects of citizen links to international civil society along with our control variables. As anticipated, the countries in which citizens had more ties to international NGOs of all kinds had higher memberships in regional TSMOs, irrespective of economic resources and rights. Ties to international society serve as conduits for various kinds of

Table 1. Regional TSMO participation

		1980	1990	2000
All countries in analysis	Mean # orgs.	6	15	24
	Stand. dev.	8	13	27
	Range min.-max.	0-33	1-63	2-121
European countries	Mean # orgs.	14	28	59
	Stand. dev.	11	20	34
	Range min.-max.	0-33	2-63	14-121
Non-European countries	Mean # orgs.	4	9	12
	Stand. dev.	3	5	5
	Range min.-max.	0-10	1-20	2-21

informational and resource exchanges that enhance opportunities to coordinate social change agendas across national boundaries.

Further, in this early year, international ties were more important for explaining variation in regional TSMO memberships than both domestic economic resources and the Europe/non-Europe regional divide.

In model 3 we test the effects on regional TSMO counts of state ties to the world polity as measured by membership in trans-regional IGOs and UN treaty ratifications. We find that both of these variables had positive, statistically significant effects. Moreover, just as civil society ties to international society eradicated the independent impact of the European regional realm on variation in regional TSMO participation, so too did state ties to the world polity. That is, countries within and outside of Europe that had more ties to trans-regional IGOs or had ratified a greater number of UN treaties had a higher number of regional TSMOs active within their borders.

In model 4, we consider the effects of regional institutional contexts on regional TSMO participation. Regional IGO memberships and regional treaty ratification were significant predictors of regional TSMO memberships, net all other factors. Moreover, when we control for these variables, the difference between European and non-European countries becomes significant once again. That is, European countries had significantly higher memberships in regional TSMOs when state ties to the regional institutional context were held constant. We attribute this finding to variation in the strength of association between state ties to regional governance structures and TSMO participation across the countries of individual regions. The bivariate correlation between regional IGO memberships and regional TSMO participation was .64 for European countries, where regionalism was (in relative terms) already robust by 1980, compared to .27 for non-European countries, where regionalism was weak during this time period. Thus, idiosyncratic patterns of regional civil society development in relation to qualitatively different forms of regionalism emerge when we control for the effects of state ties to the regional institutional context.

Table 2. Results of negative binomial regression analysis of regional TSMO counts, 1980 (N=113)†

	1	2	3	4	5
Control variables:					
GDP per capita (log 10)	.67***	.26	.53**	.44**	.18
	(.19)	(.17)	(.18)	(.16)	(.16)
Rights	.12**	.11***	.09**	.04	.05
	(.04)	(.03)	(.04)	(.04)	(.03)
Europe	.49*	.17	.30	.52**	.32
	(.20)	(.22)	(.20)	(.19)	(.21)
Citizen ties to international society:					
INGOs (log 10)††		1.2***			1.2***
		(.19)			(.29)
State ties to trans-regional political institutions:					
IGOs			.02*		-.02
			(.01)		(.01)
Core UN treaties			.09**		.02
			(.03)		(.03)
State ties to regional political institutions:					
Regional IGOs				.03***	.02**
				(.01)	(.01)
Regional treaties (log 10)				.44***	.31**
				(.11)	(.11)
Overdispersion parameter	.26***	.14***	.19***	.11***	.06***
	(.06)	(.06)	(.07)	(.04)	(.03)
Log likelihood	-282.9	-266.5	-274.4	-260.7	-251.7

Note: * $p<=.05$; ** $p<=.01$; *** $p<=.001$.
† Robust standard errors are in parentheses
†† For INGOs and regional treaties, a constant 1 was added before the log 10 transformation

But, in our final model for 1980, the difference between European and non-European countries in regional TSMO membership is not statistically significant. Our measure of citizen ties to international society once again is statistically significant, net all other factors. In fact, a closer examination of the data showed that it was these international ties that leveled out the differences in regional TSMO participation between non-European and European countries in 1980. When we excluded INGO participation from our full model, the lower TSMO participation of citizens in non-European countries relative to European countries once again became statistically significant (this model is not shown in the table). As Appendix 2 reveals, particularly in 2000, participation in international associations of all kinds was far higher in Europe than it was elsewhere. In year 2000, on average there were 2,302 INGOs per European country compared to 617 per non-European country. Because of this dramatic difference, European citizens were also advantaged in their mobilization into regional TSMOs.

Irrespective of the Europe/non-Europe divide as well as citizen ties to international society, where states were linked up to the regional governance system through IGO membership or treaty ratification, there were more regional TSMO memberships. In general, in 1980 the regional institutional realm was a more important explanatory factor in regional TSMO variation than was the trans-regional dimension of the world polity measured by non-regionally specific IGO membership and UN treaty ratification. Further evidence for this relationship is the greater reduction in error as measured by log likelihood for model 4 with regional world polity variables than for model 3 with trans-regional world polity variables (model 3 G2 = 17 and model 4 G2 = 44).

Referring to the statistically significant coefficients in model 4, for every additional IGO in which a state participated in 1980, there was a 2% increase in the number of regional TSMOs. Clearly, quantitative differences in regional TSMO participation relative to regional IGO participation were more appreciable for countries with participation in higher numbers of regional IGOs. With regard to regional treaty ratification, which is a logged variable in the model, where ratification was 10% higher than elsewhere, regional TSMO participation increased by 5%. However, state ties to international society (also logged) had the strongest quantitative impact on regional TSMO counts holding all other variables constant: a 10% increase in INGO participation corresponded with a statistically significant 13% rise in regional TSMO participation.

Next we report our results for 1990. Beginning with model 1 in table 3, we find two important differences between 1990 and 1980. Here, wealth was not a statistically significant predictor of regional TSMO participation in the model that includes our control variables only. Moreover, although not statistically significant here, we find that wealth had a negative association with our dependent variable in 1990, and that this negative relationship was retained across all 1990 models.[7] One explanation is that the relationship between GDP per capita and regional TSMO participation was confounded by population size. Smaller countries tend to be richer, and smaller countries have lower participation in transnational associations of all kinds. Thus we find, for example, that while France and Italy had lower GDP per capita than Switzerland and Luxembourg, they had higher participation in both TSMOs and international NGOs in all years under analysis. Smith and Wiest's (2005) study of variation in TSMO participation showed a significant, positive relationship between the population of a country and TSMO membership, controlling for GDP per capita. Nevertheless, when we included population size in all models for 1990

Table 3. Results of negative binomial regression analysis of regional TSMO counts, 1990 (N=113)†

	1	2	3	4	5
Control variables:					
GDP per capita (log 10)	-.11	-.34**	-.19	-.13	-.28**
	(.15)	(.13)	(.14)	(.12)	(.11)
Rights	.18***	.12***	.15***	.07**	.06*
	(.03)	(.03)	(.04)	(.03)	(.03)
Europe	.71***	.40*	.37	.88***	.69***
	(.21)	(.19)	(.23)	(.19)	(.21)
Citizen ties to international society:					
INGOs (log 10)††		1.2***			.91***
		(.16)			(.23)
State ties to trans-regional political institutions:					
IGOs			.03**		-.01
			(.01)		(.01)
Core UN treaties			.05*		-.01
			(.02)		(.02)
State ties to regional political institutions:					
Regional IGOs				.01***	.01**
				(.00)	(.00)
Regional treaties (log 10)				.65***	.52***
				(.10)	(.11)
Overdisperion parameter	.22***	.12***	.16***	.09***	.06***
	(.21)	(.04)	(.05)	(.03)	(.03)
Log likelihood	-368.7	-346.1	-356.5	-335.2	-324.3

Note: * p<=.05; ** p <=.01; *** p<=.001
† Robust standard errors are in parentheses
†† For INGOs and regional treaties, a constant 1 was added before the log 10 transformation

(and also for 2000), the negative relationship between GDP per capita and regional TSMO participation remained. We return to the conundrum of GDP per capita in our discussion of the models for year 2000.

The second difference we find in model 1 for 1990 compared to 1980 is that the magnitude of the coefficient for Europe is much larger. On average, European countries had 63% more regional TSMOs than non-European countries in 1980 holding wealth and political rights constant. This difference surged to 103% by 1990. As European regionalism deepened and expanded throughout the 1980s and into the 1990s, regional civil society also grew. The number of regional TSMOs doubled in Germany, France, Belgium and Norway, where there had been a relatively high number of TSMOs active in 1980. At the same time, citizens in Portugal, Poland and Spain, where memberships were low in 1980, also became very active in regional TSMOs over this 10 year period. Thus, by 1990, we saw the expansion of European civil society to include citizens of countries that were less active sites during the first wave of regionalization considered here.

Turning now to models 2 and 3, we find that again, ties to international civil society were a significant predictor of regional TSMO membership in 1990, as was state participation in global IGOs and ratification of UN treaties. Of interest also in model 3 is that when we control for state ties to the global dimension of the world polity through treaty ratification, the difference between European and non-European countries with respect to regional TSMO participation is not statistically significant. We note that this pattern was also found for 1980, and it suggests that state integration into global legal regimes encourages regional transnational mobilization regardless of regional context. As we will see below, however, this pattern does not hold when we control for state ties to the regional polity.

Model 4 includes our measures of state ties to regional institutions along with our control variables for 1990. As in 1980, where states were more engaged in regional governance through IGO participation and regional treaty ratification, citizens participated in significantly more regional TSMOs. This holds for European and non-European countries alike, and across all countries with various levels of economic resources and differential political rights protections. Significant differences remained between European and non-European countries, however, suggesting that greater participation in regional governance on the part of states (measured quantitatively) did not dissolve the qualitative differences between European and non-European contexts with regard to incentives and opportunities for regional TSMO mobilization.

Our final model for 1990 shows that compared to 1980, country differences in wealth and rights mattered for differential participation in regional TSMOs. Also, while there were not significant differences in regional TSMO participation between European countries and others in 1980, the difference was statistically significant by 1990. Citizens in European countries had significantly higher participation in regional TSMOs. The coefficients in model 4 reveal that net all other factors, regional TSMO participation in European countries was, on average, double that outside of Europe ($e^{.69}$). Even though several non-European countries witnessed a rise in the number of active regional TSMOs (for example, participation grew from 1 to 11 in Guinea; 6 to 16 in Indonesia; and 7 to 17 in Bolivia), they could not keep pace with the tremendous growth across Europe. Again, the evidence here supports our contention that differences in the quality, strength, and extensiveness of regional institution-building in Europe compared to other regions affected the ways in which people organized across national borders.

Citizen participation in international civil society remained significant in our final model for 1990 as did state ties to regional institutions. Irrespective of region and other control variables, where citizens were connected to the dense networks of international society, there was significantly higher participation in regional TSMOs. The coefficient for INGO ties (.91) suggests that on average, in countries where citizens participated in 10% more INGOs than elsewhere, regional TSMO participation was also around 10% higher. The regional institutional context also predicted participation in regional TSMOs. Where governments were involved in regional IGOs and party to regional treaties in 1990 there was a correspondingly higher number of regional TSMOs. Also pointing to the relevance of regional institutional contexts, model 4 containing our regional institutional variables once again fit the data significantly better than model 3, which included our global institutional variables (model 3 G2 = 24.4 and model 4 G2 = 67).

We now turn to our models for 2000, the final year under consideration here. Our first model reveals the great disparity between European and non-European countries. Neither wealth nor rights mattered for predicting participation in regional TSMOs in this first model. Instead, the European context explains all of the variation we see in regional TSMO participation when we do not take into account citizen participation in international civil society or state ties to global and regional institutions. The average number of regional TSMOs active per country was 492% higher in Europe than elsewhere in 2000, up from 233% in 1990. The regression findings once again highlight the qualitatively different approach to region building in Europe compared to other regions. Unlike in the other two years, this variable retains its significance across all of our models for the year 2000.

Models 2 and 3 report similar findings to those found for the same models in 1990. There is, however, an important difference between model 3 for 1990 and that for 2000. In 1990, both state participation in trans-regional IGOs and state ratification of core UN treaties were significant, irrespective of region. In that year, the effects of these variables were such that the disparity between Europe and elsewhere in regional TSMO counts was leveled out when we compared countries with similar levels of state ties to the global dimension of the world polity. In 2000, European countries had significantly higher participation in regional TSMOs, even in countries where governments were not strongly connected to the trans-regional dimension of the world polity, such as the Ukraine and the Czech Republic. Of importance also is that the level of statistical significance for trans-regional IGO participation and UN treaty ratification increased in 2000. Further, the fit of model 3 compared to model 1 in 2000 is much improved over that model's fit in 1990 (In 1990 G2 = 24.4 for the difference between model 3 and model 1. In 2000 G2 = 48 for the

Table 4. Results of negative binomial regression analysis of regional TSMO counts, 2000 (N=113)†

	1	2	3	4	5
Control variables:					
GDP per capita (log 10)	.12	-.22	-.12	-.19	-.27**
	(.12)	(.12)	(.10)	(.11)	(.11)
Rights	.04	.07*	.06*	.08**	.08**
	(.03)	(.03)	(.03)	(.03)	(.03)
Europe	1.4***	.89***	.80***	1.2***	.84***
	(.19)	(.20)	(.19)	(.15)	(.18)
Citizen ties to international society:					
INGOs (log 10)††		1.2***			.28
		(.18)			(.33)
State ties to trans-regional political institutions:					
IGOs			.04***		.02*
			(.01)		(.01)
Core UN treaties			.06***		.04**
			(.01)		(.01)
State ties to regional political institutions:					
Regional IGOs				.03***	.02***
				(.01)	(.00)
Regional treaties (log 10)				.66***	.36*
				(.13)	(.17)
Overdisperion parameter	.19***	.12***	.10***	.12***	.08***
	(.03)	(.03)	(.02)	(.02)	(.02)
Log likelihood	-397.7	-379.3	-373.6	-378.4	-364.8

Note: * p<=.05; ** p <=.01; *** p<=.001
† Robust standard errors are in parentheses
†† For INGOs and regional treaties, a constant 1 was added before the log 10 transformation

difference between model 3 and model 1). Both with regard to Europe as an institutional space and to the world polity space of trans-regional IGOs and UN treaties, institutional factors became more important between 1980 and 2000 in their impact on transnational movement mobilization within regions.

Turning now to model 4, the same result obtained for 1990 holds: the regional institutional context mattered for explaining participation in regional TSMOs, irrespective of wealth, rights, and the Europe/non-Europe divide. But again, there is an important difference between 2000 and 1990. In 1990, the fit to the data of model 4 with the regional institutional variables and controls was statistically better than that of model 3, which included our global institutional variables with controls (G2 = 42.6 for the difference between model 4 and model 3 in 1990, p <= .001). The same was true for 1980 as well. But in

2000, this was not the case: model 4 with regional institutional variables did not reduce error more than model 3 with global institutional variables. This finding suggests that for the population of countries under consideration here, global institutional contexts took on more significance over time in facilitating TSMO regionalization, as interactions at the regional level became increasingly nested within global institutional dynamics.[8]

Comparing our final model for 2000 to the final models for the other two years further reveals the important changes that took place in transnational civil society over the time period under analysis. First we return to the conundrum of GDP per capita. Our measure of economic resources is again negatively associated with regional TSMO participation, while our rights variable retains a significant, positive association. In 2000, the bivariate relationship between GDP per capita and TSMO participation was positive and relatively strong at .59. Yet, our results show that there was relatively higher participation in regional TSMOs among lower income countries in 2000 and that this was not the case in 1980. This is seen in all of the regions, although the trend was strongest in Africa because variation in TSMO participation was much higher there. For example, the low-income countries of Niger, Mali, and Burkina Faso stood out for their relatively high participation in regional TSMOs. Angola, Libya, and Swaziland, on the other hand, all of which had much higher GDP per capita in 2000 than the three countries previously listed, had much lower participation in regional TSMOs. In Asia, Cambodia and Singapore had the same number of active regional TSMOs in 2000 (4) even though Singapore's GDP per capita was many times higher. These findings suggest that joining in regional TSMOs may be an important means of overcoming resource obstacles to political participation in low-income countries. Also, because many UN development programs throughout the 1990s focused intensely on low-income countries, the findings may reflect the distribution of international resources available for participation in transnational, social change organizations.

Turning to our measure of ties to international civil society in model 4, we find that unlike previous years, this variable does not have a significant, independent effect on participation in regional TSMOs. We interpret this to mean that, while international NGO networks were important catalysts for the emergence of regional TSMO sectors, the importance of these diminished over time, at least with regard to the formation of and participation in regional TSMOs. As regional TSMO sectors developed and evolved, the symbolic, informational, and material resources necessary for their survival and expansion flowed more fluidly within them, thus diminishing (to some extent at least) the significance of resource flows from outside of the region. Interestingly, however, when we exclude state ties to global IGOs or state ratification of regional treaties from the model, our measure of citizen ties to international civil society once again becomes a significant predictor of regional TSMO participation. Thus, our finding regarding the decreasing significance of ties to international civil society for regional TSMO participation is being driven by the countries where ties to global and regional polities are more institutionalized.

We also find that one of our measures of state ties to the trans-regional level of the world polity–core multilateral treaty ratification–retains significance in our final model for 2000. As treaty ratification increased by one treaty, participation in regional TSMOs increased by 4%. In 1990 and in 1980, this variable was not significant when INGOs and ties to the regional institutional context were included in the models. Moreover, state ties to trans-regional IGOs approached statistical significance in 2000. As discussed above, we argue that these findings strongly suggest the nested and evolving nature of institutional contexts. Over time, regional TSMO sectors develop in relation to institutional pressures and opportunities at regional and global levels. We also note that these longitudinal findings are consistent with theories that relate institutional changes to the activities of INGOs.

The significance in this final model of our domestic measures of resources and opportunities–GDP per capita and political rights protections–points to the enduring relevance of state institutional contexts. Where citizens had more rights and freedoms, they had higher participation in regional TSMOs; where economic resources were relatively low, citizens linked to regional civil society to overcome the resource deficits that limited possibilities for social change oriented collective action in their own countries. Hence, the emergence of regional TSMO sectors can best be viewed as responses to openings at the regional institutional level facilitated by citizen engagement in the resource flows and dense networks of international civil society. Over time, however, in states with more ties to regional and global institutions, citizens in countries with fewer domestic advantages in terms of state granted rights and economic resources were able to take advantage of transnational institutional contexts to increase their involvement in regionally organized TSMOs.[9]

Conclusions

Our findings reveal the important ways international political institutions affect the organization of transnational collective action. We found that where states participated in regional governance through IGO memberships and regional treaty ratification, citizens engaged in significantly higher numbers of regional TSMOs. Our analysis also uncovered how qualitatively different forms of regionalism translate into significantly different levels of TSMO regionalization. In Europe, where the regional institutional structure was more elaborated by 2000 than elsewhere in the world, in terms of both the diversity of interests formally represented at the regional level and the extensiveness of international law as embodied in regional treaties, the number of regional TSMOs in which citizens participated outpaced that found elsewhere. This finding corroborates our expectation that regional institutional contexts matter tremendously for the emergence and development of regional TSMO sectors. Within these sectors, participation in regional TSMOs was predicted by state participation in regional governance. Thus, as state leaders established direct links to the regional institutions through IGO participation and regional treaty ratification, the relevant political space in which citizens organized their claims-making expanded beyond national boundaries to encompass the region as a whole.

But, we also found that over time, the relevant institutional space for social movements organized at the regional level expanded beyond regional boundaries. While regional TSMO participation was constrained by levels of state participation in regional governance in the early years, by 2000, states with more UN treaty commitments were also sites of higher levels of citizen engagement in regional TSMOs. In 1980 and 1990, network ties to actors outside of the nation-state as well as state participation in regional institutions catalyzed the emergence and development of regional TSMO sectors. Over time, more coherent pressures towards institutional integration at multiple levels ensued. Thus, core multilateral treaties and state participation in global IGOs became significant for explaining variation in regional TSMOs. This finding supports a 'connective tissue' argument that TSMOs are helping link local actors with transnational political spaces. Activists are forming regional organizations to address gaps between international law embodied in the core multilateral treaties and realities at the local level. Regional institutional spaces may provide more conducive settings for reconciling discrepancies between local and global policies and practices. That ties to international civil society were not as important to predicting participation in regional TSMOs in 2000 as they were in earlier years further supports this interpretation. While network ties to actors outside individual states are important conduits of information and resource exchange, and are thus important catalysts for the development of regional TSMO sectors, the expansion of the intergovernmental sphere has advanced to a point where it is creating new openings and opportunities that encourage the proliferation of regional TSMOs.

In addition to the state level institutional changes induced by both coercive and non-coercive pressures towards isomorphism as posited by world polity theorists, sociologists must pay more attention to the development of regional institutional contexts. As our research shows, there was increasing convergence between global and regional political spaces between 1980 and 2000, suggesting the multi-scalar nature of isomorphic pressures on nation-states.

The regional institutional spaces are integral world polity structures that have distinct effects on the organization of political participation and conflict worldwide. Further, the extent to which global and regional institutional layers are mutually reinforcing or divergent and conflicting likely varies across time and region. This variability has important implications for the organization of collective life, and for the sociological study of the relationship between macrostructure and collective action.

Our research also shows that domestic institutional features remain crucial to explaining the development of regional TSMO sectors and the variable levels of participation in regional TSMOs across countries. Although economic disadvantage did not necessarily limit citizen participation in regional TSMOs, citizens in states with restrictions on political rights and civil liberties had significantly lower participation in these organizations in 1990 and 2000. Even so, over time, it appears that citizens in states with more ties to global and regional multilateral processes found more ways to overcome this disadvantage and strengthen their participation in regional civil society. Thus, it is a mistake to view domestic and international politics as a dualism (see also Marks and McAdam 1996). This research supports the contention that international contexts can increasingly help activists overcome disadvantages within national settings. States are becoming further integrated into an ever-more formalized set of organizations and practices that will continue to shape domestic politics in key ways. The definitions of state interests and agendas, the context of regional political debates, and the vulnerability of governments to various types of pressures from international actors change with time and with a state's relationship to both regional and trans-regional actors and institutions. We therefore must see states as embedded in transnational political contexts whose influence over state practice and citizen mobilization has strengthened over time.

Notes

[1] This research was supported by a grant from the National Science Foundation (#SES 03-24735). Support for the early phases of the data collection work came from the American Sociological Association/NSF Funds for Advancing the Discipline Program and from the World Society Foundation.

[2] This same pattern of greater cross-regional ties among southern TSMOs and more regional ties among northern ones is found when we look at ties to other INGOs, although it is slightly less pronounced.

[3] The UNEC regions are politically rather than geographically defined, although the bulk of countries within the Economic Commission groupings are geographically proximate. For example, while the majority of countries within the UN-Economic Commission for Europe are European, Canada and the United States are also contributing members of the Commission. The other four regions represented by the Commissions are Asia and the Pacific, Latin America and the Caribbean, Africa, and Western Asia.

⁴ In order to be included in the Yearbook, an organization must have members in at least three countries.
⁵ APEC was not included in analysis because unlike ASEAN, it is not a treaty producing body. Moreover, like the Commonwealth, APEC is a cross-regional organization.
⁶ We did not include treaties established through subregional bodies in Africa, the Americas, or Europe (such as ECOWAS in Africa and NAFTA and Mercosur in the Americas) because the development of non-economically oriented IGOs affiliated with these bodies, and the production of non-economic treaties has been very limited in the smaller, non-hemispheric regions outside of Southeast Asia.
⁷ There are two major outliers in the dataset. Canada and the USA have very high GDP per capita but almost no participation in regional TSMOs. When these outliers are removed from the dataset, however, the negative association between GDP per capita and regional TSMO participation remains across models.
⁸ The relationship between global and regional institutionalization is likely to be operating two ways: ties to global institutions encourage and reinforce regionalism at the same time as regional ties are likely to encourage links to global institutions.
⁹ We pooled the data and tested the following interaction terms: Year 2000*UN Treaties, Year 2000*Global IGOs, Year 2000*Rights, and Year 2000*INGOs. The interaction terms were entered separately into NBR models that included all variables discussed above plus dummy variables for each year (Year 1980 was the omitted category). Net all other factors, the interaction of Year 2000 with UN Treaty ratification was significant ($p <= .01$). The coefficient for the interaction term was .06, interpreted as a 6% increase in regional TSMO counts in 2000 for every additional core UN treaty ratified. The partial coefficient for UN treaty ratification in 1980 and 1990 was not statistically significant. The Year 2000*Global IGOs interaction term was also significant (B =.02; $p <=.01$), while the partial coefficient for the effect of IGO membership on TSMO counts in 1980 and 1990 was not. The magnitude of the coefficient for the impact on TSMO counts of political rights in 2000 was .21 ($p <= .01$) compared to .06 ($p <= .01$) for years 1980 and 1990. In the pooled dataset, the impact of INGO ties on TSMO counts for year 2000 was statistically significant (B =.26; $p <=.05$). However, the magnitude of the partial coefficient for the effect of INGO participation on TSMO memberships for the years 1980 and 1990 was much stronger at .82 ($p <= .001$).

References

Anand, Anita. 1999. "Global Meeting Place: United Nations' World Conferences and Civil Society." Pp. 65-108 in *Whose World is it Anyway? Civil Society, the United Nations and the Multilateral Future*, edited by J. W. Foster and A. Anand. Ottawa: United Nations Association in Canada.

Ball, Patrick. 2000. "State Terror, Constitutional Traditions, and National Human Rights Movements: A Cross-National Qualitative Comparison." Pp. 54-75 in *Globalizations and Social Movements: Culture, Power, and the Transnational Public Sphere*, edited by J. A. Guidry, M. D. Kennedy, and M. N. Zald. Ann Arbor: University of Michigan Press.

Boli, John and George M. Thomas. 1999. *Constructing World Culture: International Nongovernmental Organizations Since 1875*. Stanford: Stanford University Press.

Brysk, Alison. 1993. "From Above and Below: Social Movements, the International System, and Human Rights in Argentina." *Comparative Political Studies* 26: 259-285.

Chatfield, Charles. 1997. "Intergovernmental and Nongovernmental Associations to 1945." Pp. 19-41 in *Transnational Social Movements and World Politics: Solidarity Beyond the State*, edited by J. Smith, C. Chatfield, and R. Pagnucco. Syracuse, NY: Syracuse University Press.

Clark, Ann Marie. 2003. *Diplomacy of Conscience: Amnesty International and Changing Human Rights Norms.* Princeton: Princeton University Press.

Coleman, William D. and Geoffrey R.D. Underhill. 1998. "Introduction: Domestic politics, regional economic cooperation, and global economic integration." Pp. 1-19 in *Regionalism and Global Economic Integration: Europe, Asia and the Americas*, edited by W. D. Coleman and G. R. D. Underhill. London and New York: Routledge.

Desai, Manisha. 2002. "Multiple Mediations: The State and the Women's Movement in India." Pp. 66-85 in *Social Movements: Identity, Culture, and the State*, edited by D. S. Meyer, N. Whittier, and B. Robnett. Oxford and New York: Oxford University Press.

Fawcett, Louise and Andrew Hurrell. 1995. "Introduction." Pp. 1-9 in *Regionalism in World Politics: Regional Organization and International Order*, edited by L. Fawcett and A. Hurrell. Oxford and New York: Oxford University Press.

Finnemore, Martha. 1996. *National Interests in International Society.* Ithaca, NY: Cornell University Press.

Friedman, Elisabeth Jay, Ann Marie Clark, and Kathryn Hochstetler. 2005. *Sovereignty, Democracy, and Global Civil Society: State-Society Relations at the UN World Conferences.* New York: State University of New York Press.

Giugni, Marco G. 2002. "Explaining cross-national similarities among social movements." Pp. 13-31 in *Globalization and Resistance: Transnational Dimensions of Social Movements*, edited by J. Smith and H. Johnston. New York: Rowman & Littlefield Publishers, Inc.

Khagram, Sanjeev. 2004. *Dams and Development: Transnational Struggles for Water and Power.* Ithaca: Cornell University Press.

Lewis, Tammy L. 2002. "Conservation TSMOs: Shaping the Protected Area Systems of Less Developed Countries." in *Globalization and Resistance: Transnational Dimensions of Social Movements*, edited by J. Smith and H. Johnston. New York: Rowman & Littlefield Publishers, Inc.

Mansfield, Edward D. and Eric Reinhardt. 2003. "Multilateral Determinants of Regionalism: The effects of GATT/WTO on the Formation of Preferential Trading Arrangements." *International Organization* 57:829-862.

Marks, Gary and Doug McAdam. 1996. "Social Movements and the Changing Structure of Political Opportunity in the European Union." *West European Politics* 19:249-278.

McAdam, Doug, John D. McCarthy, and Mayer N. Zald (eds.). 1996. *Comparative Perspectives on Social Movements: Political Opportunities, Mobilizing Structures, and Cultural Framings.* Cambridge: Cambridge University Press.

McCarthy, John D. and Mayer Zald. 1977. "Resource Mobilization in Social Movements: A Partial Theory." *American Journal of Sociology* 82:1212-41.

Meyer, John. 2003. "Globalization, National Culture, and the Future of the World Polity," Wei Lun Lecture- Chinese University of Hong Kong (Nov. 2001).

Meyer, John W., John Boli, George M. Thomas, and Francisco O. Ramirez. 1997. "World Society and the Nation-State." *American Journal of Sociology* 103:144-181.

Moghadam, Valentine. 2000. "Transnational Feminist Networks: Collective Action in an Era of Globalization." *International Sociology* 15:57-85.
Nepstad, Sharon Erickson. 2002. "Creating Transnational Solidarity: The Use of Narrative in the US-Central American Peace Movement." in *Globalization and Resistance: Transnational Dimensions of Social Movements*, edited by J. Smith and H. Johnston. New York: Rowman & Littlefield Publishers, Inc.
Ouguergouz, Fatsah. 2003. *The African Charter on Human and People's Rights: A Comprehensive Agenda for Human Rights Dignity and Sustainable Democracy in Africa*. The Hague: Marinus Nijhoff.
Ramirez, Francisco, Yasemin Soysal, and Susanne Shanahan. 1997. "The Changing Logic of Political Citizenship: Cross-national Acquisition of Women's Suffrage." *American Sociological Review* 62: 735-745.
Reimann, Kim. 2002. "Building Networks from the Outside In: Japanese NGOs and the Kyoto Climate Change Conference." Pp. 173-190 in *Globalization and Resistance: Transnational Dimensions of Social Movements*, edited by J. Smith and H. Johnston. New York: Rowman & Littlefield Publishers, Inc.
Risse, Thomas, Stephen C. Ropp, and Kathryn Sikkink. 1999. *The Power of Human Rights: International Norms and Domestic Change*. New York: Cambridge University Press.
Sassen, Saskia. 1998. *Globalization and its Discontents*. New York: The New Press.
Sidaway, James D. 2002. *Imagined Regional Communities: Integration and Sovereignty in the Global South*. New York: Routledge.
Sikkink, Kathryn and Jackie Smith. 2002. "Infrastructures for Change: Transnational Organizations, 1953-1993." Pp. 24-44 in *Restructuring World Politics: The Power of Transnational Agency and Norms*, edited by S. Khagram, J. Riker, and K. Sikkink. Minneapolis: University of Minnesota Press.
Smith, Jackie. 2005. "Building Bridges or Building Walls? Explaining Regionalization among Transnational Social Movement Organizations." *Mobilization* 10:251-270.
Smith, Jackie. Forthcoming. *Changing the World: Struggles for Global Democracy*.
Smith, Jackie and Dawn Wiest. 2005. "The Uneven Geography of Global Civil Society: National and Global Influences on Transnational Association." *Social Forces* 84:621-651.
Tarrow, Sidney. 1996. "States and opportunities: The Political Structuring of Social Movements." Pp. 41-62 in *Comparative Perspectives on Social Movements: Political Opportunities, Mobilizing Structures, and Cultural Framings*, edited by D. McAdam, J. D. McCarthy, and M. N. Zald. Cambridge: Cambridge University Press.
Tarrow, Sidney. 2001. "Transnational Politics: Contention and Institutions in International Politics." *Annual Review of Political Science* 4:1-20.
Tarrow, Sidney. 2005. *The New Transnational Activism: Movements, States, and International Institutions*. New York: Cambridge University Press.
Taylor, Ian. 2003. "Globalization and Regionalization in Africa: Reactions to Attempts at Neo-liberal Regionalism." *Review of International Political Economy* 10:310-330.
Tilly, Charles. 2004. *Social Movements, 1768-2004*. Boulder: Paradigm Publishers.
Tsutsui, Kiyoteru. 2004. "Global Civil Society and Ethnic Social Movements in the Contemporary World." *Sociological Forum* 19:63-87.

Tsutsui, Kiyoteru and Christine Min Wotipka. 2004. "Global Civil Society and the International Human Rights Movement: Citizen Participation in Human Rights International Nongovernmental Organizations." *Social Forces* 83:587-620.

United Nations. "Multilateral Treaty Framework: An Invitation to Participate." New York: United Nations.

Verba, Sidney, Kay Schlozman, and Henry Brady. 1995. *Voice and Equality: Civic Volunteerism in American Politics.* Cambridge: Harvard University Press.

Wapner, Paul. 1995. "Politics Beyond the State: Environmental Activism and World Civic Politics." *World Politics* 47:311-340.

Wiest, Dawn and Jackie Smith. 2006. "Regional Institutional Contexts and Patterns of Transnational Social Movement Organization." *Korea Observer* 37: 25-32.

Appendix 1. Countries included in the analyses

Africa	Americas	Southeast Asia	Europe
Algeria	Argentina	Cambodia	Albania
Angola	Bahamas	Indonesia	Austria
Benin	Barbados	Malaysia	Belgium
Botswana	Belize	Philippines	Bulgaria
Burkina Faso	Bolivia	Singapore	Cyprus
Burundi	Brazil	Thailand	Czech Republic
Cameroon	Canada	Vietnam	Denmark
Cape Verde	Chile		Finland
Central African Rep.	Colombia		France
Chad	Costa Rica		Germany
Congo	Dominican Republic		Greece
Congo D.R.	Dominica		Hungary
Egypt	Ecuador		Iceland
Ethiopia	El Salvador		Italy
Gabon	Guatemala		Luxembourg
Gambia	Guyana		Malta
Ghana	Haiti		Netherlands
Guinea Bissau	Honduras		Norway
Guinea	Jamaica		Poland
Cote d'Ivoire	Mexico		Portugal
Kenya	Nicaragua		Romania
Lesotho	Panama		Russia
Liberia	Paraguay		Spain
Libya	Peru		Sweden
Madagascar	St. Lucia		Switzerland
Malawi	St. Vincent		Turkey
Mali	Suriname		United Kingdom
Mauritania	Trinidad		Ukraine
Mauritius	Uruguay		
Mozambique	United States		
Namibia	Venezuela		
Niger			
Nigeria			
Rwanda			
Senegal			
Seychelles			
Sierra Leone			
South Africa			
Sudan			
Swaziland			
Tanzania			
Togo			
Tunisia			
Uganda			
Zambia			
Zimbabwe			

Appendix 2. Descriptive statistics for variables in analysis
All countries in analysis

		1980	1990	2000
Regional TSMOs	Mean	6	15	24
	S.d.	8	13	27
	Min.	0	1	2
	Max.	33	63	121
GDP per capita	Mean	$4,110	$4,820	$5,713
	S.d.	$5,630	$7,105	$8,533
	Min.	$123	$93	$49
	Max.	$25,868	$30,325	$34,655
Civil and political rights	Mean	4	4	5
	S.d.	2	2	2
	Min.	1	1	1
	Max.	7	7	7
INGOs	Mean	552	763	1,049
	S.d.	547	719	998
	Min.	8	8	113
	Max.	2,161	2,777	3,752
Global IGOs	Mean	30	31	34
	S.d.	11	11	9
	Min.	1	11	19
	Max.	69	64	56
Core UN treaties	Mean	3	5	9
	S.d.	2	2	3
	Min.	0	0	3
	Max.	7	9	16
Regional IGOs	Mean	17	18	16
	S.d.	10	10	7
	Min.	0	0	2
	Max.	51	44	39
Regional treaties	Mean	7	11	19
	S.d.	7	9	12
	Min.	0	0	3
	Max.	27	33	45

Appendix 2 (continued)

Countries outside of Europe

		1980	1990	2000
Regional TSMOs	Mean	4	9	12
	S.d.	3	5	5
	Min.	0	1	2
	Max.	10	20	21
GDP per capita	Mean	$2,144	$2,277	$2,621
	S.d.	$955	$3,987	$4,754
	Min.	$123	$93	$49
	Max.	$20,671	$25,891	$30,704
Civil and political rights	Mean	3	3	4
	S.d.	2	2	2
	Min.	1	1	1
	Max.	7	7	7
INGOs	Mean	339	481	617
	S.d.	290	378	518
	Min.	25	70	113
	Max.	1,528	2,051	2,858
Global IGOs	Mean	27	28	30
	S.d.	9	8	7
	Min.	1	11	19
	Max.	52	64	46
Core UN treaties	Mean	3	5	9
	S.d.	2	2	3
	Min.	0	0	3
	Max.	7	9	16
Regional IGOs	Mean	15	17	15
	S.d.	6	9	6
	Min.	1	1	2
	Max.	28	43	30
Regional treaties	Mean	6	10	16
	S.d.	7	9	13
	Min.	0	0	3
	Max.	27	33	45

Appendix 2 (continued)
European countries

		1980	1990	2000
Regional TSMOs	Mean	14	28	59
	S.d.	11	20	34
	Min.	0	2	14
	Max.	33	63	121
GDP per capita	Mean	$9,805	$12,189	$14,670
	S.d.	$7,177	$8,896	$10,606
	Min.	$1,063	$1,100	$608
	Max.	$25,868	$30,325	$34,655
Civil and political rights	Mean	5	5	6
	S.d.	2	2	1
	Min.	1	1	4
	Max.	7	7	7
INGOs	Mean	1,170	1,581	2,302
	S.d.	646	846	1,000
	Min.	8	8	428
	Max.	2,161	2,777	3,752
Global IGOs	Mean	39	41	44
	S.d.	12	11	7
	Min.	11	12	28
	Max.	69	53	56
Core UN treaties	Mean	4	6	12
	S.d.	2	2	2
	Min.	0	0	5
	Max.	7	8	15
Regional IGOs	Mean	24	20	20
	S.d.	14	12	9
	Min.	0	0	6
	Max.	51	44	39
Regional treaties	Mean	9	14	26
	S.d.	7	9	4
	Min.	0	0	14
	Max.	17	23	34

Appendix 3. Zero-order correlations

		1	2	3	4	5	6	7	8	9	10	11	12	13	14	15	16	17	18	19	20	21	22	23
1	TSMOs 80																							
2	TSMOs 90	.95																						
3	TSMOs 00	.91	.93																					
4	GDP 80	.74	.70	.67																				
5	GDP 90	.73	.69	.66	.99																			
6	GDP 00	.73	.70	.66	.97	.99																		
7	RIGHTS 80	.61	.55	.50	.71	.71	.72																	
8	RIGHTS 90	.62	.58	.51	.67	.67	.68	.85																
9	RIGHTS 00	.50	.42	.47	.57	.58	.59	.59	.69															
10	INGOs 80†	.85	.85	.88	.79	.77	.77	.58	.61	.49														
11	INGOs 90	.84	.84	.87	.79	.78	.77	.58	.61	.49	.99													
12	INGOs 00	.81	.80	.87	.77	.75	.75	.54	.57	.51	.98	.99												
13	GLIGOs 80	.54	.57	.59	.49	.49	.49	.33	.37	.17	.77	.78	.76											
14	GLIGOs 90	.61	.64	.67	.57	.56	.55	.36	.43	.20	.81	.81	.79	.84										
15	GLIGOs 00	.65	.69	.74	.58	.57	.57	.33	.39	.29	.88	.89	.90	.85	.85									
16	UNTR 80††	.44	.44	.26	.33	.32	.31	.34	.37	.21	.42	.43	.38	.37	.38	.34								
17	UNTR 90	.37	.39	.38	.26	.33	.34	.21	.31	.12	.39	.39	.37	.40	.37	.41	.80							
18	UNTR 00	.47	.49	.53	.38	.37	.36	.25	.34	.46	.50	.50	.51	.37	.41	.46	.53	.61						
19	RIGOs 80§	.64	.65	.59	.52	.51	.48	.33	.35	.27	.59	.59	.55	.41	.48	.50	.47	.45	.47					
20	RIGOs 90	.31	.40	.31	.27	.25	.22	.03	.03	-.18	.32	.33	.26	.42	.35	.35	.34	.40	.20	.73				
21	RIGOs 00	.55	.58	.52	.49	.46	.43	.33	.37	.15	.56	.57	.51	.55	.49	.52	.51	.53	.37	.79	.83			
22	REGTR 80§§	.55	.53	.38	.36	.35	.38	.41	.55	.33	.44	.42	.38	.32	.31	.30	.45	.38	.34	.37	.12	.39		
23	REGTR 90	.58	.58	.41	.41	.40	.42	.43	.58	.33	.51	.50	.45	.39	.39	.39	.45	.40	.35	.39	.17	.44	.92	
24	REGTR 00	.51	.48	.39	.34	.34	.35	.26	.46	.35	.49	.49	.50	.41	.47	.47	.31	.29	.39	.31	.03	.25	.76	.83

† Global (trans-regional) intergovernmental organizations
†† Core United Nations treaties
§ Regional intergovernmental organizations
§§ Regional treaties

3
Economic Glocalizing, Regional Embedding, and State Scaling
A Comparative Analysis of the Pearl River Delta and the Yangtze River Delta in China

Xiangming Chen

> Despite the progress in research on the renewed importance and dynamics of varied forms of regions and regionalism, there remains an void in understanding how regions may play a "middle" role in bridging and integrating global, national, and local economies. This role also turns regions into highly contested terrains where the diverse processes and outcomes of economic development and integration, or lack of it, manifest themselves. These include simultaneously competitive and cooperative policies and practices of regional and local governments vs. those of global and local firms, as well as shifting opportunities and constraints on economic development and industrial upgrading. In this chapter, I contend that regional dynamics are capable of embedding global-local economic relations in ways that either facilitate or hinder local economic growth and competition. But this regional embedding is intertwined with the spatial downscaling of the Chinese state. I examine the coupled influence of regional embedding and downward state scaling on economic development in the Pearl River Delta (PRD) and the Yangtze River Delta (YRD) in China—two of the most dynamic manufacturing regions in the world. The comparative analysis shows that regardless of the historical and geographic differences between the PRD and the YRD, their similarity in rapid economic growth and limited industrial upgrading can be accounted for by regionally embedded global-local production linkages that are subject to the shaping by the developmentally-minded local state.

Research on regions becomes increasingly important to a more comprehensive understanding of the multifaceted relationship between globalization, the nation state, and local economic development. The contemporary era of globalization has elevated the significance of regional studies, prompting Scott (1995: 59) to pronounce that "[R]egions are once again emerging as important foci of production and as repositories of specialized know-how of technological capability, even as the globalization of economic relationships proceeds apace." The resurgent interest in regions has focused on the relative momentum of two seemingly competing tendencies: a trend toward a regionalization and localization of economic activity and production due to simultaneous vertical disintegration and political/administrative decentralization vs. a tendency toward global economic integration and the resulting erosion of independent regional economies (see Amin 1993).¹

Corroborating evidence on the first trend includes successful industrial districts of closely networked and functionally specialized small- and medium-sized firms in a tightly knit space like the Italian knitwear industry in Modena (Lazerson 1993). The latter tendency, however, was reflected in the steady decline of older regional economies due to the long-term "lock-in" development and attempted recovery through continued specialization and internal coherence, as exemplified by the coal-and-steel-dominated Ruhr area of Germany (Grabher 1993). The rise of global city-regions, mostly in industrialized countries in recent years may represent a new spatial-economic form of local-regional response to global opportunities and constraints (Scott et al. 2001), as exemplified by the Southeast Region of England anchored to both London as a global financial center and involving a number of much smaller cities as booming high-tech and info-tech nodes (Hall 2001).

Introducing the renewed interest in regional studies leads to two crucial questions. The first is to what extent have the position and role of regions shifted in relation to those of the state at different spatial scales. The second pertains to what does the realigned power of the region vs. the state mean to local economic development. While the first question calls for understanding a given region's relationship to the national and local government, the second question points the analytical attention to the varied ways in which a given region is related to both the global and local economy and to how these relations, mediated by the changing state, may either facilitate or impede local economic development. In the next section, I develop the argument that while regional dynamics have become crucial in embedding global-local economic ties, their influence generally works through the porous body of the rescaled state.

A new dynamic triangle: economic glocalizing, regional embedding, and state scaling

Research on globalization confronts the challenge of understanding the complex and multifaceted global-local relationship. While this relationship has been conceptualized as interdependent and interpenetrating through such terms as "glocalization" (Robertson and Khondker 1998), it remains empirically difficult to specify and clarify how the global and local are linked and interact with each other in different socio-spatial contexts. Of all types of global-local ties, the economic ones may be most complex, extensive, and resilient because economic globalization is more advanced than cultural or political globalization and thus exerts the strongest local impact. It makes conceptual sense to characterize global-local economic ties as a nexus, which contains a web of mutually embedded linkages between the global economy and local economies. To understand how these linkages are organized at any spatial scale calls for untangling or deconstructing the global-local economic nexus (Chen and Sun 2007).

The challenge to untie the global-local economic nexus is complicated further by the varied ways in which the nexus is embedded regionally as region becomes a more enabling spatial structure that is capable of reconfiguring linked economic activities across the global-local divide. Regions have gained this strength as the nation state has been weakened by the decentralization and localization of state autonomy and power, at least in the Chinese and broader Asian contexts (Chen 2005). However, the rise of regional economies has not occurred at the total expense of the nation state as claimed by Kenichi Ohmae (1995). So what is happening exactly to the nation state and how it is reorganizing itself as it confronts deeper and more rooted global-local economic ties on the one hand, and the increasing regional embedding of them, on the other? In a new way of decoding the shifting and somewhat invisible DNA of the nation state in the vortex of globalization, Sassen (2006) points to the dual process by which the variety of micro-processes unleashed by globalization denationalize some national institutions and practices, while the nation state is also a key enabler of the global scale. As this process unfolds, the state has also rescaled itself into more differentiated political spaces (Brenner 2004) as a result of yielding some sovereign authority upward to supranational organizations like the EU and granting some autonomy and power downward to local governments. It is the latter or downscaling of state power and its development consequences that can be understood in relation to the regional embedding of global-local economic linkages in the Chinese context.

The role of regions in embedding global-local economic ties varies by how the latter are spatially and organizationally differentiated in either agglomerated or dispersed forms. This embedding process may lead to a cumulative spatial outcome shaped by aggregate decisions of various disaggregated actors such as business firms, local governments, and professional associations (Markusen 2004). Decisions by powerful actors such as multinational corporations often carry strategic reference for and bearing on multiple locations in a regional context (Ho 2000). These actors' behavior and decisions add up to a collective force that serves as a "mediating middle" between the global economy and local economies. And the downscaling of the state leads to a more active and aggressive local state, which acts on the mediating role of regional embedding from below.

If regional embedding and state scaling have a joint and interactive influence on global-local economic ties at the local level, it is crucial to specify the form and content of these ties as they reflect the larger process of globalization vs. localization and the tension between them. Rosenau (1997) argues that the integrating force of globalization and fragmenting impact of localization blend into fragmegrative (his original usage) processes that produce either complementary or contradictory outcomes. Amin and Thrift (1994) challenge the homogenizing effect of globalization by emphasizing persistent local diversity, which includes inter-institutional interaction and synergy, collective representation by many bodies, a common industrial purpose, and shared cultural norms and values. While the global and local are mutually constituted as Rosenau suggested, the local may remain distinctively local against the global (Amin and Thrift). The challenge for a regional analysis of the global-local economic nexus is to uncover how it is nested in multi-layered spatial and functional hierarchies. This analysis can benefit from perspectives on how *place* is viewed in relation to *network* and how value *chains* and industry *clusters* fit in.

Place has taken on added importance in the study of globalization, global cities, and regional development (see Orum and Chen 2003). The greater salience of place is reflected in a new geography of power produced by economic globalization, exemplified by the emergence of global cities like New York, London, and Tokyo as the command and control centers in the global economy (Sassen 2001). The role of cities or places in a globalized or globalizing region is more complex as they get tangled up with networks of value chains and industrial clusters. A networked production system in a given region involves input-output linkages among embedded places. The relative benefits for the actors involved in a regional division of labor accrue from their positions in different value chains and their power or lack of it in the governance of global value chains (Gereffi, Humphrey, and Sturgeon 2005).

Any globally integrated regional production networks contain value chains that vary in where and how they enter, extend through, and exit regions. In one region, the chains may encompass more cities and their hinterlands than in another region. Cities in one region may spread more evenly along different segments of a global value chain, whereas localities in another region may cluster around one distinctive segment of the chain (e.g., manufacturing). The uneven involvement and functions of cities as local nodes in value chains depend on the size and concentration of industry clusters specific to a region. Given the rich components of a cluster in a region, it may either occupy a single segment (e.g., manufacturing of parts and components in a particular industry) or cover multiple segments (R&D, completion of a high-value-added product, marketing) of a value chain anchored to a locality. The spatial configuration of chains and clusters in a given region matter a great deal to its development and integration by enhancing and sustaining the economic competitiveness of the places or localities that host these clusters as constituent parts of that region (Porter 2000). This logic has made clusters or cluster-based initiatives a highly desirable policy tool for many cities and regions in their efforts to increase growth, productivity, and employment (Cumbers and MacKinnon 2004), even though it was criticized as based on a problematic concept and cautioned as a policy tool (Martin and Sunley 2003).

Incorporating value chains and industry clusters into the relative importance of places and networks turns the global-local economic nexus into a highly complex phenomenon consisting of multiple functional and relational attributes. This synthetic view is crucial for studying regions hosting complete or partial global production networks that drive regional and local development through value creation and other enhancements (Coe et al. 2004; Yeung 2005). The local impact of global production networks, either positive or negative, generally works its way through layers of embedded organizational and spatial relations to producing local development outcomes. Regional embedding is about how these relations are spatially configured, while downward state scaling, which empowers local governments, directly affects the policy-making capacity of the localities that are linked together regionally. Having mapped out the relational triangle in which economic glocalizing (in the form of global-local production linkages) is subject to the coupled influence of regional embedding and state scaling, the stage is set for introducing the Pearl River Delta and the Yangtze River Delta of China as a pair of cases for comparative analysis.

A pair of regional powerhouses: the PRD vs. the YRD

If the GDP and exports for all the world's major economic regions are mapped out and up in colored bars, two regions on China's coast would easily stand out. The two regions are widely known and labeled as the Pearl River Delta (PRD) region bordering Hong Kong and the Yangtze River Delta (YRD) region anchored to Shanghai, respectively. While the PRD fueled southern China's emergence and growth as a major region for massive foreign (mostly overseas Chinese) investment and manufactured exports during the 1980s and into the 1990s, the YRD rose as the second regional driver of huge foreign investment into and export out of central coastal China during the 1990s and into the 21st century. Despite being often mentioned in tandem, the PRD and YRD have not been comparatively analyzed via the framework as outlined in the preceding section. I begin by providing a brief statistical account of the two regions' dominant shares in China's inward foreign investments and exports as powerful engines behind their rapid economic growth (see table 1).

The PRD and the YRD account for the lion's share of China's total inward foreign investment and exports, absorbing as much as 87.2% of China's foreign

Table 1. Foreign investment into and exports from the Pearl River Delta (PRD) and the Yangtze River Delta (YRD) as shares of China's totals, 2000-2005

Year	Pearl River Delta (PRD)* Surface: 42,000 sq km Population: 40.77 million GDP: $100 billion (2005)		Yangtze River Delta (YRD)** 101,000 sq km 82.82 million $208 billion (2005)	
	Foreign investment	Exports	Foreign investment	Exports
2000	36.1	43.0	27.5	28.7
2001	33.8	41.5	28.6	30.2
2002	28.8	42.2	33.3	31.2
2003	36.6	40.4	50.6	34.2
2005 (1st Half)	19.0	28.0	51.0	37.0

Note: The figures in the four columns are percentages of China's totals.
* The PRD is defined as Guangdong and Fujian provinces for data through 2003, and the data for the first half of 2005 refer to Guangzhou and eight other central cities in Guangdong province.

investment and sending as much as 74.6% of its exports in 2003. Having moved differently in recent years, however, the PRD's share of foreign investment in China's total stagnated and began to drop, while that of the YRD rose sharply after 2001. Secondly, the PRD is more export-oriented than the YRD, and has had a consistently higher export-to-foreign-investment ratio, which reached 1.47 (28% divided by 19%) in the first half of 2005. The YRD, on the other hand, maintained a rough balance between foreign investment and exports until 2005 when its foreign investment inflow exceeded exports by a factor of 1.38 (51% divided by 37%), suggesting that foreign investment in the YRD became less export-oriented. (The use of different boundaries of both regions between 2003 and 2005 in table 1 does not distort the parallel trends over time.)

The influx of foreign investment into and abundant exports from both regions have kept the economic growth of the PRD's cities at an average of almost 15% annually since the 1980s and that of the YRD's cities at the same rate since the 1990s. In fact, even with slowed GDP growth of the YRD in the first half of 2005 due to macroeconomic adjustment, half of the cities in the region maintained more than 15% GDP growth. Among them, the cities of Nantong and Wuxi led others by growing at 15.5%, closely followed by Suzhou, Zhoushan, Changzhou, and Nanjing, which grew at 15-15.4%.[2] While the total GDP of the YRD doubled that of the PRD, GDP per capita of the PRD remains higher than that of the YRD due to their population differentials (table 1). Nevertheless, the GDP per capita gap narrowed over the last decade from 55% higher in 1995 of favor of the PRD to about 35% in 2004. Folding the GDP of Hong Kong into what may be called the Greater PRD would tilt the total GDP in favor of the PRD and further widen the GDP per capita gap between the two (Fang 2005).

The PRD and the YRD are similar in having had their sustained rapid economic growth driven by foreign investment and exports, which are tied to some shared features of the two regions' industrial composition. There is a striking spatial concentration of the (huge) outputs from the clothing and related industries in the PRD and the YRD, especially the latter. However, the broad cross-regional similarity in certain spatially agglomerated industries between the PRD and the YRD masks important cross-regional differences across a range of spatially organized industries and intra-regional variations in the spatially networked production in both regions.

Regional embedding of two global-local production networks

The real development dynamics of the PRD and the YRD lie beneath the general glowing picture of their rapid growth and booming exports; they are embedded in two largely regionalized global-local production networks. The critical question here is do these networks exhibit a visible region-wide division of labor across localities of varied sizes, hierarchical positions, and functional influences. The question can be partly answered by mapping out the array of global-local economic linkages that tie the cities of either region together as local nodes of the regionalized and regionalizing production chains.

The PRD's stronger export orientation is based on a region-wide industrial system consisting of numerous factories of varied sizes in a cluster of cities that make labor-intensive products for exports. This massive export-driven growth machine has turned the PRD (with Hong Kong and Macao) into the world's 16th largest economy and tenth leading exporter, if it were a country. Over 50,000 Hong Kong-owned companies and factories in the PRD (see map 1) employ 10 million workers, more than Hong Kong's total population (Enright and Scott 2005). These factories, coupled with over 10,000 Taiwan-owned factories, churn out disproportionately large shares of China's consumer products for the world markets.

Export-oriented manufacturing in the PRD is embedded in regionalized global-local production linkages that span Taiwan, Hong Kong, and the PRD cities in Guangdong province. Figure 1 displays the complementary inputs from and the functional linkages between the four geographic nodes that connect the PRD to the global economy through different value chains. For example, in the chain of athletic shoes, multinationals like Nike and Reebok used to order the bulk of shoes from their subsidiaries or subcontractors in Taiwan,

Map 1. Huge numbers of Hong Kong-owned factories clustered in major cities of the Pearl River Delta (PRD), Southern China

which began to move their factories to in the PRD cities. Most of the raw materials were shipped from Taiwan through Hong Kong to the mainland sites, at least initially before they could be increasingly sourced locally. Each of the shoe factories would use a few Taiwanese resident managers who have been in the shoe business for years and might also speak the local dialect. Hong Kong-based staff of companies like Nike have continued to handle accounting and designs, make sure the sample and raw materials reach the factories on time, and transport the finished Nike shoes out of China through Hong Kong toward their destined markets. The chain of toys is similarly structured: toys are designed in Hong Kong, assembled in the PRD, often with a Taiwan-made chip for talking dolls, and finally packaged in and shipped from Hong Kong to world markets (see Chen 1994, 2001).[3]

Compared with the PRD, the YRD embeds a more diverse set of industries of varied global connectivity and capital and technological intensity, ranging from garments to cars and to semiconductors. The automotive industry in the YRD involves heavy capitalization and advanced manufacturing technology. Shanghai Volkswagen or SVW (a joint venture between Shanghai Automobile Industrial Corporation [SAIC] and VW) has recently built an integrated car manufacturing complex (with a Formula 1 race track nearby) in the new town of Anting on the outskirts of Shanghai, representing a spatial extension of manufacturing from Shanghai into the larger region. Hankook, a large Korean tire-maker based in the city of Jiaxing in Zhejiang province, about one hour

Figure 1. Regionalized global-local production linkages embedded in cross-border production chains in and out of the Pearl River Delta (PRD)

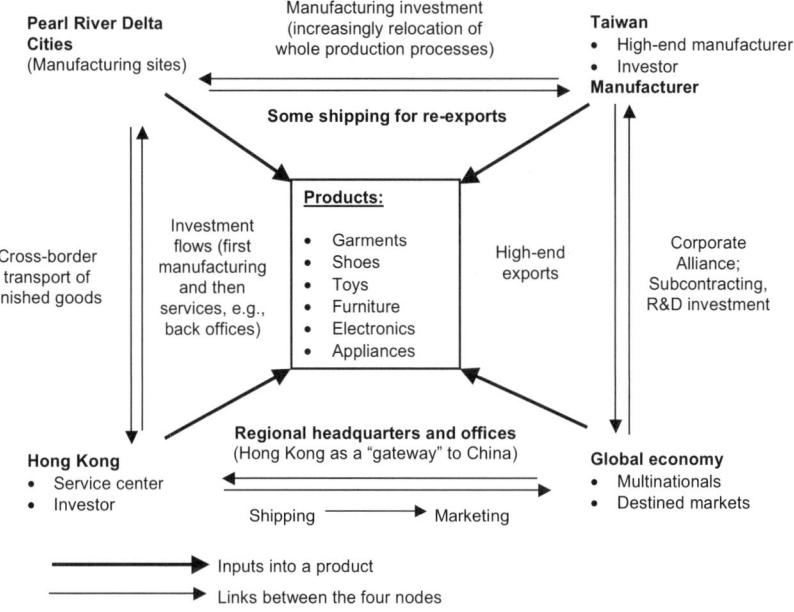

- A **multinational company** owns brand names, sets product specifications, subcontracts, and controls wholesale channels and retail markets.
- **Taiwan** contributes capital, manufacturing technology, equipment, management expertise, raw materials, and intermediate inputs.
- **Hong Kong** contributes manufacturing management, product design, accounting and legal services, customs clearance, forwarding, logistics and other producer services.
- **Pearl River Delta (PRD) cities** contribute land, labor, and some raw and semi-processed materials.

Source: Modified from Chen (2005: 70).

away from Shanghai, is a major supplier of tires to VW from the 50% of its domestic sales through its marking functions in Shanghai (see figure 2).[4]

The electronics/PC/IT industries involving primarily Taiwanese capital have become agglomerated in and around Shanghai and are more technology-intensive and advanced than their counterparts in the PRD. These industries vary in the spatial division of labor and inter-firm linkages between the global economy and the YRD and within the latter. In notebook manufacturing, the Taiwanese company of Quanta, the world's No. 1 notebook maker that accounted for a quarter of the roughly 49 million notebooks shipped in 2004, employs 20,000 workers at its $48 million factory complex in Shanghai where more than 90% of its output is generated and for Dell and HP orders back in the U.S. While manufacturing, packaging, and shipping is done in and from Shanghai, the most valuable components of the notebooks are designed and sourced overseas, with memory chips from the U.S., Korea, and Taiwan, graphic processors designed in the U.S. and Canada but made in Taiwan, and liquid-crystal-display screens from Korea, Taiwan, and Japan. However, more and more of the notebook-component production has moved to near Shanghai (Dean and Tam 2005). Beyond notebooks, Asustek makes iPods for Apple in Suzhou, while the Taiwanese firm of Hon Hai–the world's second largest electronics contract manufacturer–employs up to 100,000 workers in both Kunshan near Shanghai and the PRD to make the PlayStation 2 for Sony among other products (Einhorn 2005).

Core, secondary, and peripheral nodes in a regional hierarchy

The PRD and the YRD appear to share more similarities than differences in the regionally embedded and inter-locally linked labor-intensive and export-oriented industries. To widen and deepen the cross-regional comparison, I shift the analytical focus on the core, secondary, and peripheral cities as various nodes with different (and perhaps complementary) roles in the respective regional hierarchies. This is essentially a shift from a horizontal to a vertical analysis of how cities of different sizes and complexities function both independently and in interdependence with one another. I begin with the two core cities or regional centers of the PRD and the YRD–Hong Kong and Shanghai. While some may view Guangzhou and/or Shenzhen as core cities of the PRD, Hong Kong has dominated the region from its much more powerful position and strategic location as the major source of investment capital, management experience, and export outlet. This makes Hong Kong a fair comparison as the core of the PRD with Shanghai for the YRD.

Since the purpose of this paper and lack of space do not allow a full-fledged comparison of Hong Kong and Shanghai, I restrict the comparison to their positions and roles in the two regions. Hong Kong's development and role has been shaped by its evolved economic relations with the PRD. Tuan and Ng (2002) identified three stages in the transition of Hong Kong's economy as it became more integrated with the PRD. And they were referred as: 1) cross-border operations (1980-1987) during which Hong Kong shifted partial manufacturing operations and original equipment manufacturing (OEM[5]) to the PRD; 2) direct outward investment (1988-1992) during which Hong Kong shifted mid-stream manufacturing production to the PRD to achieve maximum re-exports; and 3) Hong Kong relocating whole plants with more service-oriented operations to the PRD since 1992 and becoming almost exclu-

Figure 2. Regionalized global-local production chains into, through, and out of the Yangtze River Delta (YRD)

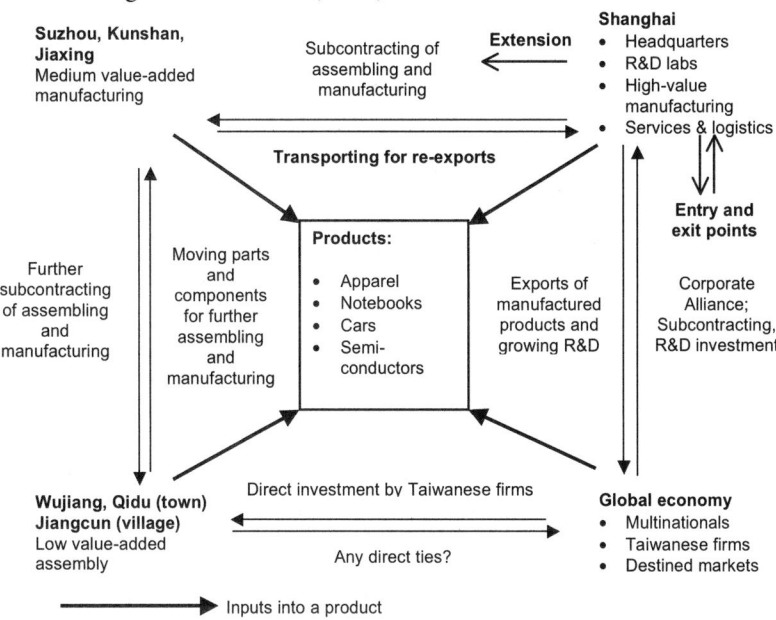

- A **multinational company** owns brand names, sets product specifications, subcontracts manufacturing, and controls wholesale channels and retail markets.
- **Shanghai** (central node of the YRD) contributes land, some capital, skilled labor, some production equipment, and management expertise; provides some producer services such as accounting, insurance, and legal services, custom clearance, shipping logistics, and increasingly R&D talent and outputs.
- **Suzhou**, **Kunshan**, and **Jiaxing** (secondary cities in the YRD) contribute medium-cost land and labor, intermediate inputs, manufacturing expertise, and also finished products to be moved (back) to Shanghai for exports.
- **Wujiang**, **Qidu** and **Jiangcun** (third-tier cities, fourth-tier towns, fifth-tier villages in the YRD) contribute lowest-cost land and labor, some raw processed materials, and ships parts and components to secondary cities for further assembling or manufacturing.

Source: Modified from Figure 1 above.

sively focused on manufacturing management (Tuan and Ng 2002: 3). What is most revealing about this shift in Hong Kong's ties with the PRD is not the continued decline of Hong Kong's manufacturing sector from 46% of total employment in 1980 to 5% in 2002 (Chen 2005). It not only has something to do with the overwhelming spatial concentration (almost 70%) of Hong Kong-owned factories in the PRD but also with how Hong Kong's role in servicing the PRD and China as a whole has shifted.

The shift has occurred along two dimensions. First, Hong Kong companies have relocated some operations of service nature such as R&D, design, prototype manufacturing, and logistics to the PRD. However, they have kept high-level services like advanced R&D, manufacturing management, and offshore trade in their Hong Kong headquarters (Tuan and Ng 2006). Second, Hong Kong has reasserted its broader service role not only by growing its traditionally strong banking and finance, but also other services such as professional services, trading, and re-exports. For example, the number of Chinese state-owned companies listed on Hong Kong's stock market increased from six in 1993 to 72 in 2004. In addition, the number of multinational corporations' regional headquarters in Hong Kong rose from 602 in 1991 to 944 in 2001 and then 1,167 in 2005, while the number of regional offices increased from 278 in 1991 to 2,631 in 2005. And 1,046 of the 1,167 regional headquarters are responsible for business in China, and more of these regional headquarters engage in wholesale, retail, and trade-related services. Hong Kong's strategic role in bridging the global economy and China's economy and in servicing the latter has become stronger (Lui and Chiu 2006) even as its dominant service function for the PRD gets consolidated.

Turning to Shanghai in the YRD, it not only has grown rapidly from inward foreign investment and booming exports but also experienced a major restructuring of its economic system and thus faced a major dilemma regarding its role at varied scales. Behind the strong push of the Shanghai government to promote the service sector and downsize the declining state-owned manufacturing industries, the industrial share of the GDP dropped from 63.8% in 1990 to 57.3% in 1995 and then to 50.1% in 2003. In terms of employment, the industrial share of the GDP declined from 54.6% in 1995 to 39% in 2003, while the services' share rose from 33.5% to 51.9% (Shanghai Statistical Bureau 2004). Within the service sector, producer services such as finance, insurance, and real estate (FIRE), which are central to a global city (Sassen 2001), grew most rapidly, as its combined employment in Shanghai's total service employment rose from 2% in 1997 to about 10% in 2003 (Shanghai Statistical Bureau 2004). This economic restructuring has facilitated the emergence of Shanghai as an attractive new hub for multinationals' regional headquarters and R&D centers (see figure 2). Fifty-five multinational companies set up regional headquarters in Shanghai after 2003, leading to increased memberships for the city's American Chamber of Commerce, while Amcham membership in Hong Kong shrunk (Overholt 2004). There was an average annual addition of 30 multinationals' R&D centers in Shanghai from 2002 to 2005. The total number of R&D facilities of multinationals in Shanghai is expected to grow from around 150 in 2005 to around 200 by the end of 2008. The R&D centers that GE and Alcatel have set recently in Shanghai rank among their top three global R&D centers, respectively (Du 2005).

Shanghai's shift from a dominant manufacturing to a more service-oriented center with increasing strength in business services and R&D moves it a little closer to the functional profile of a global city like Hong Kong. This generally favorable transition, however, has thrust Shanghai into an unfavorable scenario of balancing the continued growth of its advanced service sector, which is expected of a global city, vs. maintaining its dominance as a traditional regional manufacturing hub for the YRD. In addition to being a dilemma, it is a crucial part of Shanghai's image and functionality that are perceived quite differently from those of Hong Kong. Overholt (2004) saw Hong Kong's advantages in many business services such as accounting, law, and investment banking, and some of these have spilled over into the PRD over time and facilitated the latter's edge in logistics and supply-chain management, especially in rapidly changing product areas like toys, gifts, and fashion. Shanghai, according to Overholt, has advantages in engineering, R&D, and design due its concentrated human talent and top-notch universities, with another advantage in the economies of scale from the critical mass of heavy industries like petrochemicals, steel, automobiles, machines tools, and information technology. Overholt's conclusion was that most Fortune 500 companies focused on China's domestic market belong in Shanghai, while most exporters and many sophisticated service industries belong in Hong Kong.

Regardless of its comparative advantages against Hong Kong, Shanghai is facing new challenges in the YRD regional context stemming partly from its economic boom. Its land and labor costs in the central city, especially in the most developed industrial zones (such as Jinqiao and Waigaoqiao) have risen relative to those in the outlying areas of the city and the nearby secondary cities of Jiangsu and Zhejiang provinces (see table 2). Although these differentials do not appear to be large, they are large enough to induce new foreign and domestic companies to locate in or relocate from Shanghai to the surrounding (YRD) region, especially to booming secondary cities such as Suzhou (see map 2). While the even bigger disparity in manager salaries between Shanghai and other YRD cities reinforces this outward spill of business activities, they attract some managers in the other cities to Shanghai. This has a double-edged effect on the relative development of Shanghai vs. such booming secondary cities like Suzhou in the YRD.

To better understand a rising secondary city like Suzhou in the YRD context, I use Dongguan as both a different and similar booming secondary city in the PRD for comparison. Bordering Shenzhen (and thus close to Hong Kong), Dongguan is arguably the most favorably located secondary city in the PRD. This location, coupled with its flexible policies and incentives, has turned

Table 2. Labor costs in Shanghai and cities around Shanghai

Location	Average wage workers (RMB/month)	Average wage technicians (RMB/month)	Average wage managers (RMB/month)	Pension contribution (%)
Shanghai Jinqiao Export Processing Zone	700-1,000	1,000-2,000	2,000-5,000	44
Shanghai Waigaoqiao Free Trade Zone	700-1,000	1,000-2,000	2,000-5,000	44
Shanghai Qingpu Industrial Zone	600-800	1,000-1,200	2,000-5,000	24
Singapore-Suzhou Industrial Park, Jiangsu	600-800	1,000-1,800	1,800-3,500	22
Suzhou New District, Jiangsu	600-800	1,000-1,800	variable	40-41
Wuxi, Jiangsu	500-800	800-1,100	1,500-3,000	37
Nanjing, Jiangsu	460-600	900-1,500	1,500-3,000	42
Changzhou, Jiangsu	600-800	1,000-1,800	1,600-3,200	40
Hangzhou, Zhejiang	700-900	1,000-2,000	1,800-3,500	42
Ningbo, Zhejiang	500-700	900-1,200	1,500-3,200	42

Note: 8 RMB=1US$.
Source: Adapted from McDaniels.

Dongguan into one of the "hottest" spots for Hong Kong and Taiwanese investments in over 20,000 factories (see map 1). They account for 80% of Dongguan's gross industrial output, 62.5% of its economic growth, and 90% of its exports in 2002, pushing Dongguan up to China's third-ranked city in exports volume behind only Shanghai and its neighbor Shenzhen (Mao, Liu, and Hu 2004). A rural township surrounded by rice fields and known for growing litchis in the 1980s, Dongguan has risen to a booming manufacturing center that stretches 2,520 sq km and has over five million people. With large revenues from leasing increasingly valuable land for building factories, the local government is capable of funding the entire primary and secondary education at no cost to residents and of experimenting with completely free health insurance and old-age pensions. At the household level, the level of wealth in Dongguan is reflected in a 20-% ownership of private cars, the highest of all cities in Guangdong province and one of the highest in China (Chen 2005).

Underlying Dongguan's explosive growth is a difficult and complex process of an evolving manufacturing sector. From the 1980s to the early 1990s, Dongguan was primarily involved in simple cross-border processing and assembly of labor-intensive food, clothing, and home electronics products for

Map 2. Shanghai's spillovers to and back flows from several secondary cities and lower-tiered cities and towns in the Yangtze River Delta (YRD)

exports to and through Hong Kong. The limited IT activity in Dongguan was confined to assembling and finishing at the low value-added segment of the international production chain organized by and through Hong Kong companies based on cheap local land and labor. Since both raw materials, parts, and half-finished and finished components of IT products came from and went through Hong Kong (with the two high value-added ends being controlled from the outside), Dongguan was stuck in the low value-added middle with few inter-firm supplier-manufacturer links that benefit the local economy.

The mid-1990s ushered a new and more advanced stage for Dongguan's manufacturing sector, which began to take advantage of more Taiwanese IT companies moving more complete production networks to the PRD due to greater price pressure for OEM order from multinational corporations and growing competition from Southeast Asian IT firms. This process involved a core Taiwanese IT company with both or either OBM or ODM[6] relocating to Dongguan first and then bringing a group of its small and medium-sized suppliers of parts and components over to form a complete production and assembly network. As some Taiwanese firms have shifted more manufacturing of computer components (switch power supply units, motherboards) and peripherals (monitors, keyboards) to Dongguan, upstream suppliers of plastics, resistors, and printed circuit boards have followed them there, which was also facilitated by preexisting social networks in Taiwan that continued in Dongguan (Chen 2000, 2001, 2005). This makes it possible for a PC to be assembled and shipped in only few days within an area of 50 sq km in which specialized suppliers of such peripherals as monitors and keyboards cluster with motherboard manufacturers and final assemblers. The real local multiplier benefit is that there are now approximately 1,000 indigenous IT companies in Dongguan that can supply a whole range of parts and components like printed circuit boards and liquid crystal for Taiwanese-owned PC manufacturers (Ma, Liu, and Hu 2004). Dongguan illustrates the significant role of a rising secondary city with externally linked and specialized industry clusters in driving local economic development with some industrial upgrading (see Chen 2007).

In comparison to Dongguan, Suzhou has risen to a dynamic secondary city in the YRD from a very different background but reached a similar economic status as Dongguan along a distinctive development trajectory. Once a pleasant merchant town known for its fine silks, elegant gardens, and canal-lined streets, Suzhou is the oldest and one of the weathiest cities of Jiangsu province. It once thrived as a trading center along the Grand Canal built between Hangzhou to Beijing in the seventh century, and the silk trade and textiles remain important to its modern-day economy. Located only about 100 km west of Shanghai, Suzhou's fortune has long been tied with Shanghai through a reputation as the latter's "backyard garden." Despite and because of those fine qualities, Suzhou existed as an industrial backwater to Shanghai. With regard to the lack of industrial tradition, Suzhou was not dissimilar to Dongguan before their recent manufacturing boom.

Suzhou has pursued two different models of development as opposed to Dongguan's two sequential stages. From the early 1980s to the early 1990s, government-led development of Suzhou's economy focused on township and collective enterprises (TVEs)–the so-called "Southern Jiangsu (Sunan) economic model," which was also followed by other nearby cities. While generally successful in stimulating pent-up economic growth and rural industrialization, the Sunan model ran into serious problems from its inherent constraints such as local government interference, lack of economies of scale, duplication of production, and environmental pollution. In the next decade Suzhou switched gears, reducing the role of state-owned companies and concentrating on bringing in foreign capital. From 1997 to 2002, the share of industrial output for state and collective enterprises dropped from 58.9% to 9.8%, while that of foreign-invested entities shot from 33.2% to 55.8%.[7] What became known now as the Suzhou model (as opposed to the old Sunan model) relies heavily on careful planning and aggressive action by the municipal government to create an attractive investment environment, which differentiates Suzhou from other cities in the YRD. The most prominent and successful project is the Suzhou Industrial Park (SIP), which began as a 35-65% joint venture between the Chinese and Singapore governments in the early 1990s. The Singapore side effectively jumpstarted Suzhou's snowballing foreign investment with its technical know-how, and the large swath of land east of the old city morphed into a meticulously planned suburban community with efficient infrastructure and corporate campuses. A second large-scale planned project is the Suzhou New District (SND), which the municipal government developed in the western part of the city as a sort of rival zone to the SIP.[8]

With lower land and labor costs than Shanghai (see table 2), the SIP and the SND have attracted the operations of 107 Fortune 500 companies and most of the over 5,500 foreign enterprises in Suzhou, with over 16,000 foreign expatriates working in the two parks. Electronics and telecommunications equipment make up the largest portion of the city's broad industrial base. High-tech firms like Panasonic, Philips, Nokia and Alcatel have large presences there. Suzhou exported 16 million laptop computers (taking only five days to assemble one) valued at $10.9 billion in 2005, and makes more than a third of the world's mice as Logitech's largest production base (see later). Semiconductors have also become a major business, as chipmakers National Semiconductor, Solectron, Fairchild, and AMD have all moved into town. Besides being a manufacturing behemoth, Suzhou is also gaining a reputation as an R&D-friendly town. More than 30 top-500 companies in the city have set up R&D centers, and SIP plans to push for more growth in technological and R&D sites. Even as some firms move their assembly operations to cheaper, mid-sized cities in the larger region, they are staying in Suzhou for research.[9] This massive influx of foreign investment has fueled Suzhou's economy. In 2005, Suzhou's GDP ranked fifth in the country at $50.8 billion, and its industrial output totaled $150 billion, good enough for second place behind Shanghai after topping the list in 2004. Suzhou also received $6 billion in foreign investment in 2005, second only to Shanghai.[10]

Its prosperity aside, Suzhou's development strategy has become heavily dependent on foreign capital. Of the city's bounding growth figures in recent years, foreign investment accounts for over 70%. The massive foreign investment-driven exports not only cost huge amount of energy and resources to produce but also the local government hefty export tax rebates every year. For all the thriving foreign-invested enterprises in town, there are practically no significant homegrown businesses. The Suzhounese have become relatively poorer–while Suzhou's per capita GDP is higher than Shanghai's, its per capita income is about half that of Shanghai.[11] Local government officials see this heavy dependence on foreign investment as very imbalanced like walking on two very uneven legs, with the one based on foreign capital being long and strong and the one involving indigenous capital being short and weak. They also expressed a sense of potential crisis in which foreign companies will pick up and move to lower-cost cities in northern Jiangsu or the interior of China, leaving the local economy to weak indigenous companies.[12]

Does the rise of secondary cities like Dongguan and Suzhou have a developmental influence on the smaller cities and towns below them in the regional hierarchies? What are the opportunities and constraints for smaller and lower-ranked places to grow via their direct and indirect ties to the secondary cities and regional cores? The lowest land and labor costs, coupled with geographic proximity would seem to favor small towns as attractive and accessible sites for the most labor-intensive assembly and manufacturing operations, even though this may "lock" them into the least profitable and dependent segments of the regionally embedded global-local production chains. Both realities are illustrated by the small places with distinctive manufacturing clusters in the PRD and the YRD.

In the PRD, the concentration of IT production in Dongguan has triggered spatially clustered specialization in the manufacturing of PC peripherals and other products in its towns. The town of Qingxi, with only 30,000 residents, hosts several large-scale manufacturing facilities of seven large Taiwanese PC companies traded on Taiwan's Stock Market. The town turns out two million monitors, 700,000 keyboards, and 13 million PC boxes (20% of the world's total) a year (Chen 2005). While this was driven largely by production cost considerations and the spatial benefit from clustering, other factors make towns slightly beyond the main PRD cities attractive to overseas investors. A Hong Kong company chose to build a plant in the town of Xixiang just outside Shenzhen, because it had social connections with one local official there. In addition, Xixiang not only is close to Hong Kong but also lies beyond Shenzhen's bureaucratic regulations, which tend to be heavier than its surrounding areas (Lee 1998).

The growth of many towns in and around the PRD cities has led some making famous local brand products to register them as collective trademarks, including Houjie furniture, Nanhai Yanbu undergarments, Guzhen lightings and Xintang denims. The Dongguan town of Dalang, which is renowned for its woollen textiles, recently announced its plan for building Dalang into an International Brand Name and enhancing its international reputation. In early 2006, the Guangdong provincial government designated Dalang (China's celebrated town for woollen jumpers), Shantou's Chenghai (for toys) and Chaozhou's Fengxi (for ceramics) as pilot units for regional brand building. Dalang has asked the industry associations concerned to assist in the registration of "Dalang" and "Dalang Woollen Textiles" as trademarks. The township government of Dalang will inject over one million U.S. dollars as a start-up fund to cover expenses incurred in the hiring of experts, trademark design, and planning. There are estimated to be over 100 specialized industrial clusters in towns like Dalang in Guangdong province, mostly in the PRD. Most of these specialized towns started off as family workshops and many of them made their first large sales through carrying out OEM operations.[13]

The development of manufacturing towns in the YRD is similarly dynamic. The county city of Wujiang under Suzhou municipality (see map 2) has several specialized manufacturing towns (see the lower-left corner of figure 2). The town of Jinjiaba, with only about 50,000 residents, is crowded with several hundred small factories making and assembling steel frames used for constructing factory or office buildings, which makes the town the largest cluster with the largest output of this product in China. Everyday as many as 5,000 salesmen for these factories roam the country to sell steel frames. In two towns specialized in making cotton and synthetic fabrics and extracting silk threads, there are over 100,000 water-powered looms humming in small and often makeshift factory buildings scattered in the villages around the town centers. Many peasant households also own a couple or handful of these looms and use them for subcontracted work at home during the slow farming season. These preliminarily processed fabrics are generally sold as inputs to clothing companies in the towns of neighboring Zhejiang province, which make garments for export. Given the constant pressure on the price of the fabrics, some small factories and individual families periodically have to shut down production to avoid selling their fabrics at a loss.[14]

The town of Qidu under Wujiang city (see figure 2) shows a different aspect of how local manufacturing clusters are globally linked through a partially regionalized production network. Amidst the large number of small local cable and electrical components factories in Qidu is a large Taiwanese-owned electronics company with approximately 1,300 employees that is capable of making 600,000 key tops of computer keyboards, 480,000 sets of top/bottom cases of keyboards, and assembling over 120,000 complete keyboards a month. In fact, this company produces a large share of all the keyboards manufactured and exported by its Taiwan-based mother company, which accounts for 28% of the world's keyboards. The Qidu facility opened in 2001 to begin producing keyboards for the American company Logitech, which had just established a large factory in Suzhou one hour away (see earlier). The Taiwanese-owned factory also makes keyboards for Sony through a Japanese trading company based in Kunshan 80 minutes away (see map 2). Dell and HP also place orders for higher-end keyboards that are painted by hand after plastic injection. And all these keyboards are shipped out through the Shanghai port. Given its convenient location and in light of its multiple customers in the YRD, the Taiwanese manufacturer in Qidu tries to schedule the delivery date so that its trucks can carry the ordered keyboards to different customers located in the nearby larger YRD cities.[15]

The booming manufacturing towns in both the PRD and the YRD share three salient features in common. First, they are attractive local manufacturing sites, especially for Hong Kong and Taiwanese companies due to their lowest labor and land costs in the regions. Second, these towns' geographic proximity allows convenient and timely delivery of components and finished products to the secondary cities for further assembly or higher-value-added manufacturing (see figure 2). Third, regardless of their diverse industries, many of these towns have become directly or indirectly linked to or even embedded in increasingly regionalized economic network of global-local ties. Their positions and roles both stretch these ties spatially and solidify them in functional terms.

Making sense of cross-regional similarities and differences

Having compared the PRD and the YRD from the chain (horizontal) and hierarchy (vertical) perspectives, it is time to highlight their most important similarities and differences in development success and challenges that need to be accounted for. First of all, despite the different timing of development, the rapid and sustained economic growth of both regions has been driven by regionally grounded production networks of global-local and some local-local linkages. Second, while the industries in the regional production networks in both regions differ somewhat, they share the similar profile of being heavily foreign investment-driven, labor-intensive, and export-oriented. Third, as these general features are portrayed somewhat ideal-typically in figures 1 and 2 earlier, there are variations within and deviations from the expected capital intensity of the industries involved, the length of the production chains and the number of their segments, and the spatial organization of production linkages.

Chains and places in a regional milieu

What may explain these important similarities and differences are factors located within and beyond the production chains and places (cities and towns). The regionalized production chains have stimulated and sustained the rapid economic growth of the two regions thus far because they contain the middle segment of agglomerated factories and supportive facilities owned by foreign companies in many PRD and YRD cities, while the two ends–design and R&D

at the front and marketing and after-sales services at the back—are largely outside the regional boundaries. The cheap and abundant land and labor allow these factories to churn out huge volumes of price-competitive exports, boosting GDP and trade statistics. The "manufacturing middle" in both regions has stretched within itself and extended in both directions over time. Its internal stretching involves the development of more inter-firm ties of supply and subcontracting in certain industries, especially the IT industry. Extension to the front end of the production chain involves drawing R&D activities from the regional cores and beyond to key manufacturing nodes such as Suzhou. In extending backward, some foreign-owned factories have pulled a growing number of local domestic suppliers into their production orbit as exemplified by the IT manufacturing clusters in Dongguan.

There are however built-in constraints on the typical production chain in both regions that tend to fragment or truncate them, thus preventing their local development benefits from reaching more deeply and widely. Some chains are governed by a network or relational mechanism, which creates and sustains complex interactions between buyers and sellers based on mutual interdependence and high levels of asset specificity through reputation, or family or ethnic ties in either spatial proximity or not (Gereffi, Humphrey, and Sturgeon 2005). In the two regions, foreign companies, especially those from Korea and Taiwan that drive and control the production chains rely primarily on their transplanted supplier networks to minimize the use of local suppliers who are often perceived as cheaper but less qualified.[16] In cases where multinationals source from Taiwanese-owned factories or where the latter use local Chinese suppliers, the buyer keeps a strong price squeeze on suppliers, creating extremely fierce competition among them. This tends to "lock" small suppliers in the PRD and the YRD into a transactionally dependent relationship with large, powerful customers.

Looking beyond the explanatory factors within the chains and places to account for the cross-regional similarities and differences in development success and challenges, several larger and regional-level factors appear in sight. Both the PRD and the YRD are endowed with favorable geographic and natural conditions, and a long history of development. They are among the most populous and productive farming regions in ancient China. While the PRD has long been China's southern gateway for foreign trade and sea transportation, the YRD has always been China's central transport hub for the interior cities along the Yangtze River to link with the outside world. Situated at the southern end of the Chinese mainland, the PRD is far away from the political center of Beijing. This remote location, coupled with being separated from the vast national territory by the Nanling Mountains has fostered an outward, business-oriented, and flexible attitude among the people. In comparison, the

YRD has long been one of China's central economic regions, and Shanghai has been one of the central government municipalities since 1949. Hence, the YRD has always been more constrained by the central government. While these geographic, cultural, and historical conditions do not guarantee rapid development, they are conducive to it.

The rescaled state and rising local power

Regional embedding has had a generally favorable effect on the PRD and the YRD through the chains and places of global-local production linkages and broader regional conditions. Asserting and exerting additional influence is the new power alignment created by the process of state scaling. The beginning of this process provided the initial trigger and subsequent timing for the takeoff and development of the two regions over the past two and half decades. The PRD was the first collective beneficiary of central government policies that spurred the region (following the Special Economic Zone model of Shenzhen) to pursue open and autonomous development in the early 1980s. This allowed the PRD to take full advantage of being close to Hong Kong and Taiwan to capture the massive cross-border relocation of their export-oriented factories. The shallow and less diverse industrial foundation in the region dominated by light consumer goods industries, which was an intended historical legacy of centrally planned economy favoring heavy industries in northern cities, turned out to be unintended advantage for the PRD to develop spatially concentrated competitive toys, garments, and consumer electronics, and some IT clusters. When the favorable development policies were shifted to Shanghai and the YRD in the early 1990s, they immediately set the region off on a fast growth track. In addition, the YRD has benefited tremendously from its historical advantage in having developed a more balanced and complete mix of industries under central planning, which allowed the region to draw foreign investment into more capital- and technology-intensive industries than the PRD.

If the above account reveals the scaling down of state autonomy and power to the regional level, the further downward scaling of the state has translated into the strong and competing role of the local governments in both regions, turning them into developmentally-oriented entrepreneurial actors. Their control over and right to approve land use allows them to lease land as a both a valuable asset and financial incentive to foreign investors to build factories. Revenues from land lease are used to finance large-scale infrastructure provision, which in turn improves the transportation and logistics of manufactured goods (Chen 2005). While the autonomous and flexible policies and incentives of local governments have brought in huge and spatially uneven numbers of growth-generating foreign companies, they have led to almost unbridled competition for foreign investment that involves discounting land values and compromising on environmental protection. This has eventually put cities like Suzhou in a dilemma of foreign capital becoming "too much of a good thing" where they feel the pressure to seek a more balanced development involving more local companies and investment from Shanghai (see earlier).

Although too much foreign capital has caused concerns for the local government of a booming secondary city like Suzhou and prompted it to draw domestic investment from Shanghai, smaller and less prosperous cities in the YRD have continued their aggressive efforts to lure both foreign and domestic investors within and outside the region. The county-level city of Taicang under Suzhou municipality has taken a three-pronged approach to both competing against and cooperating with Shanghai using geographic proximity (see map 2). First, Taicang's government has staged a number of prominent promotional events in Shanghai to lure companies there to relocate to Taicang for its much lower land and labor costs, and managed to get about 300 companies to do so during 2003-2005, with another 41 in January-May of 2006. Taicang also zoned about 20 sq km of open land near the border with Shanghai as an automotive-related industrial park for new factories that could supply parts to the auto manufacturing complex in the town of Anting in Shanghai (see map 2). Second, the city of Taicang has been engaged in a large-scale upgrade of its container port off the month of the Yangtze River with funding from the central, provincial, and local governments. This project also involves connecting and coordinating with two other nearby mid-sized ports more closely to create a cluster of ports as an alternative export platform besides Shanghai. Third, Taicang has advertised and sold its new housing estates in a town bordering Shanghai to the latter's residents, some of whom have purchased the apartments at one-third of Shanghai's price.[17] Located very close to Shanghai, the city of Pinghu in Zhejiang province has also tried hard to strengthen its ties with Shanghai (see map 2). Pinghu has set up four government offices in Shanghai since 2000 to promote cooperation in investment, tourism, and agriculture. These government-led initiatives reflect the close economic relationship between the two cities, as Shanghai accounts for 30% of Pinghu's investment and 20% of its tourists, while 90% of Pinghu's agricultural products are exported Shanghai.[18]

In some ways, the aggressive governments of the cities near Shanghai appear to be harmless to the dominant regional core. If Suzhou wants to look up to Shanghai for commerce and turns to the provincial capital of Nanjing for politics, while Jiaxing approaches Shanghai vs. Hangzhou (the capital of Zhejiang) the same way, what is wrong? Nothing, especially when cities like Suzhou and Jiaxing have professed to occupy secondary, supportive, and complementary positions or niches vs. Shanghai, and described them in different metaphorical ways.[19] Suzhou government officials even played down the statistical "shock" that its total FDI (not FDI per capita) was almost neck to neck with Shanghai in 2004 and 2005. But drawing capital and companies away from Shanghai was perceived as a threat to its broad manufacturing base, prompting Shanghai to launch a 2004 policy initiative of keeping old manufacturing jobs and growing new ones in Jiading and Qingpu close to its border with Jiangsu province (map 2). While Shanghai may be losing some edge in lower-end manufacturing to the YRD's booming secondary cities, the latter keep losing white-collar professionals, especially senior managers to Shanghai due to its higher pay scale (see table 2) and quality of life. The governments and companies of Suzhou, Jiaxing, Taicang, and Pinghu not only have to offer higher salaries to keep their competent administrators and managers but also have to keep recruiting highly educated and trained talents from interior cities.[20]

All the simultaneous competitive and cooperative behaviors of the local governments in the YRD have stemmed inevitably and predictably from the broadly rescaled Chinese state driven and managed by the central government in a top-down fashion. For the local state, more decision-making power has brought about both development opportunities and pressures at the same time. While the opportunities are many and some have been explored to the advantages of some cities and towns as examined earlier, the pressures are great on top local government officials to seize the opportunities to improve their cities and towns' economic performance. And this performance has been measured in a personalized manner where local officials are evaluate annually for their efforts in bringing in both foreign and domestic investment and raising GDP, which in turn determine their chances for upward promotions to higher Party and government positions. The annual national rankings of the top 100 counties (or county cities like Wujiang, Taicang, Pinghu) only serve to heighten the personal political stakes for local officials in booming and competitive county cities in the YRD.[21]

Conclusion: toward a new global(izing) city-region

As the multi-scaled comparative analysis has shown, both regional embedding and state scaling have intersected and converged to facilitate and fuel the rapid economic growth of the PRD and the YRD. The closer and more fine-grained examination, however, has revealed emerging and potential challenges that may threaten the sustainability of the two regions' good times. To reiterate, most cities and towns in the PRD and YRD, which specialize in making low-end and medium-level standard products, qualify for what Florida (2005) called "hills." The hills may rise and fall, but the "peaks"–the world's top advanced services and innovation centers–can remain vital and dynamic.

And Shanghai may rise further from a large hill to becoming a peak like Hong Kong someday, but the rapid development of the rest of the PRD and the YRD is difficult to sustain without industrial upgrading. The YRD's prospect looks somewhat brighter than the PRD, which has relied more heavily on labor-intensive and low-tech assembly and manufacturing that not only rely on suppressed low wages and razor-thin profit margins but also lack local integration and innovation. This model of industrialization, successful as it might have been in its earlier phase, has kept some local industries and firms in a dependent and even disconnected mode in relation to the global economy. Most PRD-based firms and factories may be trapped in the assembling and manufacturing segment of the production chain and earning merely labor-processing fees rather than engaged in acquiring technology, developing their own brand-name products, and creating international markets directly. (For an extended discussion on the constraints on industrial upgrading in both the PRD and the YRD, see Chen 2007.)

The comparative analysis here has yielded certain insights suggesting that the PRD and the YRD may have become a new type of globalizing city-region with general(izable) features and a clear Chinese imprint. Generally speaking, both cases point to the more enabling role of regions in mediating and restructuring global-local economic relations. This role has a potential double-edge. It could foster local industrial upgrading through more effective and cooperative mechanisms for regional integration as one possibility. Alternatively, this regional role could delay or even derail local industrial upgrading when inter-local or intra-regional competition breeds fragmentation. In addition, the PRD and the YRD demonstrate the analytical value in rethinking and reassessing the relationship between city and region in the global city-region. This may help bridge the analytical divergence between the optimistic and sanguine view on regions as new engines of growth and the economic hope for the future vs. the pessimistic and bleak focus on cities, especially some in industrialized countries as a gathering place for economic decline and unsolved social problems (Läpple 2001).

In ways the PRD and the YRD exhibit China-specific attributes, they push us to think through their implications for the study of global city-regions more broadly. The thin theoretical and empirical research on global city-regions acknowledges both their external and internal orientations (Scott et al. 2001), having taken a cue from the perspective on global cities functioning as key nodes of the global economy but producing unequal and undesirable local consequences such as service sector and income polarizations (Sassen 2001). In the PRD, Hong Kong, with this dominant and advanced services, influences the PRD as a true global city, albeit from across a de facto international border. In the YRD, Shanghai's dominant power is complicated and compromised by its dual role as a rapidly globalizing city and traditional regional manufacturing hub, as well as by the administrative barrier of being a separate, central government municipality. Despite these distinctive characteristics, economic and spatial integration has come a long way in both regions. In the YRD, some engineers from state-owned enterprises in Shanghai on the weekends crossed the administrative boundaries to work for and provide technical assistance to small and mid-sized state or collective enterprises in Jiangsu and Zhejiang provinces as early as the mid-1980s, and thus earned the legendary title of "Saturday engineers." Today labor and goods crisscross the myriad of administrative boundaries between Shanghai, the secondary cities, and small towns, as well as among the latter, with much greater ease and frequency. The internal economic and physical linkages within the YRD are just as important as its cities and towns' increasingly strong external or global orientations.

On balance, while regional embedding of global-local production chains has created both broad (region-wide) and local constraints on industrial upgrading in the PRD and the YRD, the more autonomous and powerful local governments from downward state scaling pose a bigger challenge to developing new and more effective governance strategies for improving regional "collective efficiency." Regions like the PRD and YRD are sandwiched between the top-down (global) and bottom-up (local) governance pressures. Certain forms of global governance such as the rule-setting regime of the World Trade Organization (WTO) have introduced and reinforced global technical, social, and ecological standards, which exert considerable demands and pressures on national, regional, and local actors (Messner 2002). From the bottom, local governments in the PRD and the YRD have gained autonomy and power not only from political and fiscal decentralization but also from larger local coffers from rapid growth and land-lease revenues. In the YRD, local autonomy has not freed municipal governments from being fixated to territorially bounded and functionally independent entities. This has sustained some degree of regional and local economic fragmentation and conflicts under the legacy of the entrenched planning system. Although some of this has been ameliorated by the administrative annexation by higher-order cities of adjacent lower-ranked, county-level units as new city districts in the YRD, it has not eliminated all the hierarchical and horizontal inter-city conflicts (Zhang and Wu 2006).

The strong local state aside, an increasingly powerful non-government local and regional actor in the U.S. context is special-purpose authorities, which not only continue to undertake and run traditional infrastructure projects (highways, rapid transit, ports) but also have taken on urban redevelopment projects like convention centers and sports facilities (Judd 2003). In the PRD and YRD, non-government organizations (NGOs) and business associations have become more active and involved in local policy-making and could contribute to broader and more effective policy networks for facilitating industrial upgrading and regional integration. Environmental NGOs could work with local governments to deter approval of some labor-intensive manufacturing projects that may have pollution problems down the road. Business associations could cooperate with local governments to provide better and more targeted training programs to upgrade the skills of workers. By offering both financial (dis)incentives and market information to certain manufacturers, local governments in the regional network could redirect them to new or alternative market segments in order to reduce the current "horde mentality" of too many local Chinese companies competing to produce the same profitable products by squeezing one another's already razor thin margins.

Although cross-boundary policy networks are slow to emerge due to the traditional administrative barriers that tend to restrict horizontal ties between Shanghai and the surrounding cities, they appear to be an inevitable response to the complex challenges facing the YRD. While the PRD does not have to contend with the barrier effect of provincial boundaries, it faces a tough challenge of regulating a complex and differentiated movement of people across the Guangdong-Hong Kong border (Lin and Tse 2005). The PRD also faces a steeper climb than the YRD in upgrading from a more massive industrial system characterized by labor intensity, low wages and technology, and lack of local innovation.

In both similar and different ways, the PRD and the YRD have provided extensive and layered evidence that helps analysts recover region as a "crucial middle" that is capable of mediating the tight nexus between the global economy and local economies in conjunction with the continued rescaling of the nation state. Just as the PRD and YRD are central to China's economic development, accounting for the bulk of its FDI and exports (table 1), they also bring crucial value to continued comparative research for better understanding the broader and distinctive attributes and impacts of a growing number of global(izing) city-regions in the world.

Notes

[1] While the bulk of the empirical analysis in this chapter was abridged from "A Tale of Two Regions in China: Rapid Economic Development and Slow Industrial Upgrading in the Pearl River and the Yangtze River Deltas," which is forthcoming in *International Journal of Comparative Sociology* (April, 2007), it pushes in a different theoretical direction through an alternative conceptual framework and with some different field data on the role of the local state. In drafting this chapter, I benefited from a Faculty Scholar Award from the Great Cities Institute of the University of Illinois at Chicago during Fall 2005. My appointment as Professor in the School of Social Development and Public Policy of Fudan University in Shanghai in Spring 2006 greatly facilitated my subsequent field work in Shanghai and the Yangtze River Delta region. Professor Haoxin Liu at Fudan University arranged and

accompanied me through the field interviews in several cities, towns, and villages around Shanghai. The revision benefited from comments and suggestions from Sir Peter Hall, Dennis Judd, Mark Herkenrath, Yuemin Ning, Dajian Zhu, and two anonymous reviewers, while I am alone responsible for the content. I also thank the participants at the conference "City and State in 20th Century East Asia" at Northwestern University (October 12-13, 2006) for their feedback on my presentation on the Yangtze River Delta region. Finally, I am grateful to the World Society Foundation in Switzerland for rewarding my effort to understand the complexity of regional formations in a global world.

[2] "Growth cools in Yangtze River region," Asia Times online, reprinted and accessed on Asian Development Bank Institute (ADBI)'s Web site at http://www.adbi.org/e-newsline/index.html, June 3, 2005.

[3] In the early 1980s, when some children's dolls were made in Hong Kong, they would be designed in Hong Kong, and their molds were produced in Hong Kong where sophisticated machinery was available. Then the molds were shipped to China, where workers would shoot the plastic, assemble the dolls, paint the figures, and make the dolls' clothing. Then the dolls were brought back to Hong Kong for final-testing, inspection, packaging, which could not be done up to quality in China, and finally were distributed from Hong Kong (Interview with Victor Fung in Magretta, 1998: 105). Nowadays, though the dolls may still be contracted to and designed by a Hong Kong firm, the manufacturing process through packaging is normally completed in China, which shifts "Made by Hong Kong" to "Made by China." Hong Kong, however, still controls the front (design) and back (distribution) ends of the process. In this sense, "Made by Hong Kong" has shifted to "Made in Hong Kong but Made by China" (see Berger and Lester 1997).

[4] Hankook chose Jiaxing because its founding CEO knew Kim Gu (who, like Sun Yat-sen, was like the founding father of Korea, and his exile government in China during Japanese occupation ended up in Jiaxing where there is a Kim Gu museum) and had some sentimental attachment to Jiaxing. Hankook started making tires in 1996 with $30 million investment and raised its capitalization to $300 million by 2006. It now employs about 1,000 people and also has brought its key suppliers from Korea to be with it in Jiaxing. Author's interview in Jiaxing, May 29, 2006.

[5] OEM refers to suppliers making certain products according to the designs and specifications and with equipment from generally multinational corporations as buyers. It makes companies engaged in OEM largely dependent on multinational corporations that contract the OEM production to them.

[6] ODB (original design manufacturing) refers to companies engaged in OEM also providing designs, whereas OBM (original brand manufacturing) refers to companies owning their own brands and using them to deal with buyers of their branded products. ODM is an important upgrade over OEM, and OBM is another major advancement beyond ODM.

[7] "Silks to silicon," China Economic Review online, March 2006, accessed from http://chinaeconomicreview.com/cer/ on April 4, 2006.

[8] Due to this perceived or real competition between the SIP and the SND for foreign investment projects, the JV partners in the SIP had a falling out in the late 1990s, which led the Chinese side buying out 30% of Singapore's stake in the venture.

[9] "Silks to silicon," China Economic Review online, March 2006, accessed from http://chinaeconomicreview.com/cer/ on April 4, 2006.

[10] Ibid.

[11] Ibid.

[12] Author's interview in Suzhou, June, 2006.

[13] "Dongguan protects collective brands with trademarks," Hong Kong Trade Development Council online, reprinted and accessed on Asian Development Bank Institute (ADBI)'s Web site at http://www.adbi.org/e-newsline/index.html, July 12, 2006.

[14] Author's interview in Wujiang, Suzhou, June 9, 2006.

[15] Author's interview in Qidu town, Wujiang, Suzhou, June 10, 2006.
[16] Author's interviews with several business executives in the Yangtze River Delta, June, 2006.
[17] All the information on Taicang was obtained during the author's interviews in Taicang, June, 2006.
[18] Author's interview with government officials in Pinghu, Zhejiang province, June, 2006.
[19] Officials of Suzhou described the city as green tea growing under the shadow of the big tree (Shanghai), whereas officials of Jiaxing seemed to be content with "making a bite from Shanghai last a long time." Author's interviews in Suzhou and Jiaxing, July, 2004 and June, 2006.
[20] The government officials and business managers in the secondary cities like Suzhou and Jiaxing compared Shanghai to a big magnet sucking talents away. Author's interviews in June, 2006.
[21] After the city of Wujiang (see figure 2 and map 2) dropped from No. 10 in the national ranking of top 100 counties in 2004 to the 11th spot in 2005, the Party secretary of Wujiang was reportedly told by higher authorities that he would need to work harder for next year. The prior expectation was that this man who had been the director of a key commission of Suzhou municipality, which administers the county city of Wujiang, would be promoted to the position of a vice Party secretary of Suzhou municipality in 2005, after successfully serving a three-year term as Wujiang's Party secretary. The one-spot slipping of Wujiang from China's top 10 counties implied the lack of success for its top Party boss. Author's interview in Suzhou, June, 2006.

References

Amin, Ash. 1993. "The Globalization of the Economy: An Erosion of Regional Networks?" Pp. 278-295 in *The Embedded Firm: On the Socioeconomics of Industrial Networks*, edited by Grabher, Gernot. London and New York: Routledge.

Amin, Ash and Nigel Thrift. 1994. "Living in the Global." Pp. 1-22 in *Globalization, Institutions, and Regional Development in Europe*, edited by Amin, Ash and Nigel Thrift. London: Oxford University Press.

Berger, Suzanne and Richard K. Lester (eds.). 1997. *Made by Hong Kong*. Hong Kong: Oxford University Press.

Brenner, Neil. 2004. *New State Spaces: Urban Governance and the Rescaling of Statehood*. Oxford and New York: Oxford University Press.

Chen, Xiangming. 1994. "The New Spatial Division of Labor and Commodity Chains in the Greater South China Economic Region." Pp. 165-186 in *Commodity Chains and Global Capitalism*, edited by Gereffi, Gary and Miguel Korzeniewicz. Westport, CT: Greenwood Press.

Chen, Xiangming. 2000. "Both Glue and Lubricant: Transnational Ethnic Social Capital as a Source of Asia-Pacific Subregionalism." *Policy Sciences* 33 (3/4): 269-287.

Chen, Xiangming. 2001. "From Regional Integration to Export Competition? The Evolution of the Chinese Economic Triangle." Pp. 23-42 in *The Chinese Triangle of Mainland China, Taiwan, and Hong Kong: Comparative Institutional Analyses*, edited by So, Alvin Y., Nan Lin, and Dudley Poston. Westport, CT: Greenwood Press.

Chen, Xiangming. 2005. *As Borders Bend: Transnational Spaces on the Pacific Rim*. Lanham, MD: Rowman & Littlefield Publishers.

Chen, Xiangming. 2007. "A Tale of Two Regions in China: Rapid Economic Development and Slow Industrial Upgrading in the Pearl River and the Yangtze River Deltas." *International Journal of Comparative Sociology* 48 (2): 79-113.

Chen, Xiangming and Jiaming Sun. 2007. "Untangling a Global-Local Nexus: Sorting Out Residential Sorting in Shanghai." *Environment and Planning A* (in press).

Coe, Neil, Martin Hess, Henry Wai-chung Yeung, Peter Dicken, and Jeffrey Hendreson. 2004. "'Globalizing' Regional Development: A Global Production Networks Perspective." *Transactions of the Institute of British Geographers* 29 (4): 468-484.

Cumbers, Andy and Danny MacKinnon. 2004. "Introduction: Clusters in Urban and Regional Development." *Urban Studies* 41 (5/6): 959-969.

Dean, Jason and Pui-Wing Tam. 2005. "The Laptop Trail." *The Wall Street Journal* (June 9): B1, B8.

Dicken, Peter, Philip F. Kelly, Kris Olds, and Henry Wai-Chung Yeung. 2001. "Chains and Networks, Territories and Scales: Towards a Relational Framework for Analyzing the Global Economy." *Global Networks* 1 (2): 89-112.

Du, Debin. 2005. "Shanghai: An Emerging Global R&D Base of Multinationals." Presentation in the Session on Urban Progress and Governance, the 4th International Convention of Asian Scholars, Shanghai, August 20-24.

Einhorn, Bruce. 2005. "Why Taiwan Matters?" *BusinessWeek* (May 16): 76-81.

Enright, Michael J. and Edith E. Scott. 2005. "China's Quite Powerhouse." *Far Eastern Economic Review* 168 (5): 27-434.

Fang, He. 2005. "The Yangtze River Delta and the Pearl River Delta: Competitors or Partners?" M.A. Paper, Department of Sociology, University of Illinois at Chicago.

Florida, Richard. 2005. "The World in Numbers: The World is Spiky." *The Atlantic Monthly* (October): 48-51.

Gereffi, Gary, John Humphrey, and Timothy Sturgeon. 2005. "The Governance of Global Value Chains." *Review of International Political Economy* 12 (1): 78-104.

Grabher, Gernot. 1993. "The Weakness of Strong Ties: The Lock-In of Regional Development in the Rhur Area." Pp. 254-277 in *The Embedded Firm: On the Socioeconomics of Industrial Networks*, edited by Grabher Gernot. London and New York: Routledge.

Hall, Peter. 2001. "Global City-Regions in the Twenty-First Century." Pp. 59-77 in *Global City-Regions: Trends, Theory, Policy*, edited by Scott, Allen J. Oxford: Oxford University Press.

Ho, K.C. 2000. "Competing to Be Regional Centres: A Multi-Agency, Multi-Locational Perspective." *Urban Studies* 37 (12): 2337-2356.

Judd, Dennis R. 2003. "Restructuring Regional Politics: General Purpose Authorities and Municipal Governments." A Great Cities Institute Working Paper, University of Illinois at Chicago, June.

Läpple, Dieter. 2001. "City and Region in the Age of Globalization and Digitization." *German Journal of Urban Studies*, http://www.difu.de/index.shtml?/publikationen/dfk/en/01_2/welcome.shtml, pp. 12-36.

Lazerson, Mark. 1993. "Factory or Putting-Out? Knitting Networks in Modena." Pp. 203-226 in *The Embedded Firm: On the Socioeconomics of Industrial Networks*, edited by Grabher, Gernot. London and New York, Routledge.

Lee, Ching Kwan. 1998. *Gender and the South China Miracle: Two Worlds of Factory Women*. Berkeley, CA: University of California Press.

Lin, George C.S. and Pauline H.M. Tse. 2005. "Flexible Sojourning in the Era of Globalization: Cross-Border Population Mobility in the Hong Kong-Guangdong Border Region." *International Journal of Urban and Regional Research* 29 (4): 867-894.

Lui, Tai-lok and Stephen W K Chiu. 2007. "Becoming a Chinese Global City: Hong Kong (and Shanghai) Beyond the Global-Local Duality." Chapter 6 in *Shanghai Rising: Global Impact, State Power, and Local Transformations in the World's Most Dynamic and Rapidly Globalizing City*, edited by Xiangming Chen. Forthcoming from the University of Minnesota Press.

Magretta, Joan. 1998. "Fast, Global, and Entrepreneurial: Supply Chain Management, Hong Kong Style, An Interview with Victor Fung." *Harvard Business Review* (September-October): 103-114.

Mao, Yanhua, Wenxing Liu, and Jixia Hu. 2004. "Dynamics of SEMs Clusters and Networks: An Analysis of the Export Network Economy of IT Industries in Dongguan." *Web Journal of China Management Review* 7 (1): 49-65.

Markusen, Ann. 2004. "An Actor-Centered Approach to Economic Geographic Change." *Annals of the Japan Association of Economic Geographers* 49 (5): 395-408.

Martin, Ron and Peter Sunley. 2003. "Deconstructing Clusters: Chaotic Concept or Policy Panacea?" *Journal of Economic Geography* 3 (1): 5-35.

McDaniels, Iain. 2004. "A Critical Eye on Shanghai." *The China Business Review* (January-February): 8-9.

Messner, Dirk. 2002. "The Concept of the 'World Economic Triangle': Global Governance Patterns and Options for Regions." IDS working paper 173, Institute of Development Studies, Brighton, Sussex, England, December.

Ohame, Kenichi. 1995. *The End of the Nation State: The Rise of Regional Economies*. London: HarperCollins.

Orum, Anthony M. and Xiangming Chen. 2003. *The World of Cities: Places in Historical and Comparative Perspective*. Oxford and Cambridge: Blackwell Publishers.

Overholt, William H. 2004. "Hong Kong or Shanghai?" *The China Business Review* (May-June): 44-47.

Porter, Michael E. 2000. "Location, Competition, and Economic Development: Local Clusters in a Global Economy." *Economic Development Quarterly* 14 (1): 15-34.

Robertson, Roland and Habib Haque Khondker. 1998. „Discourses of Globalization: Preliminary Considerations." *International Sociology* 13: 25-40.

Rosenau, James N., 1997. *Along the Domestic-Foreign Frontier: Exploring Governance in a Turbulent World*. New York: Cambridge University Press.

Sassen, Saskia. 2001. *The Global City: New York, London, Tokyo*. Second Edition. Princeton, NJ: Princeton University Press.

Sassen, Saskia. 2006. *Territory, Authority, Rights: From Medieval to Global Assemblages*. Princeton, NJ: Princeton University Press.

Scott, Allen J., 1995. "The Geographic Foundations of Industrial Performance." *Competition and Change* 1 (1): 51-66.

Scott, Allen J., John Agnew, Edward W. Soja, and Michael Storper (2001): "Global City-Regions: An Overview." Pp. 11-32 in *Global City-Regions: Trends, Theory, Policy*, edited by Scott, Allen J. Oxford: Oxford University Press.

Shanghai Statistical Bureau. 2004. *Shanghai Statistical Yearbook 2004*. Beijing: State Statistics Press.

Tuan, Chyau and Linda Fung Yee Ng. 2002. "From Manufacturing Cross-Border Operations to Regional Economic Integration: Evolution of Hong Kong's Economy and the Guangdong Factor." *Web Journal of China Management Review* 5 (1): 1-14.

Tuan, Chyau and Linda Fung Yee Ng. 2006. "Hong Kong-Shanghai Metropolitan Competitiveness: Reflections from Surveys of Multinationals, 2001-2005." *Web Journal of China Management Review* 9 (2): 1-14.

Yeung, Henry Wai-chung. 2005. "Rethinking Relational Economic Geography." *Transactions of the Institute of British Geographers* 20 (1): 37-51.

Zhang, Jingxiang and Fulong Wu. 2006. "China's Changing Economic Governance: Administrative Annexation and the Reorganization of Local Governments in the Yangtze River Delta." *Regional Studies* 40 (1): 3-21.

4
East Asia: Structure and Formation of a World Region

Patrick Ziltener

> This article uses two methods of analyzing East Asia as a world region within the world system. First, a statistical, comparative country analysis shows that East Asian countries have strong traditions of highly differentiated social organization, are comparatively homogenous societies and successful post-colonial state-builders. But there are significant differences between the countries of the region, which have shaped the making and re-making of the region. Second, East Asia is analyzed as an interactional entity that came into existence in the early centuries CE and turned into a sinocentric trade-tribute-system. Colonialism did slow down regionalization, but under "open imperialism" in 18th and 19th c. economic integration increased to a high level. Intra-regional exchange hit rock bottom in the post-war period, but since 25 years economic integration has intensified rapidly while keeping the region's strong connectedness to other world regions. Increased economic interdependence does only unassertively lead to regional political cooperation.

Geographically, East Asia is a gigantic land mass at the Eastern end of the Eurasian continent, with a long stretched archipelago in the Pacific Ocean. It has almost 2 billions inhabitants, about one third of world population. Besides North America and Europe, East Asia is considered to be the third pillar of the contemporary world political economy. The region holds well over 50% of international monetary reserves. By the early 1990s, the combined economies of Japan, South Korea, Taiwan, Greater China (the People's Republic and Hong Kong) and the countries of the *Association of Southeast Asian Nations* (*ASEAN*) contributed roughly 30% to World GDP, approximately the same share as that held by North America on the one hand and Western Europe on the other. Therefore, many scholars analyze the structure of the world economy as a *triad*.[1] These are statistical constructions that obviously do not make East Asia a world region *per se* yet.

What is East Asia? The boundaries of East Asia have never been conclusively defined, neither economically nor politically. Historically, China and India have been used as reference points to structure the *oriens extremus* (*Far East*), and the area between has been given different names in relation to these (*Indochina* and *East Indies*, among others). Nowadays, two concepts are in use:

East Asia understood as an entity encompassing Northeast Asia (Japan, Korea, China, Taiwan; in the following *NE Asia*) as well as Southeast Asia (the 10 ASEAN-countries; in the following *SE Asia*), or, alternatively, *East Asia* is used to describe the first group of countries only, as opposed to *Southeast Asia*. This article uses the first concept, for reasons that will be discussed in section 4. The idea of *East Asia* as a region has been introduced to the region from the outside, by European colonial powers and the US. It has never been widely used as self-description. Historically, China considered itself not as a regional empire or state, but as the center of the civilized world. Even today, as a political scientist of the Beijing Normal University writes, "[the] great-power psychology characterized with 'China at the center and barbarians at the four directions' still remains in the subconscious of many Chinese people" (Lu 2004). In the Meiji-period Japan, the concept of "abandoning Asia, joining the West (Europe)" (*datsu-A nyu-O*) was a constitutive element of the development of Japanese modernity. For countries in the neighborhood of these two great East Asian powers, like Korea and Vietnam, national identity was hammered out of the reception of profound cultural influences combined with centuries-long defensive struggles against domination and colonization. In SE Asia, national identities were mainly formed in anti-colonial wars with Western powers. The idea of a regional association of states as a security alliance to protect national sovereignty has been quickly accepted by the political elites of the newly independent states, and the 1967 founded ASEAN has certainly been successful in creating a network among these and to provide them with more weight in the international arena as they would have had without it. However, facing ethnic, linguistic, regional and religious cleavages, many SE Asian societies are struggling with the definition of a national identity, often in differentiation from neighboring countries, and post-national or "regional" identities are rare in SE Asia as well. Both in NE and SE Asia, only a minority of the population and of the elites tend to consider themselves to be (East) "Asians," but there are interesting differences between the countries. Recent research on identities "above" the national level found that only 26% of the Japanese and 30% of the Chinese consider themselves to be "Asians"–but 88% of the Koreans.[2] If we follow an approach that relies on the concept of "imagined communities" as the constitutive element of a region, then East Asia is not a region. Or not yet: In the words of the *East Asia Study Group* (*EASG*), which consisted of thirteen senior officials of the ten ASEAN countries plus China, Japan, Korea, and the Secretary-General of ASEAN and had the mission to clarify the goals of the current intensification of intergovernmental cooperation in East Asia: "ASEAN countries, China, Japan, and Korea share a common destiny. East Asia is our natural constituency, and Northeast Asia and Southeast Asia are inextricably intertwined economically, politically, and socially" (EASG 2002: 58).

Beyond the subjective perceptions of the population or elitist projects, there are basically *two ways of defining and analyzing world regions*; both of them will be used in the article. One way consists of cross-national or comparative countries analyses, which are firmly anchored in the world of "methodological nationalism." Central dimensions (language, culture, religion, kinship structures, political regimes, business styles etc.) are defined, and empirical (quantitative or qualitative) analysis finds different values and types for countries.[3] This allows to "map the world" and to detect regional patterns. Two sub-types can be differentiated, depending on whether the group of countries that constitute the "region" is defined *ex ante*, or if it is derived from statistical analyses (*ex post*), by identifying clusters within a larger sample. A cluster analysis is static, focuses similarities and differences and cannot detect functional complementarities. The first type of cross-national analysis assesses the degree of similarities between a given group of countries and defines typical and deviant cases. From a culturalist perspective, a research project at Princeton University described a "region-wide heritage," Confucianism, as "basic worldview" of the region (NE Asian countries and parts of SE Asia, especially Vietnam and Singapore). It aimed at determining what constitutes "the common regional heritage as distinct from the specific national traditions," "examining the diffusion of the regional legacy over many centuries" and "analyzing a changing regional heritage interacting with national and interregional forces" (Rozman 1991: vii). Huntington (1996) sees culture in the sense of "subjective attitudes, beliefs, and values prevalent among the dominant groups in the society" as the "central independent variable" for socio-economic development. He distinguishes three cultures in the area that is defined here as East Asia: *Japanese* (Confucianism, Buddhism, Shinto), *Sinic* (Confucianism; China, Taiwan, Korea, Singapore, Vietnam) and *Malay* (Islam, Buddhism, Catholicism; Malaysia, Indonesia, Philippines). By relating Hofstede's value dimensions to anthropological variables, Hans-Peter Müller and I have showed that there is a distinct Asian pattern of articulating "power distance" and "uncertainty avoidance" (Müller and Ziltener 2004). In the first part (section 2 and 3), this article applies the method of comparative country analysis to East Asia. Using statistical macro-sociological methods, structural and historical factors that created similarities and differences between East Asian countries are analyzed, in the framework of a sample of 90 African and Asian countries.

The second (or better: *other*, because there is no "royal way," no superiority of one of the methods, rather complementarity) way is to analyze world regions as *interactional entities*. As Pempel (2005: 26) noted, "no self-evident and essentialist East Asia forms a single logical and self-contained regional unit ... different problems 'create' different regions." Indeed, different historical periods featured highly different degrees of "regionness" in East Asia, different levels of internal connectedness and cohesiveness. It makes sense to understand a world region as a result of transnational societal processes with variations in intensity (and of boundaries) over time. In this sense, world regions are constantly made and re-made. In section 4, it will be shown that East Asia has been economically integrating since the early centuries CE while never experiencing a period of unified political control. Before and after the short-lived Japanese "co-prosperity sphere" in the first half of the 1940s, Western powers politically dominated intra-regional relations. In mid-20th c. East Asia witnessed a dramatic fall of intra-region exchange from which it recovered only decades later. Only recently, but at a very fast pace, East Asia is reintegrating economically, followed by attempts to build up political cooperation in a regional framework. This way of analyzing East Asia as a world region has been informed by *neofunctionalist integration theory*, developed in the 1950s and 1960s to analyze regionalization in different world regions, Asia among them,[4] and *world-systems theory*. World-systems research has not analyzed world regions prominently yet because the focus traditionally was the emergence of the modern world system and the successive incorporation of the rest of the world into it. However, Abu-Lughod's (1989) seminal analysis of the world system before European hegemony and the debate on the "rise of East Asia"[5] in the 1990s have brought the question of *regions*, "*regionness*" and *regionalization* to the forefront. Abu-Lughod conceptualized the medieval world system (1250-1350 CE) as "set of linterlinked subsystems" (ibid., 353). East Asia (as defined in this article) constitutes in her analysis one of these subsystems. According to Arrighi, Hamashita and Selden (1997: 1), the "regional character" of the "East Asian miracle" challenged "world-system theories that rely too heavily on the tripartite division of the world-economy into core, periphery, and semiperiphery." Ikeda (1996: 65) argues that adding "the regional perspective" as "an additional layer" would enable "world-systemists to study the region specificity of world-systemic processes as well as the region generality of the national processes." He suggests, however, to conceptualize the region East Asia as a world-system.[6] In contrast, I suggest to analyze *world regions* as interactional entities that have qualities different from world-systems. Most importantly, they are not systemic in character which means they are *not self-contained*: The important social processes that reproduce or transform its basic structures are not all within the region (cf. Chase-Dunn and Hall 1997: 4f). Regions are open subagglomerations within a world system, they are interlinked and overlap. Not only has East Asia been connected to South and West Asia but also Africa and Europe for at least 2000 years, it has significantly influenced the development of the world system as a whole. China has been one of the core countries in the world system for centuries, translating its superior manufacturing techniques into bullion inflow from the rest of the world (Frank

1998), thereby affecting prices and economic activities worldwide. Since 500 years, European powers have tried to reshape the region and its internal relations in their interest, and have succeeded to do so, with some interruptions, since more than 200 years. Especially SE Asia has been a battleground for centuries, and in some periods it would be justifiable to count at least some areas of it as parts of other subsystems. In the 16/17th c., external powers competed fiercely to incorporate the "spice islands" as periphery into their subsystems and did everything to destroy linkages into other subsystems. World regions usually have a *core-periphery* structure. It will be shown that the formation of this structure in East Asia can be traced back to social evolutionary processes thousands of years ago and that it reproduced in different time periods. It also underwent tremendous change during the decline of China, the rise of Japan, and–in the post-war period–with the formation of a new semi-periphery in SE Asia. *Regional and global processes interact.* Like world-systems, world regions are made of intersocietal networks that undergo fluctuations and cycles, the "pulsate" (cf. Chase-Dunn and Hall 1997: 204ff). The interaction can be synchronous or asynchronous: Regional integration can intensify during the expansion of the world system, decrease during its contraction, or it can intensify in reaction to the world system's crises. For both processes empirical evidence can be found in East Asia. Therefore, regional integration[7] can be measured against the background of world system development ("global integration," since late 15th c.). Regional integration takes place when intra-regional interactions increase or intensify at higher pace than the system as a whole, and disintegration when they decrease or the world system as a whole integrates faster.[8]

As has become clear already, this article does not focus on short-term dynamics or conjunctural shifts, it rather analyzes regional integration from a long-term perspective. Obviously, the empirical measurement of processes going back 2000 years is a problem; we possess reliable data and indicators for little more than 140 years.[9] While overall regional integration and disintegration trends can be assessed relying on a large volume of research done by sector-, area- or country specialists, statements about the relative *levels* of integration in East Asia in different periods are confined to "guesstimates."

A comparative analysis of East Asian societies

East Asia is a highly diverse region, and this diversity is a major obstacle to regional integration. These statements can be found in almost all analyses of the region, but usually this diversity is not further researched beyond income levels and other indicators for economic development. In this and the following section the characteristics of–and the similarities and differences between East Asian societies are analyzed in four dimensions, both using historic indicators (precolonial development level of social organization; societal heterogeneity) and modern ones (quality of statehood; character of political regimes).

From the theory of social evolution and related empirical research, a basic, long-term evolutionary mechanism is well known: the interrelation between the development of agriculture, population growth, increasing social complexity and cultural homogeneization.[10] Where agriculture–in the case of East Asia mainly wet rice agriculture–could be practiced and has been introduced, populations grew faster and social structures differentiated. Starting in central China around 5000 BC, this process took place mainly in the big river basins, connecting other areas through waterways. Exchange intensified, states and empires were formed that led to the incorporation of neighboring population groups and to cultural homogeneization through the spread of religions and the development of a refined court culture. Even with data for modern countries in Africa and Asia this relationship can be shown: On the basis of ethnographic data, Müller et al (1999, *Atlas*) have constructed an index that measures the precolonial level of development of social organization, formed from the ranked variables "mean size of local communities," "jurisdictional hierarchy beyond local community," "class stratification" and "written language" of the ethnic groups on the territory of the postcolonial states.[11] Values for 13 East Asian countries are given: Japan, North and South Korea, China, Taiwan, Philippines, Vietnam, Cambodia, Laos, Thailand, Myanmar (Burma), Malaysia and Indonesia. This index correlates highly with their data for ethnic, linguistic and religious heterogeneity for 1960 as well as with more recent World Bank data for so-called fractionalization (Table 1).

In general, countries with a higher precolonial level of development of social organization do have a lower level of societal heterogeneity in the modern era. Even the arbitrary and sometimes absurd boundaries imposed by the colonial powers did not fundamentally alter this situation. As Table 1 shows, this relation holds for the reference sample as well as for 13 countries of East Asia, except for religious heterogeneity.[12] For further analysis of the similarities and differences between East Asian countries, the focus will be on the most significant relationship, the one between traditional social organization and ethnic homogeneity (1960). Figure 1 shows the classification of the East Asia countries (light grey symbols) in the context of the reference sample.

First, it has to be stated that East Asian countries are among the societies with the highest development levels of precolonial social organization. This is obvious for the countries that were profoundly influenced by the Chinese model of civilization (NE Asia plus Vietnam). The main influence on SE Asian countries came from Indian Hindu-Buddhist civilization which interacted with endogenous development. The results were the early "indianized states,"[13] of which traces can be found at the Central coast of nowadays Vietnam, in the big river basins of the Mekong (Cambodia), Chaophraya (Thailand) and Irawaddy (Myanmar) on the SE Asian continent and, in the archipelago, predominantly on the island of Java. In these areas, highly differentiated societies

Table 1.
Traditional social organization and modern societal heterogeneity

Correlations (bivariate)	Traditional level of social organization	
	Sample Africa/Asia (N=90)	East Asia (N=13)
Ethnic Homogeneity (% biggest ethnic group/total population, 1960)	.72 n=83	.81 n=13
Linguistic Homogeneity (% biggest language/total population, 1960)	.63 n=83	.71 n=13
Religious Homogeneity % biggest religion/total population, 1960)	.57 n=83	n.s. n=13
Ethnic Fractionalization (Ethnic Fractionalization Index, 1995)	.48 n=83	-.68* n=13
Linguistic Fractionalization (Language Fractionalization Index, 1995)	-.54 n=82	-.79 n=13
Religious Fractionalization (Religion Fractionalization Index, 1995)	-.37 n=83	n.s. n=13

Note: All correlations sig. at 0.01 level (two-tailed) (* sig. at 0.05 level)
Sources: Index for traditional level of social organization, ethnic, linguistic, religious homogeneity, 1960: *Atlas* (Müller et al. 1999); Ethnic, Language, Religion Fractionalization Index, 1995: Alesina et al (2003).

developed on the basis of irrigated rice cultivation, with kings claiming divinity (*devaraja*), a nobility and a Brahmanic caste supervising the religious cults, the construction of monumental stone temples and systems of related monasteries with important economic functions, taxation and military organizations etc. The Khmer state of Angkor (9-15th c.) was probably the most advanced in the double process of transforming former autonomous local or regional centers into provinces and in building up a centralized government (Kulke 1989). However, the "indianized states" of SE Asia did not reach the level of a rational, systematic bureaucratic organization as did the states following the Chinese model.[14] Furthermore, big areas have not been (or only superficially) integrated into these states and empires, such as the mountainous areas of continental SE Asia, or Borneo and the Eastern Indonesian islands as well as the island group that would be called "the Philippines" by the Spanish colonizers. These areas still have higher levels of societal heterogeneity than the core

Figure 1.
Traditional level of social organization and ethnic homogeneity, 1960

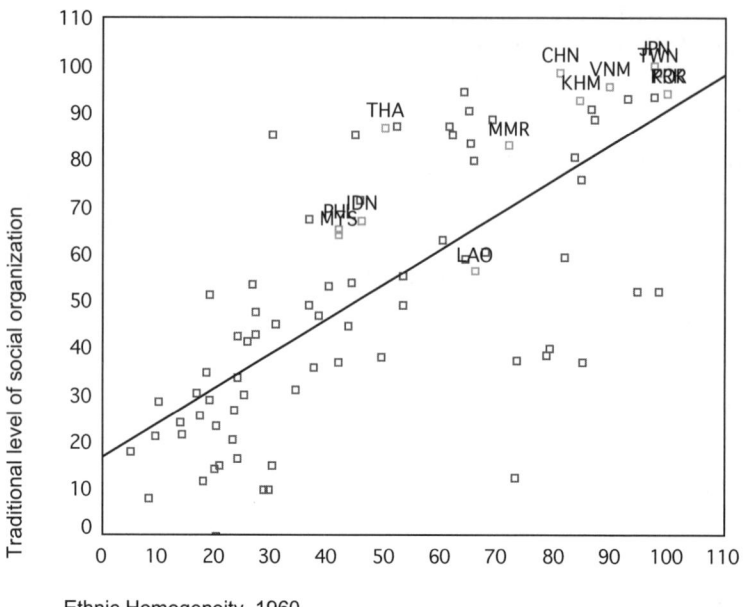

Note: Total sample: African and Asian countries, light grey: countries of East Asia (CHN: China, IDN: Indonesia, JPN: Japan, KHM: Cambodia, LAO: Laos, MMR: Myanmar/Burma, MYS: Malaysia, PHI: Philippines, PRK: North Korea, VNM: Vietnam, ROK: South Korea, THA: Thailand, TWN: Taiwan).
Sources: author's compilation based on the data from Table 1

areas of the old states and empires. Therefore, regarding the traditional level of social organization, the East Asian countries can be divided in three groups:
- countries with the highest values are those who followed the Chinese model of state-building (NE Asia plus Vietnam[15]),
- countries with high values: continental SE Asia without Laos (Cambodia, Thailand, Myanmar) and
- countries with (for East Asia) rather low values: maritime SE Asia (Malaysia, Philippines, Indonesia–with exception of the islands Java and Bali) and the hinterland of the continent (Laos).

Without two negative feedback-mechanisms, the correlation between social organization and heterogeneity would even be stronger. The first one is *empire-building*: ethnic groups with bigger populations and more complex social organization expanded territorially and subjected other groups. Cultural assimilation and social integration, however, was a slow and often incomplete process. As a result, Thailand and Myanmar are rather heterogeneous countries. China and Vietnam are examples of successful empire-building too; in these cases, the dominant ethnic group numerically dwarfs the others. Laos owes its existence to an agreement by colonial powers. Without that, it would probably have been incorporated into Siamese (Thai) or Vietnamese empire in the long-term. On the other side, Cambodia, with its Khmer empire dominating much of the SE Asian continent for centuries, owes its high level of homogeneity to the decline of the empire and the subsequent loss of territory. Today we find significant Khmer minorities in all neighboring countries (Thailand, Laos, Vietnam). The modern situation of societal heterogeneity, therefore, reflects the long-term evolutionary mechanism described above as well as the competition between states and empires–whose results have been modified by the impact of *colonialism*. In general, in areas with higher levels social of social organization, colonialism met stronger resistance. In East Asia, colonialism had its deepest impact in the SE Asian archipelago, to a smaller degree on continental SE Asia, and even less in NE Asia, where comparably stable boundaries have been in place for centuries.[16] In contrast, the SE archipelago has never been unified into a stable inter-state system or empire; it was basically a decentralized trade network, based on Islamic law and Malay as *lingua franca*. The SE Asian post-colonial states were born within the colonial borderlines. As a result, there exist entities, which are geographically bigger and have larger populations than some of the old empires of the continent, but with a much lesser degree of integration. Furthermore, colonialism modified the composition of the population in some areas significantly by organizing labor migration (the so-called "coolies" from China and India) into the areas with plantation economy. As a result, the populations of some areas like the Malay peninsula (today part of Malaysia) have been transformed profoundly. Also, ethnic trade networks all over East Asia, mainly Chinese and Malay, had an impact on the composition of mainly urban populations. By creating a new class of civil servants and military personnel under European cultural influence, and through missionary activities, the colonial powers further increased societal heterogeneity. Some of these processes were reversed by ethnic, religious and social conflicts and government policies in the immediate postcolonial period. In general, the predominant "economic nationalism" (Myrdal 1957; Golay et al. 1969) in the postcolonial period prevented transnational migration, but furthered intra-migration.[17]

As conclusion it can be stated that East Asian countries have in general rather homogenous populations and a high level of traditional social organization. However, there is no statistically defined cluster of East Asian countries; as Figure 1 shows, there are other traditionally complex and homogenous countries in Asia which are closer to the NE group than some SE Asian countries. The statistical analysis enables us to define two fundamental cleavages in East Asia: the one between the highly homogenous societies of NE Asia (plus Vietnam) with highest levels of social organization, and less homogeneous SE Asia. Within SE Asia, there is a cleavage between the areas of the socially complex continental empire-states (plus Java), and two hinterlands: the *inner continent*, the mountainous area between China, Myanmar, Thailand and Vietnam, incl. Laos, and the *outer maritime realm*: the thousands bigger and smaller islands of the SE Asian archipelago, following the degree of their distance to the continent and to the historic centers on Java and Bali. This structure still shapes modern processes of national development as well as regional integration.

The impact of historic factors on modern development

Undoubtedly, societal heterogeneity is highly relevant for modern political as well as socio-economic processes. Furnivall (1941: 61ff) analyzed the "pural colonial society" and noted a low degree of social cohesiveness between ethnic groups: "mutual relations are confined to the economic sphere ...A common social will is feeble or absent." Geertz (1967: 259ff) described postcolonial societies as "abnormally susceptible to serious disaffection based on primordial attachments (...) disaffection based on race, language, or culture threatens partition, irredentism, or merger, a redrawing of the very limits of the state, a new definition of its domain." In one of the earliest empirical analyses of the effects of societal heterogeneity in 74 countries (1957-1962) Adelman and Morris (1967: 41) concluded: "... cultural and ethnic heterogeneity tend to hamper the early stages of nation-building and growth." Recent analyses with newer data have confirmed these findings.[18] Furthermore, the traditional level of social organization proves to be a main determinant of modern development, astonishingly to an over time *in*creasing degree (Ziltener and Müller 2007 [forthcoming]). Traditionally more complex societies have stronger economic growth and reach higher levels of life expectancy for their populations. Therefore, the comparably high levels of social organization and homogeneity of East Asian societies are both factors to be taken into consideration in explaining the "East Asian miracle" (World Bank 1993) (and also in explaining the obvious differences *between* East Asian countries). In this section, the focus will be the interrelation between these historic factors and *(modern) statehood*. In general, heterogeneous countries are politically less stable, have a lower quality of bureaucracy, more corruption and an insufficient rule of law.[19] On the other side, countries with traditionally higher social organization have better post-colonial states. For a sample of East Asian countries, however, there is no significant correlation between societal heterogeneity and the quality of the state as measured by the *Governance Indicators* compiled by World Bank researchers.[20] Also, there are several cases in East Asia which do not follow the general interrelation between traditional social organization and postcolonial state quality. Figure 2 depicts the correlations for the reference sample and the East Asian countries.

Figure 2. Correlations between traditional social organization, homogeneity, and statehood

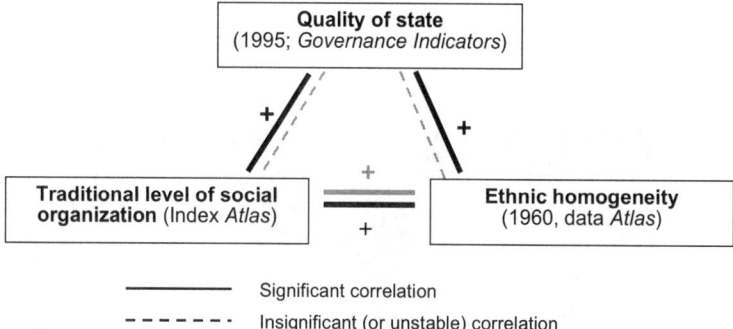

——————— Significant correlation
- - - - - - - Insignificant (or unstable) correlation

Reference sample: 90 countries in Africa and Asia; inner lines represent East Asian countries.
Note: Traditional social organization, homogeneity, quality of state are positive determinants of economic and social development (1965-95); political democracy is not significant. Source: author's results on the basis of the data from the *Atlas, Polity 98* and the World Bank *Governance Indicators*.

The focus of the analysis will be on the fact that *state quality* as measured by the *Governance Indicators* in East Asia is–in contrast to the reference sample– statistically not related to traditional organization and homogeneity. Why this East Asian exceptionalism? Table 2 shows a classification of the countries of East Asia countries regarding the dimensions of interest here. This overview makes it possible to identify the reasons behind the insignificant correlations for East Asia. Several countries with high values regarding the factors influencing the quality of modern statehood, namely traditional social organization and ethnic homogeneity, do not have a correspondingly high quality level of modern statehood. These countries are: China, Vietnam, North Korea, and in SE Asia Cambodia and Myanmar.[21]

On the other side, there are two cases with highly developed modern statehood, despite historically less favorable factors, namely Malaysia and Singapore. These two SE Asian countries belong to the very small group of countries in Africa and Asia which managed to break the tragic nexus between high societal heterogeneity and low quality of statehood.[22] Both countries (as well as ASEAN as regional organization) have developed political, educational and cultural programs in order to mitigate potentially conflictive ethnic cleavages. It has to be noted that Thailand, China and Vietnam, with high levels of traditional social organization, are (in contrast to North Korea and Myanmar) making fast progress in reforming the state, and it can be expected that they will be evaluated with more positive results in some years. As a first conclu-

Table 2.
Traditional level of social organization and ethnic homogeneity, 1960

	Trad. social organization	Ethnic homogeneity, 1960	Level of democracy, 1965-95	Quality of state, 1995
	low --------- high	low ------- high	autoc-----democ	low -------- high
Japan				
S-Korea				
N-Korea				
China				
Taiwan				
HongKong	- - -			
Vietnam				
Cambodia				
Thailand				
Myanmar				
Laos				
Philippines				
Brunei	- - -			
Malaysia				
Singapore	- - -			
Indonesia				

Note: Simplified data representation in form of a three tier scale (*low, medium, high*); --- missing data; democracy: average level autocracy-democracy for the years 1965-95 according to Polity 98, years with regime breakdown excluded, Vietnam 1975-95, Hong Kong and Brunei: author's classification.
Source: author's compilation on the basis of the data from the *Atlas*, *Polity 98* and the World Bank *Governance Indicators*.

sion, it can be stated that East Asian countries in general belong to the group of countries that were successful in post-colonial state-building, even on the basis of less homogenous societies. However, there are country cases in East Asia (Indonesia, Philippines, Myanmar) which do not follow "the East Asian way," but correspond more to the general pattern in Africa and Asia, where societal heterogeneity forms a persistent obstacle to development. Therefore, it cannot be excluded that in the long-run, East Asia's trajectory will follow the general pattern, and the correlation between quality of statehood and societal heterogeneity, or traditional level of social organization respectively, will become significant for the East Asia sample as well.

How does democracy fit into this picture? First, it has to be recalled that in general, there is no stable link between political regime and economic and social performance.[23] There is no significant correlation between democracy/autocracy and traditional social organization as well as ethnic heterogeneity. Looking at the country values in Table 2 shows that a more democratic tradition does not necessarily lead to "good governance," while some clearly autocratic regimes in East Asia reached a very high quality of statehood. The data for political democracy reflect average levels from the 1960s to the mid-1990s; therefore, the recent processes of democratization in some countries influence the values only marginally. It has to be recalled that, until present, no East Asian country ever has introduced political democracy under the conditions of political autonomy and sovereignty–and with long-term stability. In Japan political democracy has been introduced by the Allied powers after World War II, and the democratization in several East Asian countries took place only in the late 1980s or during the 1990s. Political democracy (or democratization) in East Asia, therefore, can be understood only as a result or a corollary element of successful economic development, not as its causal factor. The countries of East Asia are for a significant part responsible for the results of statistical analyses showing no correlation between democracy and development. In no other world region can as many autocratic regimes with positive economic and social development be found. This fact has sponsored the discourse on "Asian values," which caused concern in the West. The recent processes of democratization in East Asia (South Korea, Taiwan, Philippines, Thailand, Cambodia, Indonesia) however, show that as in other world regions people opt for more participatory political regimes when they are given the chance to express their preferences. However, regarding political regimes, strong differences persist in East Asia.

These results suggest that there is no interrelation between traditional social organization and homogeneity and the political regime. Average values over long periods of time, however, veil remarkably different political dynamics. There is evidence, not presented here, that regime *stability* is related to these factors: The higher the traditional level of social organization and the more homogeneous the society, the more stable the political regime (democracy or autocracy). The country with the highest variance of democracy/autocracy values is the Philippines, while the NE Asian countries qualify as the ones with highest stability (lowest variance), joined by autocratic Singapore. And there is also evidence for democratization being more successfully and effectively implemented in more homogenous countries.

For the purpose of this article it suffices to conclude with the following statements:
- East Asian countries share certain societal features: In general they have strong traditions of highly differentiated social organization, they are comparatively homogenous societies, and–related to that–they are above-average successful post-colonial state-builders, independently from the kind of political regime. As a result, East Asia has some of the socially most integrated societies and most efficient governmental institutions of the world. These factors partly explain the "East Asian miracle."
- East Asia as a region is diverse: These favorable factors are distinctive to varying degrees. As analyzed in section 1, long-term evolutionary developments have formed core and periphery areas in East Asia, as in other world regions. This structuration has a lasting impact: Modern indicators like the quality of statehood as well as economic data increasingly reflect these differences. In many countries, there is a positive dynamic of institutional reform, including more participatory forms of government. But East Asia also has some corrupt, dead-locked and ineffective political regimes,–more often in traditionally peripheral regions than in the old cores. It is also remarkable that of the few worldwide "success stories" against the odds of unfavorable historical factors, two are in East Asia: Malaysia and Singapore.[24] If they serve as models for the trajectory of other countries of the region–and they are closely studied for that purpose–then the "East Asian exceptionalism" may turn into a stable characteristic of the region. At least as plausible as the opposite scenario which could be called "return to normality": A further desintegration of the old peripheries and a more accentuated divergence of development in East Asia. The different problems that East Asian societies are internally preoccupied with (increasing social integration, preventing regional desintegration, upholding political stability, reform of institutions, extending popular participation etc.) have to taken into account when recent progress and blockades of transnational cooperation are studied.

The making and re-making of a region–a long-term perspective

From a long-term perspective, five stages of regional integration in East Asia can be distinguished, according to the dominant structuration of intra-regional relations:
1. the development of intra- and trans-regional exchange, from the first centuries CE,
2. the period of the sinocentric trade-tribute-system, 15th-17th c.,

3. the period of Western domination, 18th c.–1942
4. the period of the division of the region in the bloc confrontation, 1945-1980
5. the period of re-integration, from 1980.

As mentioned has all of East Asia in the first millennium CE been influenced by the Indian civilization, mainly by the spread of Buddhism, and SE Asia additionally by Hindu concepts of state and political rule. However, even in this early period economic exchange between SE and NE Asia has probably been of more weight than between SE Asia and South Asia. From 13th c. on SE Asia has definitely been influenced more by its relations with NE Asia than with India, though the strong Chinese impact has to be somewhat relativated by the spread of Islamic religion and culture which proceeded in maritime SE Asia at a slow but steady pace from the 13th c. on.

The development of intra- and trans-regional exchange

That intra-and trans-regional trade in East Asia goes back at least to the first centuries CE is proven by artifacts found in archaeological excavations in Oc Eo, in the Mekong delta (Higham 2001: 25ff). Trade was of high significance for an early polity it belonged to, called *Funan* by Chinese sources. Oc Eo has been a central entrepôt on the East-West route (see Map 1). Archaeologists found goods not only from other SE Asian regions and from China, but also from India, the Near East, Africa and also of Roman origin. The Mekong region itself exported mainly elephants and ivory, spices, aromatic wood and lacquer. In this early period, the trade route followed the SE Asian continental coast line closely, the goods were then unloaded in what is nowadays Southern Thailand, transported over land at the narrowest part of the Isthmus of Kra (around 65 km). Then they were loaded on ships again at the Andaman Sea coast and brought over the Indian ocean. Only from 4th-5th c. on, an all sea route through the Malacca Strait has been firmly established. The Strait is still the main East-West sea route. Since 2000 years there is an intense (economic and military) competition in SE Asia between trading ports for the central entrepôt function on this route.[25] Oc Eo was the first looser when the trading ships rerouted, and many places on the Malay peninsula and Sumatra since have shared its destiny and fell into oblivion. Only few places could keep their importance for longer periods, Malacca was among them, with changing political rule: In 15th c. it was backed by the Chinese Empire, in 1511 conquered by the Portuguese[26] and later taken by their rivals, the Dutch, in 1641.

From the early 19th c. on it was the open port of British Singapore (with Malacca and Penang as its satellites) that became the central entrepôt in SE

Asia; in NE Asia it was British Hong Kong. Historically, these port cities remained politically and militarily vulnerable and could usually not resist the power of the large land-based empires. Alliances among them were short-lived, and the exit-strategy of high mobility of traders proved to be more effective. As a result, neither intra- nor trans-regional trade could be controlled by a

Map 1. Historic sea routes and entrepôts in East Asia

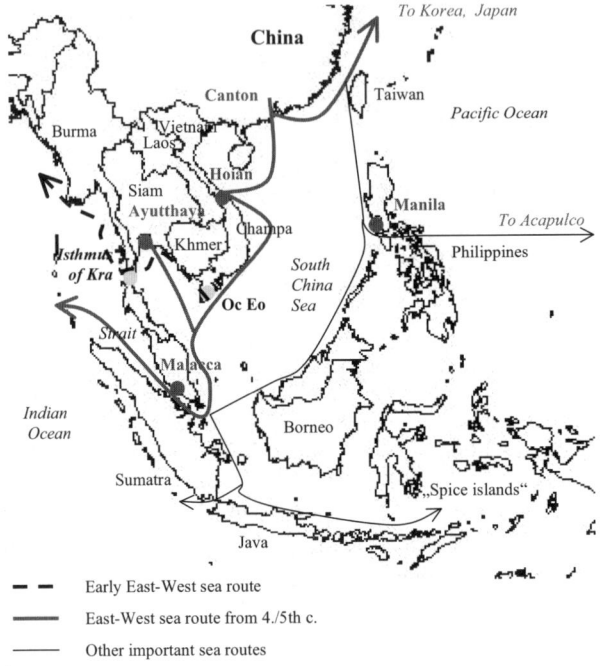

Source: author

single power.[27] Commerce in SE Asia, however, was not completely open, "free trade." It was based on the longstanding tradition of *negotiated trade*, wherein representatives of trade communities (e.g. Malay, Chinese, Indian, Javanese) negotiated with local rulers and their trade officials (who were usually traders themselves) to achieve mutually satisfactory results (Hall 1999: 18). Rulers often insisted that traders buy from them by exalted prices before being given access to the market (Tarling 1999a: 140). Furthermore, there were royal monopolies on many of the most lucrative export items, as well as tolls on international trade and taxes on markets.

In every regard–population size, economy, technology and military–*China* was by far the superior country in East Asia, from the region's earliest state formation in the centuries before CE well into 19th c. Han emperor Wu (reign 141-87 BC) already sent Chinese trade envoys to explore the oceans in the South. The single most important demand side impulse for the formation of East Asia as region came with the fall of the Han-Dynasty in 3rd and 4th c. Nomadic people invaded Northern China and interrupted land-based East-West trade, the so-called "silk road." Significant parts of the Chinese population, including its wealthy upper class, moved to the region south of the Yangtze. From now on, goods from "the West" destined for the Chinese market had to be shipped through SE Asia. Furthermore, the Chinese developed a taste for the spices from the "Southern Ocean" (*Nanyang* in Chinese) like pepper, clove, nutmeg, and others. Chinese medicine highly valued some exotic products, like Rhinoceros horns. The huge Chinese demand during the Tang and Sung dynasties (7-12th c.) had persisting effects on the formation of trading empires in SE Asia (Reid 1993: 10). By AD 987, during the Sung dynasty, the southern maritime trade provided a fifth of the total cash revenue of the Chinese state (Chew 2000: 225). The Mongol conquest of China and large parts of the region (13th c.) interrupted the process of economic integration. It was the first attempt to bring the whole region under a unified political control; it failed to do so because of the successful resistance of Japan and Vietnam. The less consolidated maritime empires in SE Asia could not be brought under Mongol rule permanently either. The following period of *pax mongolica* (13th and 14th c.) dramatically increased integration in the Eurasian world system as a whole (Abu-Lughod 1989), but had a mixed impact on the only partially conquered East Asian region. On the one hand, it opened up trade opportunities in general, but, on the other hand, by securing the continental East-West trade routes and devastating parts of SE Asia, it reduced the significance of maritime exchange in the "Southern Ocean."

The sinocentric trade-tribute system (15th-17th c.)

China was the most important market for SE Asian goods for centuries. The Chinese were not passive recipients but also active seekers of commercial gain. Recent Research shows that much more trade went on than official Chinese documents reveal, and that tribute-trade, the only type referred to in dynastic documents, was only the tip of an iceberg of unrecorded private trade. The latter seems to have almost always exceeded the former in bulk and value. Private trade expanded continuously, and intensified especially from 12th to 14th c. (Wang 1970). The first systematic and large-scale attempts by the Chinese to explore and connect the region were undertaken in early 15th c., almost a century before the first Europeans reached East Asia. The Imperial Chinese navy, founded in 1232, had been massively expanded under the early Ming dynasty. Several naval expeditions were sent by the Chinese emperors to explore the "Southern Ocean." The expeditions, equipped with up to 100 for that period gigantic ships and 20-30"000 seamen and soldiers, landed in Vietnam, Java, Sumatra, Brunei, Siam (Thailand), Malacca, crossed the Indian Ocean, stopped at Calicut and Cochin (Southwest India), Ceylon and the Maldives, several ports on the Arab peninsula, and even reached East Africa (Somalia, Kenya). The expeditions were certainly motivated by the search for exotic goods, but the goal was not to occupy trading posts or to establish colonies but to open diplomatic contacts in order to incorporate the "rest of the world" into the "Chinese world order" (Fairbanks 1968).[28] If the local rulers did not agree to send tributary missions to the Chinese capital, they were exchanged by using military force if necessary. The tributary missions, however, proved to be so attractive in terms of trading opportunities with the leading economy that the Chinese court had to send orders to several polities in SE Asia not to dispatch these missions too frequently. Some merchants even presented themselves as tribute bearers from imaginary states in order to be allowed to conduct trade in China. The key to the functioning of the tribute trade as a system was huge demand for commodities outside China and the differences between prices inside and outside China. The system was determined by the price structure of China, and on that basis the region became an integrated "silver zone" (Hamashita 1994: 96). Given the extended trade opportunities, many Chinese remained in or migrated to SE Asia. These "overseas Chinese" formed a diaspora (Chang 1991) that became one of the crucial elements of the integration of East Asia as a region. Manila e.g., whose main economic function was to serve as trading place of Chinese silk for Spanish silver from America, was inhabited in the 16th and 17th c. by 42.000 people–12.000 Spaniards and 30.000 Chinese (Flynn and Giraldez 1994: 82). In peak years like 1597, the amount of bullion sent from Acapulco to Manila exceeded the total value of trans-Atlantic trade (Andaya 1999: 13).

Maritime networks in this period were sustained by the exchange of currencies (bullion, cowry shells, minted coins) and commodities (luxuries and bulk). Around 1500 Chinese copper coins were the principal currency used in the maritime realm of SE Asia (Tarling 1999a: 140). Rice, jungle products, spices, and textiles were all among SE Asia's local products that attracted traders. In return, SE Asian producers and consumers received bullion and coinage, food, and imported luxuries such as silk and ceramics from China and also from Japan and Vietnam. The economic historian Anthony Reid (1988: xiv) concludes: "the region was manifestly better integrated by the warm and placid waters of the South China Sea then were southern Europe, the Levant, and North Africa by the Mediterranean" (Reid 1988: xiv). Another indicator for the degree of regional connectedness is the fact that in SE Asia a new ship design developed out of Chinese and SE Asian types.[29] These hybrid vessels demonstrate "an interactive maritime realm, where there was regular exchange of ideas and technology coincidental to the transaction of trade" (Hall 1999: 7).

Considering these facts, we can speak of East Asia as an economically *and* politically integrated region at least from 13th c. on. The sinocentric trade-tribute-system was a complex system of reciprocal relations that embraced both inclusion and competition, and it was in symbiosis with a network of commercial trade relations. It was definitely not an empire, from the Chinese point of view too. The Chinese concept of order and unity was based on the idea of "ranks" for all countries according to their closeness/distance to Chinese civilization, the universal acceptance of its superiority, and clearly defined and heavily regulated exchange relations with China at the center. After mid-15th c. there were no attempts by China to intervene in SE Asia, neither to protect its trade interests nor the Chinese communities. Trade with and in China was a privilege which was granted in exchange for the acceptance of and the participation in the Chinese "world order" in an appropriate manner. In the 16th and 17th c., the ideal of sinocentric unity was expanded and consolidated, with Korea, Japan, and Vietnam being particularly strongly affected (Hamashita 1994). In more distant and open SE Asia, however, China was gradually loosing its political and cultural influence, while remaining the region's economic gravity center well into the 19th c.

On the background of these facts and the analysis of section 2, we can define the traditional core-periphery structure of East Asia (Figure 3).

In the Nothern part of the region, this was a highly stable structure, with China at the center. According to the criteria like spatial location and "containing both core and peripheral forms of organization and institutional features" (Chase-Dunn and Hall 1997: 78), the semiperiphery consisted of the countries Japan, Korea and Vietnam, all three as mentioned highly influenced by the "Chinese model." They also successfully adopted Chinese manufacturing techniques and exported "high-tech" products like porcelain or silk. Regarding the criterion "mediating activities between core and periphery," Vietnam, with its strategic location at the main North-South sea route and important ports like Hoian (*Faifo*) where Chinese and Japanese traders met, belonged to the semiperiphery, while Korea and Japan in their "seclusion" period did certainly less so. Modeled on China, Vietnam also brought neighboring countries (Cambodia, Laos) into a tributary relationship. In SE Asia, however, positions were in general less stable, or, in other words, there was a competitive dynamic which allowed for a certain degree of mobility. None of the port cities, however, managed to fulfill central functions for intra- and trans-region trade for a longer period of time and therefore to rise definitely into the semiperiphery. The process of competitive state-/empire-building on the SE Asian continent led to a basically three polity-structure (Burma, Siam, Vietnam) with "shared"

Figure 3.
Core-periphery structure and mobility in East Asia, 13th-17th c.

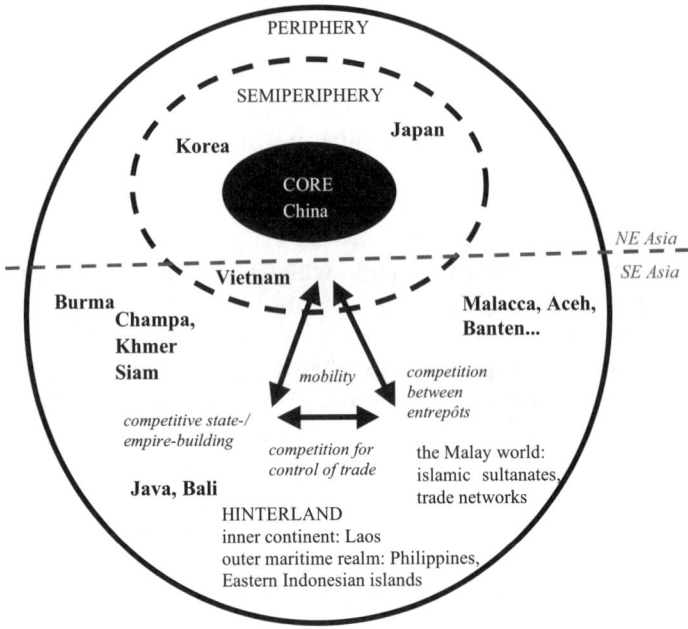

Source: author

dependencies like Cambodia. Western Colonialism terminated this historic process.

Western domination of intra-regional relations, 18th c.-1942

Being an incremental process, it is difficult to determine the beginning of the historical period of Western domination of intra-regional relations. Newer historical analyses show that the European impact on the Asian economic exchange system in the 16th-18th c. has traditionally been massively overestimated (Frank 1998). By military attacks, piracy, draining trade and successively "closing" parts of the archipelago to other traders, the European powers did steadily advance in controlling trade in SE Asia. The trading ports of Vietnam and Thailand (Ayutthaya in the 18th c. and Bangkok in the 19th c.), however, profited from evading trade and established themselves as the main entrepôts in SE Asia. And, while the European powers controlled trans-regional trade from and to their colonies, ethnic Chinese trade networks were tolerated to organize intra-East Asia trade. Therefore, a dual system of transnational exchange in SE Asia came into existence. Over a long period, Chinese merchants

Figure 4. Core-periphery structure in East Asia and the advancement of colonialism, 16th-20th c.

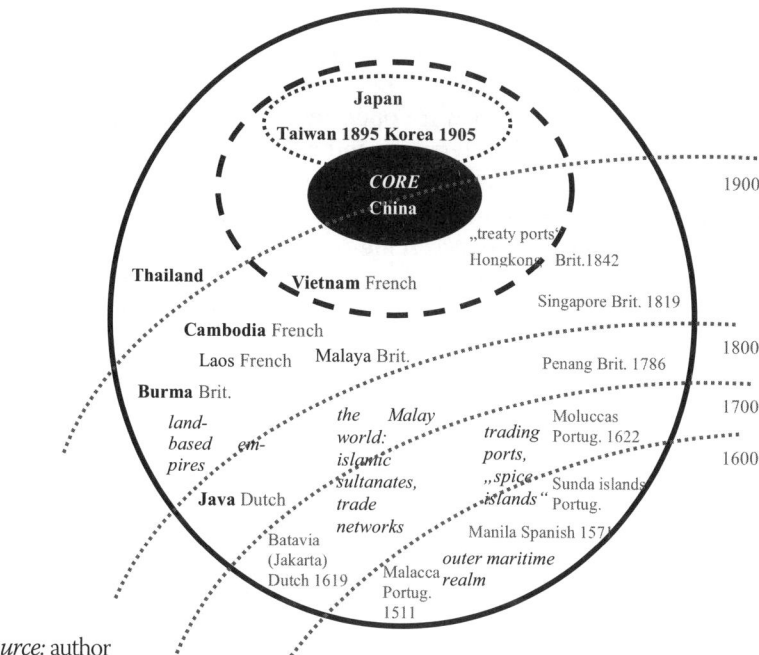

Source: author

under European protection accumulated capital, controlled increasingly also trade in rural areas and became even money-lenders to colonial governments. Government-sponsored or -tolerated anti-Chinese riots were not rare. This ethnicity-based economic structure became one of the socially and politically most divisive legacies of colonialism to the newly independent countries in SE Asia after 1945.

As Figure 4 shows, Western expansion in East Asia clearly followed the core-periphery structure. Beginning with the occupation of trading ports and the "spice islands" which were not protected by one of the land-based empires, the Portuguese and the Dutch brought parts of the lucrative maritime trade under control. The Spanish occupied a large part of the politically weakly integrated islands in the maritime "hinterland" (Philippines). The Malay trade networks, however, could not be easily destroyed, due to their inherent organizational flexibility and geographical mobility. On Java, the Dutch implemented a strategy of "divide and rule," profited from the political fragmentation and made the Javanese empire(s) the first one in East Asia to fall under Western control. China, the core country, as well as the semiperipheral countries in the region resisted successfully to Western expansionism for centuries. They channeled and tightly controlled foreign trade through closely supervised trading posts, making sure the results of economic exchange was in the interest of the country, and keeping out undesired Western influence. Only in the era of steam-powered gunboats, the Western powers had the military means to overcome these obstacles. In a series of "unequal treaties" even the formerly most powerful Asian empires had to "open the country" and to accept the loss of control over jurisdiction, territory and economic exchange. In 19th c. Britain and France succeeded in bringing all the big land-based empires in SE Asia under their control, directly, or in the case of Siam, indirectly.

Under the evolving regime of free trade-oriented, "open imperialism," East Asia integrated economically at fast pace. The significance of the new central entrepôts Singapore and Hong Kong did lay less in distributing British goods in Asia, but in redirecting and re-allocating Asian goods within Asia. As Latham (1994: 145) concludes his analysis of trade data 1868-1913, they were "the twin hubs of intra-Asian trading activity, not merely British trading outposts ... British control of these two great ports ensured the maintenance of relatively free trade in the Malacca and Sunda Straits, and the South China Sea, which was more important for the trade of East Asia than it was for the trade of Britain or the British empire." Also, between 1851 and 1900, more than two million "contract laborers" left China. Two-thirds of them were shipped to Western colonies in Southeast Asia, what enlarged the Chinese diaspora to a significant degree. In late 19th c., Japan joined the Western powers in imperialistic endeavors at the expense of the Chinese empire. After defeating China in 1895, it occupied Taiwan and subsequently the Korean peninsula, and redirected economic flows.[30] Japan also profited from Western dominance in Asia because it could sell goods successively in the Western colonies and was granted "concessions" in China equal to the Western powers. The business directory of Shanghai (or another "treaty port") in the 1930s is very revealing: Companies from all major Western countries can be found–and Japanese. In terms of its overall share of the China market, Japan quickly surpassed most of its competitors. Intra-Asian trade was negatively affected by the organization of the war economies 1914-1918 and the subsequent world market crises in the 1920s and 1930s, especially in the areas depending on the export of raw materials like rubber.

The period of Western domination of intra-regional relations in East Asia ends with the occupation of all Western colonies in East Asia by the Japanese army within a few months. US-Manila fell to the Japanese in January 1942, British Singapore in February and Dutch Jakarta in March of the same year, while French Vichy-government cooperated in Indochina. For the first time since centuries intra-regional relations in East Asia were controlled by Asians. The region's natural and human resources were mobilized for the Japanese war machinery, mostly by coercive means. The Japanese-organized "Great Co-Prosperity Sphere" proved to be short-lived, and the former colonial powers returned to East Asia. However, except for some ports and city states (Singapore, Brunei, Hong Kong, Macao), they were not able to gain back the sustained direct control over the region anymore. Especially the centers of the former land-based empires turned into the cores of anti-colonial resistance (China, Burma, North Vietnam, Java), but also the (mainly ethnic Chinese) workers in the plantation areas of Malaya formed a guerilla.

The division of the region in the bloc confrontation, 1945-1980

Through the increasing involvement of the US and the Soviet Union in the Region, the struggle for liberation and independence in East Asia, as in other world regions, quickly turned into a bloc confrontation between a "communist camp" and the "capitalist West." After a long period of bloody civil wars with the engagement of external powers, interrupted by few years of peace, East Asia was divided between a "communism"-dominated continent and a US-led maritime sphere, reaching from Japan and the US-defended Southern half of the Korean peninsula over Taiwan (dubbed "America's air carrier"), the Philippines, British Hong Kong into the Malay world. On the continent, Thailand remained as the only US-ally, capitalizing on being a front state, as did South Korea and Taiwan. Against Western plans for the creation of a regional military bloc and economic community, the SE Asian states defended their autonomy and newly won independence. Most of them joined the non-alignment movement, and ASEAN declared itself a "Zone of Peace, Freedom and Neutrality in SE Asia" (ZOPFAN) in 1971 and later a nuclear-free zone (1995). In the early years of bloc confrontation and the supremacy of economic nationalism, exchange relations were subordinated to military needs. Transnational economic flows almost completely followed the military alliances, and reached a historically unprecedented low level. It is highly likely that East Asia in its more than 1000 years history of regional integration has never been so "de-regionalized" as in the years after 1945. Intra-regional trade recovered slowly, and amounted in the mid-fifties to little more than a third of the total volume (Table 3).

Even during their years with high economic growth, the countries of the "Western bloc" were predominantly oriented towards the markets of America and Europe. Japan, after the war by far the biggest economic power in the region, conducted for decades less than a quarter of its trade within the region. Plans for deeper economic integration among the ASEAN countries bore little effect due to low complementarities between the SE Asian economies, and

Table 3. East Asian trade as share of total trade for different countries (export plus imports)

	1913	1925	1938	1955	1990
China	0.53	0.46	0.70	0.43	0.59
Indonesia	0.32	0.38	0.26	0.32	0.60
Taiwan			0.99	0.50	0.42
Japan	0.41	0.47	0.70	0.22	0.29
Korea			1.00	0.35	0.40
Malaysia	0.44	0.39	0.35	0.30	0.37
Philippines	0.18	0.15	0.11	0.17	0.43
Thailand	0.62	0.71	0.65	0.52	0.51
Simple average	0.42	0.43	0.59	0.35	0.45
- excluding Korea, Taiwan	0.42	0.43	0.46	0.33	0.47
- excluding Korea, Taiwan, Japan	0.42	0.42	0.41	0.35	0.50

Source: Petri (1993), The East Asian Trading Bloc: An Analytical History, p. 30.

close economic relations with former colonial powers prolonged, e.g. in the case of the Philippines.

After 1945, the traditional core-periphery structure in East Asia was modified. The war-torn old empires on the continent spent huge sums on vast armies and had experienced a period of economic decline. Recovery plans following the Soviet model (combined with massive military and economic aid) did not bring the results hoped for. At the same time, many Western allies were able to export to America while protecting their own markets and catching up on technology. For the US at that time, firm military alliance was more important than respect for "free trade" and intellectual property rights, what opened windows of opportunity that no developing country enjoys today. The states of Korea, Taiwan and Japan were successfully redirected from war mobilization to planned national economic development. Feudal remnants like unequal land possession were abolished. State agencies cooperated closely with big private companies in order to reach the development goals agreed upon. Increasingly huge credits were directed into "sunrise industries," creating competitors that began to challenge Western companies. Following Johnson's (1982) analysis of the Japanese Ministry of Trade and Industry (MITI), these kinds of practices were described with the term "developmental state."[31] It is hardly a coincidence that this kind of effective statehood developed in NE Asia, which has a tradition of highly differentiated social organization, including a strong state and bureaucracy.

The re-integration of a region, 1980-today

Both the Soviet-oriented policies on the continent and the nationalist economic policies in SE Asia did not lead to a pace of economic change that could measure with the countries that were economic more liberal and opted for a stronger, but highly regulated integration into the world economy. In the late 1970s and early 1980s, most East Asian countries implemented reforms, combining more internal economic freedom with more openness, but with the will to keep economic exchange under control. During the 1980s, the orientation towards the successful Japanese economic "model" became predominant in East Asia, especially in South Korea, Singapore, Malaysia, and subsequently also in China and Vietnam. In SE Asia, however, many ambitious plans to adopt Japanese policies failed due to incompetent and inefficient bureaucracies, corruption and nepotism, the failure of plans for land reforms, dependence on external capital and expertise which made autonomous policy planning impossible, the pressure by international institutions to liberalize the economy unconditionally, and internal instability due to ethnic, religious, class and regional tensions. Despite the different degrees of reform success, the new policies had an enormous impact: They enabled the economic re-integration of the region. The companies of the more developed countries followed the new opportunities in the new markets quickly. After the *Plaza Accord* of 1985, which led to a revaluation of the currencies of Japan, South Korea and Taiwan, the outsourcing of production became a central element of keeping competitiveness. Japanese foreign direct investment grew from 1986 on by 50% per year, and Japan became the biggest foreign investor in the world. Main targets of the Japanese industrial investment were the countries Thailand, Malaysia and Singapore, to a lesser degree Indonesia, and in the 1990s China (Beijing, Shanghai, Manchuria and the Southern region around Hong Kong). Korean investment flowed mainly into the neighboring Chinese province Shandong and to Indonesia, while Taiwanese companies focused on geographically close Southern China (via Hong Kong to Canton and Fukien). In SE Asia, ethnic Chinese business networks profited most from the new economic opportunities. In the 1990s, it was estimated that the private wealth of SE Asia's 20 mio ethnic Chinese alone exceeded 200 bio USD (Liu 1998: 594). The People Republic's government changed its policy towards the overseas Chinese, calling for the "unity for the cause of socialist modernization in China."[32] The material and immaterial resources of the overseas Chinese should be channeled into the development of the "homeland." Indeed, Chinese capital flew back into China, attracted less by patriotism than by the entrepreneur-friendly framework and the high returns on investment. Furthermore, since the beginning of its "go overseas" policy, the Chinese government supports linkages between the big state-owned companies and Chinese business networks all over the world to promote exports and to gain a foothold in overseas markets. The years from 1986 to 1997 were the decade of the *East Asian Miracle*. The growth rates in East Asia were the highest in the world, international trade soared, and the regional economic dynamic attracted the majority of foreign investment worldwide. In the late 1980s already the dominance of transpacific trade over intra-East Asia trade came to an end (WTO 1995). In 1993, Japan's trade surplus towards other Asian countries was higher than the one towards the US for the first time. By 1995, Japanese owned firms were manufacturing more overseas (¥41.2 trillion) than they exported from the home islands (¥39.6 trillion). The developing intra-regional division of labor follows the matrix of economic complementarities in the region. Today, a dense web of production networks in different sectors crisscrosses East Asia. In 1997, the share of intra-regional trade in East Asia's total trade exceeded 50% (Chia 2000: 102). Empirical analyses of trade relations in the 1990s reveal a fascinating pattern. The cluster analysis done by Poon, Thompson and Kelly (2000) with trade data for 1995 (intramax method) show an Asian "bloc" that contains all East Asian countries and is centered on Japan.[34] Some SE Asian-countries (Vietnam, Indonesia) are more strongly interconnected with Japan than with their ASEAN-neighbours. But the Asian "bloc" is larger than East Asia; most countries around the Indian ocean belong to it as well.[35] As a matter of fact, the Asian "bloc" detected by Poon et al. corresponds quite accurately to the world connected by the Ming naval expeditions: NE Asia, the "Southern Ocean" with India, Sri Lanka, the Arab peninsula and East Africa (incl. Somalia, Kenya). However, the region found by the cluster analysis with foreign direct investment data for 1995 corresponds more exactly to East Asia as defined here (ibid., 438f).

Characteristics of Regional Integration in East Asia

In many regards, the re-integration of East Asia during the last 25 years is "catching up" with the developments that took place in other regions over a longer time span. There is a strong regional "gravity" at work: exchange with neighboring countries tends to be more intense than with countries on the other side of the globe. Economic interdependence and the functional linkages of tasks lead to pressure to initiate and deepen political cooperation (*spill over*-mechanism). This has been analyzed prominently be the first generation of integration theorists, and in contemporary East Asia the mechanism can be studied at work. Increasing trade needs cooperation in the area of information, regulation, infrastructure and safety. Transnational production networks need the elimination of tariff, fiscal and regulatory barriers as well as measures towards harmonization and standardization. Among the characteristics of recent regional integration in East Asia, the most noteworthy is that it does not follow an institutional scheme. The relevant economic spaces as sketched above are not congruent with institutional boundaries or international treaties. ASEAN has, according to Richard Stubbs (2004: 216), evolved into "the most high profile and successful regional organization in the Third World." But, as mentioned, ASEAN economic schemes continuously have been overshadowed by region-wide processes and therefore did not have a sustained significant impact. Furthermore, since the "Asia crisis," individual ASEAN-countries strive to restructure intra- and trans-regional relations through bilateral negotiations, with Japan and other countries. The Indonesian ASEAN-Expert Soesastro concludes:

> "At the age of thirty plus, ASEAN is neither an economic community nor a political community. It has become a diplomatic community, but this too has been weakening in recent years. (...) As developments within the ASEAN region itself no longer provide an impetus to mobilize political resources and to promote political co-operation, the focus has been shifting towards the wider region and the need to build a regional political and security architecture." (Soesastro 2001: 308)

The 1989 founded *Asia Pacific Economic Cooperation (APEC)* is a transpacific organization including Australia as well as North and South American countries. Praised in the early 1990s as leading institution of the coming "Pacific century," APEC stalled within few years over fundamental differences in economic policies between the legalistic, liberalization-oriented Anglosaxon countries and the East Asian informal, consensual "managed trade" approach.[36] Truly regional organizations like the *ASEAN+3* (ASEAN plus China, Japan, South Korea) framework are still embryonic and cannot be assessed regarding their impact yet.[37] As in other world regions, *regional institutions* excerted relevant functions for regional integration. In the case of East Asia, these were the *UN Economic Commission for Asia and the Far East, ECAFE*) (founded 1947; later renamed *UN Economic and Social Commission for Asia and the Pacific, ESCAP*) and the *Asian Development Bank (ADB*, founded 1966). Although without being equipped with political power, they initiated successful projects in the re-integration of the region by networking among foreign policy elites, connecting ministries all over the region as well as steering credits and providing capacity building for regional projects. In some cases, regional institutions were crucial for the breakthrough of regional projects because they opened the political space and created the legitimacy that national initiatives were not able to provide. The Japanese-sponsored Asian Development Bank Institute (ADBI) provided the technical and organizational expertise in setting up the regional monetary cooperation in the aftermath of the financial crisis.[38]

That economic interdependence calls for cooperative macroeconomic policies became evident when exchange rate fluctuations disrupted regional economic exchange. The network of bilateral swap arrangements that developed could evolve into an Asian Monetary Fund. The recent adoption of a currency basket by China could pave the way toward the next phase in this process, adoption of a common currency basket by the main countries in the region. This is not the only area pressure is built up to deepen political cooperation in East Asia. Trade conflicts have to be resolved, opponents to be bought off, an equitable distribution of the gains of regionalization has to be organized, if the process is to be sustained and deepened. More and more actors are drawn into the process, mutual observation intensifies, and national politics start to influence each other more directly. Cooperative solutions at regional level gain plausibility. However, this is not a linear process; national rivalries, distrust and political-cultural nationalisms lead regularly to sub-optimal solutions, in East Asia as well as in other world regions. A low level of formalization and institutionalization will remain one of the characteristics of regional integration in East Asia for quite a time.

There are fundamental differences in the basic structure of the region, compared to earlier periods. The rise of Japan since 19th c. ended the traditional sinocentric unipolarity–and created for a hundred years a new one. For a long time, Japan was the "Gulliver in the region of Asian economic Liliputs" (Pempel 1999: 72); with only 10% percent of the region's population and an even smaller proportion of its total land mass, it accounted for almost two-thirds of East Asia's GNP. Its economy used to be not only ten times greater than China's, but also much larger than neighboring Korea's (about fifteen times) and Taiwan's (twenty times). Given the history of the coercive "co-prosperity sphere" and its close alliance with the US, Japan was very cautious, even reluctant, to transform its economic weight in the region into institutions under its leadership. Looking back to the last 20-30 years of uncontested Japanese economic dominance, it can be stated that Tokyo missed the chances to influence political integration, beyond the close bilateral networks with the SE Asian countries that have been built up (Sudo 2005). China is the only country that has the potential to transform the region into a truly bipolar system. Its economy has quadrupled since 1978, was the world's largest recipient of foreign direct investment for many subsequent years, and might become the second largest economy in the world soon. Politically, it is challenging Japan's political leadership in the region already. The People's Republic has developed a proactive policy in securing a positive environment for the continued "peaceful resurgence" (the official Chinese term) of the country. Economically, China has become more dependent on market access for its exports and on the import of resources from overseas. It joined the trend to conclude bilateral free trade agreements, and managed to overtake Japan in its negotiations with ASEAN. China also sees the necessity of a strategic regionalist policy to avoid the emergence of Japanese-dominated regional institutions. The political competition in and for the region is certainly going to increase in the years to come. Given the sustained military role and economic importance of the US, Japan and other US-allies in the region, it cannot be excluded that a future transition of China towards a more aggressive stance to challenge the US-dominated world order will put heavy strain on East Asia's still moderately developed political integration.

Conclusion: East Asia as a world region

This article has used two methods to analyze East Asia as a region: a comparative country analysis and a macro-analysis of regional integration and disintegration. *First*, it has been shown that East Asia countries share certain societal features like comparatively high levels of traditional social organization and societal homogeneity. However, East Asia as a region cannot exclusively be statistically defined, as a cluster of countries with a high degree of similarities. These features are distinctive to varying degrees, which can be explained by social evolution and different types and degrees of external civilizational influences. Even traditionally less complex and ethnically more heterogeneous societies in East Asia managed to achieve a rather high development level of post-colonial statecraft. These features constitute country-specific trajectories, which partially explain recent economic performance and the development of East Asia as a region, compared to other world regions.[39]

Second, East Asia has been analyzed as interactional entity. Figure 5 summarizes the development of regional integration in East Asia over the last 1700 years. In a very rough manner, it depicts two dimensions of regionalization, economic and political integration in East Asia, by abstracting from short-term shifts and crises such as the world market turbulences of the 1930s or the Asian financial crisis (1997-99). Economic integration is a long-term process, beginning in the early centuries CE and increasing steadily until the impact of colonialism. Colonial regimes directed economic flows partially away from the region, but as soon as imperialism entered its more open phase in 19th c., economic regionalization took powerfully up again. Four processes can be subsumed under political integration: the failed attempt by the Mongols to conquer the whole region militarily and to turn it into a tributary empire (1), and the Ming tribute-trade-system (2) favoring incentives for incorporating other countries into the Chinese "world order," instead of direct domination. From a world-systems perspective, the traditional political structure has been object of a discussion, which is not terminated yet. It definitely does not fall under the notion of "world-empire," in which the intersocietal division of labor is encompassed by a single overarching imperial polity (Wallerstein) resp. in which the territorial economic network is largely contained within a single state apparatus (Chase-Dunn). East Asia was an inter-state system, but the there was only one core country, China, which had for a long period no challenger

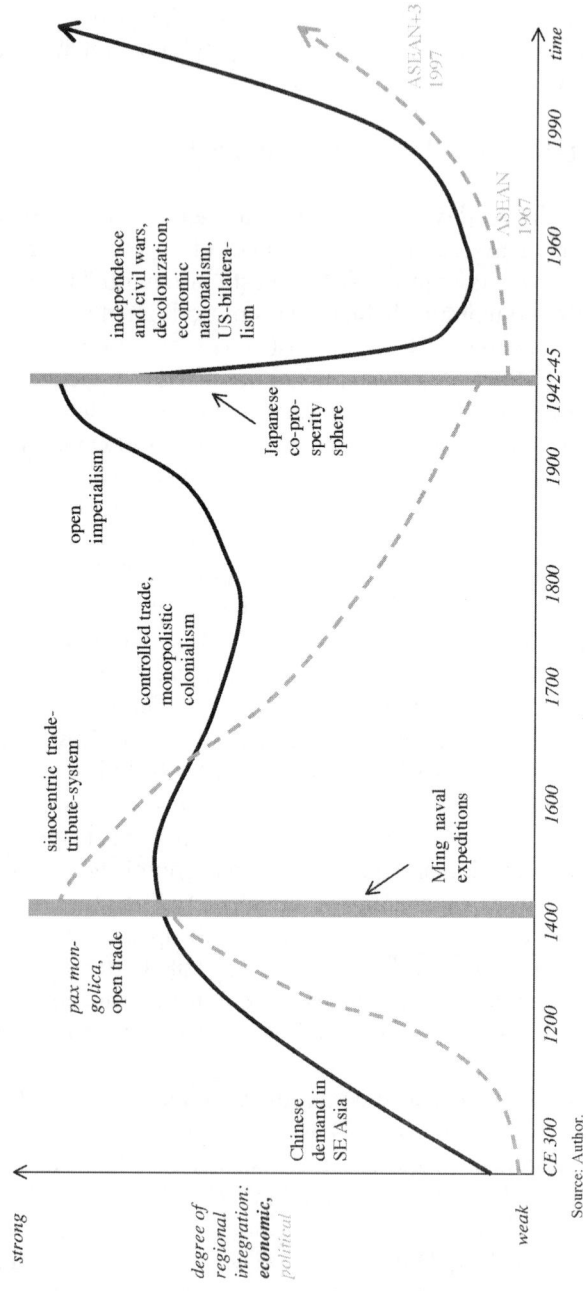

Figure 5. Long-term development of regional integration in East Asia

within the region. Given the sustained centrality and superiority of the largest polity, it has been called a "core-wide empire" (Chase-Dunn and Hall 1993). Furthermore, all the NE Asian countries achieved a high degree of internal stability and managed to control exchange relations. The development of SE Asia took a different turn: Being gradually incorporated into the subsystem dominated by the European powers, the maritime realm became a "shared periphery." On the SE Asian continent, the process of inter-state competition went on. But even the surviving three polities (Burma, Siam, and Vietnam) were no match for the European powers and were politically incorporated into the Colonial empires. Economically, however, East Asia integration advanced further, especially under "open imperialism" in the 18th and 19th c. The core-periphery structure was fairly stable, with China as the core country, and the semiperiphery consisting of Japan, Korea, and Vietnam. The rest of SE Asia formed the periphery; only temporarily certain SE Asian port cities and/or trading empires acquired a different position.

The traditional SE hinterlands did not participate in the "East Asian miracle" and are still the areas with the lowest per capita income. The semiperiphery in East Asia was, as world-systems theory conceptualizes it, the "seedbed of change," from where China's regional challenger stemmed, Japan. Adopting colonial and imperial techniques of coercion at end of the 19th c., the Japanese empire (3) incorporated within 40 years the entire region, from Manchuria to the Indonesian archipelago. Post-war East Asia was dominated by anti-colonial (anti-Western as well as anti-Japanese), nationalist movements. Beginning with the formation of ASEAN in the 1960s (4), however, for the first time in East Asian history a process of political integration without coercion, of co-operation between sovereign states in the region at their own terms, began. From a long-term perspective, the processes of the last 25 years represent a *re*-integration, a return to the historic "normality" of a highly interdependent East Asia.

World region and world-system: This article aimed at showing that it is possible and fruitful to study world regions as subunits of the world system. Regions can be analyzed as clusters and interactional entities, adding information to the understanding of the social world. Although geography (proximity, similarity of ecological basis for subsistence, natural land and sea routes etc.) is–even under the conditions of modern communication and transport means–a powerful force, regions cannot be considered to be natural, they are produced and reproduced through social interaction which is determined through many other factors than geography. Interactional depth, frequency and density can be measured and related to indicators of national and global integration. East Asia has been an area of intensified interaction since about 1700 years. However, it always has been connected to other regions, to different degrees in different periods. Taking into account all the facts, starting with the influence of Indian civilization in the early centuries CE, makes it impossible to consider East Asia a world-system. It could not be upheld that the interaction with the world outside of East Asia (long distance trade on the "silk road" and through maritime SE Asia, attracting bullion from the rest of the world, Islamization, the Mongol conquest and Western colonialism) was not an important condition of the reproduction of the internal structures of the composite units. On the other side, East Asia was the subsystem, which contained the biggest and most advanced economy for centuries, and therefore we observe a exceptionally high degree of "gravity" affecting the neighboring countries.

The main challenge to this article, probably, will not be analyses aimed at proving that East Asia did not have the quality of "regionness" or that it did constitute a world-system on its own, but that suggest different definitions of the region in the Eastern part of the Eurasian land mass, which would make more sense than the one argued for in this article.

Notes

[1] Highly influential was Ohmae (1985), Triad Power; cf. Poon, Thompson and Kelly (2000).
[2] The question was "do you consider yourself being part of a larger group that includes people from other countries, for example, as European, Asian, Chinese, Islamic etc.", year: 2000, nine Asian and nine European countries (Inoguchi 2003). According to Inoguchi, another 30% of the Chinese seem to think of "Chinese as supranational identity." "The Chinese cognitive map seems to be shaped by the single dimension: Chinese versus the rest. Asia does not sit well with Chinese." (p. 2). "Traditionally Japanese Asian identity has been weak. Japan is very much like Britain vis-à-vis their respective Continent. Keeping arm's length is the best phrase to characterize their relationship with the Continent. To them, the Continent is a potentially troublesome place; but from some distance you must keep engaged with them; you must discourage them from attempting awful things etc." (ibid.).
[3] Or, in the case of anthropological cross-cultural analyses, the basic unit is the "ethnic group."
[4] See Lindberg and Scheingold (eds., 1971). The bibliography therein lists 21 publications on regional integration in East, SE and South Asia integration (p. 415f).
[5] See Arrighi (1996a, b, 1998), Arrighi et al. (1993, 1997, 2003), Ikeda (1996), Wallerstein (1997, 1998).
[6] He defines the "East-Southeast Asian world-system" as one of the "Asian world-systems" (pass.). Lee (2000: 776) speaks of the "collision between the expanding European world-economy and the East Asian regional system."
[7] Cf. Nye (1968: 858): "The concept of integration, verbally defined as forming parts into a whole or creating interdependence, can be broken down into economic integration (formation of a transnational economy), social integration (formation of a transnational society), and political integration (formation of transnational political interdependence)."
[8] Cf. Katzenstein (1997: 1) who argues that, in the contemporary period, "international and national developments are increasingly shaped by regional dynamics."

[9] The Asian Historical Statistics Project (ASHSTAT) at the Institute of Economic Research of the Hitotsubashi University, Tokyo, is improving the situation successively (see Ichimura 2000, website: www.ier.hit-u.ac.jp).
[10] See Lenski and Nolan (1984) and the newer research mentioned in Ziltener and Müller (2007 [forthcoming])
[11] The national values are computed according to the ethnic composition of the population in 1960. For details of the index construction see the website www.developmentsociology.ch and Ziltener and Müller (2007 [forthcoming]).
[12] This has to do with effects of missionary activities in the colonial and postcolonial period as well as, in the case of the Fractionalization Index, with problems of coding the widely syncretistic religious practices in East Asia.
[13] Coedès (1971), in the French original $1944^1/1964^3$ "états hindouisés." Cf. Higham (2002: 287f): "The traditional view arose in the context of a pessimistic if not patronising view of indigenous culture, associated with a paucity of information. This view held that Indian expansion encountered a stone-age society of little complexity. Within this framework, such innovations as metallurgy were late and derivative, and the acceptance of Indian religious and political ideas were passive and inevitable, just as blotting paper absorbs water. (...) The Indian colonialist and Indianisation models are no longer tenable. (...) the Indian presence as but one of several variables whose successive conditions reflect their mutual interplay."
[14] China began its civil service examinations in 587 CE, as a measure against the domination of hereditary aristocracy (Miyazaki 1976) According to Winzeler (1976:234), "[b]ureaucratic modes of organization were everywhere weakly developed or nonexistant" in SE Asia.
[15] The Chinese influence on the development of the state in Vietnam is analyzed in detail by Woodside (1971).
[16] Cf. Tarling (1999: 4) on boundaries in SE Asia: "International relations in Southeast Asia came to be increasingly European. The frontiers were drawn so as to avoid disputes among the European powers. As a result, especially at the margins, the bore no firm relation to economic, social, cultural, ethnic or even geographical realities. The concept of a national frontier in Southeast Asia was applied in the general absence there of the relevant concept of nation. And it was applied with additional arbitrariness since it was designed to avoid conflict elsewhere." Lieberman (1993: 571) concludes: "The territorial creations of the Dutch, Spanish, and eventually the British in the archipelago bore little relation to precolonial political or ethnic boundaries. By contrast, once they arrived on the mainland the British and French were obliged to accept the tripartite division that had been emerged since 1350. Of course, Laos Cambodia, and the northern Malay states, all of which were as yet poorly assimilated into the still expanding Thai empire, were detached; but the interrelated trends towards territorial, ethnic, and commercial integration in Burma, Thailand, and Vietnam survived, and in many ways intensified, during the nineteenth and twentieth centuries."
[17] E.g. the *transmigrasi* from densely populated Java and Madura to the outer islands of the Indonesian archipelago or the migration into the river deltas of the Irrawaddy (Myanmar) and the Mekong (Vietnam).
[18] See Easterly and Levine (1997) and Alesina et al. (2003, 2004).
[19] See Easterly and Levine (1997), La Porta et al. (1999), Alesina et al. (2003). Rauch and Evans (2000), however, did not find a relationship between fractionalization and the quality of bureaucracy in 35 developing countries.
[20] Kaufman, Kraay and Zoido-Lobatón (1999, 2000).
[21] The case Myanmar can partly be explained by the legacy of rather high level of societal heterogeneity, regarding the religious situation amplified by colonialism, which also led to a complete breakdown of the traditional state.

[22] This finding is confirmed with data for the quality of bureaucracy (*Weberianness Scale*) by Evans and Rauch (1999).
[23] The variance of performance of autocratic systems is by far higher than in the case of political democracies, or, as Przeworski and Limongi (1997: 166) conclude: "Democracies are less likely to generate both miracles and disasters than dictatorships." Cf. Przeworski et al. (2000).
[24] These cases prove that further analysis of country-specific factors are necessary; for Malaysia see Trezzini (2001a,b).
[25] Cf. Abu-Lughod (1989: 311): "... the 'natural' role of the ports along the Strait was that of comprador (or 'agent' for trade), a role that is both politically contingent and economically unstable. (...) Being the chief international port along a waterway all must frequent depends not only on geographic advantage but on the ability of that port to attract a variety of different foreign merchant firms by assuring security of person and goods and freedom of action. Most importantly, the entrepôt must 'guarantee' that other traders will be using the same interchange. Clearly, not all of these variables are within the control of the port itself." On the rise and demise of the SE Asian port cities see also Kathirithambi-Wells and Villiers (eds., 1990), Latham (1994).
[26] In and around Malacca, an estimated 20,000 Malaysians still identify themselves as descendents of the Portuguese colonizers. They speak an old Portuguese dialect with strong Malayan grammatical influences (Kristang) and practice Catholic rituals.
[27] Only the monopoly-oriented practices in the outer archipelago by the Dutch and Spanish colonizers, mainly in the spice trade, were successful to a significant degree.
[28] The actual goals of the expeditions are not known. Apart from the search for valuable goods, especially spices, the Chinese emperor might also wanted to probe new horizons for conquest, although the missions had no military objectives. The Cambridge History of China (Vol. 7, p. 232) numbers several motivations of the Chinese emperor: "to search for treasure, to display his power and wealth, to learn about the plans of Timur and other Mongols in Western Asia, to expand the tributary system, to satisfy his vanity and his greed for glory, and to make use of his eunuch staff. ... these activities reflected this restless emperor's concept of imperial world order and of foreign relations as applied to the South Seas."
[29] This was the type of ship that the first Europeans encountered in SE Asia; the Portuguese called it "junco," after the Malay word "jong." They were surprised that these ships were larger than their own; Portuguese ships could carry less than half of the cargo of the largest SE Asian ships (Hall 1999: 5f).
[30] See Myers and Peattie (1984), Tsunoyama (1994), Schran (1994).
[31] Cf. Johnson (1999) and the other contributions to Woo-Cumings (ed., 1999), Leftwich (2001).
[32] Under the slogan "all patriots are one family"; Barabantseva (2005:9).
[33] See Arrighi, Ikeda and Irwan (1993), Hatch and Yamamura (1997).
[34] Poon, Thompson and Kelly (2000: 437) found that "the only 'truly' continental or natural region for both years [1985, 1995] is the Japan region, the membership of which consists of a majority bof East Asian countries."
[35] Regarding trade, Australia and New Zealand belong to the Asian "bloc," regarding foreign direct investment they are part of the Anglo-Saxon world (Poon, Thompson and Kelly 2000: 439).
[36] For evaluations of APEC see Rüland et al. (2002) and Feinberg (2003). Cf. Peng (2000: 21, 31): "The non-litigiousness of East Asian legal cultures has endured for thousand of years... Although Western-style legal systems have greatly influenced East Asia, fundamental differences remain... avoiding formal and legalistic procedures continues to be a dominant social norm in Asia." Haas (1989: 2-10) describes the "Asian way" as preference for working toward shared objectives through informal incrementalism rather than by drawing up grand blueprints or timetables; "Asian incrementalism" stresses the utility of noninstitu-

tional frameworks for discussion, while operational activities are entrusted usually to organizations without elaborate constitutional specifications.
[37] See Webber (2001), Stubbs (2002), Zhang (2005).
[38] See Lin and Rajan (2001), Manupipatpong (2002), Bull and Boas (2003).
[39] This complex of factors can be subsumed under "heritage" or "legacy," which gives the concept a meaning that is not vague and all encompassing, as in many culturalist analyses; see the critique by Arrighi, Hamashita and Selden (1997).

References

Abu-Lughod, Janet M. 1989. *Before European Hegemony. The World-System A.D. 1250-1350.* Oxford: Oxford University Press.
Alesina, Alberto, Arnaud Devleeschauwer, William Easterly, Sergio Kurlat, and Romain Wacziarg. 2003. "Fractionalization." National Bureau of Economic Research (NBER) Working Paper No. 9411. Cambridge, MA: NBER. (Published in *Journal of Economic Growth*, 2003, 8 (2): 155-194).
Alesina, Alberto and Eliana La Ferrara. 2004. "Ethnic Diversity and Economic Performance." National Bureau of Economic Research (NBER) Working Paper No. 10313, Cambridge, MA: NBER.
Andaya, Leonard Y. 1999. "Interactions with the Outside World and Adaptation in Southeast Asian Society, 1500-1800." Pp. 1-57 in *The Cambridge History of Southeast Asia, Vol. 1, Part 2: From c. 1500 to c. 1800*, edited by N. Tarling. Cambridge: Cambridge University Press.
Arrighi, Giovanni. 1996a. "The Rise of East Asia and the Withering Away of the Interstate System." *Journal of World Systems Research* 2 (15): 1-35.
Arrighi, Giovanni. 1996b. "The Rise of East Asia. World-Systemic and Regional Aspects." *International Journal of Sociology and Social Policy* 16 (7): 6-44.
Arrighi, Giovanni. 1998. "Globalization and the Rise of East Asia. *International Sociology* 13 (1): 59-77.
Arrighi, Giovanni, Satoshi Ikeda, and Alex Irwan. 1993. "The Rise of East Asia: One Miracle or Many?" Pp. 41-65 in *Pacific-Asia and the Future of the World-System*, edited by R. A. Palat. Westport and London: Greenwood Press.
Arrighi, Giovanni, Takeshi Hamashita, and Mark Selden. 1997. "The Rise of East Asia in World Historical Perspective." Paper prepared for the Planning Workshop held at the Fernand Braudel Center, State University of New York at Binghamton, December 6-7, 1996 (fbc.binghamton.edu).
Arrighi, Giovanni, Takeshi Hamashita, and Mark Selden. 2003. *The Resurgence of East Asia. 500, 150 and 50 Years Perspectives.* London and New York, NY: Routledge.
Barabantseva, Elena. 2005. "Trans-nationalising Chineseness: Overseas Chinese Policies of the PRC's Central Government." *ASIEN* 96: 7-28.
Bull, Benedicte and Morten Boas. 2003. "Multilateral Development Banks as Regionalising Actors: The Asian Development Bank and the Inter-American Development Bank." *New Political Economy* 8 (2): 245-261.
Cambridge History of China, Vol. 7, The Ming Dynasty, 1368-1644, Part I, edited by F.W. Mote and D. Twitchett, Cambridge: Cambridge University Press, 1984.
Chang, Pin-tsun. 1991. "The First Chinese Diaspora in Southeast Asia in the Fifteenth Century." Pp. 13-28 in *Emporia, Commodities and Entrepreneurs in*

Asian Maritime Trade, C. 1400-1750, edited by R. Ptak and D. Rothermund. Stuttgart: Steiner.

Chase-Dunn, Christopher. 1998. *Global Formation: Structures of the World-Economy*. Oxford: Rowman & Littlefield (updated edition).

Chase-Dunn, Christopher and Thomas D. Hall. 1991. "Conceptualizing Core/Periphery Hierarchies for Comparative Study." In: *Core/Periphery Relations in Precapitalist Worlds*, edited by C. Chase-Dunn and T. Hall. Boulder, CO: Westview.

Chase-Dunn, Christopher and Thomas D. Hall. 1997. *Rise and Demise: Comparing World-Systems*. Boulder, CO: Westview.

Chew, Sing C. 2000. "Neglecting Nature: World Accumulation and Core-Periphery-Relations." Pp. 216-234 in: *World System History: The Social Science of Long-Term Change*, edited by R. Denemark et al. London: Routledge.

Coedès, George. 1971. *The Indianized States of Southeast Asia*. Honolulu: University of Hawaii Press.

East Asia Study Group (EASG). 2002. *Final Report of the East Asia Study Group*. Jakarta: ASEAN Secretariat.

Easterly, William and Ross Levine. 1997. "Africa's Growth Tragedy: Policies and Ethnic Divisions." *Quarterly Journal of Economics* 112 (4): 1203-1250.

Evans, Peter and James E. Rauch. 1999. "Bureaucracy and Growth: A Cross-National Analysis of the Effects of 'Weberian' State Structures on Economic Growth." *American Sociological Review* 64: 748-765.

Fairbanks, John K. 1968. *The Chinese World Order: Traditional China's Foreign Relations*. Cambridge, MA: Harvard University Press.

Feinberg, Richard E. (ed.). 2003. *APEC as an Institution. Multilateral Governance in the Asia-Pacific*. Singapore: Institute of Southeast Asian Studies (ISEAS).

Flynn, Dennis O. , and Giraldez, Arturo. 1994. "China and the Manila Galleons." Pp. 71-90 in: *Japanese Industrialization and the Asian Economy*, edited by A. J. H. Latham and H. Kawakatsu. New York, NY: Routledge.

Frank, André Gunder. 1998. *ReOrient. Global Economy in the Asian Age*. Berkeley, Los Angeles, and London: University of California Press.

Haas, Michael. 1989. *The Asian Way to Peace. A Study of Regional Integration*. New York: Praeger.

Hamashita, Takeshi. 1994. "The Tribute Trade System and Modern Asia." Pp. 91-107 in *Japanese Industrialization and the Asian Economy*, edited by A. J. H. Latham and H. Kawakatsu. New York, NY: Routledge.

Ichimura, Shinichi. 2000. "Asian Historical Statistics Project: Difficulties and Expectations." *ASHSTAT- Newsletter* No.16 (www.ier.hit-u.ac.jp).

Ikeda, Satoshi. 1996. "The History of the Capitalist World-System vs. the History of East-Southeast Asia." *Review* XIX (1): 49-77.

Inoguchi, Takashi. 2003. "Does Identity Matter in Facilitating or Hindering Regional Cooperation in East Asia?" Paper presented at the Wilton Park Conference, Gotenba, Shizuoka, 28.9.-1.10. 2003 (www.glocom.org).

Johnson, Chalmers. 1999. " The Developmental State: Odyssey of a Concept." Pp. 32-60 in *The Developmental State*, edited by M. Woo-Cumings. Ithaca: Cornell University Press.

Kathirithambi-Wells, Jeyamalar and John Villiers (ed.). 1990. *The Southeast Asian Port and Polity: Rise and Demise*. Singapore: Singapore University Press.

La Porta, Rafael, Florencio Lopez-de-Silanes, Andrei Shleifer, and Robert Vishny. 1999. "The Quality of Government." *Journal of Law, Economics, and Organization* 15 (1): 222-279.
Latham, Anthony J. H. 1994. "The Dynamics of Intra-Asian Trade, 1868-1913. The Great Entrepôts of Singapore and Hong Kong." Pp. 145-193 in *Japanese Industrialization and the Asian Economy*, edited by A. J. H. Latham and H. Kawakatsu. New York, NY: Routledge.
Latham, Anthony J. H. and Heita Kawakatsu (eds). 1994. *Japanese Industrialization and the Asian Economy*. London: Routledge.
Lee, Su-Hoon. 2000. "The Rise of East Asia and East Asian Social Science's Quest for Self-Identity." *Journal of World Systems Research* 6 (3): 768-783 (jwsr.ucr.edu).
Leftwich, Adrian. 2001. *States of Development: On the Primacy of Politics in Development*. Oxford: Polity Press.
Lieberman, Victor B. 1990. "Wallerstein's System and the International Context of Early Modern Southeast Asian History." *Journal of Asian History* 24 (1): 70-90.
Lieberman, Victor B. 1993. "Local Integration and Eurasian Analogies: Structuring Southeast Asian History, c. 1350-c. 1830." *Modern Asian Studies* 27 (3): 475-572.
Lenski, Gerhard, and Nolan, Patrick D. 1984. "Trajectories of Development: A Test of Ecological-Evolutionary Theory." *Social Forces* 63 (1): 1-23.
Lin, Chang Li and Ramkishen S. Rajan. 2001. "The Economics and Politics of Monetary Regionalism in Asia." *ASEAN Economic Bulletin* 18 (1): 103-118.
Lindberg, Leon N. and Stuart A. Scheingold (eds). 1971. *Regional Integration. Theory and Research*. Cambridge, MA: Harvard University Press.
Liu, Hong. 1998. "Old Linkages, New Networks: The Globalization of Overseas Chinese Voluntary Associations and Its Implications." *China Quarterly* 155: 582-609.
Lu, Benlong. 2004. "Evolution of New China's International Identification; A New Frame to Understand the Foreign Policy of New China." *International Review* 35 (Summer 2004), Shanghai Institute for International Studies (SIIS, www.siis.org).
Manupipatpong, Worapat. 2002. "The ASEAN Surveillance Process and the East Asian Monetary Fund." *ASEAN Economic Bulletin* 19 (1): 111-122.
Miyazaki, Ichisada. 1976. *China's Examination Hell. The Civil Service Examinations of Imperial China*. New York, NY, and Tokyo: Weatherhill.
Myers, Ramon H. and Mark R. Peattie. 1984. *The Japanese Colonial Empire 1895-1945*. Princeton: Princeton University Press.
Müller, Hans-Peter, Claudia Kock, Eva Seiler-Schiedt, and Brigitte Arpagaus. 1999. *Atlas of Precolonial Societies: Cultural Heritage and Social Structures of African, Asian and Melanesian Countries*. Berlin: Reimer (see www.development-sociology.ch).
Müller, Hans-Peter and Patrick Ziltener. 2004. "The Structural Roots of Values: An Anthropological Interprtation of Hofstede's Value Dimensions." Pp. 122-140 in *Comparing Cultures. Dimensions of Culture in a Comparative Perspective*, edited by H. Vinken, J. Soeters, and P. Ester. Leiden: Brill.
Ohmae, Kenichi. 1985. *Triad Power. The Coming Shape of Global Competition*. New York: Free Press.

Pempel, T. J. 2005. "Emerging Webs of Regional Connectedness." Pp. 1-28 in *Remapping East Asia: The Construction of a Region*, edited by T.J. Pempel. Ithaca: Cornell University Press.

Peng, Shin-yi. 2000. "The WTO Legalistic Approach and East Asia: From the Legal Culture Perspective." *Asian-Pacific Law and Policy Journal* 13: 1-34.

Poon, Jessie P.H., Edmund R. Thompson, and Philip F. Kelly. 2000. "Myth of the Triad? The Geography of Trade and Investment 'Blocs.'" *Transactions of the Institute of British Geographers* 25: 427-444.

Przeworski, Adam and Fernando Limongi. 1997. "Democracy and Development." Pp. 163-194 in *Democracy's Victory and Crisis*, edited by Axel Hadenius. Cambridge, MA: Cambridge University Press.

Przeworski, Adam, Michael E. Alvarez, José Antonio Cheibub, and Fernando Limongi. 2000. *Democracy and Development: Political Institutions and Well-Being in the World, 1950-1990*. Cambridge, MA: Cambridge University Press.

Rüland, Jürgen, Eva Manske, Eva, and Werner Draguhn (eds). 2002. *Asia-Pacific Cooperation (APEC). The First Decade*. London: Routledge Curzon.

Rauch, James E., and Peter B. Evans. 2000. "Bureaucratic Structure and Bureaucratic Performance in Less Developed Countries." *Journal of Public Economies* 75: 49-71.

Schran, Peter. 1994. "Japan's East Asia Market, 1870-1940." Pp. 201-238 in *Japanese Industrialization and the Asian Economy*, edited by A. J. H. Latham and H. Kawakatsu. New York: Routledge.

Stubbs, Richard. 2002. "ASEAN Plus Three: Emerging East Asian Regionalism?" *Asian Survey* 42 (3): 440-455.

Stubbs, Richard. 2004. "ASEAN: Building Regional Cooperation." Pp. 216-233 in *Contemporary Southeast Asia. Regional Dynamics, National Differences*, edited by M. Beeson. Basingstoke: Palgrave/Macmillan.

Sudo, Sueo. 2005. *Evolution of ASEAN-Japan Relations*. Singapore: Institute of Southeast Asian Studies (ISEAS).

Trezzini, Bruno. 2001a. "Institutional Foundations of Malaysia's State Capacity." *Asian Journal of Public Administration* 23 (1): 33-63.

Trezzini, Bruno. 2001b. "Embedded State Autonomy and Legitimacy: Piecing Together the Malaysian Development Puzzle." *Economy and Society* 30 (3): 324-353.

Tsunoyama, Sakae. 1994. "Sino-Japanese Trade and Japanese Industrialization." Pp. 194-200 in *Japanese Industrialization and the Asian Economy*, edited by A. J. H. Latham and H. Kawakatsu. New York, NY: Routledge.

Wallerstein, Immanuel. 1997. "The Rise of East Asia, or The World-System in the Twenty-First Century." Keynote Address at the Symposium on "Perspectives of the Capitalist World-System in the Beginning of the Twenty-First Century." Institute of International Studies, Meiji Gakuin University, Jan. 23-24, 1997 (fbc.binghamton.edu).

Wallerstein, Immanuel. 1998. "The So-called Asian Crisis: Geopolitics in the Longue Durée." Paper given at International Studies Association Annual Meeting, Minneapolis, March 17-21, 1998 (fbc.binghamton.edu).

Webber, Douglas. 2001. "Two Funerals and a Wedding? The Ups and Downs of Regionalism in East Asia and Asia Pacific after the Asian Crisis." *Pacific Review* 14 (3): 339-375.

Woodside, Alexander Barton. 1971. *Vietnam and the Chinese Model. A Comparative Study of the Nguyen and Ching Civil Government in the First Half of the Nineteenth Century*. Cambridge, MA: Harvard University Press.
World Bank. 1993. *The East Asian Miracle: Economic Growth and Public Policy*. Oxford: Oxford University Press.
World Trade Organization (WTO). 1995. *Regionalism and the World Trading System*. Geneva: WTO.
Wang, Gungwu. 1970. "'Public' and 'Private' Overseas Trade in Chinese History." Pp. 215-225 in *Sociétés et companies de commerce en orient et dans l''Océan Indien*, edited by M. Mollat. Paris: S.E.V.P.E.N.
Woo-Cumings, Meredith (ed.). 1999. *The Developmental State*. Ithaca: Cornell University Press.
Zhang, Yunling. 2005. "Emerging New East Asian Regionalism." *Asia-Pacific Review* 12 (1): 55-63.
Ziltener, Patrick and Hans-Peter Müller. 2007 (forthcoming). "The Weight of the Past–Traditional Technology and Socio-political Differentiation in African and Asian Societies: A Quantitative Assessment of their Impact on Socio-economic Development." Forthcoming in *International Journal of Comparative Sociology*.

5
Islam in the World System

Amir Sheikhzadegan

The purpose of this paper is to provide an overview of the role and status of Islam in the modern world system. The study begins by examining, from an historical perspective, the development of the Muslim community from a tribal society to an Empire, which defeated the Sassanid Empire and conquered Persia as well as vast territories of the Eastern Roman Empire. Following a brief discussion of the subsequent metamorphosis of the Islamic world up to the modern times, the paper then focuses on its development during the last two centuries. This part of the analysis begins with a description of the devastating impact of colonialism upon the Islamic world, which gave rise to a series of Islamic revivalist movements.

The study then examines the emergence of nationalist movements in Islamic countries leading to the creation of modern nation states. Furthermore, it shows how the modern nation states, whether capitalist or socialist, turned out to be repressive autocratic systems, thus alienating the civil society. The study also demonstrates how the defeat of Arab armies in their wars against Israel in 1948 and 1967 as well as the Arab-Israeli conflict deepened the delegitimization of Western ideologies, which at the time prevailed in most Islamic countries.

The analysis also explores the dynamics of a religious reawakening throughout the Islamic World in the 1970s, which reached its peak in the Islamic Revolution of 1979 in Iran. The paper further analyzes the development of the Islamic revivalist movements in their interaction with the industrialized world after 1979, examining the impact of the end of the Cold War on the role of Islam in the World system. Finally, the study discusses the recent political developments in the World System triggered by the terrorist attacks on the World Trade Center on September 11, 2001. More specifically, it examines the characteristics of the new militant Islamist groups, the appeal of Islamist ideologies for the Muslim masses, the political consequences of poor developmental achievements in the Islamic World, and the growth of a global Muslim identity, facilitated by the modern communication systems.

Emergence of Islam

In the year 610 A.D., Muhammad, a caravan driver from Mecca, declared to be a prophet of the one and only God, Allah, with the task of converting the people to *Islam* ("dedication to God"). This was the dawn of a new religion that would forever alter the course of world history.

At the time of declaration of Islam, the Arabian Peninsula lay in the spheres of influence of Eastern Rome and Persia. The rivalry between these two great powers of the time gave the Arabs a certain degree of autonomy. The Arabs, including those from the Quraish tribe who ruled in Mecca, used this autonomy to conduct a rather flourishing economy by participating in trade on the Silk Road. The people from Mecca also took commercial advantage of the fact that a great number of Arab tribes would travel every year to Mecca to worship their idols in Kaaba.

The monotheistic and egalitarian teachings of Muhammad were perceived by the aristocracy of Mecca as a serious threat to their own interests. Thus, he had to contend with the incensed persecution of his followers. Having no other choice, in 622 Muhammad emigrated to Yathrib (later called al-Medina al-Nabi–the City of the Prophet–or simply al-Medina–the City) where he succeeded in founding an Islamic state. Out of a tribal society there emerged an Ummah (community), in which the universal principle of faith in God seemed to abolish all the individual differences between the community members.

The founding of an Islamic State meant at the same time a shift of focus in the teachings of Muhammad from eschatological to practical issues. The new state soon proved to be capable of both maintaining order as well as facing the military challenges if its enemies.

Rise of the Caliphate

The death of Muhammad in 632 gave rise to two developments with lasting impact on the future of the Muslim community. On the one hand, the question of Muhammad's succession[1] led to a split in a political system, which was tied together mainly by the charismatic leadership of the Prophet. On the other hand, the rebellion of some Arab tribes against the Muslim state forced the first Caliph, Abu-Bakr, to devote his short rule (632-634) entirely to suppressing the rebels. Once the military operations reached a certain momentum, they went beyond combating the rebels. Under the second Caliph, Omar (634-644), the battles spread into the neighboring regions, even if Omar had not really intended it.[2] Soon, there followed the conquest of Persia and some Eastern Roman territories–including Syria, Palestine and Egypt. Even though the Muslim conquests had come about rather by chance than according to a missionary plan (Halm, 2002: 25), there soon emerged out of a small Ummah an Empire, which stretched from the Atlantic to the Sind.

Omar found himself forced to accept the *fait accompli* situation and to yield some administrative authority to the leaders of the Islamic armies within their conquered areas. With this, there emerged a political tradition, which was to be practiced for centuries by the Caliphs: The reluctant legalization of the usurpers. In this way, Mu'awiah, whom Omar never really trusted,³ was designated as the Governor of Syria. Mu'awiah increased his influence under the third Caliph, Uthman (644-656), after whose death he organized a revolt against the fourth Caliph, Ali (656-661)–the first Imam of the Shi'is.

Of the first four Caliphs⁴ (632-661), the second one (Omar) was stabbed to death by an Iranian slave; the third one (Uthman) was killed in a mob of discontent; and the fourth one (Ali) was assassinated by a Kharijite.⁵ A tradition of murder of the political elite was thus initiated.

Following Ali's assassination, the power-conscious Mu'awiah founded Umayyad dynasty (661-750) in Damascus—a regime, which followed the Byzantine and Sassanid models of an Empire rather than the Islamic tradition of the Caliphate.

The excessive, non-Islamic practices of the Umayyad, their shift from Islamic universalism to Arab particularism (being expressed by their favoring of Quraishi clan as well as by their open contempt for the increasing non-Arab population of the Islamic Empire), and their atrocities against the family of the prophet⁶ led to a mass uprising⁷ whereby the dynasty of Umayyad were wiped out and replaced by the Abbasids (750-1258)–a new dynasty related to the prophet Muhammad.⁸

The process of empire-building, however, went on also under the Abbasids. From their seat in Baghdad and leaning on the legacy of Persian civilization they managed to build up an amazing empire. Soon, the Iranians were to occupy a prominent position, not only in the administration of the state, but also among the poets, technicians, scientists and philosophers.

The Abbasids soon proved to be great promoters of science, art and philosophy.⁹ Under their rule, a large number of works of Persian, Greek and Indian civilizations were translated into Arabic.¹⁰ Of particular interest for the Muslim scholars was the reception and continuation of the Greek heritage. The spread of the Arabic language in all corners of the Islamic world facilitated the confluence of the old civilizations, giving birth to a new multi-faceted civilization. As Halm (2004) has remarked, with Arabic there emerged "a medium of communication, which was used from the borders of China to the marches of the Franks, and which enabled a cultural transfer, that the world had only experienced once before in the Classical Greek epoch" (Halm, 2004: 42; my translation of the German original).

Decline of the Caliphate

Even though the Abbasid Caliphs tried to imitate the Persian model of governance, they were hardly able to cope with the task of the administration of their growing Empire. Moreover, their atrocities against the Shi'is, without whose help they would most probably not have succeeded in coming into power, diminished the legitimacy of their rule. Therefore, they were forced either to deliver the control of peripheral lands to their military slaves[11] or to recognize usurpers, to at least maintain a nominal control over the Empire.

Through the legalization of usurpers there emerged several Iranian, Turkish or even Arab dynasties. Since the actual power lay in the hands of these dynasties, this development led to a *de facto* separation of worldly power, controlled by the military slaves or the usurpers, from the religious authority of the Caliphs (Halm, 2002: 50). The new parallel dynasties represented not only a political challenge to the Caliphs, but also at times a serious doctrinal threat. For example, the Iranian dynasties of the Saffarids (861-900) in South Eastern Iran, Buyids (945-1058) and Hashashin[12] (1090-1273) in Northern Iran, as well as the Arabic dynasty of the Fatemids[13] (909-1171) in Northern Africa and Syria, belonged all to the Shi'i community. The Samanids (819-999) in North Eastern Iran even strove for a revival of the teachings of the ancient Iranian prophet, Zoroaster, and espousing it to Islam. While the Caliphs had to share their political authority with the parallel dynasties, their religious authority was increasingly challenged by a social group called *Ulama* (the Learned). With Ulama there emerged also the *science* of religion–the *theology*.

Another important doctrinal challenge to the new political order came from the mystics. The mystical understanding of Islam is as old as Islam itself. For its early beginnings can be traced back to Hasan al-Basri (d. 728), a contemporary of the Prophet. The Islamic mysticism is in search of the true meaning of Islam behind the surface of Shari'a. Not satisfied by simply obeying religious regulations, it strives to attain union with God. The tendency of the mystics to ignore or even despise the Shari'a has always been a source of tension between them and the Ulama. Even though some of the great scholars, in particular Al-Ghazzali (d. 1111), tried to reconcile mysticism and theology, the tensions between the two spiritual worlds could not be overcome.

As a reform movement, mysticism came also to grips with corrupt authorities. The critical attitude of the mystics to worldly matters, including political issues, led to tensions between them and the rulers, sometimes with fatal consequences for the former. The cruel lynching of the great Persian mystic, Hallaj, in 922 by order of the Abbasids is but an example.

From the 12th century on, Islamic mysticism underwent a very important development with a lasting impact on the Muslim community: With the emergence of Sufi[14] orders and brotherhoods, Sufism–so far a free movement of the elite–became a popular institution. Due to the difficult conditions of admission to the Sufi orders and the high level of obedience to the leader (*Sheikh* in Arabic, *Pir* in Persian), the brotherhoods soon acquired a significant, hardly influenceable socio-political power. The Sufi religious orders played an influential role in the spread of Islam amongst the Mongols, in India, in Indonesia, and in black Africa.[15] The Sufi religious orders were also often active in the liberation wars against foreign rulers.

Invasions of the "infidels"

Had the Muslim community been plagued in the last centuries of the first millennium by power struggles between different Islamic dynasties, towards the end of the eleventh century they were confronted with a new challenge: In 1095, an alliance of Christian armies followed the appeal of the Pope Urban II and set out eastwards to "liberate" the holy land–Jerusalem–from the "Mohammedan infidels." The Crusades, which persisted till 1270, had a very deep and lasting impact on the relationship between Muslim and Christian worlds thereafter. After a long series of conquests and losses, the Crusades ended with the victory of the Muslims. However, the gains of these wars for the Europeans far exceeded those for the Muslims: Europeans, who had set out to the "Holy Land" to combat the "barbarians," were perplexed to face in Islamic lands a fascinating civilization, which had succeeded in reviving and developing the great Greek heritage, then almost totally unknown to the Europeans. Thus, a new wave of reception of the Greek heritage, meditated by the Muslims, was soon initiated in Europe. The second major impact of the Crusades on Europe was rather a material one. The necessity of huge transportations of soldiers, weapons and goods from Europe to Palestine led to the emergence of major centers of commerce and shipment in cities like Venice and Genoa, laying thus the fundaments of capitalism in these areas. These two trajectories merged soon to give rise to a historical phenomenon of unprecedented significance: modernity.

Shortly before the last Crusade, the Islamic world was shocked by an event no Muslim could have ever imagined. A huge, dreadful army coming from Central Asia suddenly invaded the Muslim lands: The invasion of the Mongols had already started.

This event was indeed the first destructive blow against the Islamic self-confidence. For several centuries, the Muslims had interpreted their military success, as well as their continuing expansion, as a proof of their fighting for the right path of Islam. And suddenly, they were besieged by pagan "barbarians" who did not even shy from killing the leader of the Muslim community, the Abbasid Caliph, al-Musta'sal (1258). The widespread devastation by the Mongols had serious effects on the Islamic civilization for the centuries to come. The Mongols were finally stopped in the Levant by the slave dynasty of the Egyptian Mamlukes (1250-1517).

The spectacular military victories of the Mongols were not only due to their tremendous fighting spirit and inner cohesion (or *assabiyyah*–to use Ibn Khaldun's terminology). The doctrinal as well as political split of the Islamic world into conflictive fractions further facilitated the Mongols' advance.

The Mongols could not avoid a gradual acculturation to the far superior Islamic-Iranian civilization. As shamanists, however, they showed more interest in the saint cults of the Shi'is and Sufis than for the abstract teachings of the orthodox Sunnis.[16] More specifically, the Sufis fascinated the Mongols with their miracles and were thus instrumental in converting them to Islam. Once more, the doctrinal variety of Islam played an integrative role. But this power of integration had a price to pay: the doctrinal split in the Islamic world assumed now even geopolitical contours: Whilst in the Mamlukes' territory in the Levant and in Egypt the Sunni orthodoxy prevailed, a great variety of saint cults unfolded under the rule of the Mongols in the Northeast, predominantly in Persia.[17]

Hardly had the lives of the Muslims been given a chance to normalcy, the Islamic world faced a new Mongol invasion, this time led by Timur Lenk (1328-1405). With the advent of the Timurdis (1409-1506), the Mongol supremacy in the Islamic world spread well into the sixteenth century, and in the Indian subcontinent even into the nineteenth century.

Islamic civilization, already affected by the dominance of military forces during the Crusades, could never really recover form the Mongol invasion.

The frequent subjugation of the sedentary populations by nomadic peoples was not limited to invasions from Central Asia. There were also nomads from other regions, in particular from North Africa, whose invasions to the cities showed a similar pattern. This ever-recurring pattern inspired the Tunisian historian, Ibn Khaldun (1332-1406), to develop his evolutionary theory on the dynamics of emergence and decline of dynasties.

Colonialism

At the beginning of the sixteenth century the Islamic world was divided into three empires: the Ottomans (1300-1923) extended their control from Asia Minor up to the Balkans, Eastern Europe, the Middle East and North Africa. The Safawids (1501-1732) controlled Iran. And the Indian subcontinent was ruled by a branch of Timurid Mongols (1504-1858).

The sixteenth century witnessed also the advent of the colonial powers and their gradual penetration into the Islamic world. While, in 1942, the Spaniards in Granada were able to end the last Muslim rule in Spain, the Portuguese, thanks to the rounding of Africa by Vasco de Gama in 1498, began to build up their colonial empire in the Indian Ocean without having to pass through uneasy Islamic lands. Furthermore, the conquest of Kasan, the capital of the Tartars, in 1552 by the Czar, Ivan the Terrible, initiated the Russian expansion into Central Asia. Another important event of the time was the settlement of the British East India Company in India in 1612–the very first stage of British Colonialism in the Indian subcontinent. Two and a half centuries later, the British, having swept away the Mongols from India, expanded their rule over the whole subcontinent.

The Ottomans, ruling over a vast empire from Caucasus to North Africa, began, from the end of the seventeenth century on, to lose major territories in Eastern Europe, the Balkans, the Crimea and North Africa to the colonial powers. One of the most bitter of all was the loss of Crimea in 1774 as a result of the Ottoman-Russian wars. Moreover, the invasion of Egypt, then an Ottoman province, by Napoleon in 1798 is generally considered to be the first shock to the self-consciousness of the Muslims.

In Persia, the effect of colonialism meant, in a first stage, long, exhaustive wars against the Russians leading to the loss of large Iranian territories in Caucasus. In the second half of the nineteenth century, Persians experienced an increasing political and economic penetration by the colonial powers of Russia and Great Britain into their country. In 1907, in a secret treaty, these two big powers even divided up Persia into two regions of influence. The increasing control of the colonial powers over the economic resources of Iran provoked the protest of the local population. The tobacco uprising of 1891, triggered by a *fatwa* of the high rank cleric Mirza Hasan Shirazi, set a political process in motion, which led, within a few years, to the constitutional Revolution (1906-11) in Iran. The tobacco uprising had another very important impact on the contemporary history of Iran: The politicization of the Iranian Shi'i clergy.

By weakening or even eliminating of the great empires of the Islamic world, the colonial powers managed to control major Islamic lands. Around the year 1900, from a total of 200 million Muslims some 160 Millions lived under colonial rule (Schulze 2002: 39). Even those regions still independent were mostly under a massive influence of the colonial powers.

After the Mongol invasion in the thirteenth century, the Islamic world experienced once again a widespread wave of conquests by "non-believers," this time the colonialists. The impact of the new conquerors was, however, essentially more striking and lasting. For, compared to the Mongols who were regarded by the Muslims as heathen barbarians, the Europeans fascinated the Muslims by virtue of their superior technology, science, organizational structures, economy, educational systems and more. Compared to the Mongols who were quickly Islamized, the Europeans threatened to undermine not only the religious fundaments of the Muslims, but also their cultural identity.

Anti-colonial movements

The first Muslim reactions against colonialism came in the nineteenth century from the so-called *Folk Islam*, represented mainly in the rural areas. Of great significance were the uprisings of Sufi orders–including those of Qadiriya and Rahmaniya in Algeria, Sunusiyah in Libya, Tidjaniya in West Africa, as well as that of Imam Shamil and his followers in Caucasus and Central Asia–who fought bitter battles against the colonialists. Furthermore, there were a few armed, messianistic movements here and there, including the uprisings of Bu Ziyan and Bu Maza in Algeria and that of Mahdi in Sudan.

Once the colonial powers managed to suppress the armed religious movements in the country-side, there emerged towards the end of the 19th century a new kind of anti-colonial opposition, which was rather urbane and intellectual. This new generation of anti-colonialists, well known as Islamic modernists, sought the salvation of the Islamic world in a new interpretation of Islam, more compatible to the requirements of the modern world. Islamic modernism was initiated by the Persian scholar al-Afghani (1838-97) who strove for unity of the Muslim world against colonialism. The Islamic modernists idealized the early Islamic Ummah as an egalitarian, intellectually orientated and science-friendly society and called for a revival of the original Islam. Only through such a revival would the Islamic world be able to liberate itself from the yoke of colonialism. The somewhat diffuse ideas of al-Afghani were systematized by his pupils, most notably the Egyptian scholar Muhammad Abduh (1849-1905). The most brilliant pupil Abduhs, the Indian scholar Muhammad Iqbal (1877-1938), reintroduced this doctrine in a more elaborate form into Indian Muslim communities.

Whereas the majority of the Islamic modernists were against colonialism, a few of them, including the Indian scholar Sir Seyyed Ahmad Khan (1817-98) opted instead for cooperation with the colonialists.

The idea of a return to the pure teachings of Islam was also shared by the reformist movement led by Mohammad Abdul Wahhab (d. 1791) in the Arabian Peninsula.[18] In contrast to the Islamic modernists, however, the Wahhabites represented a very conservative conception of reviving the "original" Islam. Because of their emphasis on the classical form of Islam both these movements, Islamic modernists as well as Wahhabites, are occasionally called *Salafiyya* (Salaf=ancestor).

A third reaction to the colonial situation in the Islamic world was Secular Modernism, which pleaded for a full assimilation to the modernity. The following statement of the Iranian modernist, Taqizadeh (1921), aptly reflects this new ideology: "Iran must, externally and internally, physically and spiritually, become Western. That's it!"[19]

Nationalism

In all four constitutional revolutions in the Islamic world (in the Ottoman Empire, in Persia, in Egypt, and in Tunisia) the secular modernists were in charge, even though in the case of Persia a considerable part of the clergy took part in the movement. None of the constitutional revolutions was, however, blessed with lasting success. In Tunisia and in the Ottoman Empire, the newly founded Parliaments were dissolved by Muslim rulers (in Tunisia in 1864; in the Ottoman Empire in 1878); in Egypt, it was the British who closed down the parliament; and in Persia, an alliance of the royal court and the Russians was responsible for the closure of Parliament (in 1908 by means of Russian canons; in 1911 by a Russian ultimatum).[20]

After the failure of the democratic movements, the longing for modernity took on a new form of articulation: From the 1920s on, the Islamic world witnessed the emergence of modern national states headed by modernist dictators: In 1921, Reza Khan, a former Cossack officer, came to power in Persia and founded in 1926 the Pahlavi Dynasty. In 1923, the so-called Young Turks, led by Mustafa Kamal, dissolved the Ottoman Empire and founded the modern Turkey, based on radical Secularism.[21] To speed up the modernization process, the Kamalists even replaced the Arabic writing with the Latin one. Soon there emerged other modernist national states all over the Islamic world.

Hardly recovered from the penetration of Islam-unfriendly colonialism, Islam had to face now a new local anti-Islamic autocracy. However, Islam was not the only victim of the modernist autocracies. The ethnic minorities, regarded as a threat to the national unity, had also to suffer from the nationalist zeal now thriving throughout the Islamic world. The Armenian genocide of 1915 by the Ottomans was indeed the most tragic example of this conflict.

With the emergence of modernistic dictators the path to democracy seemed for the time being to be blocked. Thus, the civil society was mostly excluded from active participation in the modernization process.

These socio-political turbulences had a deep impact on the movement of Islamic modernism. While some of the Islamic modernists, for example, Taha Hussain (1889-1973), were seized by the frenzy of secular modernism, others, for example, Rashid Rida (d. 1935), took on a more conservative attitude. The latter tendency finally led to the foundation of conservative organizations that were skeptical of, if not adverse to, the modernity: the *Ikhwan-al-Muslimin*, founded in 1928 in Egypt by Hasan al-Banna (1906-1949), *Fada'ian-e Islam* founded in 1945 in Iran by Navvab Safavi (1923-56) and *Jama'at-i Islami*, founded in 1941 in India by Mawdudi (1903-79), were the most renown. These groups, called the "Neo-Salafi," gradually acquired militant traits struggling for founding of an Islamic state. The modernistic regimes answered with bloody repression. With the execution of Navvab Safavi in 1956 in Iran and Sayyid Qutb in 1966 in Egypt both neo-salafi organizations were banned in their respective countries. Only in the state of Pakistan, founded in 1947, the Jama'at-i Islami was allowed to carry on its existence. The significance of these movements cannot be overestimated. Islamic fundamentalism emerging from the 1970s on, no matter in what historical or geographic setting can be traced back to the neo-salafi movements.

The Cold War

The concentration of oil in the Middle East turned this region in the post-war era into one of the most important arenas of the Cold War. Whilst capitalist countries, including Turkey, Iran, Jordan, Saudi Arabia and the Golf states, joined the Western camp, many Arab nationalistic regimes (like Egypt, Syria, Iraq, Libya etc.) sought for support in the socialist camp. This split was also seen in other parts of the Islamic world. Thus, peoples of the same belief were divided into two antagonistic camps. Fear of each other's respective ideology led, in both camps, to a radical elimination of any democratic structure. There soon emerged all over the Islamic world anti-capitalist or anti-communist police states, heartily supported in their build-up of modern repression systems by their respective "patrons." The antagonism between these two camps gave also rise to a dramatic arms race in the Middle East.

One of the victims of the Cold War in the Middle East was indeed Mohammad Mosaddegh's liberal nationalist government (1951-53) in Iran. Mosaddegh enjoyed an immense popularity among the Iranians as well as in the larger Islamic world for his successful liberation of the Iranian oil from the British control in 1951. Thanks to his popularity, Mosaddegh was designated by Shah of Iran, Mohammad Reza Pahlavi, in 1951, as the new prime minister. Two major achievements of Mosaddegh during his short-lived office as prime minister were, firstly, the promotion of an unprecedented degree of democracy; secondly, the running of the Iranian economy without oil revenues, as the British navy in the Persian Gulf succeeded in preventing the sale of Iranian oil.

Unable to destabilize the Mosaddegh administration by impeding the export of Iranian oil, Great Britain changed its tactic and planned, together with the United States, which seemed to be preoccupied by the "red threat" in Iran, an overthrow of Mosaddegh administration. Indeed, the Soviet friendly Communist Party in Iran (*hezb-e tudeh*) took any possible advantage of the fostering democracy in Iran to propagate its communist ideology. Finally, in 1953, the Americans launched a coup against Mosaddegh administration replacing it with a royalist, pro-American, military government.

The overthrow of Mosaddegh administration led, on the one hand, to a discrediting of the West and, on the other hand, to an alienation of the Iranian people from the monarchic regime of Shah–two processes, which ended up 26 years later in the "Islamic" revolution of Iran.

One of the most important arenas of the Cold War in the Middle East was undoubtedly the Arab-Israeli conflict. It was mainly the humiliating defeat of a large alliance of Arab armies against the state of Israel in 1948, which destabilized many Arab regimes and led to the emergence of Soviet-friendly nationalist regimes. The Arab Nationalism found a passionate and charismatic leader in Gamal Abdel Nasser (1954-1970). Two years after taking power, Nasser nationalized the Suez Canal. After the nationalization of Iranian oil, this was the second biggest victory in the nationalistic movements of the Islamic world.

Thanks to the new communication medium, radio, the whole Arab world seemed to melt into a single nation. Through this magic box all Arab nations could listen to the fiery speeches of Nasser as well as the fascinating Arab songs of great musicians like Umm Kolthum, Muhammad Abdul Wahab and Farid al-Atrash. The vision of a modern, strong and united Arab world aroused an immense euphoria among the Arab peoples. Nasserism soon triggered off in the whole Arab world a series of nationalistic movements, of which the War of Independence in Algeria (1954-1962) against the French colonialists was the most spectacular.

The humiliating defeat of the Arabs in the Six Day War against Israel in 1967, however, meant the end for Arab Nationalism: Nasser had linked Nationalism much too closely with the Arab-Israeli conflict; and he had counted too much on the support of the Soviet Union.

Indeed, the impact of the Arab-Israeli conflict on the worldview of Arabs, as well as on that of many other Muslim nations, can hardly be overestimated. By founding the Israeli State, the crumbling colonialism seemed to be brought back to life. In the eyes of the Muslims, Israel became a monument embodying both western neo-colonialism and the powerlessness of the Islamic world (Esposito, 1983: 12). As a result, the romantic attitude of the Arab modernists towards the West began to fade. The West was no longer considered as a model worth emulating since it was perceived as the emanation of injustice.

Haddad comments the lasting effects of the Arab-Israeli conflict on both the Arabic and Islamic view of world politics as follows (1982):

> Western historians and social scientists will never be able to understand fully the Arabic/Islamic interpretation of the current state of affairs in the Arab world as well as the Muslim view of historical process without coming to terms with the meaning of the existence of Israel for Arabs. [...] It is crucial to the understanding of the Islamic view of history to see that for Muslims the existence of Israel is a condemnation and a sign that the forces of darkness and immorality, of wickedness and apostasy, have for reasons yet unexplained, taken the ascendancy in the world. [...] Many publications refer to Zionism as a modern version of the Crusades, an insidious conspiracy of the Western Christian world and its continued hatred and enmity towards Islam. (Haddad 1982: 33–34)

Islamic fundamentalism

As already mentioned, the defeat of Arab armies in 1967 by the Israeli army had a deep negative impact on the legitimacy of the modern ideologies. Neither modernism in the sense of emulating Western liberal models nor a socialist modernity was able to restore the Muslims' sense of dignity being symbolized by territorial integrity. The argument among Islamists that the current plight of the Islamic world was to be found in an abandoning of the true belief started to echo through Islamic countries. "As once happened after the destruction of Baghdad by the Mongols, the Arab world retreated into its shell. Faced by a desolate present and an uncertain future, it fled to its 'glorious past' and sought salvation in the pure, original teachings of Islam" (Heller und Mosbahi 1998: 15; my translation).

When Nasser's successor, Sadat, commanded the Egyptian army in 1973 to stage a surprise attack against Israel, he used Islamic slogans and symbols–an action, which clearly demonstrated the weakening of the nationalist ideology. The victory of the Egyptian army showed that he was right in regarding Islam as a better way of mobilizing the public. The founding of OPEC as well as the worldwide oil crisis of 1973/1974 caused by the Arab oil embargo were other victories of the Arab world, bringing about a new light of hope, not only in the Arab countries, but also in the greater Islamic world. Supported by astronomical oil revenues, the conservative monarchy in Saudi Arabia launched a comprehensive program of Islamic propaganda in the Islamic world, which due to its anti-communist potential also enjoyed the support of the Western camp.

Iranian "Islamic" Revolution

At the end of the 1970s a political event in Western Asia radically changed the status of Islam in the world system. In this year, the Western-orientated monarchic regime in Iran was toppled by a nation-wide revolution. What distinguished this revolution from other political turbulences in the Third World was the fact that it was led by a high rank cleric–the Grand Ayatollah Khomeini. The fact that Khomeini succeeded in replacing the modernistic regime of the Shah with a theocratic order demands an explanation.

The encounter with modernity in Iran was problematic from the very beginning. For the modernization of the country had been constantly shaped by the interests of the Great Powers. This was not any different during the Cold War either. Modernization by dictatorial means and without any integration of civil society damaged the image of the Modernity and favored Islamic ideologies. Repression and lack of a political culture made Iranians susceptible to radical impulses from the world system–abundant in the 1960s/1970s–as well as to populist ideologies. Dissociated from the civil society, the Iranian dependent rentier state lost its balance mainly by two "blows" (Abrahamian 1989: 27-28): Whereas the sharp increase of oil prices in the 1970s destabilized the Iranian economy, the human rights policy of Jimmy Carter facilitated the public expression of the discontent.

A verbal assault against Ayatollah Khomeini in an anonymous newspaper article–most probably ordered by Shah himself (Ahrar 1979)–led to the engagement of the clergy in the protest movement. The radicalization of the protest movement as a result of the rapidly increasing repression led to a shift of leadership of the "Islamic revolution" from moderate clergy to Ayatollah Khomeini, whose radical rhetoric could hardly be surpassed. The leadership of Khomeini was soon underpinned by his growing international fame: In their desire for sensationalism, the global mass media concentrated on Khomeini, whose black-and-white comments were more appealing to the Western masses than the cautious statements of the moderate clergy. Thus, an Islamist cleric was fashioned into a superstar. Instead of offering a program of reforms, Khomeini concentrated on demonizing the Shah–an easy task as Muhammad Reza's failed modernization programs, his dictatorial regime, and his closeness to Israel had made him highly unpopular.

The power-deficient middle and low ranking clerics, despised for decades by the modernists for being "back-warded," were blinded by the prospect of a take-over of power and joined the Islamist cause of Khomeini, thus turning their backs to the high ranking moderate Ulama. Due to their countrywide network, the clerics dominated the autonomous public sphere and were instrumental in winning over the deprived masses. The most important social groups being attracted by the Islamist propaganda, however, were the urban poor, mostly migrants from the rural areas. The secular political groups (either liberal or Marxist), lacking a substantial base among the masses, were soon overshadowed by the rapidly spreading Islamist ideology. Since the Western powers, deeply concerned about the "red threat" in Iran, considered an Islamic solution as a basically negotiable alternative to the monarchic regime, the Islamists did not face any serious opposition from the Western camp as they seized the power in 1979. The Soviets welcomed the regime change in Iran, as it meant the overthrow of one of the most important allies of the West in the Middle East.

The global impact of the Iranian Revolution

The Iranian revolution of 1979 had a threefold global impact: Firstly through its radiation, secondly as a result of its doctrinal shift, thirdly and finally through its anti-American focus.

Global radiation

As Esposito and Piscatori (1990: 1) have remarked: "Few events in the second half of the twentieth century have provoked as much disquiet as the Iranian revolution of 1979."

Shortly after the victory of the revolution, the dominating clerics announced their intention to export the "Islamist" revolution. Since 1979 many Islamist movements around the globe, especially in the countries with a considerable Shi'i population, have been reported to have received financial, logistical or at least political support from Iran.

But most importantly, it is the radiation of the Iranian revolution, which has inspired many Islamist movements in the world. The Islamist regime in Iran has served, however, more as an inspiration than a model for other Islamist movements (ibid., 4-5).

While direct influence of Iranian revolution has been limited to a few countries, most importantly Lebanon, Bahrain, and Iraq, its indirect influence, at least at the very beginning, has been observed in many parts of the Islamic world including Egypt, Algeria, Nigeria, Persian Gulf states, Muslim populations in former Soviet Union, Malaysia, Indonesia, Philippines, Sudan, Nigeria and to some extent Libya, Tunisia, and Afghanistan.[22]

However, the revolutionary appeal of the Iranian revolution for Muslim masses in other countries has been of a rather short-term character. The long-term impact of the Iranian revolution on Muslim populations all over the world has been much less spectacular than anticipated.

Constant reports of the repressive policies of the dominating clerics in Iran led soon to a reduction of sympathy of Muslim nations for the cause of the Iranian Islamists. Moreover, the increasing emphasis of the clerical regime in Iran upon Shi'i observations during the Iran-Iraq war (1980-88) alienated the Sunnis–the overwhelming majority of the world Muslim population–from the ideals of the Iranian revolution.

Indeed, many moderate Islamic leaders regarded the Iranian revolution as rather negative for their own cause: On the one hand, the constant violation of human rights by the Iranian state damaged the noble image of Islam they usually propagated. On the other hand, the merciless prosecution of the higher officials of the monarchic regime in Iran alarmed other dictators in the Islamic world, leading to an enhancement of repressive measures against Islamic movements almost in all Islamic countries. Moreover, the situation of Shi'i minorities in countries with a Sunni or non-Muslim majority has deteriorated as a result of the relentless efforts of Khomeinists to export their revolution.

Nevertheless, the indirect global impact of Islamism in Iran remains substantial. Since the Iranian revolution, Islam has turned into a political factor of global importance. In almost every Islamic country and even in countries with a considerable Muslim minority one could observe a politicization of Islam, mostly unseen before 1979.

Doctrinal shift

Despite the rhetoric of the leading Islamists in Iran and their insistence on installing a "genuine" Islamic state according to the Islamic principles, the new theocratic regime in Iran carried many footprints of modern political systems. Most importantly, it showed many similarities with the secular totalitarian regimes in the modern world system (Siebertz, 2004).

As for its totalitarian character, the Islamist regime was, firstly based on an all-encompassing ideology, which delivered explanations for the whole human history. Secondly, it relied upon a charismatic leadership. Thirdly, by glorifying the "Islamic revolution" and demonizing its enemies it used similar propaganda methods as other totalitarian regimes. Fourthly, it used pseudo-democratic means–such as manipulated parliamentary system and referendums–to institutionalize an antidemocratic political order. Finally, it strove for a total monitoring of pubic as well as private life of its citizens.[23]

The totalitarian character of the new state in Iran was underpinned by a radical change in the dominant religious doctrine. Excessive practices of the Islamist regime–such as repression of any critic, even if exerted by grand ayatollahs, use of torture, assassination of dissidents, approval of hostage taking, disregard for private ownership, and so on–reflected a doctrinal shift of the

Iranian Islamists from the traditional perception of Islam. Attainment of power and its preservation, no matter by what means, was now regarded as the highest religious principle. The ethical "mission" of Islam with its goal of individual salvation–so far the focus of the traditional Islamic discourse in Iran– was replaced overnight by the new objective of collective liberation of Islamic nations from non-Islamist political orders. As the new state was headed by a grand Ayatollah (namely, Khomeini), this new religious credo had to be justified theologically. This justification was found in the controversial principle of *welayat-e faqih* ("guardianship of the theologian"), according to which the supreme theologian had unlimited authority to adapt the Islamic code to the necessities of the Islamic state as well as to enforce his interpretations by any means he would regard as appropriate–a competency, which, according to the traditional Shi'i theology, was reserved for the prophet and the twelve holy Imams.[24]

The reaction of other Islamic movements to the doctrinal shift of Islamists in Iran varied from rejection to fascination. Whereas the moderate Islamic groups all over the world distanced themselves from Iranian Islamists' view of Islam, the more militant groups were fascinated by the new Islamist ideology. Especially, militant leaders with modest Islamic knowledge were more receptive to the Iranian Islamist ideology than to the sophisticated traditional theology. In this sense, the most important long-term impact of the Iranian revolution has been on the extremist, militant Islamist movements.

Anti-American focus

Even though Ayatollah Khomeini had always criticized the monarchic regime for its dependence on the USA, Anti-Americanism did not seem to be an intrinsic part of his ideology. The common anti-communist interests could have even been a basis for a better mutual understanding between the new Islamist state and the USA. This might have been, as already shown, the main reason why Americans did not show any substantial resistance toward a transfer of power from the monarchic regime to the Islamists. The Soviet military operations against Mojahedin in Afghanistan could have even fostered an amicable relationship between the USA and the Islamist Iran.

Khomeini intensified his anti-American rhetoric mainly as the Carter-administration refused to turn over the disposed Shah–then residing in the USA for medical treatment–to Iran. The subsequent occupation of the American embassy in Teheran by the radical Islamist students on November 4, 1979 and their taking of embassy staff as hostages put the already started crisis between the two countries on an irreversible course.

The anti-American rhetoric of the Islamists in Iran soon proved to be very instrumental in cementing their newly won power. Firstly, it was a flattering signal to the Soviet Union, which, with its long border with Iran, was a much bigger threat than a US government presided by Jimmy Carter. The Soviet invasion into Afghanistan had clearly demonstrated the seriousness of the Soviet Union in defending its strategic interests. Secondly, the radical factions of the Islamist regime could successfully use anti-American slogans to weaken their liberal rivals in the administration. Thirdly, the "anti-imperialist" slogans of the Islamists, coupled with their social radical rhetoric, served to ideologically disarm Marxist groups. Fourthly, every now and then, some documents–allegedly reconstructed out of the shredded documents of the US-embassy–were published to discredit the dissidents for having "contacts" with the US authorities. Fifthly and finally, having an enemy as powerful as USA was masterly exploited by the Islamists to demonstrate the global importance of Khomeini's "divine mission." In the holy war against the "Great Satan"–as Khomeini described the USA–no sacrifice was too big.

Suicide bombings

With the outbreak of the second Intifada in 2000, Islamism assumed a new feature: With suicide bombing, a new method of combating the "enemy" was introduced into Islamist movements, unprecedented in the history of Islam. Originally initiated by Japanese Kamikaze pilots during World War II, the concept of committing suicide in order to damage the enemy was later on applied by the PLO against Israeli citizens. The introduction of suicide bombings into the Palestinian Islamist movements had several significant outcomes. Firstly, the Palestinian-Israeli conflict was expanded from occupied territories into the everyday life of the Israeli, giving the conflict a new dimension. Secondly, a new fighting spirit captured the Palestinians. Thirdly, the Islamists assumed a leading role in the Palestinian public opinion. Fourthly and finally, the sympathy of the world community for the Palestinian cause diminished as the Intifada, so far symbolized by the picture of stone-throwing youngsters, was dominated by suicide bombers.

With al-Qaida's strike on the World Trade Center towers and the Pentagon on September 11, 2001, Islamist suicide bombing in its Kamikaze version assumed a global dimension. The attack against the twin towers was indeed the biggest and most devastating attack ever launched against the USA. In this sense it was the biggest demonstration of power of an Islamist group against the most powerful nation of the world. In its aggressiveness it surpassed by far the hostage taking of the American embassy staff in Iran in 1979, which was regarded on its own as an extremely daring aggression against the USA up to that point. Regarding its impact on the world economy as well as on global politics it certainly surpassed the impact of the oil embargo of 1973.

According to Byman (2003: 153-156), al-Qaida's status as the most formidable terrorist organization is derived from the following reasons: "Its ability to tap into broader resentment in the Muslim world; its "mix of elements of hierarchy and global network," the remarkable diversity of its members regarding ethnicity, age, education, expertise, geography, wealth and social position; its being composed of elites; its remarkable bureaucracy with myriad committees of specialists; its extreme sensitivity to operational security; its "ability to adapt its methods and structures to setbacks or failures"; its unusual patience; its ability to penetrate military and intelligent services; its remarkable tolerance toward other Islamist organizations, no matter what ideology they prescribe; and, finally, its strategic view of terror, seeking, for example, "to use the reactions of the United States and its other adversaries against them."

Al-Qaida and other militant Islamist groups, having emerged in the last two decades of the 20th century, interpret Islam in a new way: Jihad is regarded not anymore as one among other Islamic duties, but, as Schulze has remarked, as "the anthropological meaning of being, [the only way,] through which one can become a 'true human being' (Muslim)"[25] (Schulze 2004: 215). Another important feature of the notion of Jihad in the ideology of these militant Islamist groups is that they subscribe to declaring Jihad even against other Muslims who are regarded as less pious (Byman 2003: 146; Benjamin and Simon 2002: 48-55).

The grievances of al-Qaida, as expressed in their statements, are mostly political (Bergen 2002, Byman 2003). In his analysis of 5 major texts on al-Qaida,[26] Byman (2003) identifies the following main points of grievances of al-Qaida, or rather their accusations against USA:
- A blasphemous military presence (in the Islamic holy centers in Arabia and elsewhere)
- A blinding bias toward Israel
- Support for a range of corrupt regimes in the Muslim world
- The destruction and enslavement of Iraq
- Subordination of the Muslim world
- Forcing Muslim oil producers to sell their oil at artificially low prices
- A willingness of the USA to tolerate, or even inflict, Muslim deaths in struggles around the world (Byman, 2003: 144-45).

Some hundred years after al-Afghani, al-Qaida emphasizes once again the global frame of reference in addressing the Malaise of the Islamic world. One again, the liberation of the Islamic world from domination by the "infidels" becomes the most important goal in the agenda of an Islamic movement.

Social appeal of Islamism

Poor developmental achievements of the Islamic states have always been used by the Islamist organizations to criticize their respective governments for their corruptness as well as their dependence on the "enemies of Islam." Indeed, a majority of the Islamic countries show but a modest progress in their development programs. As shown in table 1, with the exception if the Gulf states and Brunei, all Islamic countries have a HDI rank higher[27] than 50. Even Brunei and the Gulf States (with the scores 33 and 44) lie behind the Western countries–ranking between 1 (Norway) and 27 (Portugal).

A majority of Islamic countries (35 out of 55) show a HDI rank higher than 100. As many as 16 countries with a HDI rank of 150 and more can be even characterized, regarding their level of human development, as highly underdeveloped.

One key issue being criticized by the Islamists is the highly underdeveloped state of the welfare programs. Many Islamist organizations, such as *Ikhwan al-Muslimin* in Egypt and some other Arab countries, the Algerian *FIS*, the Palestinian *HAMAS*, the Lebanese *Hizbullah* and other similar groups, have at the same time proved to be able to develop highly efficient solidarity networks with very strong welfare programs. Addressing the shortcomings of the Islamic states in the production of knowledge,[28] the Islamists also offer vast educational programs for the deprived Muslim masses.

Concluding remarks

Let me conclude this historical analysis of the role and status of Islam in the world system with the following reflections:
1. After two centuries of longing for progress and prosperity, the Islamic countries are mostly underdeveloped. Regarding the chronic weaknesses of welfare programs of Islamic states as well as the ongoing rise of demands for social services in Islamic countries (Schulze 2004), one should expect a perpetuation of the presence of Islamist organizations in the public life of the Muslim nations in the near future. Poverty, social inequality, hopelessness could simply drive the affected social groups and classes into the arms of Islamist groups.
If neo-liberalism as the doctrinal basis of the new Western societal model (Bornschier 2005) is supposed to extend to the Islamic world, one should even expect a worsening of the already precarious status of the welfare state in the Islamic countries. Indeed, the World Bank and the IMF have been instrumental in enforcing neo-liberal policies in the developing countries including the Islamic states.

Table 1. The Human Development Index (HDI[29]) rank of the members of OIC[30] (Organization of Islamic Countries), according to UNDP Human Development Report 2005: Highest rank: 1; lowest rank: 177 (data from 2003)[†]

HDI Rank	Country	HDI Rank	Country
33	Brunei	119	Egypt
40	Qatar	122	Tajikistan
41	U. A. E.	123	Gabon
43	Bahrain	124	Morocco
44	Kuwait	132	Comoros
58	Libya	135	Pakistan
61	Malaysia	139	Bangladesh
68	Bosnia-Herzegovina	141	Sudan
71	Oman	143	Togo
72	Albania	144	Uganda
77	Saudi Arabia	148	Cameroon
80	Kazakhstan	150	Djibouti
81	Lebanon	151	Yemen
86	Suriname	152	Mauritania
89	Tunisia	155	Gambia
90	Jordan	156	Guinea
94	Turkey	157	Senegal
96	Maldives	158	Nigeria
97	Turkmenistan	162	Benin
99	Iran	163	Côte d'Ivoire
101	Azerbaijan	168	Mozambique
102	Occup. Palestin. Territories[††]	172	Guinea-Bissau
103	Algeria	173	Chad
106	Syria	174	Mali
107	Guyana	175	Burkina Faso
109	Kyrgyzstan	176	Sierra Leone
110	Indonesia	177	Niger
111	Uzbekistan		

Notes: [†] No data for Afghanistan and Iraq; [††] no OIC member.

2. Beside the welfare state, a key issue of social importance is globalization. Given the relevance of social dislocations for religious fundamentalisms (Marty & Appleby 1993),[31] one should expect a growth of fundamentalist tendencies all over the world as globalization—as a major source of dislocations—proceeds.
3. Lack of priesthood in its strict sense has made Islam susceptible to decentralized, grass roots movements. Theoretically, every Muslim, no matter how knowledgeable in Islamic theology, could lead an Islamic movement. Indeed, none of the Islamist movements—with the exception of the one led

by Ayatollah Khomeini[32]–had a high rank theologian as their leader. Many have even had leaders with modest Islamic knowledge.
4. Even though al-Qaida has lost much of its appeal due to its jeopardizing, if not consciously targeting of, the civilians, its "savage violence" (Kepel 2002), its reactionary ideology–demonstrated by its alliance with the Taliban regime–and its hostility towards Shiism, its symbolic impact remains significant for the time to come. Moreover, as a global Muslim solidarity network (Schulze 2004),[33] it has still some potential to grow.
5. Islamist groups are facing a major problem: None of the states ruled by Islamists, neither Iran, nor Afghanistan under the Taliban, nor Sudan, has been ever able to fulfill its promises of freedom, progress and prosperity. On the contrary, all nations under the Islamist rule had to experience a continuous worsening of their life conditions. The Islamist dream seems to be out-dreamed. As Kepel (2002: 320) has remarked, the use of violence by militant Islamist groups reflects a lack of grassroots support. Iran as the first country to experiment with a political system based on an Islamist ideology has brought about a new generation of Islamic reformists who passionately endorse some kind of Islamic secularism.
6. The Internet and Satellite TV, as two major modern communication systems, can give rise to a new global Muslim identity. This might promote the mobilization potential of the Islamist organizations. Given the chaotic nature of the Internet, however, it could also undermine the traditional authorities. Moreover, both devices could strengthen the civil society structures in Islamic countries and foster thereby pluralistic worldviews.
7. The conflicts of Muslim nations with the Super Powers have so far had a negative impact on the legitimacy of Western ideologies. There is no reason why this trend should change in the near future. Specifically, the Palestinian-Israeli conflict lies at the heart of Muslim international solidarity. If the Super Powers do not succeed in bringing about a just and lasting resolution to the Palestinian question, the existing distrust of the Muslim masses toward the West will continue to develop.

Notes

[1] The Sunnis believed that Muhammad's successor should be elected by a committee of his disciples. The Shi'is, on the other hand, were of the opinion that Muhammad had already designated his cousin and son-in-law, Ali bin Abu-Talib, as his successor.
[2] Omar was originally of the opinion that Islam should be limited to the Arabian Peninsula. He was, however, overtaken by the reality of the advancing Muslim conquests (Nagel, 1998:15)
[3] Muslims were generally distrustful of the late-convert Quraishi aristocrats like Mu'awiah. Besides, Mu'awiah's loyalty to Islam was doubted because his father, Abu Sufyan, was known as one of the archenemies of the prophet.

4 The Sunni Muslims call the first four Caliphs *Khulafa- al-Rashidun* ("the Righteous Caliphs") and regard their rule as just and truly Islamic. This "Golden Era of Islam" has also served as the ideal model for an Islamic state by Sunni reformists as well as fundamentalists.
5 The Kharijis were originally Shi'is. However, after a discord with Ali during his wars with Mu'awiah, they turned their backs to him.
6 The brutal massacre on Hussain–the grandson of the Prophet and the third Imam of the Shi'is–and his family and companions in 680, ordered by Mu'awiah's son Yazid, was indeed the climax of atrocities of the Umayyads against the family of the prophet. Up to the present time, the most important processions of the Shi'is take place at the anniversary of this massacre–on the so-called *Ashura*.
7 The rebellion was led by a coalition of three groups (Halm, 2004: 34): Firstly, Arabs who were discontent with the "unfair" distribution of the loots of the wars; secondly, Iranians, to whom the universalistic interpretation of Islam was much more appealing than the particularistic, Arab-biased Islam of the Umayyad; and Thirdly, the Shi'is.
8 A branch of the Umayyad continued its rule in Maghreb (756-1036) and in 929 founded the Caliphate of Cordova, which soon became an amazing center for science, philosophy, art and technology.
9 The Islamic world experienced under the Abbasids a boom in a long list of disciplines, such as Alchemy, Astrology, Astronomy, Ethnography, Geography, History, Literature, Mathematics, Medicine, Theory of Music, Mysticism, Natural History, Pharmacy, Philosophy, Physics, Theology and so on.
10 Rudolph (2004: 12-14) mentions three reasons for the great interest in cultural heritage of other civilizations under the Abbasids: Firstly, the administration of the great empire required the acquisition of techniques and sciences unknown to the Arabs. Secondly, the Abbasids regarded themselves, in contrast to the Umayyads, not simply as the dominant Arab elite, but as the legitimate representatives of all Islamic peoples. Thirdly and finally, the reception of the old civilizations obtained soon some auto-dynamism.
11 The Caliphs recruited their armies primarily from the slaves. Military slaves had two major advantages for the Caliphs. On the one hand, they had seldom access to the local social networks and could, therefore, hardly get involved in any conspiracies against the Caliphs. On the other hand, they were, at least theoretically, bound to absolute obedience to the Caliph. The institution of military slaves was maintained up to the 19th century, to be abolished only as the Ottomans dissolved their slave troops (the so-called Yenitchar army).
12 Out of the hardly accessible mountains in Northern Iran, the Iranian Shi'i sect of Hashashin (1090-1273) fought the Sunni supremacy by trying to murder its political elite. It could only be defeated by the Mongols.
13 In 909 the Fatemids even took on the title of Caliph.
14 Since the mystics were often wrapped in coarse woolen cloth (Suf), they were called Sufis.
15 See for example Schimmel, 1995: 340-41.
16 See Nagel, 1993: 70ff.
17 Ibid: 83ff.
18 The current regime in Saudi Arabia stems from an alliance of the Saudi family with the followers of Abdul Wahhab–the so-called *Wahhabites*.
19 *Kave*, 1920, Number 1, page 2.
20 Shortly after the closure of the Parliament in 1908 there came to a major military showdown between the revolutionaries and the Royal forces ending up with the triumph of the constitutionalists. The newly elected Parliament, however, was dissolved in 1911 upon a Russian ultimatum. Iranian Parliament was established once again in 1914. However, with the occupation of Iran by the great powers during World War I, it only had a sham exis-

tence. The post-war chaos and takeover of power by Reza Khan in 1921 prevented the Iranian parliament from restoring its due significance.

[21] Reza Shah took the modernization program of Mustafa Kamal (Attaturk) as his model and closely followed it (Keddie 2003: 92).

[22] See for example Willis (1996), Bayat/Baktiari (2002), Nasr (2002) as well as the valuable contributions in Esposito (1990).

[23] My discussion of the totalitarian character of the Islamist regime in Iran is mainly based upon the elaborate analysis of this phenomenon delivered by Siebertz (2004).

[24] This explains the great emphasis of the leaders of the Islamic Republic on the principle of *Welayat-e faqih*. This also helps understand the importance of Ayatollah Shariatmadari's protest against the anchoring of this doctrine in the new constitution (For a detailed discussion of Khomeini-Shariatmadari conflict see Sheikhzadegan 2003).

[25] My translation of the German original.

[26] These five texts are written by Benjamin & Simon (2002), Bergen (2002), Gunaratna (2002), Kepel (2002) and an anonymous intelligence officer (*Through Our Enemies' Eyes: Osama Bin Laden, Radical Islam, and the Future of America*, Washington, D.C.: Brassey's, 2002).

[27] It goes without saying that the higher the rank of a country is, the lower is its level of human development.

[28] Shortcomings in the acquisition and production of knowledge in Arab countries are best reflected in the UNDP Arab Human Development Report 2003. According to this report, major obstacles of a knowledge society in the Arab countries are deficits in the areas of *freedom, women's empowerment* and *access to knowledge*. In the closing section of this report, the authors put forward a strategic vision for creating knowledge societies in the Arab world. According to them, this strategy should be based on five pillars: guaranteeing key freedoms; disseminating quality education; embedding science; shifting towards knowledge-based production; and developing an enlightened Arab knowledge model.

[29] HDI was gained as an arithmetic average of three indices: life expectancy at birth; schooling index as a composite of adult literacy rate (weighed 2/3) and schooling registration ratio (primary, secondary and tertiary levels combined) (weighed 1/3); PPP (Purchasing Power Parity) in US$.

[30] In some of the sub-Saharan Muslim countries on the list (like Togo, Mozambique, Benin or Uganda) the Muslims do not build the majority of the population. I did not exclude these countries from the list simply because they are members of OIC.

[31] Marty & Appleby (1993: 620) formulate this thesis as follows: "[...] religious fundamentalisms thrive in the twentieth century when and where masses of people living in formerly traditional societies experience profound personal and social dislocations as a result of rapid modernization an in the absence of mediating institutions capable of meeting the human needs created by these dislocations. [...] religious fundamentalisms are concerned with defining, restoring, and reinforcing the basis of personal and community identity that is shaken or destroyed by modern dislocations and crises." As possible sources of dislocations these authors mention mass migration from rural to urban areas, unsynchronized social, economic and cultural transformations and uneven schemes of development, failures in educational and social welfare systems and the collapse of "long-held assumptions about the meaning and purpose of human existence" (ibid.).

[32] Even in Iran, Ayatollah Khomeini's new doctrine was not endorsed by any other Grand Ayatollah. However, only a few (like Ayatollah Seyyed Kazem Shariatmadari or Ayatollah Seyyed Hasan Tabataba'i al-Qomi) dared to protest against him. The Islamist regime answered with decloaking and house arrest. The other Grand Ayatollahs either drew back into their habitual Shi'i quietism (e.g. Ayatollah Abul Qasem al-Kho'i or Ayatollah Ahmad Khansari) or tried to find some diplomatic let-out (e.g. Ayatollah Mar'ashi Najafi, or Ayatollah Golpayegani).

[33] In his typology of Islamic solidarity networks, Schulze (2004) classifies al-Qaida as a *global* type of solidarity networks, even though he puts the word global into quotation marks. The other 4 categories in this typology are philanthropic, transnational, national, and local networks.

References

Abrahamian, Ervand. 1989. *The Iranian Mojahedin*. New Haven & London: Yale University Press.
Ahrar, Ahmad. 1979. "Ahmad-e Rashidi-ye Motlaq shakhs-e Shah bud" ("Ahmad Rashidi Motlaq was Shah himself"), in: *Ettelaat*, 29. Bahman 1357 [18.2.1979]
Anonymous. 2002. *Through Our Enemies' Eyes: Osama Bin Laden, Radical Islam, and the Future of America*. Washington, D.C.: Brassey's.
Bayat, Asef, and Baktiari, Bahman. 2002. "Revolutionary Iran and Egypt. Exporting Inspirations and Anxieties." Pp. 305-326 in *Iran and the Surrounding World*, edited by Keddie, Nikki R., and Matthee, Rudi. Seattle and London: University of Washington Press.
Benjamin, Daniel and Steven Simon. 2002. *The Age of Sacred Terror*. New York: Random House.
Bergen, Peter L. 2002. *Holy War, Inc.: Inside the Secret World of Osama Bin Laden*. New York: Simon and Schuster.
Bornschier, Volker. 2005. "Varianten des Kapitalismus in reichen Demokratien beim Übergang in das neue Gesellschaftsmodell." Pp. 331-371 in *Vom Manager- zum Finanzmarktkapitalismus*, Sonderheft der Kölner Zeitschrift für Soziologie und Sozialpsychologie, edited by Windolf, Paul. Wiesbaden: VS Verlag für Sozialwissenschaften.
Byman, Daniel L. 2003. "Al-Qaeda as an Adversary: Do We Understand Our Enemy?" *World Politics* 56: 139-63.
Esposito, John L. 1983. "Introduction: Islam and Muslim Politics." Pp. 3-15 in *Voices of Resurgent Islam*, edited by Esposito, John L. New York/Oxford: Oxford University Press.
Esposito, John L. (ed.). 1990. *The Iranian Revolution: Its Global Impact*. Miami: Florida International University Press.
Esposito, John L., and Piscatori, James P. 1990. "Introduction." Pp. 1-16 in *The Iranian Revolution: Its Global Impact*, edited by Esposito, John L. Miami: Florida International University Press.
Gunaratna, Rohan. 2002. *Inside Al Qaeda*. New York: Columbia University Press.
Haddad, Yvonne Yazbeck. 1982. *Contemporary Islam and the Challenge of History*. Albany: State University of New York Press.
Halm, Heinz. 2002. *Der Islam*. München: C. H. Beck
Halm, Heinz. 2004. *Die Araber*. München: C. H. Beck
Heller, E. and H. Mosbahi. 1998. "Einführung." Pp. 7-28 in *Islam, Demokratie, Moderne: Aktuelle Antworten arabischer Denker*, edited by Heller, E., and Mosbahi, H. München: C. H. Beck.
Ibn Khaldun, Abd al-Rahman ibn Muhammad. 1958. *The Muquaddimah*, translated by Franz Rosenthal. New York: Pantheon.
Keddie, Nikki R. (2003): *Modern Iran: Roots and Results of Revolution*. New Haven and London: Yale University Press.

Kepel, Gilles. 2002. *Jihad: The Trail of Political Islam*, translated by Anthony F. Roberts. Cambridge: Harvard University Press.
Marty, Martin E., and Appleby, R. Scott. 1993. "Conclusion: Remarking the State: The Limits of the Fundamentalist Imagination." Pp. 620-643 in *Fundamentalisms and the State: Remarking Politics, Economies, and Militance*, edited by Marty, M. E., and Appleby, R. S. Chicago and London: The University of Chicago Press.
Nagel, Tilman. 1993. *Timur der Eroberer und die islamische Welt des späten Mittelalters*. München: Beck.
Nagel, Tilman. 1998. *Die Geschichte der islamischen Welt bis 1500*. München: Oldenbourg Grundriss der Geschichte.
Nasr, Vali. 2002. "The Iranian Revolution and Changes in Islamism in Pakistan, India, and Afghanistan." Pp. 327-354 in *Iran and the Surrounding World*, edited by Keddie, Nikki R., and Matthee, Rudi. Seattle and London: University of Washington Press.
Rudolph, Ulrich. 2004. *Islamische Philosophie*. München: C. H. Beck.
Schimmel, Annemarie. 1995. *Mystische Dimensionen des Islam. Die Geschichte des Sufismus*. Frankfurt a.M. and Leipzig: Insel Verlag.
Schulze, Reinhard. 2002. *Die Geschichte der islamischen Welt im 20. Jh*. München: C. H. Beck.
Schulze, Reinhard. 2004. "Islamische Solidaritätsnetzwerke." Pp. 195-218 in *Transnationale Solidarität: Chancen und Grenzen*, edited by Beckert, Jens et al. Frankfurt a.M.: Campus.
Sheikhzadegan, Amir. 2003. Der Griff des politiscche Islam zur Macht: Iran und Algerien im Vergleich. Bern etc.: Peter Lang Verlag, Reihe Europäische Hochschulschriften.
Siebertz, Roman. 2004. "Totalitarismus im modernen Iran." Paper presented at the 29th Conference of German Orientalists (29. Deutscher Orientalistentag) in Halle, Germany.
Willis, Michael. 1996. *The Islamist Challenge in Algeria: A Political History*. New York: New York University Press.

6
Northeast Asian Competition for Russian Far East Natural Resources
Possibilities of Russo-Chinese Geo-economic Integration

John Gulick

Many historical sociologists contend that East Asia is reclaiming its former status as the "center among centers" in the global order. This discourse neglects the elementary geographical fact that the Russian Far East (RFE) is part of East Asia, namely Northeast Asia. The collapse of the Soviet Union and the gradual drawing of the RFE's plentiful though remote natural resources into Northeast Asia's zone of gravity has transformed this overlooked geographical fact into a patent reality of regional political economy. The emergence of a regional division of labor has been punctuated by more friction than anticipated by pundits and technocrats who forecast in the early 1990's that the opening of the RFE's factors of production to Northeast Asia and points beyond would lead to a positive-sum outcome eagerly embraced by all concerned parties. To a great extent this friction stems from the increasing demands the metropoles of Northeast Asian states are imposing upon the vast raw materials hinterland of the RFE, in the context of a complex and fluid situation in which 1) RFE elites remain wary of rising Chinese demographic and economic influence, while at the same time 2) Moscow and Beijing are bent on furthering energy cooperation arrangements that marginalize if not altogether exclude Japan, especially insofar as Japan is regarded as a proxy of the US in its determination to prolong the US-centered global order. The possibility exists that Russia and China will strengthen their "strategic partnership" and transform this relationship toward geo-economic integration. This path is consonant with the desire of both countries for a multiply centered world order. Moreover, upward pressure on the world price for oil assures that hydrocarbon deposits in eastern Siberia will become commercially viable to exploit and that Russia will enjoy windfall revenues from peddling said deposits to China, while establishing a trans-border accumulation regime with Russia may be China's best hope for surviving the coming age of hydrocarbon energy deficits.

What with Japan's rapid industrial growth after World War II, soon followed by that of South Korea and Taiwan, and now most especially by that of mainland China, there is a gathering consensus among many world-systems scholars that East Asia is reclaiming its former status as the "center among centers" in the global order (Arrighi 2005a, 2005b, 1994; Frank 1996). Often neglected in the discursive hype about the reemergence of East Asia is the elementary geographical fact that the Russian Far East (RFE) is too part of

East Asia, namely Northeast Asia (Kotkin and Wolff 1995). As long as the RFE was little more than a hidebound outpost guarding the eastern frontier of the Soviet Union, in a country at bilateral odds with its Northeast Asian neighbors (North Korea excepted), this oversight was excusable. But the implosion of the transcontinental empire that was the Soviet Union well more than a decade ago, and the attendant weakening of formerly subsidized linkages between the RFE and European Russia, transformed this oft-overlooked geographical fact into a more obvious political-economic fact (Minakir 1995; Thornton and Ziegler 2002: 4-8). At the very least, the contraction of Kremlin military spending in the RFE, the scuttling of energy and transport subsidies binding the RFE to European Russia and western Siberia, and the relaxation of Moscow's highly centralized political authority all gave rise to speculation that the stranded region's economic inputs and outputs would surely be drawn into the orbit of a Northeast Asian accumulation regime (Minakir 1995). Think-tank pundits and multilateral technocrats from many Pacific Rim countries (most notably Japan and the United States) forecast and endorsed a mutually advantageous division of labor in Northeast Asia, one commingling abundant Japanese and South Korean capital, cheap Chinese labor, and plentiful RFE natural resources (Kim et. al. 1992; Rozman 2004: 12; Rozman 1995; Valencia 1995). Furthermore, imbued with a sensibility that later became institutionalized as Washington Consensus ideology, these scholars and officials blithely presumed that such a Northeast Asian division of labor would not take the form of a regional fortress, but to the neo-liberal contrary, would be receptive to extra-Northeast Asian investors and responsive to extra-Northeast Asian markets. Given these kindred expectations and hopes, the "Northeast Asian-ness" of the RFE not only manifested itself as geographical fact and political-economic prospect, but could also be regarded as a socio-ecological prospect, with the RFE possibly consigned to the unenviable role of a primary commodity-exporting enclave undergirding industrial growth to its immediate south and east, and to more distant locales as well.

In the more than ten years which have passed since the Soviet Union self-destructed, the natural resources of the RFE, as well as its transport infrastructure and its bulk ports on the Sea of Japan, have been drawn into Northeast Asia's economic zone of gravity, although more fitfully and less rapidly than many prognosticators anticipated (Rozman 2004: 9). But the gradual emergence of a regional division of labor has also been punctuated by much more geopolitical friction than anticipated by those who forecast that the opening of the RFE's factors of production to Northeast Asia and points beyond would lead, in textbook Ricardian fashion, to a positive-sum outcome eagerly embraced by all concerned states (Rozman 2004: 1-2, 9). Steeped in triumphalist sentiment typical of the post-1991 moment, those who envisioned the opening of the RFE also envisioned the easing of outmoded Cold War hostilities among the states of Northeast Asia, regarding the former as an inevitable and desirable precondition of the latter (Rozman 2004: 9; Thornton and Ziegler 2002: 3-4). That is, they avowed what were soon to be proven flawed articles of faith: that a fundamental reorganization of the RFE's economy could be accomplished seamlessly, that entrenched inter-state tensions would magically dissolve in the face of the post-socialist "new world order," and that tethering the region's raw materials, biological resources, and commodity transport systems to extra-regional markets could somehow be a dynamic innocent of geopolitical maneuvering (Rozman 2004: 9).

I pursue two objectives in this paper. The first is descriptive; the second, diagnostic. Objective one is to present empirical evidence regarding these geopolitical frictions, many of which stem from the increasing environmental demands the metropoles of Northeast Asian states (especially China) are imposing upon the vast hinterland of the RFE (Rozman 2004: 336-337). I will focus on one case of momentous global significance–the contest between China and Japan to influence the routing of long-distance oil pipelines being extended from eastern Siberia and transecting the RFE. I will also touch upon two cases of admittedly modest global significance, but of notable regional significance nonetheless: a) active Russian and Chinese disagreement over the leasing and improvement of coal bulk ports on the RFE coast and b) latent Russian and Chinese disagreement over the migration of land-poor and landless Northeast Chinese peasants into the huge and uncultivated agricultural frontier north of the Heilongjiang River. Objective two is to draw from these cases and offer both a provisional interpretation of the ongoing maturation of the Russo-Chinese "strategic partnership" and a preliminary diagnosis of the prospects for mutually complementary accumulation regimes on both sides of the Russo-Chinese border. In order to furnish a framework for understanding one of the most crucial axes around which all aspects of my inquiry revolve, I begin by surveying the vagaries of the Russo-Chinese relationship during the last 15 or so years.

A potted history of post-Soviet Russo-Chinese bilateral relations and RFE-Northeast China economic integration

A paradox of great importance threads through the recent course of Russo-Chinese bilateral relations. On the one hand, the simple revival of normalized ties in the late 1980's was eventually succeeded in 1996 by the formal construction of a "strategic partnership" (Wishnick 2001: 128-130). The elevation of the bilateral relationship involved both states recognizing their shared subscription to similar principles and goals, most notably those dealing with issues of global governance and big power geopolitics, and the reciprocal adjustment and conscious coordination of policies in the service of advancing said principles and goals (Achcar 2000: 130-131). Not least among the concrete elements of the "strategic partnership" was a putative commitment by Russia to assist China in its quest to meet its exploding demand for primary energy imports (Thornton and Ziegler 2002; Page 2003). On the other hand, lingering apprehension in Moscow but more specifically in the RFE toward rising Chinese demographic and economic influence in the RFE stymied cross-border economic integration (at least until very recently) and enabled other Northeast Asian states to figure prominently in the extraction, transport, and sourcing of the RFE's natural resources, undermining or at least compromising Russia's grandiose pronouncements about its "strategic partnership" with China. One helpful way of getting a handle on this paradox animating Russo-Chinese relations in the post-Cold War context, then, is to conceptualize it as a complex and changing interplay between the increasingly amiable "high politics" of Moscow and Beijing and the tenacious uncertainties of on-the-ground geo-economics in the RFE-Northeast China border region.

Despite the Yeltsin government's short-lived flirtation with unequivocally aligning Russia with the advanced capitalist West, by 1993 or 1994 it had become quite clear that Moscow had committed itself to building upon the normalization of Russo-Chinese relations set in motion by Gorbachev and the Soviet reformers (Wishnick 2001: 121-123). No longer predicated on the rudimentary norms of mere "peaceful coexistence"–vowing to settle differences amicably, respecting one another's internal affairs, and so on (Wishnick 2001: 104-105)–the Russo-Chinese relationship ever so subtly began to be informed by a joint distrust of resurgent US "hegemonism" and a mutual interest in engineering some kind of equilibrating balance in the China-Russia-US "triangle" (Wishnick 2001: 126). By 1994 the Russo-Chinese relationship had been officially upgraded to one of "constructive partnership," a designation given substance by the retargeting of their atomic arsenals so their nuclear missiles were no longer pointed at one another (Achcar 2000: 132; Wishnick 2001: 126). On a more practical level, by the mid-1990's China had also established itself as the largest customer of Russian military hardware in the post-Soviet era, purchasing more than a quarter of the value of Russia's arms exports between 1992-1994 (Achcar 2000: 131).

However, by no means did increasing friendliness between the Russian and Chinese central governments automatically translate into increasingly harmonious economic integration between a natural resource-rich RFE and a cheap labor-rich Northeast China. One of many windows into making sense of the asymmetry between improving Russo-Chinese relations and stagnating RFE-Northeast Chinese economic integration is the addressing of China's long-ignored claims to territory on the RFE-Northeast China border, specifically islands in the Amur (i.e., Heilongjiang) River and land straddling the Tumen River. As part of the deepening of the resurrected bilateral relationship, the Yeltsin government promised to abide by a 1991 treaty dealing with the redrawing of the Russo-Chinese border, a treaty that included a framework for acceding to China's claims to the aforementioned islands and land (Achcar 2000: 132; Wishnick 2001: 116-117). Although fruitlessly interfering with Moscow's neighborly concessions to Beijing's territorial claims would obviously reduce the extent and the slow the pace of economic integration in the RFE-Northeast China border zone, the RFE's post-Soviet political elites did just that well into the 1990's (Ni 2002; Vinogradov 1996; Wishnick 2001: 176-182; Wishnick 1995). Such obstructionism was consistent with a larger strategy employed by political elites to win and hold electoral office in RFE provincial governments: piquing the populace's widespread fear that China sought to take back lands it ceded to Tsarist Russia in the mid-Nineteenth Century through stealth demographic conquest, i.e. by means of legal and illegal Chinese migration into the southern RFE (Kiselyov 1996; Larin 1995; Ni 2002; Rozman 1995). Exercising their newfound freedom from the discipline of the Kremlin, RFE elected officials who played the "yellow peril" card not only violated the spirit of Russo-Chinese camaraderie favored in both Moscow and Beijing, but also undercut whatever momentum existed toward the fomentation of cross-border economic integration.[1]

Sudden and severe economic dislocation in the post-Soviet RFE made the popular fear of the "Chinese threat" all the easier to marshal. The abrupt end to central economic planning in post-Soviet Russia subjected the distant RFE to terrible shortages of food and consumer goods, and by dint of necessity Russia's easternmost provinces increasingly imported these items from Northeast Asia, especially Northeast China (Larin 1995; Minakir 1995). The spontaneous reorientation of the RFE's economy toward its southern flank temporarily gave trade on the RFE-Northeast China border a shot in the arm. But it also set loose a series of processes that inflamed anti-Chinese xenophobic sentiment among RFE residents and led to an attenuation of cross-border trade that lasted far into the 1990's. In the early 1990's, cross-border economic exchange predominantly took the form of highly unregulated barter trade orchestrated by Chinese merchants, many of them unlicensed (Wishnick 1995). Industrial machinery stripped from factories, intermediate goods such as cement, and RFE raw materials (e.g., aquatic products harvested from the Sea of Japan and timber cut from the forests of Primorsky Krai) were swapped for fruits and vegetables grown in Northeast China and textiles and housewares re-exported from the special economic zones of coastal southern China

(Minakir 1995; Wishnick 2001: 159-162). As Moscow relaxed export controls on natural resources, primary commodities constituted a bigger and bigger portion of the goods crossing into Northeast China from the RFE (Wishnick 2001: 163). At the same time, RFE consumers routinely complained that wage good imports from China were poor in quality (Skosyrev 1994; Wishnick 2001: 164). Accordingly, the cross-border barter trade precipitously earned a bad reputation for being "uneven"–the RFE's precious natural wealth pawned off to fuel China's industrial accumulation and exchanged for China's pesticide-poisoned food and shoddy garments sold at a premium to feed and clothe the RFE's idled workers and their dependents (Larin 1995; Tayler, 2001; Wishnick 1995). Under the chaotic conditions of the RFE being effectively severed from European Russia, the makeshift division of labor on the RFE-Northeast China border actualized the nightmare of the region's nationalists: before their eyes the RFE was being rapidly transformed into an exporter of unprocessed and undervalued raw materials (Wishnick 2001: 163, 184; Wishnick 2002: 298-299). This emergency jolt of cross-border trade meant that trade between the RFE and Heilongjiang Province made up a much higher percentage of Russo-Chinese trade than previously, but because of the unsavory form this trade took it began to slacken in absolute terms after 1993 (Larin 1995; Mikheyev 1994; Wishnick 2001: 159-162). In other words, social fallout from the short-term uptick in cross-border economic integration resulted in the medium-run delegitimation of said integration.

The overarching trend delineated above–against the backdrop of warmer and more cooperative relations between the Foreign Ministries of Russia and China, continuing paranoia in the RFE about the sinister aims of Chinese investors, settlers, and traders in the region–has more or less persisted into the present, although of late there are some indications that the RFE's political elites are finally coming to understand the positive role that rejuvenated cross-border economic integration might play in boosting regional growth (Brooke 2004). It did not take long for Moscow and Beijing to upgrade their "constructive partnership" to the status of "strategic partnership." At the time of its formation in 1996, the glue of the Russo-Chinese "strategic partnership" was a common desire by the two Asian powers to enhance an inclusive and fluid international order, rather than one rent into inflexible blocs, most especially a bloc dominated by the US "hyperpower" (Achcar 2000: 132-133; Wishnick 2001: 128-130). Spurred by the near showdown with US carrier groups in the Taiwan Straits, China secured a pledge from Russia to oppose a Taiwanese run for independence, and in turn vowed to remain silent about Russia's ruthless war against Chechen separatists (Achcar 2000: 132; Wishnick 2001: 126-127). For the express purpose of acquiring the capability to overcome US intervention on behalf of a breakaway Taiwan, China also purchased from Russia new naval assets and air defense systems (Achcar 2000: 131-132). Later in the decade, China backed Russia's (unsuccessful) rejection of the eastward expansion of NATO, Russia returned the favor by backing China's (successful) bid to enter the WTO, and both countries strongly upbraided the "hegemonist" US for bypassing the UN Security Council and dragooning NATO into the bombing of Serbia (Achcar 2000: 131-132; Wishnick 2001: 131-132). And in July 2001, Moscow and Beijing strengthened their "strategic partnership" by inking the "Treaty of Neighborliness, Friendship, and Cooperation," which underscored their mutual hostility toward the U.S.' unilateral abandonment of the 1972 Anti-Ballistic Missile (ABM) Treaty and thus reaffirmed their twin commitment to a multipolar international order (Lukin 2001; Ni 2002).

Despite the ratcheting up of Russo-Chinese coordination in the sphere of global geopolitics, Russo-Chinese trade figures fell far short of the US $20 billion mark envisaged early in the decade, and economic integration along the RFE and Northeast China boundary continued to flag (Ni 2002; Wishnick 2001: 131-133). Both Moscow and Beijing chose to confine the "strategic partnership" to grand issues of international power politics; neither Moscow nor Beijing was willing to make pecuniary sacrifices that would give the "strategic partnership" the kind of economic content necessary for it to resemble anything like a reciprocal accumulation regime (Wishnick 2001: 153). On the one hand, the only big-ticket items China would buy from RFE industrial producers were military aircraft, and Chinese FDI in the RFE tended to be small-scale and natural resource-plundering rather than capital-deepening in character (Larin 1995; Ni 2002; Wishnick 2001: 134, 144-146, 172). On the other hand, the Kremlin refused to allocate to the RFE precisely those expenditures that would lower the resistance of the region's elites and masses to the activity of Chinese investors, settlers, and traders–funding for better border management and improved social and physical infrastructure (Wishnick 2001: 155). Nonetheless, at the tail end of the 1990's trade between the RFE and China began to show new signs of life, picking up by 24 percent between 1997 and 1998 and 27 percent between 1998 and 1999 (Ni 2002: 376). This upsurge in RFE-Northeast China trade coincided with the collapse of the ruble, and so to some unknown degree was being driven by pauperized RFE consumers substituting low-grade Chinese wage goods imports for high-grade wage goods imports from other countries (Wishnick 2001: 175). But unlike the early 1990's, this time the upsurge in trade outlasted the depths of Russian crisis, as China clearly established itself as the RFE's leading trade partner by the inaugural years of the Twenty-First Century (Brooke 2004; Ni 2002: 377; Rozman 2004: 335).

The US' opportunistic response to the terrorist attacks of September 11–namely using them as a springboard to augment its geostrategic presence in

Central (and Western) Asia, and thus as a potential solvent of the emerging cooperative alliance between Russia and China that for quite some time had been a source of increasing alarm in Washington DC (Achcar 2000)–immediately impacted the Russo-Chinese "strategic partnership" in multiple and contradictory ways, but its medium-run effect has been to strengthen the relationship. In part because Russia had already surrendered authority in its former Central Asian sphere of influence, and in part because China did not want to jeopardize its economic modernization strategy by directly confronting the state that controlled access to its leading export market, both countries stood by idly as the US leased military bases and flyover rights in numerous republics to the north of Afghanistan. However, in some respects both Russia and China were also making the best of a bad situation, turning the US' declared "war on terror" into a chance to gain some ground against Muslim fundamentalist and ethnic separatist insurgencies that had long troubled their southern and western perimeters, respectively (Anderson 2002: 14). More importantly, the US drive to establish a permanent military presence, or at least a reliable set of military clients, in Central Asia did nothing to depress Russian and Chinese aspirations for bilateral trade to constitute a more prominent part of their "strategic partnership." With the deliberate aim of expanding Russo-Chinese trade relations beyond the familiar pattern of exchanging military hardware and natural resources for low-end consumer goods, on several occasions in 2001 and 2002 Russia and China each hosted high-level trade delegations (Rozman 2004: 334-336).

Of course, the fundamental cause for the firming of the "strategic partnership" in the post-September 11 environment was the Bush Administration's determination to invade and occupy Iraq despite the strenuous objections of the vast majority of international civil society and the tepid objections of Russia and China themselves. The US-led campaign in Iraq flouted all of the principles and goals underlying the Russo-Chinese "strategic partnership": the US flagrantly disrespected consensual decision-making in the UN Security Council, it rushed to war to advantage its own narrow imperial interests, and in rushing to war it cynically deployed "democracy promotion" rhetoric strongly distasteful to both Russia and China (Blagov 2004b). While the US' unabashed display of unilateralism and its blatant violation of international law prompted Russia and China to deepen their "strategic partnership," the US' discredited reputation on the world stage and its growing immobilization in the political quagmire of post-Saddam Iraq afforded Russia and China the room to do so without inviting heavy sanction from the US. On a state visit to Moscow in May 2003, Chinese President Hu unhesitatingly called for a "multipolar world"–code for Russo-Chinese unity to brake predatory US dominance–in a speech that received a welcome reception in the Kremlin (Isachenkov 2003).

By 2005, Russia and China through the forum of the Shanghai Cooperation Organization (SCO) were demanding that the US draft a plan to end its airbase leases in Kyrgyzstan and Uzbekistan (Radyuhin 2005), and even more provocatively, conducted joint war gaming exercises ("Friendship 2005") for the first time since the Sino-Soviet split of the late 1950's (Blagov 2005a). It would still be fair to say that Russia and China each values the "strategic partnership" largely because tighter bilateral links bolster each country's leverage in their respective individual dealings with the "indispensable" US (Achcar 2000: 133; Rozman 2004: 332-338). For example, as the Pentagon and the US Congress in 2005 ratcheted up demagogic rhetoric about China's supposed expansionist ambitions in the western Pacific, its central bank's so-called "manipulation" of the value of the yuan, and other alleged misbehaviors, China's diplomatic corps gamely the played Russo-Chinese "strategic partnership" card to prompt the militarist and protectionist wing of the US ruling class to de-escalate its complaints (Lomanov 2005; Petras 2005). Yet a threshold of mutual trust between Russia and China appears to have been crossed, and it is increasingly the case that changing world-systemic realities have placed the "strategic partnership" on a footing independent of the imperative for each big Asian power to triangulate against the US, as I will show in sections to come.

Representing a fourfold increase from 1999, by 2004 Russo-Chinese bilateral trade surpassed the long-sought magical mark of $20 billion (Brooke 2004). On the strength of a few high-profile investment agreements, this figure was expected to increase by perhaps as much as another 35-40% in 2005 (Financial Times Information 2005), and officials on both sides of the border optimistically seek the figure to top US $60 billion in five years' time (Lomanov 2005). Crucially for advancing the cause of RFE-Northeast China economic integration, by the early 2000's the value of Chinese joint ventures with RFE firms surpassed that of Japan, South Korea, and the U.S. combined (Brooke 2004); China's aspirations to continue ramping up the amount of direct investment in the RFE now appear to be better attuned to Russian wishes that a greater proportion of this direct investment be raw material-transforming rather than merely raw material-extracting (Lomanov 2005). Despite lingering concerns about border demarcation, illegal immigration, and the smuggling of protected natural resources (Rozman 2004: 333-334), a fresh crop of provincial governors in the RFE now welcomed rather than shunned Russo-Chinese collaboration to modernize and expand cross-border infrastructure, with public sector actors on both sides of the border plowing tens of millions of dollars into inter-connected road, rail, and other commercial freight investment projects (Brooke 2004; Rozman 2004: 333). Nonetheless, it is too early to conclude that the RFE is destined to become a priority supplier of natural resources and/or intermediate goods to an energy-hungry and biomass-poor

China, or a transportation depot for the export of Chinese goods to Pacific Rim and European markets, as some Western journalists have prematurely suggested (Brooke 2004). Teeming trade and investment links between the RFE and Northeast China may illustrate that RFE political elites' current approach to regional economic integration at long last mirrors Moscow's embrace of "strategic partnership" with China. But from the Kremlin's point of view, its restored bond with Beijing has never been about letting Chinese industrial accumulators have privileged access to the RFE's mineral and vegetable wealth or its commercial freight infrastructure (Lomanov 2005), as the following case-studies will reaffirm.

Sino-Japanese competition over East Siberian oil

As of April 2003, Japan was the world's second largest importer of oil (Blagov 2003). Over the course of the preceding ten years, Japanese users of imported oil had become more and more reliant on suppliers specifically from the Persian Gulf. In 1991, Japan imported 70 percent of its oil from the Middle East; by 2003, this figure had reached about 86 percent (Brooke 2003). In January 2004, the International Energy Agency (IEA) announced that in 2003 China passed Japan to become the second-largest crude oil-consuming economy on the planet, its ravenous appetite driven by its booming industrial export sector (Bahree 2004) and the hothouse "automobilization" of its urban transport rolling stock (Luft and Korin 2004). Moreover, by 2005 about one-half of China's teeming demand for crude oil was sourced abroad (Klare 2005), with dramatically rising import dependence forecast decade-on-decade into the future (Bryce 2005; Klare 2005). During 2003 the rate of China's oil import growth was 31% (Mallet 2004) and astonishingly that rate shot up to 35% in 2004. Extrapolating from current trends, by 2010 Persian Gulf states should supply more than three-quarters of China's crude oil imports (New York Times 2000).

Yet because of several interrelated factors, neither China nor Japan may come to rely so disproportionately upon the Persian Gulf as their chief source of imported oil to the extent these projections and trends suggest. For years most OPEC states have deliberately overstated the volume of their proven oil reserves in order to be allotted higher production quotas (Heinberg 2003: 94; Maass 2005). Ghawar, the mega-field that girds more than half of Saudi Arabia's total oil output, is suffering from unexpected intensification of saltwater intrusion and showing surprisingly early signs of irrevocable exhaustion (Gerth 2004; Maass 2005). In any event, ongoing and possibly cascading unrest in the region might limit just how much of these reserves can be safely pumped to the surface and released to the world market. For example, the deeply unpopular presence of the US in Iraq has unleashed a new torrent of radical Islamist terrorism directed against the personnel and property of Western oil transnationals active in Saudi Arabia (Bryce 2005; Mathiason and Townsend 2004), just as Saudi Arabia requires heightened levels of transnational collaboration and investment to keep up with surging global demand for its oil exports (Klare 2004). Not only would shortfalls or disruptions in Persian Gulf oil output result from such geophysical and socio-political constraints, but the world market price for oil would also be kicked up to such a level that it would become profitable to explore and develop oil fields in remote and inhospitable locales in eastern Siberia and the Russian Far East (Filippov 2004).[2] Given that China and Japan are the closest large markets to presently untapped oil deposits in eastern Siberia and the Russian Far East, it is hardly far-fetched to speculate that the current drift of revelations and events in the Persian Gulf will soon compel China and Japan to replace a sizable share of its expected Middle East oil imports with imports from Russia (Bremmer and Clark 2003).

For their part, Russian state energy planners intend to augment Russia's crude oil output, almost all of it for export, by some 1.5 million barrels per day by the end of the decade (Helmer 2003b). A pivotal element of this plan is the cultivation of new clients in the Asia-Pacific region, not in the least because the Kremlin is concerned that the eastward expansion of NATO has created a belt of US satellites lodged between Russia and its Central and Western European petroleum customers (Kandiyoti 2005). According to the Kremlin's scheme for energy sector development, the so-called "Main Provisions of the Russian Energy Strategy to 2020" adopted in late May 2003, by 2020 Russian crude oil exports to the Asia-Pacific region could well constitute one-third of Russia's total petroleum exports, topping 2 billion barrels per year (Ivanov 2003). The recent inflammation of territorial disputes between China and Japan over potentially oil-rich rocky atolls in the East China Sea suggests that Sino-Japanese competition to secure petroleum supplies pumped in and exported from Russia will be fierce (Bajpaee 2005; Mortished 2005).

At a summit in late May 2003, Russian President Putin and Chinese President Hu signed a document declaring Russo-Chinese energy cooperation, with Russia playing the role of trusted oil and natural gas supplier and China the role of preferred customer, to be a top priority in the bilateral relationship between the two Asian giants (Page 2003). An agreement of portentous import for world energy markets and both global and Northeast Asian geopolitics, it raised the possibility that in coming years Russia would deliver hydrocarbon energy inputs to China on favorable terms while the international oil market was thrust into inflationary disarray by interruptions in the flow of low-cost oil from the Persian Gulf (Lavelle 2004). It also seemed to reinforce and add substance to the Russo-Chinese "strategic partnership."

Putin and Hu's declaration ostensibly gave official blessing to an endeavor long in the works between Russian private capitalist oil extractors and Chinese state enterprise oil refiners. The summit provided a stage for Russia's Yukos (Corporation) and China's National Petroleum Company (CNPC) to finalize a preliminary agreement several years in the making (Oil and Gas Journal 2000). The deal stipulated that beginning in 2005 and continuing until roughly 2030, Yukos would ship a grand total of about 5 billion barrels of oil to CNPC facilities in northeastern China (Isachenkov 2003). The oil would be transported in a yet to be built 2400-km pipeline connecting Angarsk in eastern Siberia to the petroleum complex of Daqing in China's northeasternmost province, Heilongjiang. Russia's public sector oil pipeline monopoly, Transneft, would put up the money to cover the construction cost of the Russian leg of the pipeline (roughly US $6-7 billion) and would also retain ownership rights over said portion (Helmer 2003b).

In fact, rather than effectively christening the Angarsk-Daqing pipeline, the high-profile protocol merely marked one of many twists and turns in the still unresolved drama of growing Sino-Japanese competition for the potentially bounteous but largely undeveloped hydrocarbon energy resources of eastern Siberia and the RFE. After a year-and-a-half of calculated stalling, the Kremlin proclaimed on the final day of 2004 that in lieu of approving the Angarsk-Daqing pipeline, it had given the green light to a rival proposal: a significantly longer (4130 km) and significantly more expensive (between US $11 and $16.2 billion) pipeline running from Taishet (more than 1000 km northwest of Angarsk) to Perevoznaya Bay, near Vladivostok on Russia's Sea of Japan coast (Blagov 2005b, 2004b; Kandiyoti 2005). Consistent with this scheme, supertankers docking at bulk depots would ferry oil to multiple Pacific Rim clients, especially but not exclusively Japan, who would pay spot market prices for the offtake. Despite its avowed commitment to energy cooperation with China, the Kremlin found opting for a Sea of Japan rather than a Daqing terminus irresistible for a variety of reasons. An offer made by a Japanese state development bank to back the expense of this very costly pipeline extending all the way to the Sea of Japan with up to US $14 billion in soft loans, or up to 80% of construction costs, was a necessary if not sufficient part of the equation (Blagov 2005b, 2004b; Brooke 2005, 2003). Equally crucial was Japan's eventual willingness to spend an additional US $2 billion underwriting oilfield discovery and development efforts in eastern Siberia's Irkutsk and Yakutsk basins (Al Madani 2005; Wonacott et. al. 2003). This gesture was indispensable because the Kremlin, on the basis of reputable geological surveys, fundamentally believed that without new petroleum exploration and recovery efforts, not enough proven and readily exploitable crude oil existed in eastern Siberia to warrant a pipeline to the Sea of Japan rather than a cheaper and hence less risky one to Northeast China (Helmer 2005a, 2005b; Jubak 2005; Kandiyoti 2005). Another critical factor was Japan's decision to retract its initial demand that all oil sent through the pipeline be exclusively shipped to Japan until the soft loans it extended Russia were fully serviced (Helmer 2003c), thus preserving what from the standpoint of the Kremlin was one of the most appealing aspects of a pipeline to the Sea of Japan: it would permit Russian crude oil producers to access a diverse array of purchasers, allocating output to each in accordance with shifting market conditions, rather than a single purchaser (the CNPC) paying a predetermined and thus conceivably sub-optimal price. Finally, a less recognized but surely significant dynamic compelling the Kremlin to announce its support for the Taishet-Perevoznaya Bay pipeline was the steadily increasing world market price of oil, with no end in sight, as the gamesmanship between Russia, China, and Japan unfolded throughout 2003 and 2004. With the price of oil progressively mounting relative to the cost of building a 4130-km pipeline across challenging terrain, the Kremlin's fears that the east Siberian oil fields do not and will not yield enough recoverable oil to operate at full capacity a pipeline all the way to the Sea of Japan became less paramount. What is more, with the balance of power in the global oil market once again resting more in the hands of sellers than buyers, being able to sell east Siberian oil to a range of purchasers at spot prices rather than a single purchaser at a negotiated price became all the more appealing to the Energy Ministry and other relevant players in Russia.

Russia's apparent retreat from approving the pipeline to Daqing was not driven by a combination of Japanese haggling and shifting conditions in the international political economy of oil alone. Another source of this apparent retreat was the Kremlin's growing determination to alter the course of Russia's approach to economic development. Russia's boom of the last few years has been thinly predicated upon rising world market prices for its raw material exports, particularly its hydrocarbon exports, but no meaningful revival of its productive capital stock, much less its social infrastructure, has taken place during this time (Cohen 2003; Anderson 2007). Throughout 2003 state officials and policy intellectuals associated with Putin's circle made increasingly bold pronouncements about the necessity of taxing windfall natural resource export rents so that these rents would be reinvested in Russia's industrial renewal rather than parked in the offshore wealth havens of the oligarchs (Cohen 2003; Anderson 2007). Sensing that the salad days of robber baron rentier capitalism were coming to an end, some of Russia's oligarchs began transferring their inflated shareholdings in raw material conglomerates to foreign investors (Cohen 2003). Forced to defend its new accumulation model before it ever got off the ground, for both symbolic and substantive purposes the Kremlin chose Yukos' principal shareholder, Mikhail Khodorkovsky, as its first target, arresting him in October 2003 on charges of tax evasion, embezzlement, and fraud (Cohen 2003). With the institutional stability of Yukos, the putative supplier of oil in the Angarsk-Daqing pipeline project, thus thrown into doubt, so too was the prospective future of a pipeline directly linking eastern Siberia and northeastern China. The uncertainty surrounding Yukos and an oil pipeline terminating in Daqing bought Japan the time it needed to raise the stakes with its offers to help fund east Siberian petroleum field discovery and development and to allow the offtake from a Sea of Japan pipeline to be exported to any and all Asian-Pacific clients.

To unseasoned observers, Russia's momentary reversal on the initial Yukos-CNPC proposal might have signaled the scotching of acclaimed Russo-Chinese energy cooperation and perhaps even the fatal weakening of the Russo-Chinese "strategic partnership." Any such rush to judgment turned out to be hasty. First, as a sort of consolation prize for denying China the trunk of the pipeline departing from Angarsk, Putin endorsed the plans of Russia's state-owned railway to double oil shipments to China within one year and to try to boost the volume of oil delivery to China to 300,000 barrels per day/15 million tons per year by 2006 (Blagov 2005b, 2004b; Lomanov 2005; Kandiyoti 2005). These were not idle promises: close to 10 million tons of oil passed by rail from Russia to China in 2005 (Romanenkova 2005). Second, Russia's Energy Ministry publicly encouraged CNPC to buy a 20% stake in Rosneft, the Russian state-owned company that had taken over the hydrocarbon extraction assets of a unit Yukos was forced to auction to reduce its back-tax bill (Blagov 2005b, 2005c; The Russian Oil and Gas Report 2005a). Putin himself held out the possibility that CNPC might be permitted to directly manage some portion of those assets as well (Blagov 2005b). It later came to light that in fact through an intermediary, banks affiliated with CNPC had fronted Rosneft US $6 billion to support its acquisition of Yukos' oil production division, with the implicit understanding that down the road Rosneft would enter into a long-term supply contract with CNPC (Blagov 2005c; The Economist 2005).

Then, four short months later, the Russian Energy Ministry disclosed its blueprint for the inaugural stage of the east Siberian pipeline's construction. According to the blueprint, the first segment of the pipeline would indeed begin in Taishet, but rather than spanning all the way to the Sea of Japan, it would terminate about halfway to Perevoznaya Bay in the Russian hamlet of Skovorodino, a scant 69km north of the Chinese border and conveniently connectible to Daqing by railway spur (The Economist 2005; Helmer 2005a). Moreover, Kremlin and Transneft officials cast doubt on the fate of the second stage of the pipeline, overtly suggesting that its very viability depends on the presently unknown volume of oil reserves to be developed in eastern Siberia and future trends in the world market price of petroleum (Kyodo News Service

2005; The Moscow Times 2005; The Russian Oil and Gas Report 2005b). More provocatively yet, they also clearly intimated that if the second segment were eventually proven feasible, ground on the project would probably not be broken until 2012 and its ultimate destination would be determined by geopolitical factors (i.e., the evolving status of Russo-Chinese and Russo-Japanese relations, respectively) rather than purely economic criteria (Prime-Tass Business News Agency 2005; Zubkov 2004). The shoe really dropped at the annual G8 summit in July 2005, when Putin diplomatically but unequivocally indicated that once the east Siberian pipeline is completed to Skovorodino in three years' time, 20 million tons of crude oil per annum will be forwarded by rail to northeast China, while only half that amount will be shipped to an upgraded bulk liquid depot in or near the RFE city of Nakhodka on the Sea of Japan (Helmer 2005b). October 2005 news reports suggested that the Putin Administration and Rosneft alike were urging Transneft, which had already successfully arranged US $6.6 billion of project financing through international bond and credit markets, to immediately begin extending the east Siberian pipeline to Skovorodino without further bureaucratic delay (The Russian Oil and Gas Report 2005c).

A host of cross-cutting factors edged the Kremlin away from its short-lived approval of a pipeline all the way to the Sea of Japan, and to hedge its bets and authorize the building of the first (and perhaps the only) pipeline segment no further than Skovorodino. During early 2005 meetings to determine exact financing commitments, Japanese negotiators tried to make the amount of soft loans on offer contingent on Russia fulfilling the demand that all four Kuril Islands be transferred from Russian to Japanese sovereignty (Blagov 2005c). Not only was such a proposal entirely unacceptable to Moscow, but Japan's brazen attempt to use a favorable resolution of the territorial dispute as a bargaining chip also engendered the suspicion of the Russian negotiating team. Energy Ministry officials, formerly among the most enthusiastic Russian advocates of a Sea of Japan pipeline, questioned whether Japan would abide by its generous financing terms (Al Madani 2005)–terms that had to be retained in order for such a long pipeline with such monumental upfront costs to be commercially feasible. The resulting atmosphere of dissension gave Transneft officials, long partisans of extending a pipeline to or near China, the opportunity to repeat a favorite cautionary message, this time with extra punch: that eastern Siberia does not now nor will it for the short-run future feature readily exploitable oil deposits ample enough to warrant massive expenditure on a pipeline all the way to the Sea of Japan, regardless of the generosity or the stinginess of Japan's soft loan offer (Helmer 2005a, 2005b; Jubak 2005; Kandiyoti 2005). But, Transneft officials contended, private sector lenders girdling the globe would be more than happy to underwrite the construction of a shorter pipeline to

Skovorodino, a claim verified by investment bank analysts in London and elsewhere (Gorst 2005; Nicholson 2005). Moreover, as the pecuniary rationales for the Energy Ministry to restrict the routing of the pipeline to Skovorodino became more evident, the Kremlin was becoming increasingly troubled by the shape of the reconstituted US-Japan security alliance. Accommodating the most alarming trends in Japanese neo-nationalism, but at the ultimate service of US imperial ambition, the reconstituted alliance more and more seemed to be aimed at the "emerging big powers" of continental Asia, primarily China but also Putin's Russia, limiting their room for maneuver in the global system (Auerback 2005, Engdahl 2005a, 2005b)–including limiting their leverage over the basis upon which they engage with the commodity, money, and productive circuits of the capitalist world market. Cementing Russo-Chinese energy cooperation and "strategic partnership" by spurning the Sea of Japan pipeline availed itself as a necessary response to these shifting circumstances.

However, even had the Kremlin stuck with its temporary choice of a Sea of Japan pipeline, this would not necessarily have signified a terrible setback for the wider pattern of maturing Russo-Chinese "strategic partnership." In fact, a bundle of interactive causes-and-effects could very well further enhance the Russo-Chinese "strategic partnership." This bundle of prospective causes-and-effects is best understood in relation to two powerful trends already in motion: 1) the enormous and still widening US current account deficit, and the likelihood of the dollar's continued fall in global foreign exchange markets, and 2) the decreasing ability of the US to ensure the stable flow of cheap Persian Gulf oil to the world market, given its irreparable failure to engineer a stable political order in post-Saddam Iraq. Despite the voluminous hydrocarbon export revenues Russia has enjoyed, the fall of the dollar is cutting more and more deeply into Russia's terms of international trade, because the lion's share of its dollar-denominated oil exports are effectively exchanged for European and (to a lesser degree) Japanese manufactured goods (Rifkin 2004). The dollar's fall may thus force the Kremlin to exercise an option about which Putin has publicly mused: accepting euros rather than dollars as the preferred means of payment for Russia's sale of oil on the world market (Hoyos et. al. 2003). If it comes to pass that China relies less than currently forecast on the Persian Gulf and more on Russia to meet its soaring oil consumption needs, and if China will need a large stash of euros at its disposal to source its increased quotient of Russian oil, then China's central bank would be prompted to accelerate the repositioning of its currency reserves from dollar-denominated to euro-denominated liquid assets. Were this to happen, it would be a crippling blow to US financial-monetary primacy–including the ability of the US to parlay its seigniorage privilege into virtually free primary energy imports–and a striking triumph for the multipolar world order that is the stated aim of the Russo-Chinese "strategic partnership."

Russo-Chinese conflict over ownership and use of southern Primorskii bulk ports

While attending the meeting of a Russo-Chinese economic cooperation working group in April 2003, the Chinese representatives made a controversial, even inflammatory, request. On behalf of Northeast Chinese steam coal exporters, the representatives asked the Russian Ministry of Transport to consider granting a Chinese parastatal agency 49-year leases at the bulk ports of Posyet and Zarubino, abutting the Northeast China border in the far southeastern tentacle of the RFE (Helmer 2003a). The representatives explained that coal export terminals were not being sufficiently upgraded or expanded under current management at either port, both of which are the most convenient sea-land depots between the mines of Northeast China's Tumangan district and thermal coal clients in Japan and South Korea (Helmer 2003a). If the Chinese government were awarded very long-term licenses to operate the two ports in southern Primsorkii Krai, it would ensure that more commodity tonnage would pass through them than at present, the representatives contended (People's Daily Online 2003). Surely neither the Russian central government nor the Primorskii Krai provincial government could summarily dismiss such an opportunity, especially insofar as both entities had recently indicated publicly their commitment to increasing Chinese trade (imports as well as exports) through RFE ports (People's Daily Online 2003). Yet although the Russian Ministry of Transport did not immediately reject the Chinese proposal, and although it expressed support for Chinese export cargo moving through Russian ports, it categorically stated that it opposed the notion of transferring "ownership" of port licenses to the Chinese government (Helmer 2003a). After some delay, the Russian Ministry of Transport's official decision to refuse the proposal was announced in March 2004, its logic seconded by the Transportation Department of Primorskii Krai (Helmer 2004).

At the time the Chinese interests broached the idea of the 49-year leases, Russian capitalist conglomerates held controlling shares in both the ports of Posyet and Zarubino. The port of Posyet was mostly in the hands of a Moscow-based corporation known as Moskovsky Delovoi Mir (MDM) Group, which directed its subsidiaries to acquire a dominant majority stake in 2000 (EastWest Institute 2002). Although when it acquired the port of Posyet the MDM Group vowed to modernize and enlarge its bulk facilities, to the degree that any new cargo moved through Posyet's gates under the watch of MDM, it was Japan-bound coal from mines also part of the MDM Group's horizontally-integrated empire (Helmer 2004). Quite obviously, the MDM Group had taken over the license to operate the port of Posyet in order to support its other raw material-exporting concerns, especially its Siberian and trans-Baikal coalmines, rather than to boost the port's net throughput. Its spokespersons plainly admitted as much when they voiced their hostility to accepting shipments of exported Northeast Chinese coal, much less the Chinese government's scheme to obtain long-term leases at the bulk ports of southern Primorskii Krai (Helmer 2003a). It should be entirely evident why the MDM Group, a classic post-Soviet oligopoly in the sense that its oligarchic investors sought to reap super-profits by claiming strategic physical assets and using their management of these assets to subdue or lock out rivals, was stridently against the Chinese government's port takeover proposal and lobbied furiously against it. But why did the Primorskii Krai provincial and Russian central governments also line up against the proposal, especially considering that a) both entities had upped their verbal and material support for improving linkages between southern Primorskii Krai ports and their Northeast China hinterland, b) the MDM Group's approach to managing the port of Posyet was emblematic of the oligarchic capitalism that Putin's government has attacked with increasing aggression from 2003 or so forward, and c) the Russian license-holders at the port of Zarubino were apparently eager to transfer their shares to proxies of the Northeast Chinese thermal coal exporters Helmer 2004)?

There is indeed little doubt that both Vladivostok (the seat of Primorskii Krai provincial government) and Moscow are solidly behind enhancing physical infrastructure connections between Primorskii Krai's Sea of Japan littoral and a Northeast China that is not far inland at all, as evidenced by the RFE spending still scarce public funds on the paving of cross-border roads (including one terminating near Posyet and Zarubino), and the Kremlin urging it to do so (People's Daily Online 2003). It also seems that there is little love lost between the MDM Group and the Putin administration, which as of March 2004 appeared to be pressuring MDM to liquidate various parts of its empire, including its license holdings in the port of Posyet (Helmer 2004).[3] Moscow's antipathy toward the Chinese government obtaining exclusive long-term leases at the ports of Posyet and Zarubino is not rooted in resistance to increasing cross-border economic integration, or in capitulation of the administrative apparatus to oligarchic capitalism, but in the Kremlin's general determination to recover leverage over national development policy it lost in the 1990's. While Moscow would welcome Russian and Chinese investors jointly collaborating to upgrade and expand RFE bulk ports, making it possible for Northeast Chinese steam coal exporters to reach their favored Japanese and South Korean markets in the quickest and cheapest manner, it does not welcome a Chinese parastatal agency effectively getting long-term operational control over those ports, encroaching upon the Russian central government's capacity to administer trade according to its own developmentalist prerogatives.

Potential Russo-Chinese tension over Chinese peasant migration into the RFE

When it joined the WTO in January 2002, China thrust an uncertain fate upon its estimated 600 million peasants–notably those who grow cotton, grains, livestock feed, and soybeans, and faced the prospect of being swamped by cheap agricultural commodities imported from capital- and energy-intensive producers of the Western Hemisphere (Fang 2000). Chinese Communist Party (CCP) officials, multilateral bank technocrats, and neo-liberal economists muffled the cries of alarm that a massive, rapid, and destabilizing rural-to-urban exodus of displaced peasants was in the making. They claimed that to the extent that land- and machinery-poor Chinese peasants were actually menaced by the prospect of cheap agricultural commodity imports, the cold bath of the international market would force these peasants to switch their crop mixes toward labor-intensive horticulture, in which China is globally competitive under the new regime (Lin 2000). Critical political economists inside and outside of China contended that the neo-Ricardians were whistling past the graveyard. They countered by drawing attention to an inexorable long-term trend: since World War II, in the core countries, the relative cost of producing agricultural commodities has unceasingly plummeted; outside the metropolitan centers, it has stayed flat (Amin 2003). This dynamic and ongoing pattern augurs badly for China's cotton, grain, livestock feed, and soybean growers now subjected to the global law of value. Surely the advocates of China joining the WTO underestimated the degree to which it will uproot land- and machinery-poor peasants from agricultural employment, perhaps doubling the uncertain number (150 million?) of "permanently floating" Chinese (Forney 2002; Schaffer 2003).

Proponents of China's WTO entry forecast a rosy future for the soybean farmers of Northeast China's Heilongjiang Province. Despite the fact that the terms of China's WTO entry radically slashed tariffs on imported soybeans, the WTO boosters insisted that Heilongjiang's soybean farmers would meet the challenge for two reasons: a) studies showed that China's soybean production costs were slightly below world market prices, and b) Heilongjiang's relatively low population density would allow for productivity-enhancing enlargement of acreage/soybean farmer and machinery/soybean farmer ratios without triggering catastrophic rural-to-urban migration streams (Mead 2001). But the serious danger WTO accession poses was validated by actions taken in 2003 by Chinese state bureaucrats to temporarily shelter the welfare of soybean farmers and thus to stave off the social instability that would otherwise result. Risking the elevation of already burgeoning trade conflict with the US, Chinese government agencies erected administrative roadblocks to the entry of imported soybeans, generating charges of non-compliance with WTO stipulations (Goodman 2003). Because the majority of Heilongjiang's industrial assets remain in the antiquated SOE sector, with further factory privatizations, downsizings, and closures expected per the requirements of China's WTO entry (Cheng 2005; The Straits Times 2003), most displaced soybean farmers confront dim hopes of ever being absorbed into urban industrial labor markets unless they are willing to migrate long distances to Chinese cities, provinces, and regions where they possess no rights of residency.

Even then, although China continues to boast torrid rates of fixed investment in industrial plant and equipment, the increasingly capital-intensive nature of this investment (especially that directly or indirectly marshaled by transnational corporations of the core countries) has actually yielded a net loss in the size of China's urban industrial labor force over the last half-decade or so (Lague 2003). Owing to China's WTO accession, among other factors, neither small- or medium-sized light industrial cooperatives (TVE's) in the countryside nor big-sized heavy industrial state-owned enterprises (SOE's) in the cities are up to the task of soaking up the labor-power of former peasants displaced from the land by cheap agricultural commodity imports (Chandrasekhar 2002). One potential migration frontier for Heilongjiang's displaced soybean farmers is fertile yet uncultivated territory to the north in the border zones of the Russian Far East (RFE) (Daniszewski 2001). When the Heilongjiang-RFE border was virtually uncontrolled in the years immediately following the Soviet collapse, anti-Chinese political demagoguery was sky high in the RFE. The border is much more controlled now, but the looming plight of Heilongjiang's soybean farmers augurs a repeat of the rampant anti-Chinese xenophobia of the early-to-mid-1990's, posing the possibility that progress toward cross-border economic integration will be set back, and even that the Russo-Chinese "strategic partnership" will be soured.

Conclusions

A global political-economic order that does not in the final instance pivot around China exporting labor-intensive consumer goods to the world market and investing the proceeds in US government bonds—or, to put it less gingerly, around the super-exploitation of China's export sector working class in support of prolonging US hegemony—is already assuming embryonic form on a host of Russian, Chinese, and Russo-Chinese fronts. Recognizing that China's growth model is too dependent on external demand in general and demand from the enormously debt-leveraged US in particular, the Chinese Communist Party (CPC) vowed at its 2004 national legislative session to redirect China's accumulation regime toward raising peasant and rural incomes and meeting neglected internal social needs (Xinhuanet 2004). Part and parcel of this new tack is an evolving recognition of Brundtland Commission principles by the CPC's technocratic-scientific elite, i.e. the notion that China's continuing industrial growth is in jeopardy unless a larger share of the total social output is devoted to radically improving the energy efficiency of the means of value production and circulation (as well as to the restoration of damaged ecosystems and the protection of imperiled ones) (Landler 2004). Radically curtailing its energy consumption-GDP ratio, and reining in its runaway energy expenditures, is not only what China must do to assure future improvements in popular welfare, but also to afford the undeniably more expensive hydrocarbon fuels and feedstock Russia will be increasingly selling it in the future. And by no means does a China more attentive to radically improving its energy conversion rate interfere with the artfully conceived ambition of Putin's Kremlin to displace Saudi Arabia as the world oil market's "swing producer" and to use its state powers of coercion, persuasion, regulation, and taxation to ensure that rising petroleum monopoly rents are cycled into domestic poverty reduction efforts. On the contrary–both China's newfound sensitivity to sustainable development and Russia's concerted drive toward broad-based economic revitalization presuppose and are bolstered by the "end of cheap oil," an era that is arriving with full force (see footnote two). In other words, by conscious scheming and by dint of circumstance, China's and Russia's preferred development strategies are coming to complement one another, as evidenced by escalating bilateral trade figures and follow-through on a hodgepodge of individually small but collectively big infrastructure integration projects in the northeast China Russian Far East border zone (Brooke 2004).

What is most interesting about the socio-ecological division of labor that may be arising between Russia and China is that it calls into question the perspective insisting that interdependency between non-renewable natural resource exporters and states and regions that industrially transform these resources is necessarily exploitative (economically and environmentally) of the former (for one example of such a view, see Bunker 1984). The unparalleled use-value of oil as a natural resource, and the peculiar geo-historical context in which incipient Russo-Chinese energy cooperation is coming into being, confounds this perspective. However devoted China's leaders and cadres may be to markedly improving China's energy efficiency performance and eventually transitioning China to renewable sources of primary energy, the many indispensable qualities oil possesses as a feedstock and a fuel–including its unmatched capability to sponsor innovations in energy-efficient and renewable energy technologies—ensure that China will not be able to readily substitute its way out of growing reliance on east Siberian oil. Given the irrefutable fact that the world market price of petroleum will only escalate in the medium- and long-range future, it strains credulity to argue that as China's priority supplier of oil, Russia will be getting the short end of the stick in Russo-Chinese energy cooperation arrangements. When one factors in the observation that the Kremlin has pulled off a nearly impossible balancing act with startling success—i.e. outflanking the petroleum oligarchs while simultaneously burnishing Russia's profile as a credible marketer of primary energy to the world (Lavelle 2004)—the conclusion that Russia will not succumb to the "Dutch disease" (Lynn 2001: 10-11) seems more and more probable.

Notes

[1] It was not unusual for corrupt provincial administrations to demagogically court electoral favor by denouncing Moscow for selling the RFE out to the "Chinese threat" while collecting bribes and other forms of payment from illegal Chinese petty merchandisers and small-time investors at the same time. Nor was it unusual for opportunistic regional politicians to make secessionist noises on the grounds that Moscow was doing little to protect the RFE from the "yellow peril," and then cynically accept federal subsidies on the condition that they muffle their threats. See Kiselyov 1996; Wishnick 2001: 160.

[2] Whether the world market price of oil will ever again temporarily settle below pre-2004 levels is nearly impossible to predict. There is, however, a gathering consensus among petroleum geologists, energy economists, and other oil industry observers that neither enough spare capacity nor enough commercially recoverable conventional petroleum exists on a global scale to return the price to the level of the 1986-1999 period. Even putting the more apocalyptic "peak oil" prognosticators aside, in 2005 a growing chorus of reputable experts concur that total conventional petroleum output from the non-OPEC nations will probably plateau and then decline sometime around 2010, and that the same type of output from non-OPEC nations will flatten out and then fall sometime around 2015, or 2020 at the very latest (Bryce 2005; Cavallo 2005; Maxwell 2004). Perhaps the most telling figures are these: in a world where the ratio of new barrels of oil discovered to old barrels of oil consumed has plunged to 1:6, by 2010 a breathtaking 50 percent of projected world oil consumption will have to be met by reservoirs that are untapped as of yet (Naparstek 2004; Gerth 2004). Given the gravity of the looming situation it is easy to envision the world market price of oil escalating to such heights that it becomes profitable to bring onstream currently unexploited oil deposits in distant Russian Far East and eastern Siberia—that is, unless the escalating cost of primary energy resources throttles world accumulation to such an extent that neither enough investment capital can be mobilized to explore and develop these remote fields as well as build the very long pipelines transporting extracted oil from these fields to centers of processing and consumption, nor enough effective demand exists to induce the mobilization of such expensive up-front investments.

[3] The same cannot necessarily be said about relations between the MDM Group and Primorskii Krai elected officials, however. Some journalists have commented on a pattern of increasing penetration of the Primorskii Krai economy by Moscow-based oligarchic capitalists once regional leadership change was effected in the late 1990's and early 2000's.

References

Achcar, Gilbert. 2000. "The Strategic Triad: USA, China, Russia." In *Masters of the Universe*, edited by Ali, Tariq. London: Verso.
Al Madani, Abdullah. 2005. "The battle for Siberian oil." *Gulf News*, October 30.
Amin, Samir. 2003. "World Poverty, Pauperization & Capital Accumulation." *Monthly Review*, October 2003.
Anderson, Perry. 2002. "Force and Consent." *New Left Review* 17: 5-30.
Anderson, Perry. 2007. "Russia's Managed Democracy." *London Review of Books* 29 (2). http://www.lrb.co.uk/v29/n02/ande01_.html.
Arrighi, Giovanni. 1994. *The Long Twentieth Century*. London: Verso.
Arrighi, Giovanni. 2005a. "Hegemony Unravelling–I." *New Left Review* 32: 23-80.
Arrighi, Giovanni. 2005b. "Hegemony Unravelling–II." *New Left Review* 33: 1-34.
Auerback, Marshall. 2005. "What Could Go Wrong in 2005?" http://www.tomdispatch.com/index.mhtml?pid=2141.
Bahree, Bhushan. 2004. "Chinese Oil Demand Puzzles Market." *Wall Street Journal*, May 14.
Bajpaee, Chietegj. 2005. "China fuels energy cold war." *Asia Times*, March 2.
Blagov, Sergei. 2005a. "China knocking on Russia's door." Asia Times Online, July 6. http://www.atimes.com/atimes/China/GG06Ad02.html.
Blagov, Sergei. 2005b. "Russia walks thin line between Japan and China." Asia Times Online, January 11. http://www.atimes.com/atimes/Central_Asia/GA05Ag01.html.
Blagov, Sergei. 2005c. "Russia's hydrocarbon geopolitics." Asia Times Online, February 3. http://www.atimes.com/atimes/Central_Asia/GB03Ag01.html.
Blagov, Sergei. 2004a. "Russia hails partnership with Beijing ... sort of." Asia Times Online, March 25. http://www.atimes.com/atimes/Central_Asia/FC25Ag01.html
Blagov, Sergei. 2004b. "Putin to expand strategic partnership with China." Asia Times Online, March 12. http://www.atimes.com/atimes/Central_Asia/FC12Ag01.html
Blagov, Sergei. 2003. "Russia eyes new oil markets in Asia-Pacific." Asia Times Online, April 2. http://www.atimes.com/atimes/Central_Asia/ED02Ag02.html
Bremmer, Ian and Bruce Clark. 2003. "The Other Great Game." *Moscow Times*, May 12.
Brooke, James. 2005. "Disputes at Every Turn of Siberia Pipeline." *New York Times*, January 21.
Brooke, James. 2004. "Russia Catches China Fever." *New York Times*, March 30. Section W; Page 1; Column 3.
Brooke, James. 2003. "Russia's latest oil and gas oasis." *New York Times*, May 13.
Bryce, Robert. 2005. "Running on Empty." Salon.com, March 15.
Bunker, Stephen. 1984. "Modes of Extraction, Unequal Exchange, and the Progressive Underdevelopment of an Extreme Periphery: The Brazilian Amazon, 1600-1980." *The American Journal of Sociology* 89 (5): 1017-1064.
Cavallo, Alfred. 2005. "Oil: Caveat empty." *Bulletin of the Atomic Scientists* 61 (3): 16-18.
Chandrasekhar, C.P. 2002. "A challenge in China." *Frontline* 19 (7).
Cheng, Eva. 2005. "China: Sweeping privatizations spark criticism." Green Left Weekly, March 16. http://www.greenleft.org.au/back/2005/619/619p20.htm.

Cohen, Stephen. 2003. "The struggle for Russia." *The Nation*, November 24.
Daniszewski, John. 2001. "Far East void eats at Russia." *Los Angeles Times*, July 19.
EastWest Institute. 2002. "Major Russian companies purchasing Primorskii Krai ports." Russian Regional Report 7 (23). www.isn.ethz.ch/researchpub/publihouse/rrr/docs/rrr020123.pdf.
The Economist. 2005. "King Solomon's Pipes; Russian Oil." May 7.
Engdahl, William. 2005. "Japan and China Tensions and Washington's Asia Geopolitics." Www.globalresearch.ca, April 2. http://globalresearch.ca/ articles/ENG504A.html
Engdahl, William. 2005. "Running into a 'BRIC' wall with Eurasia?" Current Concerns, February 11. http://www.currentconcerns.ch/archive/2005/01/20050102.php
Fang, Bay. 2000. "Growing troubles down on the farm." *U.S. News and World Report*, May 29.
Filippov, Yuri. 2004. "Russia to help cool down oil markets." *RIA Novosti*, June 7.
Financial Times Information. 2005. "China Daily: Sino-Russian Energy Links to Expand." *Global News Wire*, November 4.
Forney, Matt. 2002. "Workers' wasteland." Time Asia, November 1. http://www.time.com/time/asia/covers/1101020617/cover.html.
Frank, Andre Gunder. 1996. *ReOrient*. Berkeley, CA: University of California.
Gerth, Jeff. 2004. "Forecast of rising oil demand challenges tired Saudi fields." *New York Times*, February 24.
Goodman, Peter. 2003. "China Trade Policy's Ripple Effect." *Washington Post*, November 11.
Gorst, Isabel, and David Pilling. "Tokyo in threat to withdraw from $11 billion oil pipeline." *The Financial Times*, April 30.
Heinberg, Richard. 2003. *The Party's Over*. Gabriola Island, BC: New Society.
Helmer, John. 2005a. "China beats Japan in Russian pipeline race." Asia Times Online, April 29. http://www.atimes.com/atimes/Central_Asia/GD29Ag01.html.
Helmer, John. 2005b. "China to get first crack at Russian oil: Putin." Asia Times Online, July 16. http://www.atimes.com/atimes/China/GG16Ad01.html.
Helmer, John. 2004. "Russians reject Chinese bid for port." Asia Times Online, March 11. http://www.atimes.com/atimes/Central_Asia/FC11Ag01.html.
Helmer, John. 2003a. "China in surprise move on Russian ports." Asia Times Online, April 10. http://www.atimes.com/atimes/Central_Asia/ED10Ag01.html.
Helmer, John. 2003b. "Kremlin decides Russia pipeline on new terms." Asia Times Online, March 4. http://www.atimes.com/atimes/Central_Asia/EC04Ag01.html.
Hoyos, Carola, Christopher Swann, and Andrew Jack. 2003. "Putin's idea to price oil in euros may hurt dollar." *Financial Times*, October 9.
Isachenkov, Vladimir. 2003. "China, Russia issue multipolar world call." Associated Press wire service, May 28.
Ivanov, Vladimir. 2003. "Russia emerging as energy powerhouse." *Daily Yomiuri*, June 13.
Jubak, Jim. 2005. "From Russia, with love: $60 oil." *MSN Money*, April 26. http://moneycentral.msn.com/content/P113995.asp
Kandiyoti, Rafael. 2005. "Asia: In The Pipeline." *Le Monde Diplomatique*, May 1.
Kim, Won Bae, Burnham O. Campbell, Mark Valencia, and Lee Jay Cho. 1992. *Regional Economic Cooperation in Northeast Asia: Proceedings of the Vladivostok Conference*. Vladivostok: Northeast Asia Economic Forum.

Kiselyov, Stepan. 1996. "Nazdratenko: Power, Geopolitics in Far East." *The Current Digest of Post-Soviet Press*, XLVIII 40.
Klare, Michael. 2005. "Revving Up the China Threat." *The Nation*, October 13.
Klare, Michael. 2004. "US: Procuring the world's oil." Asia Times Online, April 27 http://www.atimes.com/atimes/Global_Economy/FD27Dj02.html.
Kotkin, Stephen and David Wolff (eds). 1995. *Rediscovering Russia in Asia: Siberia and the Russian Far East*. Armonk, NY: M.E. Sharpe.
Kyodo News Service. 2005. "Russia may stop building pipeline to Pacific if oil reserves low." *Japan Economic Newswire*, April 28.
Lague, David. 2003. "China public spending explodes." *Far Eastern Economic Review*, January 30.
Landler, Mark. 2004. "China Pledges To Increase Use of Alternative Energy Sources." *New York Times*, June 5.
Larin, Viktor (1995): "'Yellow Peril' Again?" in *Rediscovering Russia in Asia: Siberia and the Russian Far East*, edited by Kotkin, Stephen and David Wolff. Armonk, NY: M.E. Sharpe.
Lavelle, Peter. 2004. "Putin's oil cartel." United Press International Wire Service, June 2 http://www.untimely-thoughts.com/?art=591.
Lin, Justin Yifu. 2000. "China's Accession to WTO: Impacts on Agriculture and Financial Sector." China Center for Economic Research. Working Paper Series, No. E2000009, November 3.
Lomanov, Aleksandr. 2005. "Without Leaders and Led." *Vremya Novostei*, July 1.
Luft, Gal, and Anne Korin. 2004. "The Sino-Saudi connection." *Commentary* 117 (3).
Lukin, Alexander. 2001. "Russia and China: Friends or Rivals?" *Nezavisimaya Gazeta*, August 3.
Lynn, Nicholas (2001): "Resource-based Development: What Chance For the Russian Far East?" In *The Russian Far East and Pacific Asia: Unfulfilled Potential*, edited by Bradshaw, Michael. Richmond, UK: Curzon.
Maass, Peter. 2005. "The Breaking Point." New York Times, August 21. http://www.nytimes.com/2005/08/21/magazine/21OIL.html?pagewanted=print.
Maxwell, Charles T. 2004. "The Gathering Storm." *Barron's*, November 15.
Mallet, Victor. 2004. "China unable to quench thirst for oil." *Financial Times*, January 21.
Mathiason, Nick and Mark Townsend. 2004. "Saudi horror sparks fears of oil crisis." *The Observer*, May 30.
Mead, Robert. 2001. "Rural China following WTO admission." Draft paper prepared for presentation at the Western Economic Association Meetings, San Francisco, July 5-8, 2001.
Mikheyev, Vladimir. 1994. "Parts of Maritime Territory Have One Chinese Foreign Resident for Every Inhabitant." *Current Digest of Post-Soviet Press*, XVLI, 16.
Minakir, Pavel (1995): "The Russian Far East: From a Colonial to a Borderland Economy" in *Rediscovering Russia in Asia: Siberia and the Russian Far East*, edited by Kotkin, Stephen and David Wolff. Armonk, NY: M.E. Sharpe.
Mortished, Carl. 2005. "China begs fuel as Japan patrols 'oil-rich' islands." *The Times of London*, July 9.
The Moscow Times. 2005. "Tokyo Casts Pipeline Financing in Doubt." May 3.
Naparstek, Aaron. 2004. "The coming energy crunch." WWW.NYPRESS.COM, June 1.

The New York Times. 2000. "Fueling China's Growth." Editorial, December 24.
Ni, Xiaoquan. (2002): "China's Threat Perceptions and Policies Toward the Russian Far East." In *Russia's Far East: A Region at Risk*, edited by Thornton, Judith and Charles E. Ziegler. Seattle: University of Washington Press.
Nicholson, Alex. 2005. "Russian oil pipeline operator pledges that China and Japan will get adequate supplies." *Associated Press Newswire*, May 3.
Oil and Gas Journal. 2000. "Pipeline will move Siberian crude oil to China." June 12, p. 75.
Page, Jeremy. 2003. "Russia, China to step up oil cooperation." *Reuters wire service*, May 27.
People's Daily Online. 2003. "Russian Media Play up the Tune of China's Port-renting." April 28. http://english.peopledaily.com.cn/200304/28/ eng20030428_115951.shtml
Petras, James. 2005. "Statism or Free Markets? China Bashing and the Loss of US Competitiveness." *Counterpunch Online*, October 22-23. http://joun.leb.net/petras10222005.html
Prime-Tass Business News Agency. 2005. "Khristenko says Far East oil pipe may be launched in 7 years." *Prime-Tass English-language Business Newswire*, April 22.
Radyuhin, Vladimir. 2005. "Shifting balance in Central Asia." *The Hindu*, July 20. http://www.thehindu.com/2005/07/20/stories/2005072007771500.htm
Rifkin, Jeremy. 2004. "The perfect storm that's about to hit." *The Guardian*, March 24. http://www.guardian.co.uk/oil/story/0,11319,1176624,00.html
Romanenkova, V. 2005. "Fradkov Reports to Putin on His Talks in China." ITAR-TASS News Agency wire service. November 7.
Rozman, Gilbert. 2004. *Northeast Asia's Stunted Regionalism*. Cambridge, UK: Cambridge University Press.
Rozman, Gilbert (1995): "Spontaneity and Direction Along the Russo-Chinese Border" in *Rediscovering Russia in Asia: Siberia and the Russian Far East*, edited by Kotkin, Stephen and David Wolff. Armonk, NY: M.E. Sharpe.
The Russian Oil and Gas Report. 2005a. "Ministry of Industry and Energy Khristenko on Results and Prospects." January 26.
The Russian Oil and Gas Report. 2005b. "Minister of Industry and Energy Victor Khristenko Signed an Order on Construction of the First Part of the Oil Pipeline from Eastern Siberia to Pacific Ocean." April 29.
The Russian Oil and Gas Report. 2005c. "President Putin Issued Instructions on Acceleration of Construction of the Eastern Oil Pipeline." October 26.
Schaffer, Harwood. 2003. "China and Free Trade: 145 Million Job Seekers." Unpublished manuscript. Agricultural Policy Analysis Center, University of Tennessee, Knoxville.
Skosyrev, Vladimir. 1994. "Chinese 'Shuttles' Have Difficulty Obtaining Russian Visas." *The Current Digest of Post-Soviet Press*. XVLI, 16.
The Straits Times. 2003. "Chinese province grapples with high jobless rate." February 6.
Tayler, Jeffrey. 2001. "'Street of Russian goods welcome'". *The Atlantic Monthly*, April 2001.
Thornton, Judith and Ziegler, Charles E. (2002): "The Russian Far East in Perspective" in *Russia's Far East: A Region at Risk*, edited by Thornton, Judith and Charles E. Ziegler. Seattle: University of Washington Press.

Wishnick, Elizabeth. 2002. "The Regional Dynamic in Russia's Asia Policy in the 1990's," in *Russia's Far East: A Region at Risk*, edited by Thornton, Judith and Charles E. Ziegler. Seattle: University of Washington Press.

Wishnick, Elizabeth. 2001. *Mending Fences.* Seattle: University of Washington Press.

Wishnick, Elizabeth. 1995. "Whose Environment? A Case Study of Forestry Policy in Russia's Maritime Province" in *Rediscovering Russia in Asia: Siberia and the Russian Far East*, edited by Kotkin, Stephen and David Wolff. Armonk, NY: M.E. Sharpe.

Wonacott, Peter, Jeane Whalen, and Bushee Bahree. 2003. "China's growing thirst for oil remakes world market." *Wall Street Journal*, December 3.

Valencia, Mark (ed.). 1995. *The Russian Far East in Transition*. Boulder, CO: Westview.

Vinogradov, Zakhar. 1996. "NG Makes Nazdratenko's Case Against Border Cession to China." *The Current Digest of Post-Soviet Press*, XLVIII, 40.

Xinhuanet wire service. 2004. "Development strategy readjustment looming in China." www.chinaview.cn, March 4.

Zubkov, Vasily. 2004. "The politics of pipelines: Economics takes a back seat in project decisions." *Russia Profile*, November 29.

7
The Chad-Cameroon Pipeline Project and the Making of World Society in Central Africa

Yves Alexandre Chouala

This research paper analyses the dynamics of world society in Central Africa through the Chad-Cameroon Pipeline mega-investment Project. It demonstrates that the Pipeline Project constitutes a vector of the diffusion of international economic codes and standards and the spread of the managerial culture of multinationals and international financial institutions. The Chad-Cameroon Oil and Pipeline Project also forms a pathway for the expansion of world political values such as the rule of law, human rights, democracy, transparency, human security and sustainable development. With the help of the Pipeline Project, Central Africa in general and Chad in particular have been integrated into world society. The Project therefore constitutes a road to globalisation thanks to its diffusion of liberal economic culture, democratic values and its strengthening of local capacities. The Prowject is thus referred to in this paper as a civilisational process, that is, a process of expanding and transplanting widespread world economic, political, technological and cultural standards into a marginal zone. Meanwhile, the capacity of the pipeline to drive local development remains weak because of the insignificant share of Chad and Cameroon in the Project and the limited capacity of these countries to absorb new technology. At the same time, the pipeline has produced social issues such as prostitution, crime and rebellion.

This study deals with the dynamics of expansion of world standards, codes and values and the ways in which they affect regional and local societies. Its main purpose is to analyse the social life of globalisation outside of its core countries. It is, in a way, a study of how globalisation shapes an underdeveloped world through mega-investment projects whose potential for the standardisation of economic culture worldwide is remarkable. The specific case on which the study is built is the Chad-Cameroon Pipeline Project, considered as the introduction of world society into Central Africa. The construction of an oil pipeline of about 1070 km linking the Chad oil-producing region of Doba to the seaport of Kribi constitutes one of the largest development projects so far launched in sub-Saharan Africa. The project, which cost about 3.7 billion USD, involved various partners: states, international financial institutions and multinational oil companies (World Bank 2000: 48, box 4.1.). The Chad-Cameroon Pipeline investment has been considered to be a very good example of the financing of an interstate development by international financial institutions and multinational corporations (World Bank 1998). It has also been held up as a model of development opportunities provided by the internationalisation of capital.

In an international context in which economic considerations and market imperatives influence state behaviour and determine their international trajectory (Foucher 1996, Luttwak 1995), it seems pertinent to perceive the Pipeline Project as a consequence of the expansion of liberal economics. The Chad-Cameroon Pipeline Project could therefore be interpreted as a pathway to the integration of central Africa in the process of globalisation. With this integration, the region has undergone a transformation as far as its economic position, geopolitical status and its own adjustment to globalisation is concerned. The flow of capital through the region owing to oil exploitation is transforming the region which now belongs to the world's core of oil producers (Chouala 2004) as defined in American geopolitics (National Energy Policy Development Group 2001).

Because capital is not neutral vis-à-vis social norms and political values, the Chad-Cameroon Pipeline Project constitutes a vector of the diffusion of international economic codes and standards, of the exportation of the managerial culture of multinationals and international financial institutions (Reiffers 1982). It clearly appears here that geo-economy is linked to geopolitics and geo-culture (Wallerstein 1992; Luttwak 1995). A study of the manner in which the Chad-Cameroon Pipeline Project is shaping Central Africa in line with world society can therefore use the intersection of geo-economy, geopolitics and geo-culture as an analytical framework.

- Geo-economy permits one to analyse Chad and Cameroon as an example of how territories are mastered. Geo-economy is also analytically relevant because its strategic and competitive components recall game theory when analysing the international, regional and social life of the pipeline.
- Geopolitics is also of heuristic insight in that it focuses on the grand jeu of international powers, be they states or non-state actors. Security issues related to the pipeline and the redistribution of global influences over oil can readily be discussed from a geopolitical perspective.
- Lastly, geo-culture is important in analysing the cultural flows and the civilisational permeation that have occurred as consequences of the Pipeline Project. Because it considers "culture as the ideological battleground of the modern system" (Wallerstein 1992), geo-culture provides a fruitful analytical approach to the discussion of cultural stakes in the Pipeline Project.

This framework facilitates the discussion of the following questions: how has Central Africa met the Chad-Cameroon Pipeline Project? How does this project contribute to the expansion of world culture throughout the region? How is that culture adopted at local, national and regional level? Which modes or cultures of participation have emerged and are being consolidated? To summarise, what are the socio-political, economic and geopolitical impacts of the pipeline in Central Africa?

The study argues that, although the Chad-Cameroon Pipeline Project's primary aim is the extraction and export of oil, it has brought great social transformations to the oil production areas

(1) Being a modern western project located in Africa, the pipeline is a technology transfer and so constitutes a factor integrating Central Africa in world society. Conversely, as the construction of an oil enclave in Africa, the Pipeline Project presents an aspect of ghettoisation, that is, a pathway to marginalisation and domination. In both situations, the project appears to be a pied-à-terre of globalisation in Central Africa.

(2) The Pipeline Project provides a new model and practice of development, namely of development based on the transparent management of oil revenue. The coupling of oil, transparency and development constitutes a shift from the "paradox of plenty" or "devil's excrement" paradigm to that of developmental oil. It is an ethical or democratic conception of development in which natural resources such as oil cease to fuel civil wars, thus impeding development, and become opportunities for reducing rampant poverty and improving living conditions.

(3) The pipeline has brought a new business management culture to Chad and Cameroon. In fact, companies working in the pipeline domain have, as will be demonstrated, been constrained to adopt modern management procedures and equipment. The main fact here has been a shift from a traditional approach to business activities to modernisation and rationalisation according to international standards. Because of this standardisation of business and administrative methods, the Pipeline Project has therefore initiated a dynamic of capacity building and strengthening of local potentialities. Also, thanks to the Pipeline Project, a reinforced civil society, integrated with international civil society, has emerged at local, national, regional and international levels. The Pipeline Project helps to replicate the worldwide dynamics of the globalisation of civil society (Kaldor 2003: 583-593). Last, but not least, the Pipeline Project has also led to the international reclassification of Central Africa which has shifted from a marginal position to a more central one. Central Africa now belongs to the world's core of oil producers and has consequently been projected as the new frontier of radical Islamism in Sub-Saharan Africa by the United States of America (Chouala 2004).

These are the core issues that the study will develop. The study is, firstly, a theoretical study (pipeline as a path both to globalisation/modernisation and to marginalisation/domination), secondly, a policy analysis (the international policy of financing development through oil mega-projects), and thirdly, the testing of a scientific hypothesis (the hypothesis that the pipeline brings world society to Central Africa through the pipeline).

The pipeline mega-investment project: a path to globalisation and modernisation or to marginalisation and domination?

The Chad-Cameroon Oil and Pipeline Project is a mega-project that constitutes a concrete case of the way in which private capital determines key spheres of investment and drives development efforts and priorities worldwide (Dunning 1992; Vernon 1998). As a mega-project involving multinational corporations, international financial institutions, state governments and civil society organisations, the pipeline investment surely constitutes a channel through which globalisation and modernisation are being diffused in Central Africa. The pipeline integrates the region into a large oil market on the one hand and favours its modernisation through the building of development and social infrastructures on the other.

However the globalisation process carried out by the pipeline reflects the dynamics of inclusion and marginalisation/domination that characterise it. Globalisation does not mean the levelling of world inequalities. As a process, globalisation has a centre and a periphery.[2] What therefore genuinely constitutes globalisation is the worldwide expansion of its core interests. It is the reason why globalisation is associated with domination or the new imperialism (Radice 1975). Thus, since African partners of the pipeline are poor countries which are not able to afford the cost of building the pipeline, they therefore occupy a marginal position within the process. From this critical point, the pipeline leads to the marginalisation and domination of Central Africa in the oil global market, as illustrated by the insignificant proportion of shares held by African actors in the pipeline business. Consequently, while the Pipeline Project assists the integration of Central Africa within the process of globalisation and so favours its modernisation, at the same time it integrates the region in a specifically marginal position.

Making the global oil economy local: the oil and pipeline project as a part of the globalisation wave

The Chad-Cameroon Pipeline Project drives the globalisation process in Central Africa. It illustrates the dynamics of oil multinational companies towards emergent markets of the South. In fact, the pipeline makes globalisation a palpable reality in the region through a great movement of capital. It is accompanied by technological and human flows. The reality of the pipeline as a vector of globalisation can be seen at three levels at least: (1) the nature and origin of invested capital, (2) international technological transfer and (3) the transnationality of the pipeline's actors.[2]

(1) The Chad-Cameroon Pipeline Project is an instance of the international flow of capital, which no longer has frontiers. It is the logic of the expansion of international private capital which was the main force behind the launching of the project. Here, international financial institutions such as the World Bank and state governments were brought into the project by oil multinational corporations. The initiative and the implementation of the project was realised not by states or international development institutions but rather by multinational corporations whose primary aim was to realise great profits through the exploitation of oil resources.

The financial arrangement of the Pipeline Project gives an illustration of the transnationalisation of capital characteristic of economic globalisation. The project is carried out by a consortium of oil companies consisting of Exxon Mobil and Chevron of the United States with 40% and 25% of the global capital respectively, and Petronas of Malaysia with a 35% contribution. The export system is owned and operated by two joint venture pipeline companies, one for the portion located in Cameroon–the Cameroon Oil Transportation Company (COTCO), and the other for the portion located in Chad–the Chad Oil Transportation Company (TOTCO). Chad holds 15% of shares in TOTCO's global capital and the consortium 85%, while in COTCO Cameroon holds 15% of the shares, Chad 5% and the consortium once again holds the lion's share of 80%. As is clear when one takes into account the origin of capital and firms, the Pipeline Project is essentially a US-Malaysia business venture. Firms from these two countries have the biggest shares of capital invested in the project: 3.7 billion US dollars. Strictly speaking, there is no African capital in the project. Even the 2.1% of the global investment attributed to Chad and Cameroon has been financed through loans from the World Bank and the European Investment Bank. Viewed financially, the Oil and Pipeline Project is a US-Malaysia project located in Central Africa.

(2) The project is also a process of international technological transfer (Safarian and Bertin 1987; Howells 1998). In fact, the technology implemented in the project is entirely a western one. The French firms dominated the building of the pipeline with 60% of the cost of 800 million US dollars: "Bouygues and Cegelec for oil field infrastructures (roads and pathways...) and the pumping stations; Europipe for the pipeline manufacture; Spie-Capac for the laying of the pipes, Sogea-Satom (infrastructures); SDV (Vincent Bolloré) for the conveying of material and logistics; Corris for the telecommunica-

tions" (FIDH 2000: 13; author's translation). Furthermore, the construction of the pathway all the way along the pipeline went to David Terrassement, a subsidiary company of Bouygues in Chad. Another French firm, Eurest, won the maintenance of the building sites, while Catering International Service (CIS) supplied the Doba region with food.

The American presence in the pipeline's building was quite insignificant. Only the US firm Wilbros participated directly by joining the French firm Spie-Batignolles in the construction of the pipeline. According to Géraud Magrin, the "great number of French employed by the consortium indicates both the recognition given in Africa to French expertise and the difficulty faced by Esso in recruiting Americans to work in a remote part of Africa ill placed in the transatlantic professional imagination" (Magrin 2003: 44; author's translation). As for the Malaysian Petronas, the firm was absent from the pipeline building site.

(3) The growth of human flows towards the oil and pipeline region and the cosmopolitan transformation of the Doba area are also among the greatest social changes brought by the pipeline. This cosmopolitan growing world includes a diverse collection of people: natives, aliens, job-seekers, trans-border traders, Latin Americans, Europeans etc. The Doba area has been transformed into a melting pot as far as human composition is concerned.

The project first led to great displacements of peoples both at national and international level. Thousands of Chadians moved from their places of origin to the oil zone. That massive displacement included jobless people, traders, truck drivers, prostitutes and criminals. In Moundou, the launching of the oil building site accelerated the installation and movement of traders and truck pushers coming from the capital city N'djamena or the Bornou region in the north of Chad. The migration flows related to the pipeline also involved foreigners. Most of these foreigners are from the neighbouring states of Cameroon, Central African Republic, Sudan, Libya etc. The Sudanese, mainly represented by the Zaghawa - a cross-border ethnic group from Sudan and Chad - dominate the inter-urban trucking business. Cameroonians are well established in the informal trans-border trade while Libyans are progressively taking control of the tourist sector with the building of small hotels. One should also note the appearance of Lebanese and Egyptians, who control the supermarket sector of Moundou. In addition, Koreans formerly established in Bangui (Central Africa Republic) have migrated to Chad where they have opened photo shops in N'djamena and Moundou. The human landscape of Doba and Moundou has also been enriched by the Latin Americans; mainly the Colombians working on the pipeline. Called the amigos, these Colombians are among the best customers of prostitutes because of their very high salaries compared to local standards. In sum, the pipeline has transformed Doba into a cosmopolitan place and favours the advent of a world society in Chad.

Being simultaneously a foreign direct investment, according to the proportions of capital tapped, and an international technology transfer and export process, the Pipeline Project appears to be the transplantation of western modernisation into Central Africa. What the anthropologist Arjun Appadurai describes as "glocalisation" (Appadurai 1996), that is, the encounter and intermixing of local and global, or, better still, the local life of global flows, could constitute a fruitful framework for analysing the pipeline's transformation of Central Africa. The Pipeline Project is the channel through which the global economy is being expanded at the African periphery. With the pipeline, Central Africa is being connected into the world system.

The pipeline's integration of Central Africa into globalisation: a subaltern mode?

While mega-projects in Africa permit foreign direct investment and favour international technological transfer as well as the exportation of competence, the question is, do they really lead to an autonomous and beneficial introduction of the states of the continent to globalisation? What kind of world integration do mega-projects structure and help to implement? These questions are decisive in the discussion of the way in which huge and costly investment projects connect Africa with the world system.

(1) As the reality of the Chad and Cameroon Pipeline Project clearly indicates, mega-projects paradoxically do not integrate African states at the heart or the centre stage of globalisation. Mega-projects do not open the gates of globalisation as a haven for select developing countries. Contrary to expectations, they are vectors of a subaltern integration into world global integration (Madeley 1999). What seems to really take place in the launching process of mega-projects in underdeveloping societies is the extension of central areas of globalisation to the periphery and not the opening and integration of periphery into the central areas. Instead of transplanting development and prosperity in their areas of building, mega-projects rather reveal the profound underdevelopment or the gap between local agrarian or informal economies and the sophisticated rich economies of western countries (Madeley 1999; Watkins 1997). In such a way mega-projects not only inhibit local development potentials because of the grafting of technology which cannot be owned by local actors; they also structure an "anticompetitive dominance" highlighting the inability of local economic agencies to interplay with them (Kadah, nd: 1 ; Blomström and Kokko 1997).

At the heart of these negative influences of mega-projects on African globalisation is the inability of developing states to fund them. As far as the pipeline is concerned, Chad and Cameroon hold only 2.1% of the total capital of the project. This amount is insignificant and straightforwardly marginalises Chad and Cameroon in the project. In addition, the two countries are under the financial tutelage of the World Bank which provided, with the European Investment Bank, the financial contribution of Chad (32,5 million USD) and Cameroon (43,5 million USD) to the project as loans. Without financial capacity and power, Cameroon and Chad's share of influence in the pipeline is very weak. It is therefore quite impossible for these local actors to convert the pipeline into a tool of their international affirmation. Rather these two states are now under external control (Massey and Roy 2005: 253-276). This situation led the July 2000 International Human Rights Federation Report to point out that "Chad and Cameroon are not ... the principal beneficiaries of the World Bank loan and other credits mobilised in this business" (FIDH 2000: 11; author's translation). This same observation is underlined by Géraud Magrin concerning Chad's involvement in the pipeline: "Chadian business operators occupy a weak place in the oil construction business ... Esso regrets the weak capacity of [Chadian] actors regarding its needs ... Moreover, Esso, like its subcontracting firms, prefers to buy from suppliers having a bank account, a regular tax status, a phone number and fax - in brief, all the attributes of formal sector firm" (Magrin 2003: 50; author's translation). Thus, the pipeline mega-project seems to be an esoteric oeuvre because of its inadequacy in improving locals' everyday businesses. It appears therefore as an oil enclave with only a weak capacity to propel local economies into globalisation. The Pipeline Project constitutes the process of placing Central Africa under technological and scientific tutelage and therefore a subaltern mode of linking Central Africa to world system.

(2) Mega-projects are subaltern and marginal ways of connecting Africa to globalisation in the sense that they rely on technologically based modernisation that cannot really be owned at grassroots level. In fact, the mega-project, as Mohamed M. Kabah well underlines it, "has become the most important source of economic growth, competitiveness, wealth, power, prestige, and even independence ... With the increasing globalisation of business activities, knowledge and information have been gaining importance as vital elements of any firm's success in today's global economy. In fact, we are moving from an industrial age to an information age, in which technology has become the most decisive factor of competitiveness" (Kabah, nd.: 1). It goes without saying that states ill-endowed with technological potentials and means cannot play in the global arena of today. Chad and Cameroon are confronted with this reality in the Pipeline Project. Not only can these two countries not afford the

sharp and sophisticated technology of oil exploitation, but their technological absorptive capacity is, in addition, practically non-existent. The Pipeline Project therefore does not enhance local technological capacities either as it has nothing to do with local engineering. Contrary to the optimistic discourse on the importance of technology in poverty-combat battles and development efforts in developing countries (Kabah, nd; Pack and Saggi 1997: 81-98), it should be noted that international technology transfer does not go along with knowledge flows and economic performance, as is the case with the Pipeline Project. Many analysts of the pipeline economic and social effects doubt that the application of capital, technology and competence that accompanies it will have any positive or development effects on Chadian society, which will remain at the margin of globalisation. Some radical analysts have predicted it will become a "pipeline of misery" (cf. CED 1998).

The extractive logic that characterises the Pipeline Project also militates in favour of the continuing marginalisation of the region. The creation of subcontracting firms bound to disappear once the building comes to an end clearly illustrates this extractive logic. The technology gap has simply been exploited by western firms, which made a clean sweep of the pipeline market. Esso and its subcontractors have not collaborated at all with local firms, which stood by as spectators in the distribution of the pipeline contracts. Instead of strengthening the technological capacity of Chad and Cameroon in the oil domain, powerful multinational firms seem to have avoided oil technology transfer to the two African states concerned with the project. What the mega-project of the pipeline seems to have produced is the changing status of Chad from a rural economy to an oil trading post. The white gold of cotton has given way to the black of oil within the same colonial logic of the trading post (Magrin 2001).

(3) A brief political economy of social uses of the pipeline as well as its effects on the local economy permits one to better appreciate the pattern by which it integrates Africa into the global world. Three points can rapidly be surveyed: the African expertise in the pipeline building, the pipeline's disturbance of the local economy and the social uses of pipeline money.

The pipeline integrates Africans in the world job market as subaltern workers or labourers. Labourers and subaltern workers are the only job positions Africans can occupy, considering the scarcity of local human resources skilled with oil technology and knowledge. In Chad, the consortium employed foreigners coming mainly from emerging countries such as Latin America, Asia, South Africa and Cameroon in qualified positions. Executive and managerial posts go almost automatically to American and French technicians. French employees of the pipeline are predominantly retired military officials formerly engaged in intelligent units. Being unskilled, Chadians can only pick up subaltern posts such as drivers, gatekeepers, office boys, cooks etc. Chadians often complain that job announcements regarding the pipeline's construction were made in a way that excluded Chadian candidates because of the required 5 to 8 years of international experience. How could people who have never exploited oil meet this requirement?

The pipeline also seriously disturbs the local economy. All the labourers working in its construction are former farmers, administrative and sanitary agents who abandoned their traditional occupations so that Chad no longer has people committed to civil service and rural or agrarian activities, thus introducing the Dutch disease. One rather notes the emergence of what may be termed a pipeline rent-seeking population. Small business around oil installations mobilise the local labour force. The direct consequence is the lack of substantial and sustainable development projects. On another serious note, the pipeline has deeply affected the education system in Chad; gatekeepers, for example, are recruited from among schoolboys. Many teachers have also left classrooms for pipeline activities where salaries are more substantial. The visible impact of this pernicious phenomenon is the relationship between pipeline and the increasing numbers of early school leavers. The pipeline paradoxically promotes illiteracy, hardly a triumph of globalisation. Ironically, the construction of school infrastructures has been planned in the pipeline compensations strategy (GCA 1998).

The use of oil money by local people has definitely shown that the pipeline will not bring Chad and Cameroon into world society as an equal partner. "Of what use is money in a madman's hands?" asked a Cameroonian singer, observing the use of the pipeline money boom. In fact, the huge sum of money injected without any preparation into a rural milieu exerts no positive effect. The money has been misused and primarily invested in soporific expenses: alcohol, enjoyments, sex and so forth dominate the disposal of pipeline money by the workers. In addition, the pressure of relatives and the launching of ephemeral businesses due to the absence of preparation left people who initially benefited from pipeline compensation in poverty.

Pipeline and local development stakes

The Oil and Pipeline Project represented an unprecedented opportunity of financing development for the World Bank, the Chadian government and other actors intervening on the development field. According to former French Prime Minister Michel Rocard, the project was "a striking example of the manner in which governments and the international private sector can work in concert with multilateral institutions to transform the prospects of a poor country" (Rocard 2000). As for the World Bank, it strongly believes that the project will generate new resources to finance development, as one can read on the Bank's website: "The Chad-Cameroon Oil and Pipeline gives Chad an opportunity to reduce rampant poverty and improve living conditions by using oil revenues to fund development (social) project." The same vision was propagated by the Chadian government, which presented the opponents of the oil project as enemies of the nation. Development and poverty alleviation were therefore the main stakes around the oil project debate. Here, two old issues were brought back into discussion: the possibility of multinational corporations to favour development and the transformation of oil into a resource for development.

The local test of a global debate: multinational corporations and development

What emerges from the debate about the implementation of the Chad and Cameroon Oil and Pipeline Project is a renewal of the international policy of financing local development through the investments of multinational corporations. In fact, the debate on multinationals and development is an old one (Buckley and Clegg 1991; Buckley and Mucchielli 1997; Dixon and Drakakis-Smith 1986, Dunning 1992) and has attracted great attention from scholars and development actors. The dominant view in this debate is that "despite the gigantic resources at their disposal, [MNCs] have not been a major player in the development of third world countries, at least not in a positive sense. Where a development transition has taken place, the policy has been based on the generation of international resources and strategic role of the state" (Lieten 2001: 113).

This argument was reversed by the pipeline supporters and, as a result, the multinational corporations recovered their appearance as benefactors of development. The former French Prime Minister quoted above presented the project as "a chance for Africa" (Rocard 2000) because it fundamentally constituted an opportunity to fight against poverty. This position was also defended by the World Bank, which used three major arguments. Firstly, Chad is a country that does not have the public means to ensure decent living conditions for its population. The Chad-Cameroon Pipeline Project therefore constituted a unique opportunity to considerably ameliorate conditions in Chad and to help it out of extreme poverty. Secondly, the Project also constitutes a way in which the Bank can attain its aim of reducing poverty and establishing a basis for sustainable growth. Thirdly, the Project provides the opportunity to improve development prospects by generating additional fiscal revenues for the financing of education, health and infrastructure (Nain Kuma 2001: 36-37). With a total cost of 3.7 billion USD invested, the Project represented the most important private investment in Africa and, if well used, would surely have positive impacts on development building.

This optimistic vision was shared by the Chadian authorities, who presented the project as a reward for the great suffering and deprivation endured by Chad and the means to put an end to "a long period of poverty, misery and despondency" (Cameroon Tribune, n° 7210/3499, October 20 2000: 13-14). President Idriss Déby insisted on the fact that the investment mobilised by the project as well as direct and indirect gains generated by it, made the project a unique opportunity for the development of Chad. The revenues from the project were also supposed to increase the government's capacity to move towards a true economic policy (Nain Kuma 2001: 51). In Cameroon, President Paul Biya also saw the pipeline as "a powerful instrument of development." In a speech during the launching ceremony of the project in Kribi, he held that "This major project will constitute for both countries a significant booster to our economic and social development policies, and therefore contribute to the prosperity and well being of our people. The project can be a driving force of prosperity and progress, especially in terms of job creation, establishment of small and medium-sized enterprises, expansion of our industrial fabric thanks to the predictable transfer of technology, improvement of some of our road infrastructure and even new opportunities for tapping our mineral resources. These favourable prospects point to the acceleration of the economic and social development of Cameroon" (Paul Biya, in Cameroon Tribune, n° 7210/3499, October 20, 2000). In all, the Pipeline Project was viewed favourably from all sides as a developmental project.

However, a closer look at the first half-decade of the pipeline reveals that the benefits of investment flows brought by oil multinational and the World Bank are going to western firms controlling the building site market. It is not unusual for host countries to have a negative experience of oil multinationals, but what seems quite unreasonable or understandable is the optimism shown by the World Bank and the states of Chad and Cameroon about the pipelines' capacity for generating development. Whilst, "[d]evelopment, as Kristoffel Lieten stresses, in its common meaning, involves a multi-structural process with a solution to at least four basic problems: the generation of means of investment, the integration of diverse sections of the economy in a forward and backward functionality, the productive use of growing magnitude of labour market entrants and modernisation of the production process" (Lieten 2001: 111). Unfortunately, this process seems unlikely to be replicated in the Pipeline Project. The MNCs involved in the Pipeline Project have not yet made any positive contribution towards implementing the development process or dynamics described above. Local development therefore will not be supported by oil multinationals.

Up to now, the Pipeline Project has not generated substantial investment means. Examining early trends, it appears that the priority is the reimbursement of the Chadian debt to the World Bank and the European Investment Bank, as witnessed by the following passage: "The oil money was included in the 2004 state national budget as 94 million Euro, so 12.5% of the budget of about 750 million Euro ... The first bank transfer arrived in the offshore account in December 2003. The connecting account is an account at the London Citibank. This account should receive the crude sales money on the 15th of every month, after the consortium has taken its part. Chad's debt to the IBRD (International Bank for Reconstruction and Development of the World Bank Group) for its participation in TOTCO is paid according to an established schedule from this account. The payments outstanding to the IAD (International Development Association) of the World Bank Group are likewise deducted from this account. After the World Bank, it is the European Investment Bank's turn to receive its due. Reserve accounts for the reimbursement of coming date of payment in case of the crude slump or the decrease of dollar value re also fed from this account ..." (Petry and Bambé 2005: 329).

Analysing the repartition of pipeline benefits, the IFHR Report indicates that "5 billion USD invested corresponded to prospecting activity and construction, of high technology value, realised by the firms and their subcontractors; thus salaries and incomes for the firms ... of theNorth or elsewhere: not for Chadian and Cameroonian firms. Likewise 4 billion operational cost ... remunerates labour: but not really the labour force of local firms" (IFHR 2000: 14). It therefore appears that the pipeline is simply a nexus of financial flows whose final destinations are in the northern countries. The benefits from Chad and Cameroon's stakes in the Project do not permit the financing of small or medium-size enterprises. Thus there is no evident relationship between oil multinational and local development.

Developmental oil? The reality of a new international illusion.

The Chad-Cameroon Oil and Pipeline Project brings Central Africa to the centre of the worldwide debate on oil and development. Regardless of the past and present role oil has played in national economies, it is the idea that oil can help to build development that prevails and finally legitimises the Chad-Cameroon Pipeline Project. The rationale of the project for the World Bank economists was to "test in a small country their theory of the fight against poverty through oil production" (Petry and Bambé 2005: 34). This idea is now shared by many analysts and decision-makers worldwide.

The African Oil Policy Initiative Group (AOPIG), formed in the United States, considers African oil as a priority for African development. "African oil is not an end, but a means to ... more rapid African economic development" (AOPIG 2002: 1, 9). The report issued by the Group strongly underlines that "one way to achieve this is to engage with energy-producing countries in a way that fosters and encourages the development of middle class, rather than allowing petro-dollars to flow into hands of a small number of corrupt leaders and their associates" (AOPIG 2002: 9). The report of the Center for Strategic and International Studies (CSIS)'s Task Force on Rising U.S. Energy Stakes in Africa, entitled "Promoting Transparency in the African Oil Sector," also expresses a belief in the relationship between oil and development. One can read from this report that "[T]he Nigerian government's oil earnings between 2004 and 2010 will likely exceed $110 billion. The Angolan government's earnings in this same period could reach $43 billion, while Equatorial Guinea's will be approximately $10 billion. Such abundant revenues, ... potentially provide these states a chance to develop their political and economic institutions, reduce poverty, expand opportunity and for the first time in their histories, widely share their national wealth with their citizens" (CSIS 2004: 2). Oil as a development factor is also a notion propagated by multilateral organisations. The 8th meeting of the United Nations Conference on Trade and Development (UNCTAD) on oil in Africa, held in Marrakech, Morocco, advocated an oil exploitation which favours the financing of social development. The World Bank required and obtained guarantees from Chad, as well as clear directives about the utilisation of oil income for developing the social sector.[3] The first forum on oil industry in Central Africa, held in Malabo (Equatorial Guinea) from 2 to 4 October 2001, was also devoted to the search for best practices in oil production and ways of readjusting development policies and strategies (c.f. Conchiglia 2002: 42).

Meanwhile, the question of the basis of this new oil optimism remains open. Historically, oil has not been a development factor for African countries. Economic and social development has not taken off in such oil producing countries of the developing world as Nigeria, Gabon, Angola, Congo-Brazzaville, Cameroon. (Karl 1997; Hodges 2001; Ahmad Khan 1994; OCLD 1996). It is therefore difficult, in the absence of any hopeful indicators, to imagine a great, even a magic, transformation of oil from "the excrement of the devil," a major impetus of war, social inequalities and state domination, into a force for development. For, no one really believes that the new oil boom in West and Central Africa in general and Chad in particular will be different from previous developments associated with petroleum. The proceedings of the symposium on African oil held on 25 January 2002 at the University Club of Washington by the Institute for Advanced Strategic and Political Studies clearly express doubt about the linkage of oil with democracy and transparency: "Oil companies cannot always invest in democratically governed countries. It would be ideal if it could be guaranteed that the head of an African country where a US Oil Company invested was, in fact, and advocate of democracy and always respected human rights. Unfortunately, that is not a realistic expectation in today's Africa or in most other oil producing regions of the world" (Wihbey & Schutz 2002: 6).

Despite all the measures taken by the World Bank and Non-Governmental Organisations to ensure a transparent management of oil income, Chad has remained engulfed in bad governance, corruption and military authoritarianism. Chad was classified as the world's most corrupt country in 2005 by Transparency International. Moreover, oil is not pacifying the country; rather it exacerbates political disagreements and avarice. Factional groups criticising the management of oil revenues by the Déby system have resumed armed stugles in order to overthrow the regime, engulfing Chad once more in political disorder and instability, which clearly cannot create favourable conditions for development. Likewise the high growth rate of about 150% registered by Equatorial Guinea owing to its oil boom does not produce any concrete improvement in the peoples' welfare. Poverty remains the thing shared by most in the country. After several years of prosperity due to oil exploitation, Gabon and Congo-Brazzaville have not taken off and remain poor places where people are daily confronted with shortages of every kind and endemic violence. In conclusion, one can agree with Peter Rosenblum that "mineral wealth rarely translates into economic or social progress for the majority of a country's population. Transformed expectations, increased corruption, reinforced authoritarianism, yes, Democracy, development, transparency and participation, no. Africa is filled with mineral-rich failures, including Nigeria, Angola ... former Zaire [and one should add Equatorial Guinea]" (Rosenblum 2000: 198).

The pipeline shaping Chad and Cameroon's socio-political order: transformation figures and trends

Roughly speaking, social shaping is the structural modification of the core nature of a society; its physical configuration, rules of play, power distribution structures as well as its value system and philosophical foundation. It is the rebuilding of social architecture and the adjustment of people's minds and convictions to changes in the legitimate framework of action and thought. The notion of social shaping is therefore comparable with the concept of social transformation which, according to Nikolay Genov, "refers to the change of society's systemic characteristics" (Genov 2005: 109). This, as with the first notion, is within the transition framework, that is, a shift from one social configuration characterised by specific rules of play to another. The pipeline can certainly be seen as a factor of social transformation in Chadian society and to some extent in Cameroon's too. The pipeline therefore constitutes a very good area for monitoring social transformations which the whole of the Central African region is undergoing. These transformations could, on the one hand, be seen as a civilising process when considering improvements to infrastructure, and the adoption of democracy as the principle of political life, governance and transparency it tries to introduce to the culture of public affairs management. However, the transformation also has a pervasive dimension regarding the powerful influence of money, which inhibits justice and impacts negatively on human security building. Justice therefore seems to be the major missing link of pipeline social transformations.

Pipeline social and political transformations: towards a civilising process?

This part of the study relies on Nikolay Genov's analysis of societal transformations which, according to him, roughly implies the realisation of a "new quality"; that is a renewal of at least four parameters of the societal system. "First, the productive infrastructure is expected to bring about new technological chains and new patterns of participation in the international division of labour ... Second, new infrastructures of economic organisation are evolving ... In the given context, the key issue of economic restructuring is the adjustment to the increasingly globalised markets. Third, the distribution and use of political power takes various forms, which are qualitatively different from the [old] ones ... This implies substantial changes in the structure and performance of state institutions but also other decision-making bodies and control. They have to adapt the current worldwide wave of democratisation. Fourth, the normative value systems change in a way which allows for the emergence and stabilisation of new institutions. The very core of the developing new value system is the modern system of universal human rights" (Genov 2005: 109). These four levels of measuring societal changes can be operationalised in the Chad-Cameroon Oil Pipeline area. A particular emphasis will meanwhile be put on the grassroots impacts of these societal transformations. The aim here is to see the social/local life of the pipeline as a transformative device and the way in which the transformations concretely reshape the whole social, political and economic architecture of the region.

(1) There is no doubt that the pipeline has brought "new technological chains" to Central Africa. As previously indicated, the Pipeline Project is first of all a salient instance of international technology transfer. With its advent, the Chad and Cameroon technological landscape has undergone a number of major changes (Petry and Bambé 2005; Magrin 2003; Mbembe 1999: 14). These are first of all physical with the building of new and original technological infrastructures which have given a new face to the region. "Apart from the

drilling and the pipeline," note Martin Petry and Naygotimti Bambé, "a great quantity of modern infrastructure has been produced: a network of pipes for conveying the oil to the central treatment and pumping station, a dense network of roads, housing for hundreds of collaborators from countless firms from al over the world, a satellite communication system, huge warehouses, maintenance sheds and workrooms, an international airport set aside solely for the project, and a power station of 120 megawatts, using oil produced. It is five times more than the circa 25 megawatts until then produced in Chad. In Cameroon, roads and bridges have been built along the pipeline, pumping stations and the off-shore terminal" (Petry and Bambé 2005: 24). With the advent of the pipeline, Chad and Cameroon present a new landscape which reflects the modern developed economies of the North. The installation of pipeline infrastructures was coupled with a technological restructuring of the region which is now highly endowed with oil technology.

Meanwhile, the "new quality" of technology that the pipeline diffuses in Central Africa does not induce a completely new pattern of participation in the international division of labour. It is true that Chad and Cameroon are now, from the perspective of oil geopolitics, part of the world's heartland. In this sense, Cameroon and Chad are central to the multinational corporations' world, even though they occupy subaltern positions within it. To borrow Pierre Bourdieu's figure, Chad and Cameroon are dominated actors of the oil dominant majors. The idea of an oil modernity enclave suggested in the first part of this study seems fruitful. The enclave status recalls that the Pipeline Project is, from the global geo-strategic standpoint, part of the vast reorientation of the U.S. oil market. The U.S. is in the process of adjusting its oil market by substantially reducing its reliance on the Middle East following the spread of radical anti-American Islamism in the region. This adjustment, as well as the Structural Adjustment Program (SAPs) imposed on African economies during the 1990s, has brought no modification to historical postures and roles in North-South business, cooperation or partnership. As far as the pattern of participation in international labour is concerned, the "new quality" technology brought to Africa by the pipeline has not actually changed the logic of the colonial or trading post economy which characterises European economic engagement towards Africa. Chad and Cameroon are trading posts for oil raw materials which are transformed into finished products within western refineries. What is really taking place within the pipeline mega-investment project is simply the delocalisation of oil extractive technology and not the creation of oil industries at the local level which would have impacted positively on the international position of Chad and Cameroon. The Pipeline Project therefore inaugurates a new form of domination in Chad: aWorld Bank-multinational corporation collaboration.

The reduplication of the colonial mode of oil exploitation leads to a clash between local needs and the global capital invested in the project. While local expectations of the pipeline focus first on the improvement of social conditions and standards of living, that is, oil exploitation with a human face, the multinational corporations' main priority is the extraction of oil at low cost in order to realise maximum profits. What follows is the inability of the Pipeline Project to address and satisfy local expectations. This situation also leads to the popular or grassroots condemnation of the Pipeline Project. The pipeline has thus been perceived as a dirty trick which has resulted in more sufferings and damages than in providing benefits. For example, oil wells and pumping stations sprouted on indigenous farmlands. Pipeline explosions and leakages also devastated forests and lands and generally left people without goods, infrastructure, housing or cultures (CED 1998).

(2) It is undeniable that the Chad-Cameroon Oil and Pipeline Project has provoked an evolution of the economic organisation of the two states. This is more visible in Chad, where the economic infrastructure was quite non existent because of several years of civil wars. The war economy revolved around shady transactions, and informal exchanges, alongside ethnic- and religious-based business networks characterised the Chadian economy at the time of the launching of the project. With the advent of the pipeline, this traditional economy underwent substantial changes. To enter the oil and pipeline market, businessmen were obliged to adopt the standards and codes of the formal economy. "The arrival of the oil consortium revolutionised the professional practices of Chadian traders" (Magrin 2003: 50; author's translation). Henceforth, business criteria which matter for western firms have dominated Chadian business practices: legality, specialisation, product quality, reliability of services, and punctual delivery. In N'djamena and Moundou, some traders are trying to adapt to these new requirements.[4]

Likewise, following the increasing demand for food in the pipeline area, some initiatives were taken to improve agricultural production. Thus, in the Chadian locality of Moundou, the Mayor created a small NGO, the Office for Support and Promotion of Local Development Initiatives (BAPILD) with the main aim of diffusing new methods of farming in order to increase the local production of food.

In summary, the pipeline has led to the distillation of a new economic culture in Chad. The definition of rigorous rules and procedures applicable to all its subcontractors by Esso excluded the collaboration of the informal sector. The adaptation of local firms has given a new face to local economic activities.

(3) The great advantage associated with the notion of developmental oil is the diffusion of world values. Oil therefore becomes the road to the diffusion

of world democratic and transparent values. In fact, oil not only brings sophisticated technology to Central Africa; it also transplants the core elements of western political civilisation to the region. The Chad-Cameroon Pipeline Project constitutes a vector of the exportation of liberal democracy norms, codes and standards. Liberal democratic values have been promoted as the most appropriate framework for answering the fundamental question of "what policy changes should be implemented, both domestically and internationally, to promote the efficient management and fair allocation of oil revenues in the manner benefiting the power" (Gary and Karl 2003: 5). The pipeline shall consequently be considered as a channel of exportation of neo-liberal political values, hence the hypothesis of the pipeline as a civilising process. This hypothesis can be demonstrated by examining four issues: (a) the graft of the rule of law discourse onto the Pipeline Project and its use as a state capacity-building vector; (b) the pipelines' greening of regional politics; (c) the building of a regional civil society, and (d) its establishment as an Islamic frontier.

(a) The Chad-Cameroon Pipeline Project has been identified with the building of the rule of law, human rights and governance system in the host countries. The transition to the rule of law was both a precondition and the main target of the project. For many analysts and political planners, the pipeline represented a very good opportunity to end authoritarian politics in Chad by pressuring the government to adopt democratic rules and governance. The pipeline was therefore a means of democratising the authoritarian regime led by the Chadian president, former guerrilla fighter Idriss Déby. While the World Bank, which plays a major role as the leading partner, primarily insisted on the transparent management of oil revenues by improving the state governance system, international NGOs and local civil organisations put an accent on the respect of human rights and the installation of the rule of law system. Because poor governance is said to undermine both national and regional stability, David L. Goldwyn and J. Stephen Morrison recommended that the "United States must make every effort to promote equity in development, democratic norms, respects for human rights, responsible environmental stewardship, and effective emergency response to inhuman suffering. ... ... [For], no policy of promoting transparency, stability, or development can succeed where freedom of expression, association, political participation, and the press are inhibited. The United States cannot seek energy security and turn a blind eye to poverty, degradation, and abuse of human rights. The United States should not invest U.S. taxpayers' money in helping countries in which national revenues are stolen or diverted for the personal gain of corrupt government officials" (Goldwyn and Morrison 2004: 11-12). It clearly appears here that oil exploitation is not a moral and value free task. On the contrary, it is a vector of the worldwide diffusion of neo-liberal principles. The Chad-Cameroon Oil and Pipeline Project is therefore also the western civilisation pipeline.

Under the combined pressure of the World Bank, NGOs and the U.S. administration, the government of Chad on 11 January 1999 finally voted a bill on the management of oil revenues. The general spirit of this bill was to promote the struggle against poverty through transparent and accountable use of oil money. The bill stipulated that oil money should be deposited in specific accounts controlled and audited by the World Bank. The bill also provided that 85% of oil money should be primarily invested in social sectors such as education, health, social services and agriculture. Taxes and benefits were to be used to finance the state budget. The World Bank can be considered a catalyst of good governance in Chad. In contrast to the World Bank, human rights defence organisations insisted for their part on democratisation and the rule of law, because "poverty is intimately linked to the lack of democracy, to power excesses of representatives of order and to their total impunity" (FIDH 2000: 28; author's translation). Many human rights defence groups and associations have therefore campaigned for an oil exploitation which preserves and safeguards peoples' rights. Prominent among these organisations were the Chadian Association for the Promotion of Human Rights, the Human Rights-Chad Working Group, the International Christian Service for Peace, the Centre for Environment and Development, The Chadian Human Rights Working Group, Amnesty International, the Movement for Human Rights and Freedom Defence)

The Pipeline Project also serves to improve the capacity-building of Chad and Cameroonian states. Once again, the World Bank was at the centre of this capacity-building program by providing money for its implementation. The money provided served to finance a capacity building project in economic management for Chad and for environmental and technical management in the petroleum sector. "The aim of capacity building in Chad was to put in place a management strategy for petroleum revenues and to ensure that these revenues are used efficiently" (Nain Kuma 2001: 40). The capacity-building project on environmental and technical management in the petroleum sector was aimed at reinforcing Chad's capacity to manage petroleum resources adequately in environmental and social terms. It was aimed at reducing and managing possible negative impacts in the project zone, and finally to establish a reasonable framework for future development in the Chadian petroleum sector. For Cameroon, a capacity-building project carried out in environmental management and in the petroleum sector aimed at establishing a national capacity in Cameroon for the management and environmental maintenance of the Pipeline Project and, in the long term, to ensure the sustainable development of the project, programmes and policies of the petroleum sector at the environmental level. Also, nationals have been trained to track the revenue, managed by an Oversight Committee with members of the civil society.

(b) One of the worlds' main values diffused in Central Africa by the Pipeline Project has been the sustainable environmental economy labelled by Lester R. Brown as "eco-economy" (Brown 2001). In fact, the environmental effects of the Pipeline Project received more attention and importance during its feasibility studies period. The environmental cost of the pipeline and the ways through which it affects the conservation of nature and the lives of the people were among the main local and international concerns (nn 2002, Horta 2003). Owing to the pipeline, Chad and Cameroon have witnessed the diffusion of environmental norms and values. The pipeline entails the "greening" (Litfin 1998a) of regional politics in Central Africa, which is a kind of ecological accountability which tends to decrease states' and multinational corporations' capacity and autonomy of action. From the ecological battles around the Pipeline Project, one can readily accept that the "meaning of territory, along with its place in the set of practices associated with sovereignty is being modified by environmental responses" (Litfin 1998b: 11).

(c) The Pipeline Project favours the emergence and consolidation of a transnational civil society in Central Africa. The transnational or global dimension of the pipeline led the civil society to rely on the interconnected nature of social groups, networks, and organisations whose early areas of action were the national territory of states. With the Pipeline Project, a new race of "activists without frontiers" whose combined actions nurture a kind of a global civil society, emerged in Cameroon and Chad. Here social organisations from the North worked side by side with those of the South. This indicates the formation of a new network of civil organisations.

(d) The Pipeline Project should also be viewed in light of the global fight against the spread of radical Islamism. In this sense, the Chad-Cameroon Oil and Pipeline Project appears to be a frontier of radical Islamism. In fact, what was observed in Chad following the French disengagement was an intensive penetration of radical Islamism coming from Libya and Sudan. Chad was then slowly but surely falling within the sphere of radical Islamism. The discovery and the exploitation of oil and the diffusion of western political and economical codes, standards and values that accompany the exploitation will reverse this tendency and remove Chad from radical Islamic influence. The pipeline installations and money represent the power and the prestige of the western economic pattern in the popular mind, and so constitute a means of converting people to a western outlook and lifestyle. As the pipeline is projected as a symbolic and ideological western attraction, it definitely protects Chad from Islamic encroachment.

Because the pipeline is instrumental in bringing the rule of law and human rights, of economic governance channels and radical Islamic containment, it can therefore be referred to as a civilising process.

(4) The normative value systems promoted by the Pipeline Project can only lead to the stabilisation and sustainability of socio-political institutions. Rule of law, human rights, transparency and accountability, democracy, and civil society participation, which are the core political values attached to the Pipeline Project, constitute the genuine basis for the stabilisation of social and political institutions. It is important to recall that all these values were adopted in order to avoid what is known as the "Niger Delta syndrome," the Nigerian oil rich potlatch area (Olojede et al. 2000).

However, it should be pointed out that the political values mentioned above have not been fully implemented and partly remain sterile slogans. In Chad as well as in Cameroon, the rule of law state remains limited. Transparency in oil revenues management is not assured and civil society is still under-informed and excluded from decision-making regarding oil management. In spite of all the precautions taken by World Bank and multinational corporations, oil money remains concentrated in the hands of the minority controlling the state (CCSRP 2005).

The "excrement of the devil"? Oil and pipeline project social ravages

The founder of OPEC, Juan Pablo Perez Alfonzo described oil as "the excrement of the devil." Developing this idea, Terry L. Karl has spoken of "the paradox of plenty" to underline the fact that most of the oil exporting nations have been unable "to translate their fabulous windfalls into a self-sustaining, equitable and stable development path" (Karl 1997: 4). The early trends of oil exploitation in Chad unfortunately confirm this tendency. In fact, the Pipeline Project has brought about a revolution in the Chadian daily way of life with the appearance and generalisation of types of social behaviour which was unimaginable a while ago: prostitution, crime and so forth have increased greatly due to oil exploitation.

The pipeline's construction has introduced "Satan" to the community of Kome, the oil exploitation zone in Chad. The settlement which has sprung up by the Kome base has been dubbed "Kome Satan." Satan is a place teeming with people and full of bars, restaurants, video clubs, and hotels used for prostitution and many other dark transactions. The prostitution practised around the Kome oil site has led to the propagation of AIDS on a very large scale. A recent unpublished World Bank report has estimated the AIDS infection rate along the pipeline route at 90%. The main reason for this is the lack of an

AIDS prevention plan, which should have been implemented along with the project.

In Kome Satan, the only value that matters is the earning of money, by any means. This money-earning logic principle shapes social behaviour as well the decision-making of policymakers and economic entrepreneurs. Thus, the Pipeline Project not only brings about the globalisation of capital and liberal values; it also generates a subaltern globalisation among the mass of poor people.

The pipeline has also led to inflation and rendered access to housing very difficult. In Doba, Kome or Kribi, rent increases attained unimaginable proportions. Furthermore, the duration of leases was extended from a month to two or three years, a period that local people were not able to afford. In addition, community values have been seriously disturbed by the arrival of pipeline money. One can take the example of land access and ownership and exploitation. Traditionally, land has belonged to the community and only crops to the farmers, who have been seen simply as the users of the land. With the advent of the pipeline and its policy of compensation, which was a financial windfall for local people, there has been a change in the land's traditional status. This land has ceased to belong to the community and become the property of particular individuals. This situation has led to several conflicts over land ownership involving individuals as well as entire communities.

Conclusion

This study has addressed three important sets of questions. The first discussed the issue of whether or not the Pipeline Project was a road to the globalisation/modernisation or marginalisation/domination of Central Africa. The second, both theoretically and practically, focussed on the old and controversial debate on the role of multinational corporations in poor countries' development on the one hand and the relationship between oil and development on the other. And the final topic was the pipelines' reshaping of Chad and Cameroon politics.

As the discussion revealed, the Pipeline Project constitutes a firm implantation of globalisation in Central Africa. The Pipeline Project is the consequence of the growth of global corporations whose far-flung operations transcend national borders and allegiances. It is also linked with the mobility of money, labour, ideas, values, and new technologies, which also transcend borders, reinforce international transactions and create a more global economy. With the Pipeline Project, Central Africa in general and Chad in particular have integrated world society. The Pipeline Project therefore constitutes a road to globalisation thanks to its diffusion of liberal economic culture, democratic values and its strengthening of local capacities. The project has thus been referred to as a civilising process, that is, a process of expanding and transplanting widespread world economic, political, technological and cultural standards, norms and codes into a peripheral zone.

However, if the pipeline appears as a road to globalisation, its capacity for driving local development and a beneficial integration of Africa into globalisation remains very weak. The Pipeline Project thus appears to be a marginalising and dominating process. The share of Chad and Cameroon in the project is insignificant, and local participation in the building of the project has not been vigorously improved. In addition, the wealth brought by the pipeline has had no effects in reducing poverty and power inequalities between state and society. Moreover, some social problems have been associated with the project, such as prostitution, crime and a massive exodus of people. The Pipeline Project is therefore to be seen as both a civilising process and the devil's excrement. Some lessons, which are also challenges for the future, can now be drawn.

(1) If the pipeline mega-investment project is a globalising element, it does not equate to a modernising one. The main reason for this is the extractive logic which dominates the pipeline. Because of this, the globalisation of the world by multinational companies will be, for developing countries, an unequal and marginal framework of access to globalisation. The challenge for analysts and development partners is therefore to look for a modernising form of globalisation.

(2) Despite its claims of modernisation and its investment ambition, the pipeline has failed to create favourable conditions for development. That is because, instead of integrating Central Africa into the world production system, the pipeline mega-project rather reveals the technological and financial rift between the North and the South. In addition, technology transfer throughout the project does not occur because of the lack of technological absorptive capacity at the local level. The challenge here is to address, from a southern perspective, the question of whether there are alternative practices of development by MNCs that do not entail relationships of domination.

(3) The coupling of oil exploitation with the ethic of transparency, accountability, human rights and development that constitutes the strategy of the World Bank in Chad and Cameroon has not succeeded in converging local expectations and aspirations and the interests of MNCs and international financing institutions. Providing oil exploitation with moral principles is not relevant because, on the one hand, oil all over the world is associated with secrecy and, on the other hand, the moral standards promoted in Chadian oil are globally centred and not locally generated. In addition, there is no guarantee that the agents of oil moralisation are themselves democratic and transparent.

The Pipeline Project therefore reveals the gap between people who make decisions and people who are affected by it. And the association of the World Bank with multinational corporations is very critical in this respect, for the Bank has appeared as an ally of these gigantic commercial interests. What is significant in this respect is that the oil agreements concluded in Sudan were better and more beneficial that those concluded with Chad and Cameroon with the assistance of the Bank ,which presents itself as a poverty alleviation machine.

(4) At the international level, the dark side of the pipeline appears to be the limitation of the rule of law. This limitation is a consequence of the focus on money, which transcends any other value. The power of money constitutes a great obstacle to the rule of law in the pipeline domain both in Cameroon and Chad. There were no possibilities for powerless people working in the area of the pipeline to claim their rights when faced with the financial mammoths of the oil consortium (Djiraibe, Horta and Nguiffo 2004). As a result, the pipeline construction area continues to be a space devoid of rights, where the firms in charge of its construction do not respect any labour law and corrupt judges and labour inspectors authorities charged with the maintenance of law and order. It is therefore clear that, among the world values diffused by the Pipeline Project, there is one which is missing: justice. Justice, as the backbone of the rule of law, is the missing link in the pipelines' diffusion of liberal civilisation. In fact, globalisation opens the world's scene to very powerful actors while some states -those of Africa- are weak and poor. For example Chad's budget of 170 billion CFA equates to that of the successful film "Titanic" and the 204 billion USD of Exxon Mobil's annual budget is five times higher than that of Chad. Here multinational corporations are more powerful than states. What follows is that the access to justice is not democratised and globalised.

Notes

[1] As Olivier Dolfus well underlines it, "The central areas around which globalisation organises itself are essentially situated in the great metropolitan areas of the 'North'" (Dolfus 1991: 38-39, author's translation).
[2] This is what Miles Shaw, Exxon Mobil's spokesman, explained in an interview in 2001: "We have sought the participation of the World Bank in the context of political risks: the role of the World Bank constituted a part of the effort to minimise political risks. We can accept economical risk but the expertise of the World Bank and its relationship with the government [of Chad] endorses the political risk..." (cited in Petry and Bambé 2005: 34).
[3] Chad voted a bill N° 001/PR/99 which determines the use of oil revenues. The bill stipulates the creation of an off-shore account, the use of direct oil revenues for the funding of the social sector (health, education, infrastructure, agriculture, environment, water supply), the disposal of 5% of the revenue to the oil region and 10% to an account for future generations. The bill also stipulates the creation of an Oversight Committee to control the management of oil revenue.

⁴ As the case of. A. O, a trader of 45 years old testifies: before the pipeline, A. O. used to work alone in his business, with one or two brothers assisting him from time to time. Owing to the pipeline project, A. O. has recruited three people to work in the office, three at the steel house, and five other people have been recruited and sent to Cameroon for training. Another recruit has taken over the accountant's position and computerised the management of stocks.

References

Ahmad Khan, Sarah 1994. *Nigeria. The Political Economy of Oil*. Oxford: Oxford University Press.

AOPIG (African Oil Policy Initiative Group). 2002. "African Oil: A Priority for U.S. National Security and African Development." AOPIG white paper. URL: www.iasps.org/strategic/africawhitepaper.pdf.

Appadurai, Arjun. 1996. *Modernity at Large: Cultural Dimensions of Globalisation*. Minneapolis: University of Minnesota Press.

Blomström, Magnus and Kokko, Ari. 1997. "How Foreign Investment Affects Host Countries." World Bank Policy Research Working Paper WPS 1745.

Brown, Lester R. 2001. *Eco-Economy. Building an Economy for the Earth*. New York: W. W. Norton & Company Ltd.

Buckley, Peter J. and Clegg, Jeremy. 1991. *Multinational Enterprises in Less Developed Countries*. London: Palgrave Macmillan.

Buckley, Peter and Mucchielli, Jean Louis. (eds.) 1997. *Multinational Firms and International Relocation*. Cheltenham: Edward Elgar Publications.

CCSRP (Collège de controle et de surveillance des ressources pétrolières). 2005. "Rapport de mission sur sites des projets financés sur ressources pétrolières." URL: http://ccsrp-tchad.org/site/index2.cfm.

CED (Centre pour l'Environnement et le Développement, Yaoundé). 1998. "The Chad-Cameroon Oil Project–Project for Hope or Pipeline of Misery," Yaoundé: CED.

Center for Strategic and International Studies (CSIS). 2004. "Promoting Transparency in the African Oil Sector." A Report of the CSIS Task Force on Rising U. S. Energy Stakes in Africa, Washington.

Chouala, Yves Alexandre. 2004. "Le Golfe de Guinée dans le Projet du Nouveau Siècle Américain: Entre Pétrole, Gouvernance et Puissance." Paper presented at the AISA/DPMF Joint Conference on "Africa and Global Governance in the Aftermath of 9/11: Prospects and Challenges," December 6-8, Addis-Ababa, Ethiopia.

Conchiglia, Augusta. 2002. "L'Afrique centrale, pôle de développement de l'industrie pétrolière." Le Courrier ACP-UE, Janvier-Février.

Dixon, David C. and Drakakis-Smith, David. 1986. *Multinational Corporations in the Third World*. London: Routledge.

Djiraibe, Delphine, Horta, Korinna. and Nguiffo, Samuel. 2004. "Access to Justice from Local Village to Global Boardroom: An Experience in International Accountability." N'Djamena: ATPDH, Washington: Environmental Defense; Yaoundé CED. URL: www.environmentaldefense.org/ documents/4065_AccessToJustice.pdf

Dolfus, Olivier. 1991. " Mondialisation et particularisme." In: *L'intégration régionale dans le monde: innovations et ruptures*, ed. by GEMDEV. Paris: Karthala.

Dunning, John. 1992. *Multinational Enterprises and the Global Economy*. Wokingham: Addison-Wesley.
FIDH. 2000. "Tchad-Cameroun. Pour qui le pétrole coulera-t-il? Rapport de mission internationale d'enquête." Paris: FIDH.
Foucher, Michel. 1996. *Les cartes de la globalisation. Les enjeux du G7. Regards croisés sur la mondialisation*. Paris: Economica.
Gary, Ian and Karl, Terry. L. 2003. *Bottom of the Barrel. Africa's Oil Boom and the Poor*. Baltimore: Catholic Relief Services.
GCA (Groupe de concertation et d'action). 1998. Séminaire international d'information et d'échanges sur le projet pétrolier et d'oléoduc Tchad-Cameroun, 25-27 Août 1998, Yaoundé, Rapport général.
Genov, Nikolay. 2005. "Path Dependence or Quality Choice? Comparing National Transformations" Pp. 107-123 in *Postsocialist Transformations and Civil Society in a Globalizing World*, edited by Meier-Dallach, Hans-Peter and Juchler, Jakob, New York: Nova Science Publishers, Inc.
Goldwyn, David L. and Morrison, Stephen J. 2004. "Promoting Transparency in the African Oil Sector. Recommendations for U.S. Policy." A Report of the CSIS Task Force on Rising U.S. Energy Stakes in Africa. URL: http://www.csis.org/.
Hodges, Tony. 2001. *Angola: From Afro-Stalinism to Petro-Diamond Capitalism*. Bloomingtom: Indiana University Press.
Horta, Korinna. 2003. "The Chad-Cameroon Oil and Pipeline: Reaching a Critical Milestone." Environmental Defense, Washington.
Howells, Jeremy. 1998. "Innovation and Technology Transfer Within Multinational Firms." In *Globalization, Growth and Governance. Creating an Innovative Economy*, edited by Michie, Jonathan and Grieve-Smith, John, Oxford: Oxford University Press.
Kadah, Mohammed. M. nd. "Foreign Direct Investment and International Technology Transfer to Egypt." ERF Working Papers Series, Working Paper 0317. URL: www.erf.org.eg/uploadpath/pdf/0317_final.pdf
Kaldor, Mary. 2003. "The Idea of Global Civil Society." *International Affairs* 79 (3): 583-593.
Karl, Terry. L. 1997. *The Paradox of Plenty. Oil Booms and Petro-States*. Berkeley, Los Angeles, London: University of California Press.
Lieten, Kristoffel. 2001. "Multinationals and Development: Revisiting the Debate." Pp. 99-115 in *Globalization and Development Studies. Challenges for the 21st Century*, edited by Schuurman, Frans J., London, Thousand Oaks, New Delhi: Sage Publications.
Litfin, Karen T. (ed.). 1998a. *The Greening of Sovereignty in World Politics*. Cambridge, Massachusetts, London: The MIT Press.
Litfin, Karen T. 1998b. "The Greening of Sovereignty. An Introduction." Pp. 1-30 in *The Greening of Sovereignty in World Politics*, edited by Litfin, Karen T. Cambridge, Massachusetts, and London: The MIT Press.
Luttwak, Edward. 1995. *Le rêve américain en danger*. Paris: Odile Jacob.
Madeley, John. 1999. Big Business, Poor Peoples: The impact of Transnational Corporations on the World's Poor. London: Zed Books.
Magrin, Géraud. 2001. *Le sud du Tchad en mutation. Des champs de coton aux sirènes de l'or noir*. Paris: Sepia, PRASAC.

Magrin, Géraud. 2003. "Les enjeux d'un enrichissement pétrolier en Afrique centrale. Le cas du Tchad." Paris: Grafigéo, Collection mémoires et documents de l'UMR PRODIG.
Massey, Simon and Roy, May 2005. "Dallas to Doba: Oil and Chad External Controls and Internal Politics." *Journal of Contemporary African Studies* 23 (2): 253-276.
Mbembe, Achille. 1999. "A la lisière du monde. Frontière, territorialité et souveraineté en Afrique." *Bulletin du Codesria* 3&4: 4-18.
Nain Kuma, Vivian. 2001. "The World Bank and The Chad-Cameroon Pipeline Project." M. Phil Dissertation in International Relations, Yaoundé, IRIC.
National Energy Policy Development Group. 2001. "Reliable, Affordable, and Environmentally Sound. Energy for Americas' Future." Report of The National Energy Policy Development Group. Washington DC: Government Printing Press Office.
nn. 2002. "The Chad-Cameroon Oil and Pipeline Project: A Disaster Scenario Becoming Real: NGO Comments on World Bank Management Response to the Inspection Panel Report on a Claim Filed by Chadian Citizens." URL: http://bankwatch.ecn.cz/eir/reports/Vol4_chadcam_report.html
Olojede, I., B. Fajonyemi, I. Akhape & S.O. Mudashiru (2000), "Nigeria: Oil pollution, Community Dissatisfaction and Threat to National Peace and Security," African Association of Political Science, Harare, Occasional Paper Series, Vol.4, No.3.
OCLD. 1996. *Dossier noir du pétrole camerounais.* Paris: L'Harmattan.
Pack, Howard and Saggi, Kamal. 1997. "Inflows of Foreign Technology and Indigenous Technological Development." *Review of Development Economics* 1 (1): 81-98.
Petry, Martin and Bambé, Naygotimti. 2005. *Le pétrole au Tchad. Rêve ou cauchemar pour les populations?* Paris: Karthala.
Radice, Hugo (ed.). 1975. *International Firms and Modern Imperialism.* Harmondsworth: Penguin.
Reiffers, Jean-Louis. (ed.). 1982. *Transnational Corporations and Endogenous Development. Effects on Culture, Communication, Education and Science and Technology.* Paris: Unesco.
Rocard, Michel. 2000. "L'oléoduc Tchad-Cameroon: une chance pour l'Afrique." Le Monde, May 30.
Rosenblum, Peter. 2000. "Pipeline Politics in Chad." *Current History. A Journal of Contemporary World Affairs* 99 (637): 195-199.
Safarian, A.E. and Bertin, G.Y. (eds.). 1987. *Multinationals, Governments and International Technology Transfer.* London and Sidney: Croom Helm.
Vernon, R.Wilhert 1998. "Multinational Corporations: Where Are They Coming from, Where Are They Headed?" In *Transforming International Organizations,* edited by Egelhoff, W., Cheltenham: Elgar.
Wallerstein, Immanuel. 1992. *Geopolitics and Geoculture. Essays on the Changing World.* Cambridge: Cambridge University Press.
Watkins, Kate. 1997. "Globalisation and Liberalisation: Implications for Poverty Distribution and Inequality." UNDP Occasional Paper, 32.
Wihbey, P. M. and Schutz, B. (eds.). 2002. "African Oil: A Priority for U.S. National Security and African Development." The Institute for Advanced Strategic and Political Studies (IASPS) Research Papers in Strategy No. 14. (Proceedings of

the IASPS Symposium on African Oil: A Priority for U.S. National Security and African Development, Washington, DC, January 25.) URL: http://www.iasps.org/strategic/.

The World Bank. 1998. "The Chad-Cameroon Petroleum and Pipeline Project, Questions and Answers," October.

The World Bank. 2000. *Annual Report 2000*. Washington: The World Bank. URL: http://www.worldbank.org/html/extpb/annrep2000/down.htm

8
The Resilience of Cultural Diversity
Reinventing Local Identity in Ireland as the *Gesamt* creation of Enterprise, State and Civil Society

Martha C.E. Van Der Bly

Everybody who has lived abroad and has regarded himself for one moment as a "global citizen" knows the individual metamorphosis the sheer mentioning of this qualification brings about. Who chooses all might be left in a void. Which sports team to support? Being a national citizen is intrinsically different from being a global citizen – if such a thing is truly possible. Similarly, a civil society largely associated with the nation-state is quintessentially different from a global civil society. The latter might eventually be so alienated of its mould that the concept might be rendered obsolete and in need of being replaced by the more all-inclusive concept of the world society.

However, just as the cultural logic of an emerging world society might not follow the cultural logic of traditional societies embedded in nation-states, this article explores the extent to which the cultural logic of an emerging global civil society might intrinsically differ from a civil society with "realms outside the power of the state" (Hahn 1996: 5).

This article states that on the micro-level the manifestations of two apparently opposite processes of globalization can be found, namely economic globalization and secondly processes of cultural globalization, that are both conflicting and reinforcing each other. Yet, the dynamics between these processes do not follow the traditional borderlines between civil society, state and enterprise. On the contrary, the new global cultural assemblage, I argue, is the *Gesamt* creation of social agents representing the local civil society, the foreign investors and representatives of the local government.

This hypothesis is empirically scrutinized through an explorative-intensive case study of a local community subject to strong processes of economic globalization, located in one of the most globalized national economies in the world: the Republic of Ireland. The small town of Leixlip, co. Kildare just outside of Dublin has the highest proportion of foreign direct investment (FDI) in Ireland due to the large manufacturing plants of both Intel and Hewlett-Packard.

I conclude that within the global context, the local civil society reinvents the nation-state as a buffer against what is felt as the global penetration of the local community. At the same time, I observe that in an effort to prevent polarization within the local community, the globalized multinationals stimulate the emerging local culture. Quintessentially fuelled by the fear of "losing it all," a new local identity is created, which through the channels of the multi-nationals is dispersed worldwide in an unprecedented mechanism of globalized local diversity that will be characteristic for the future world society. Social mechanisms related to national societies are not necessarily applicable to the new all-inclusive society. For the emerging world society might have a cultural logic of its own.

Introduction: songs of sameness

Often globalization is thought to bring about homogeneity of cultures. This article however, argues theoretically and empirically that behind the diffuse contours of globalization a new global cultural assemblage is emerging, characterized by local diversity. Being neither homogenous nor the sole product of Western capitalism, this global cultural assemblage is quintessentially the triangular *Gesamt* creation of social agents within civil society, the foreign investors and representatives of the (national) government. Yet the observed emerging local diversity does not occur outside the realms of globalization, but must be considered as being part of globalization. This implies that we might have to review the very concept of globalization itself.[1]

Friedman writes: "Globalization has a distinctly American face: It wears Mickey Mouse ears, it eats Big Macs, it drinks Coke or Pepsi and it does its computing on an IBM or Apple laptop, using Windows 98, with an Intel Pentium II processor and a network link from Cisco Systems" (Friedman 2000: 309). Under the cultural homogeneity thesis the culprit is clear. Profit-maximizing multinationals[2] operating within the capitalist system (Wallerstein 1979) are driving the world towards a monoculture and that process is called globalization. Cultural diversity–if any–then must emerge from other segments of society: beyond the market. Even more so: beyond the nation-state that, as some argue, has lost its power to global capitalism (Hertz 2001). Or as one of my respondents stated:

> "This is the problem of multinationals you see, the state authorities will do nearly anything to please them." (Respondent V–Leixlip resident)

If state and market are equally inclined to produce a uniform world culture, diversity then is left to the domain of civil society. One of the analytical conceptualizations of civil society within the global arena refers to the recent expansion of transnational social activism and cultural innovation from below (Holton 2005: 133). However, if local re-orientations within civil society necessarily coincide with a spread of a homogenous world culture driven by the market, then the concept of globalization is essentially ambiguous–and not uni-dimensional or driven by a singular logic. Then it needs to be redefined as being more than Friedman's American face. Could globalization have multiple faces?

A multi-faced concept of globalization, we can argue, is essentially composed of opposite, possibly conflicting developments. But is the ambiguous nature of the concept of globalization (Van Der Bly 2005) simply divided along the lines of the sectors in society, with the market pushing towards cultural homogeneity and global civil society towards diversity?

Not necessarily. For within the global market cultural diversity is sometimes encouraged, for example as a means towards product diversification and the growth of a consumer market. Similarly within civil society a tendency towards a variant of cultural homogeneity might occur: a global civil society bound by the fact that it aims *not* to share, to be unique, to distinguish. Homogeneity is not the exclusive birthright of state and market, nor is cultural diversity the sole flagship of civil society.

Neither can we assume that the cultural diversity initiated by local civil society is *per se* identical to cultural innovation. Sometimes what we foresee as the future and perceive as innovation is in fact the recreation of an imagined past. Counter-movements do not always truly innovate, sometimes they merely re-orientate. Sloterdijk (2005) argues that while the nautical phase of globalization of the fifteenth century created an atmosphere of cosmopolitanism, the current phase of globalization is leading to a global provincialism. Cosmopolitan versus provincial elements within the container concept of globalization might occur simultaneously as well, possibly mutually reinforcing each other: the stronger the cosmopolitan development, the more the need might be felt for a retreat into the comforts of provincialism.

Almost four decades ago in McLuhan's (1968) "global village," change referred to the "global" becoming an inevitable adjective to every "local," the village. Yet the local remained the main noun, the primary unit of orientation and belonging. Maybe the reverse is happening in our times: the local as the distinctive adjective to the noun of a unifying global. Could we now equally witness a gradual emergence of a "village-fashioned world society," a "provincial world," with the global the main unit of orientation and the local, the traditional, the familiar, as the indispensable, necessary adjective?

Re-defining globalization

This article theoretically and empirically discusses the interaction between processes of economic and cultural globalization on the micro-level. Starting with the cultural homogeneity thesis it was expected that under the influence of the presence of strong processes of economic globalization in the shape of (American) foreign direct investment, an abating local identity, local history and local language would occur alongside an increasing affiliation with a global identity, global culture and language. Under this thesis, variety, if any, would be expected to emerge from local civil society, possibly mainly as a response to a changing economic global environment. Depending on the nature and the shape of the development of local culture instead of cultural homogeneity, cultural polarization then emerges on the local level consisting of two poles: a global culture generated by multinationals versus a local culture emerging from civil society.

Beside the homogenization and the polarization hypotheses, a third scenario is possible. When globalization does not follow a singular logic but is a multi-dimensional and essentially ambiguous concept of processes that are both conflicting and reinforcing each other, the dynamics between these processes do not necessarily have to follow the borderlines between civil society, state and enterprise. On contrary, a new *global cultural assemblage* might emerge on the micro-level as the triangular *Gesamt* creation of social agents within local civil society, the foreign investors and representatives of the (national) government. That hypothesis is in this article empirically scrutinized through an explorative-intensive case study of a small community subject to strong processes of globalization.

When aiming to empirically research globalization as an ambiguous concept, first Friedman's definition, so frequently used in the common sense, has to be left behind. Globalization will have to be defined as a rather empty concept—with the potential of many faces, albeit some might at the moment be more to the forefront on the world stage than others. Elsewhere I have argued that whereas economists have succeeded in coming to a more or less commonly accepted definition as leading towards an "open economy," sociologists have failed to come to a similar consensus[3] (Van Der Bly 2005). Aiming to come similarly to a sociological consensus on globalization as leading towards an "open society," I have suggested a definition of globalization, following Albrow (1990) as: "Globalization refers to all those actions and processes incorporating all the peoples of the world into one world society."

These actions and processes are not limited to economic processes of globalization, but refer above all to processes of connection and interaction. They are therefore essentially social. Neither are they time-bound nor essentially cosmopolitan. As any society, the world society might be divided into provinces and regions, too. Nonetheless on some level, these processes refer to a unity, a perception of a whole, as with societies associated with the boundaries of the nation-state. Unlike the *"global village,"* what I call *"the provincial world"* has the world society as its first point of reference, as the noun that can be refined by various adjectives. Also, in the above-mentioned definition, I have explicitly included "actions" to highlight the element of individual agency within these processes, to make a distinction with conceptualizations of globalization as an intangible macro-concept.[4]

Having globalization redefined, expanded and in a way opened up, this article presents a theoretical and empirical exploration of what Friedman calls "globalization" and what here is argued to be a specific and contemporary manifestation of a process of economic globalization[5]: the global movement of (American) foreign direct investment. What are its cultural responses within the local civil society? With such a broad and rather explorative theoretical research question, the empirical research design could go in only one direction: a modest approach on a small-scale. Therefore it was decided to explore the interference of processes of cultural and economic globalization on a micro-level, through intensive research within the context of a small geographic area: the vast subject of globalization on one little clod of earth.

While globalization can literally be studied everywhere in the world, the selection of the research population has been based upon the principle of theoretical sampling.[6] At the outset of this research, the intention was to research the cultural effects of globalization defined in the "classical" way as "global expansion of American multinationals," and it was assumed it would generate cultural homogeneity. Since theoretical sampling contains the dangers of tautology,[7] it was decided that the only selection criterion would be the independent variable.

Therefore a research area subject to strong processes of foreign direct investment had to be selected, preferably in a national context of a starkly globalized economy. The nation-state argued to have the most globalized economy[8] in the research period[9] was the Republic of Ireland.[10] Within Ireland the town with presumably the highest per capita proportion of foreign direct investment has been selected as a case study: Leixlip in Co. Kildare. On the lands of this town of just over 15,000 inhabitants, Intel Inc. has built its largest manufacturing plant outside of the United States of America, while Hewlett-Packard shortly after Intel's arrival established a large inkjet factory in Leixlip. Once the case study had been chosen, the research was carried out over a period of two years as a triangulation of qualitative and quantitative research methods.[11]

Just a Global Village: Leixlip, Co. Kildare

Leixlip in county Kildare is a small town just across the border of County Dublin at the confluence of the rivers Rye and Liffey. It used to be famous for its salmon leap, which attracted many visitors in the nineteenth century.[12] During the seventies Leixlip's population increased significantly[13] mostly as a result of suburbanization and intra-national migration: people from Ireland's Midlands working in Dublin who preferred to live relatively close to home.

Beginning in the early 1970s local groups, including the Community Council and the Combined Residents Association put forward the idea that a Town Commission for Leixlip would be the most effective way to give local people control over the preservation and development of their own town. A survey was carried out and, in the words of senior library-assistant of Leixlip Library:

> "armed with this result a group of local people began what was to be a long struggle to gain a measure of 'Home Rule' for the town." (Nelson 1990: 66).

Finally in 1987, Leixlip was granted Town Commission Status, which is the lowest form of local authority in Ireland, merely serving as a representation of local residents. Two years later, in October 1989, Intel decided to locate its manufacturing facilities in Ireland and in 1990 Intel commenced production on the hundred fifty hectares of a former farm at Leixlip. The site in Leixlip is Intel's fourth largest manufacturing site overall and the largest outside the United States. It produces microprocessors and communication silicon chips and Intel has invested some five billion euro in the site. Employment on site is 5,150 with both direct employees and indirect long-term contractors.[14]

Hewlett-Packard located an inkjet cartridges factory in Leixlip in 1995. Currently the factory has 2,400 employees on the site in Leixlip, with about 1800 involved in the inkjet factory and the rest in Sales and Services, Hewlett-Packard International Bank, and Contracting and Media Products. The employees are young, with an average age of 27, and relatively high educated: seventy percent of the employees are college graduates and thirty percent are in continuing education.[15]

The coming of the multinational Intel was a result of global, European, national and regional developments, however, the town itself seems to have had little involvement in it.

> "So the national Industrial Development Authority, they found this site. They purchased the land from the landowners and then they sold the land to Intel." (Respondent B–spokesperson Intel)

The site was located on the land of Leixlip, Co Kildare.

> "Kildare County Council owned most of the land, it was earmarked for industry, but Intel bought up all the farmland around the plant. They like to have a sterile ehm... area. They don't like neighbours near them." (Respondent A–spokesperson Town Council)

Even though the residents had long campaigned for local autonomy, for "Home Rule" for Leixlip, the decision that would influence the town most profoundly seems to have been taken largely without the involvement of the local residents.

> "I read the news in the national papers." (Respondent N–Member Town Commission 1989)

A study, carried out by an independent consultancy firm at the request of the current Town Commission, concluded in 2002 that:

> "The problems facing Leixlip town center are somewhat unusual. While the town does not suffer from significant unemployment or other economic problems, there is a perception that the town has not benefited from the growth in recent residential and employment development as much as expected. (...) Major new employment centers (HP and Intel) are even further removed."[16]

The report concludes that "there is a perception that the rapid pace of new development has to some extent overwhelmed the town."[17] Yet Intel has been on the grounds of the former stud farm in Leixlip for over fifteen years and shows no signs of leaving. Hewlett-Packard, after moving to Leixlip largely as a consequence of what Krugman (1997) calls "demonstration and cascade-effects"[18] in 1995, has just announced an enlargement of the site. If there are no major economic problems, then which developments do we see in the cultural field? Let's explore the town for traces of globalization.

Two sides of the town: an expansive and an explanatory identity

Bottles on the ground and a sign in the sky

A special train service called the *Arrow* connects the inner city of Dublin with its outer suburb, Leixlip, just across the border between County Dublin and County Kildare. There are two stations: *Leixlip Confey* and *Leixlip Louisa Bridge*. It is October 2002, the first day of the fieldwork and just before the Arrow enters Louisa Bridge station a wall emerges on the left side of the station. In enormous black graffiti three letters are written on it: I R A . The train slows down. The doors open.

Louisa Bridge station seems to be in the middle of nowhere. There is one long highway. There are new housing estates on the other side of the road, in the far distance. There are cars. It is windy. There is no pub. That is very unusual. Every central meeting point in Ireland seems to have a pub nearby. Not here, in Leixlip Louisa Bridge. Where is the centre of this town? There is no information. In this land that belongs to no-one, the town does not seem to exist. There is just only one sign: blue letters on a yellow background. It points towards the left and says: *Hewlett-Packard, 2.5 km.*

At the base of the Hewlett-Packard sign empty Coca-Cola bottles are left behind in the high grass. Between the green leaves of the bushes they light up colorfully: a new layer of artificial flowers covering the earth, uniform, ubiquitous and recognizable to all of its inhabitants.

In the distance a block of identical suburban houses with identical red cars parked in front of almost identical lawns looms across the highway. If urban life expresses diversity then suburban life seems to express sameness: a homogenous extract of the population has left to build walls of reassuring sameness around the ancient, yet disturbingly fast-changing city. Now a new circle of uniformity seems to have been drawn worldwide. No longer is sameness the privilege of the suburb. It is everywhere. Globalization, conceived in this way, seems everywhere.

From the Coca-Cola bottles on the ground to the Hewlett-Packard sign in the sky, the picture is clear: a layer of homogenous culture has been laid upon humanity–like grass was once laid upon the earth–and this ubiquitous presence is by origin and by nature American. Or so it seems. Much seems to confirm the idea of uniformity and Americanization. Yet this first impression is superficial and a closer look at the community reveals different, far more complex social mechanisms.

Welcome to Leixlip

The visitor who does not arrive by public transport but by car, for example coming over the Station Road, will see a different sign. There it is, on her left hand side: "Welcome to Leixlip." The signboard is placed just after the visitor in her car has past the wide stretch of Intel's buildings and car parks–as if the town's boundaries only begin when the global industrial activity is left behind. Hewlett-Packard's signpost near Louisa Bridge just indicates the name of the global market player and the distance in kilometres. It is an effective sign, reflecting the values Ritzer (1995) attributes to McDonaldization: efficiency, predictability, and calculability. As a sign it mainly seems to aim to "instruct the visitor to get where we are, assuming that you know who we are."

On the other hand, the very visible Leixlip-sign defines Leixlip, sketching the framework of an identity that is seemingly not self-evident. This signboard reflects a dynamic, contested identity that is in the process of construction and at pains to explain itself. This is a complex constellation of references to local, national and international belongings and separations, presented in a detailed and–certainly considering the context of an ordinary signboard–long-winded way that can hardly be qualified as efficient or by references to calculability. Emphasizing distinction rather than sameness, it thus does not reflect any of the values associated with McDonaldization (Ritzer 1995) or Americanization.

It is so large and full of information that it can hardly be considered efficient. It does not include any numbers, not even the distance to the town centre and it is disputable to what extent it aims to increase predictability. On the other hand, its main purpose seems to be to "explain to the visitor who we are and what we stand for assuming that you do not know who we are." In that sense the Leixlip-sign reflects an *explanatory identity* rather than an *expansive identity*: an identity that is in the process of construction and at pains to explain itself.

This signboard seems merely designed to express the local identity to the visitor. To the visitor? Or possibly not just to the motorist who will drive too fast to be able to carefully read the signpost, but to its own inhabitants as well, through sketching the content and values of an identity that is not self-evident. If all relevant parties were to know what Leixlip is and what it stands for, then the signboard would be redundant. Yet this is an identity in an explanatory phase, rather than an identity that is in a process of expansion. For an identity that is in an expansive phase does not need to explain itself. It just needs to mention the name, indicate the distance and show the way.

While under the homogeneity thesis it is expected that local identity recedes in favor of a more global identity, this gigantic sign that welcomes the stranger to Leixlip does not show any sign of an abating local identity. The explanatory identity manifests itself on this signboard–instructing the stranger how to perceive Leixlip while reminding the Leixlip inhabitants who they are–on four levels: a) which languages they speak, b) to which nation-state they belong, c) what their shared history is and d) with whom they share their present. If we want to understand the Leixlip identity, this sign board needs to be carefully examined, bearing in mind that it was erected in the early nineties, just after Intel's arrival. What is the explanatory identity that needs to be explained and is not a known fact?

Four levels of Leixlip's explanatory identity

Language: Fáilte go Léim an Bhradáin

First of all, the visitor is told that this is a bilingual, Irish-speaking town. The signpost does not just welcome the visitor to Leixlip in English, but in Irish as well: *Fáilte go Léim an Bhradáin*. The practical use of a welcome in Irish on this board is relatively limited. How likely is it that the visitor in her car is an Irish-speaking visitor who does not understand English? How many Irish-speaking visitors who cannot understand English will come to Leixlip on an annual basis? Neither is it specifically designed in order to express hospitality by welcoming visitors in their native languages. For then it would have been more plausible to welcome the stranger in the language of Ireland's largest immigrant population (China) or in the languages of the largest proportions of its tourists: the Spanish, the Italian, the German or the Japanese.

With the practical use being limited, the *symbolic* meaning is significant in at least two ways. Unlike other European languages spoken outside of the boundaries of one nation-state as well, the Irish language is exclusively associated with Ireland. Therefore the marking of Leixlip as an Irish-speaking town is not only a strong act of local distinction, singling Leixlip out from many other towns in Europe and indeed the world, but this linguistic distinction flags nationalism a well.[19] This flagging of nationalism is indirect: through the intermediating variable of language and not explicitly based upon geographical boundaries or geopolitical territoriality.

A town consists in general of land and people. When seeking local distinction, Leixlip could have chosen to distinguish itself by referring to the borders of its geographical land, explicitly including everybody in that area as being part of the Leixlip community–and those people only. This then would *exclude* everybody living outside of the town's boundaries but for example explicitly *include* the African surgeon who lives in Leixlip and who took part in my research as well. Singling out Leixlip geographically as a town on the island of Ireland and attributing a Leixlip identity solely to that geographic area would be a very strong distinguishing act, separating Leixlip from all other towns in Europe and indeed the world. This would have referred to what Smith (1986: 94) has qualified as "the compactness of territory and the defensibility of borders," as a mechanism in the survival of communities.

However, as Smith argues, the importance of geopolitical strategic aspects of location in the survival of communities has diminished. So the borders of Leixlip's identity are not geopolitical, but social; referring not to the land, but to the people. Interestingly, this act of separation is at the same time an act of connection. While Leixlip has chosen to separate itself from other people rather than from other lands, it reaches out to all those people who do not inhabit the land, but who master the Irish language.

This Irish-speaking people include the Irish Diaspora in America, in South Africa, in Australia and everywhere else in the world. But does it include as well the old man who has lived all his life in the North of the Netherlands, who is a member of the Russian Orthodox Church, but is fluent in Irish and has translated stories of the Irish writer Padraig Pearse in Dutch? And the Sudanese anthropologist I was told about, who has fluent Irish?

Through the emphasis on the Irish language, civil society in Leixlip, or at least their representatives in the Town Commission, while reaching out to some, establish an act of implicit separation from others, possibly even from people within the town's border: those who do not speak Irish. Yet at the same time a unity is created with another people outside of the town's borderlines: Irish-speaking strangers: a unity and an inclusion, though created by explicit and deliberate exclusion. While geopolitical borders by definition create local cohesion as Smith (1986) argues, borders drawn based upon social characteristics can cause local division.

The creation of national myths on a local level

The explanatory identity manifests itself on a second level on the signboard. This time nationalism is not indirectly flagged through the language, but directly, through symbols. In the case of Ireland, the indigenous language is directly related to the nation-state. The act of deliberate intensification of the place of the Irish language in Irish society is therefore implicitly an act of Irish nationalism. However, a national identity is much broader than a language, it refers to symbols and to heroes as well. On the signboard that welcomes the visitor to the town, Leixlip is advertised as "The original home of Guinness," with Guinness still being a strong element of the Irish identity.

Through emphasizing Leixlip as the original home of Guinness, the town is legitimately placed in the centre of the imaginary identity-boundaries of the Irish nation-state, while at the same time the visitor is reminded that he or she walks on Irish soil, in an example of Billig's "banal nationalism." Forgetting is part of the operation of banal nationalism. The nation is flagged, but the flagging itself is forgotten as the nation is mindlessly remembered (Billig 1995: 143). However, the examples Billig provides us with are mostly derived from the British context. In Leixlip nationalism is not just mindlessly remembered. In Leixlip, within the Irish context, nationalism is actively, deliberately and consciously created.

A mechanism that seems to have the form of "defensive banal nationalism" first emerged in an interview with one of the local historians. I had noticed both in brochures about Leixlip and physically in several places in the town how Leixlip prides itself on being the home of Guinness. Without at that stage giving too much meaning to that observation, I just wanted to know the historical background. My question was simply: "Why does Leixlip present itself as the home of Guinness?," to which a local historian replied:

> "Well, as far as I am aware, historically.... Yes.. the first Guinness operation was in Leixlip and I think that it is *historically safe*... Arthur Guinness set up the first Guinness brewery here in Leixlip...and I think that is broadly accepted and historians are reasonably happy as to where the actual site was, just off the Main Street Bridge." (Respondent M–local historian; italics added)

The answer is not a straightforward explanation, but seems to set off with a defence. The respondent uses the expression "historically safe" to justify the explanation, as if to vindicate a stronghold that somehow seems to belong to the domain of the disputable rather than to the obvious. Leixlip might have another interest in canvassing itself as the home of Guinness, turning the historical fact into a crucial instrument in a defensive strategy. But what needs to be defended? And who are the attackers?

There is no museum built around the historical Guinness site, so the emphasis placed on the historical fact seems not as much meant to attract visitors.

> "No, there is no Guinness museum in Leixlip. There is one in Dublin. It should be moved here!" (Respondent K.–Leixlip resident)

Leixlip is not just competing with the capital, global city Dublin for the ownership of national symbols, but with adjacent towns as well.

> "The people of Cellbridge [=an adjacent town]) claimed that Guinness was brewed there first. Now it might be true Arthur Guinness lived there a little while, but the first Guinness was not porter, but ale. And ale was brewed here." (Respondent N.–local historian)

National emblems seem to be symbolic assets worth fighting for in a sub-national competition. Yet interestingly enough while the plain historical fact that Arthur Guinness set up his first brewery for a very short time in Leixlip was known, the idea of Leixlip as the "Home of Guinness," seems to be a recent creation.

> "Up until relatively recent times I don't think it was a very big factor or selling point-for Leixlip.... but in more recent times, particularly since the Town Commission became aware of it, the fact of Guinness has been widely promoted, certainly compared to when I came to Leixlip in the 1970's... I was aware of it, but it was not constantly mentioned or promoted, where as the present everybody seems interested in promoting it ..." (Respondent M–local historian)

Shortly after Hewlett-Packard and Intel were erecting the signs pointing to their grounds, signboards were posted advertising Leixlip as the Home of Guinness. Smith (1986) argues that part of nationalism is the creation of a national mythology general consisting of several myths, including a "myth of origin in space, i.e. when the community was born" (Smith 1986: 192). Through redefining Leixlip as the Home of Guinness, Leixlip is placed at the heart of the origins of the Irish nation-state. Through the promotion of this historical fact the local identity is defined by "building the nation-state within the locality."

Leixlip is not just a town in Ireland, it is an Irish town, closely connected to one of the success stories of the Irish-nation state: Guinness. As Smith (1986) argues "a myth of the golden age," is another motif in any national mythology. Guinness has expanded, wandered over the country's borderlines and been exported to foreign shores, just like the Irish Diaspora, yet Leixlip is still where it once was: at the heart of Ireland, a primordial home. All else might be gone and scattered over the earth, yet somewhere the origins can be found.

While Hewlett-Packard erects a clear and efficient signpost near Louisa Bridge station, Guinness sponsors the massive signboards on the borders of the town claiming a unique local identity. The two sides of the town seem a battlefield over multi-national ownership, with the national competing with the global. Signs sponsored by Hewlett-Packard point the visitor in one direction, a global direction. The signs sponsored by Guinness point to the national, Irish direction. National? Ironically, Guinness is no longer Irish-owned but part of the global company Diageo, with its headquarters in London- the capital of the former colonial power.[20] The global fights over the local and reinvents the national in the process, or so it seems.

The harp is not just Ireland's national symbol, it is a patented trademark of Guinness as well. Every Irish euro bears on one side the harp as the distinctive national symbol and on the other hand the uniformized European economic value. Yet these apparent separate entities, national symbolism on one side and European economic policy on the other side, might in fact be two sides of the same coin: literally.

While global, European and national interests merge, to some extent the local falls apart. Once, the ruins of the Guinness brewery were the playgrounds for the children of the small community. An older Leixlip residents tells about the fifties, when Leixlip had around a thousand inhabitants:

> I–"Do you remember the Guinness brewery back then?"
> RD–"Oh yes. We used to play near the River Rye... and we played on the ruins of the old factory... Leixlip was always an integrated community." (Respondent D–Leixlip resident)

This respondent immediately links in his memory the ruins of the Guinness brewery to his perception that Leixlip was an integrated community, being an intrinsic part of what was local. Yet now the local ruins have been turned into the pillars of the symbolic building of the nation-state and what was once a common local playground has changed to a distinctive selling point on a global marketplace. The historical fact has now become a unique selling point for Leixlip. But to whom is Leixlip to be sold?

Somehow this lifting out of what once belonged to the local community to incorporate it into the national context–a defensive act in a battle fought on the global field–is an act of local disintegration. The local ruins of the brewery were a playground for all local children, even for this child whose father came from Northern Ireland to Leixlip in the forties–yet the ruins as a national symbol for the Irish nation-state are not open to all. Sometimes national and even global integration can cause local disintegration.

Banal localism: the town crest

Apart from flagging nationalism on two levels on the signpost, a third level of the explanatory identity comes in the shape of an interesting display of what I call *"banal localism"*–albeit this is not a forgotten reminder of locality, but a deliberate act to establish a local identity.[21] On the gigantic signboard the complete town crest is included. It was created in 1989 at the same time that Intel first arrived in Leixlip and this crest includes several references to the history of the town (Nelson 1990). Previously I have discussed the establishment of a distinction between other people in the here and now of contemporary society through symbolic use of language, something that I call *global horizontal segregation*.

However, *global vertical segregation* can be established, too, in time–even within the context of what Castells (1999) has called a "global economy characterized by simultaneity." Global vertical segregation through time refers to a separation of people who do *not* share the same history that in the wording of one of Leixlip's local historians: "reflect the different traditions that have made us what we are" (Kelly, (2000: 10). An act of exclusion based upon global horizontal segregation can be redefined in the here and now: people speak or do not speak Irish. Yet the act of exclusion based upon global vertical segregation is mythical, invisible and therefore in a certain way nonnegotiable. Global vertical segregation is probably the most powerful and persistent of all segregations amongst peoples. Indeed, when Smith describes an ethnic community or what he calls an *ethnie*, he argues that "Ethnie are nothing if not historical communities built up on shared memories. A sense of common history unites successive generations" (Smith 1986: 25).

If globalization refers to the expansion of smaller communities into a larger society, possibly the largest society, the world society, then indeed it implies the integral dissolution of all ethnic communities. The idea of a "shared history" then will have to recede in significance as a source for segregation. Yet a concept of "shared history" has different dimensions. Interestingly, Leixlip's town crest symbolizes a shared history based upon a) local, b) regional, c) national and d) European (or possibly global) history.

At the base of the shield, a wavy effect symbolizes Leixlip's location on the rivers Liffey and Rye. Two leaping salmon, recalling the origins of the town's name, flank the long ship. The crimson rose at the top is taken from the coat of arms of the Whyte family, who occupied Leixlip Castle for over two hundred years (Nelson 1990: 68). These symbols then refer to a *shared local history*.

The crown symbolizes the kingdom of Meath and is modeled on one that appears on the crosier of Cormac MacCullinan, King of Munster. This indeed refers to a *shared regional history*, shared with all the descendants of the Kingdom of Meath. The black harp, emblem of Arthur Guinness and Sons "whose empire was founded in Leixlip in the 1750s" (Nelson 1990: 68), refers to a *shared national history*, a past shared with all the people of Irish descent.

However, at the same time the elements for a shared history beyond the local, regional and indeed national borders are incorporated in the crest. "The basic colours of the shield are azure blue and yellow: these are Scandinavian colors which recall the Viking origins of Leixlip and this theme is repeated in the centre of the design where a Viking longship is depicted" (Nelson 1990: 68). The shared history of the *ethnie* of Leixlip then refers to all peoples of Scandinavian origin, something that possibly can be called either a *shared European history* or to some extent even a *shared global history*. In conclusion: the local identity as symbolized in the crest is multi-layered and based upon multiple shared histories: local, regional, national, European and possibly even global.

The crest does not just include references to the past. It includes a reference to the future as well. Its motto is: Léim ar Aghaidh, or "Leap Forward!" "While the coat of arms looks back to Leixlip's past, the accompanying motto–*Léim ar Aghaidh*–looks forward to future developments and growth" (Nelson 1990: 68). At the time of the design of the town crest the contours of that future had become vaguely visible. The town crest was launched at a reception in Leixlip Castle on 1 December 1989, two months after Intel announced their intention to build a major industrial plant in Leixlip.

> I–"Did you know that Intel would come to Leixlip at the time when the crest was designed?"

> RN (*defensive*)–"That had nothing to do with Intel!..... (*hesitating*) It was an imposition really. There was no consultation with the local people. We were not informed. We had heard about Intel. But we did not know anything of this company. Certainly the impression was not given that Intel was a chemical processing plant." (Respondent N–Member sub-committee of Town Commission for Design of Town Crest)

Through the design of the crest the local community designed the local identity. Globalization knocked at the town's borders in a process that by some was perceived as something that was imposed, as a product of dominion over the local and not of local autonomy. With the economic and political power of the Town Council being limited, what was left were the instruments of symbolic power.

Global connections: town twinning

The shared history, a source for the display of what I call banal localism, shows traces of globalization in ancient times: the Viking invaders literally left their colors as a legacy to Leixlip's town crest. Yet a fourth dimension on the signboard exposes an explicit and contemporary globalized element of Leixlip's explanatory identity. Leixlip announces on the board to be "twinned with Bressuire in France and Niles in the United States of America."

> "Bressuire was first. Niles was added later in the nineties. I did not want an American town. I wanted a Northern Ireland or UK town, or possibly a French or Spanish town. But that did not happen. They chose an American town." (Respondent F.–Leixlip Resident)

The explanatory identity is not solely constructed through the social mechanisms of social exclusion and inclusion, but also through a social mechanism of distinction based upon geographic *connectivity*. Leixlip is twinned with Bressuire in France and with Niles in the United States of America and therefore it is unique: there will be presumably no other towns in this world that have the same connection.

Whereas every social mechanism of connectivity assumes a certain grade of exclusiveness as well (in this case explicitly excluding all the other towns that are *not* related to Bressuire *and* to Niles) the mechanism of town twinning is based upon geographic distinction and not upon the characteristics attributed to a certain people. It refers to *all* people who live in Bressuire and in Niles and interlinks these people with *all* people who live in Leixlip–without necessarily arguing that these people need to be Irish or have an Irish history. For not all of them do.

At the time when I was taking the photographs of the signboard, a group of Intel workers dressed in blue uniforms was just behind the sign waiting for the bus to Dublin to arrive. I walked up to one of them. We had problems communicating extensively, but he told me where he is from: from China. Later I discovered that the original picture shows his silhouette through the piles of the enormous signboard "Welcome To Leixlip," his head almost out of frame, his Intel blue uniformed body sitting down on the kerb, waiting.

Not an ordinary village, but a village with a past: creating local history

Sometimes an outer appearance of homogeneity hides inner diversity. The homogeneity thesis does not seem to be supported in the field of "identity" in Leixlip. An emerging homogenous world culture would imply the gradual vanishing of a local and indeed national identity. Yet in Leixlip I observed the actual *emergence* of local identity through the awareness of local history and symbols. Besides an emerging local identity, the national identity is created and reinforced on the local level.

One might argue that in Leixlip two developments coincide rather than having a causal relationship with each other. In other words, the coming of economic globalization did not cause diversity in the cultural field, but coincided with the different, parallel process including the search for a local identity of a town that just was granted Town Commission status.

However, even when the foundations were laid at the same time as Intel arrived and its consequences were not known, under the homogeneity thesis a diminishing effect is expected: a fading out of the need for a local identity in favour of adapting a global identity, a fading out of interest in local history in favour of a global outlook on the world. Yet the opposite development seems to be taking place. To what extent is that development taking place within local civil society?

The Town Council erected the signboard. While under the most recent legislation, "the function of Leixlip Town Council generally is to provide a forum for the democratic representation of the local community, to provide civic leadership and to promote community interest,"[22] one might argue that the Town Council can be identified with the (local) government and not as such with local civil society. Yet within local civil society a similar development is taking place: the interest in Leixlip's local history *sui generis* is growing. In the last one and half decade numerous historical studies on Leixlip have been published.[23] The local civil society redefines itself not just as being "Irish" but also as distinctively "local." When I ask one of the local historians about the origin of local history writing, it appears that in many ways the history of Leixlip itself is a recent development.

> I–"Have there been any historical studies on Leixlip before 1990?"
> RM–"I know that Leixlip is referred to in a number of works, but just in passing… and there are comments by travellers, which are known, but I don't think there is a history of Leixlip as such…" (Respondent M–local historian)

While local history is written, national history functions as ghostwriter. Another dimension of any national mythology is a "myth of liberation; i.e. how we were freed" (Smith 1986: 192). As the Irish nation-state is rebuilt in Leixlip, long-forgotten national heroes are rediscovered in the locality. One local historian tells how he discovered a 19th century nationalist hero and made him part of Leixlip's identity.

> "There was a 19th century Fenian leader, William Roantree, the Republican Movement of that time, and he was born here in the Main Street." (Respondent M–local historian)

However, this native son, this national hero, is not part of the oral local history for:

> "Nobody had ever heard about him. Nobody knew where the house was." (Respondent M–local historian)

It is interesting to see how the memories of what is now called "Leixlip's Famous Fenian"[24] were locally long gone.

> "There was a lot of studying in the National Library involved and in the National Archives…going to the prison record… to the cemetery in Glasnevin and finding his tomb…his grave… and just generally rediscovering him." (Respondent M–local historian)

While the national hero might on a national level still be remembered (the National Library, the National Archives), he had locally sunk into oblivion. No longer part of his own local history, he had become part of the domain of national history and national history only. Now he needs to descend from the national level, return to the local level: his present connection needs to physically and visibly become part of Leixlip.

> "It took a lot of effort to even get a memorial sign on his house. I worked with various Town Commissions on that…"(Respondent M–local historian)

In 1996 the plaque funded by the national Bord Fáilte, the Tourist Board, was unveiled by the Cathaoirleach (mayor) of the Leixlip Town Commission.

> "Well, the plaque... Oddly enough I should mention the fact that they have been taken down the plague. Because the house is in decay and the house is reconstructed... it has been taken down for safety... Hopefully it will be rebuilt. Hopefully. Rather ironically he got years of limelight and now he is gone again..." (Respondent M–local historian)

The plaque was "erected on the front of Roantree's house in *his honour*" as another local historian writes (Kelly 2002: 32, italics added). The emergence of the Fenian leader within the streets of Leixlip is not just a historical discovery. It is a patriotic act, ultimately aiming to pay tribute to a hero who made a significant contribution to the establishment of the Irish nation-state. Yet the patriotic act occurs almost eighty years after the hero's death and the establishment of the nation-state.[25]

Connor (1993) argues that a distinction needs to be made between patriotism and nationalism, with nationalism being an irrational, primordial force, an emotional attachment to one's people appealing to blood ties (Connor 1993: 374). Nationalism, he argues, arises in ethnic groups that claim common origins of blood. Yet why does this patriotic act emerge now in prosperous, peaceful Leixlip? And to what extent does this patriotism or this form of nationalism appeal to blood ties, an irrational, primordial force? Why here, why now?

> "I hope they will restore the plaquette, just to tell to younger generations... and new people... to share our knowledge..." (Respondent M–local historian)

While the respondent here refers to younger generations and to blood ties, he refers to new people as well. The remembrance of the Fenian is a way to share knowledge, yet it is more than that. Knowledge is not just shared for the sake of spreading knowledge but to get a message across, or, as the historian continues:

> "To make clear that this is not just an ordinary village, but a village with a past..." (Respondent M–local historian)

Why is the discovery significant? To tell the future generations that Leixlip is not an ordinary town. The discovery is an act to highlight distinction, to establish the particular, the unique, and it does so by relating the local to the national. Leixlip is unique, because it is Irish. Through incorporating national heroes and symbols within the local boundaries, the local bolsters its own identity.

At the same time through this mechanism the national identity is strengthened by the need of the local to defend its own identity. But against whom? To whom might Leixlip seem an ordinary village?

Not only has the interest in local history only begun since the coming of Intel to Leixlip (*post hoc*) it seems that there are some indications that there is a causal relationship as well (*propter hoc*), as one of my respondents replies when I ask him if he sees any relationship between the coming of Hewlett-Packard and Intel and the emergence of numerous local history studies.

> "I suppose that there is a feeling–certainly amongst my age group–that if it is not collected... and noted... and here and now...with the sheer level of pace and development... that we will lose it all." (Respondent M–local historian)

Yet the national heritage of Leixlip seems very much something that is created rather than preserved from vanishing. The question then can be posed: what will be lost? For there seem to be a lot at stake: "else we lose it all."

Under the cultural homogeneity thesis we would expect an abating local identity, a diminishing interest for local history, yet we observe the opposite. In addition, somehow the fume of a smouldering cultural polarization becomes visible. We might distinguish an American culture and its values on one hand and an Irish culture on the other hand, whereby the American identity seems self-evident, self-explanatory and ready for expansion, while the Irish identity needs to be explained and possibly justified. Even on home ground.

Voice of the Irish people: speaking Irish in Leixlip

Can you speak Irish?

One might argue that the above-mentioned impressions are anecdotal, based upon the simple analysis of a sign and the observation of a growing interest in local history: hardly enough grounding in empirical evidence to reject a hypothesis of growing sameness. Identity is hard to quantify and to empirically measure. Which developments do we see in the field of language?

A gradual homogenization under the influence of forces of globalization assumes a gradual decline of the relative importance of indigenous language in favour of emerging world languages. As Huntington argues: "If a universal civilization is emerging there should be tendencies toward the emergence of a universal language and a universal religion" (Huntington 1996: 59). Homogeneity then implies the emergence of one or possibly a limited number of world languages replacing indigenous languages, such as Irish, the indigenous language of Ireland. Since cultural homogeneity is argued to be the result of economic globalization, a very strong manifestation of this mechanism is expected in the town with the highest per capita proportion of foreign direct investment, in the country with the world's most globalized economy.

Yet the opposite seems to occur. The following figure reflects the answer on the question *"Can you speak Irish"* as a percentage of the total population of three years or older based upon Census data for the period 1981-2002.[26] If the homogeneity thesis operates, a decline in Irish speakers is expected, but the reverse seems to be true. Not only is the percentage of Irish speakers not declining from the moment that the Census has extended a question addressing the ability to speak Irish: it has grown significantly, from 33% to half of the population in 2002.

This reverse effect is not only true for Leixlip but holds for the total of the Republic of Ireland as well. As mentioned before, since Ireland is the country with the highest degree of economic integration into the world economy,[27] under the homogeneity hypothesis we would expect a strong decline in the indigenous language. However, the opposite effect is true, as figure 2 shows.

This reverse homogenization effect manifests itself not only on the level of the nation-state, but also within the nation-state: in the town that is very significantly subject to processes of economic globalization, the growth of Irish speakers between 1981 and 2002 is significantly stronger than the national average (17% for Leixlip versus 11% for Ireland).

In what is argued to be the most globalized nation-state in the world, an increase of the percentage of speakers of the indigenous language can be observed, while even *within* this nation-state a region which is very strongly effected by economic globalization shows a stronger increase of the percentage of Irish speakers. Based upon these figures, it cannot be argued that the increase is caused by globalization, for there might be other disturbing variables. Yet there is no empirical support for the homogeneity thesis either.

The evidence of the development of the Irish language as reflected in the statistics is supported by the observations of one Leixlip respondent.

> I–"Do you feel there is a change in the appreciation of Irish in Leixlip over the years?"
> RK–"Yes, I do. One of our primary schools teaches entirely through the medium of Irish."
> I–"Do your children go to that school?"
> RK–"Well they did, they are grown up now, but yes. The school has a reasonable influence in the town, in so far that when it holds activities they are well supported, hundreds of events ... their influence ripples out into the community... Their influence is growing..."
> I–"It is?"

Figure 1. Irish speakers in Leixlip as percentage of total population

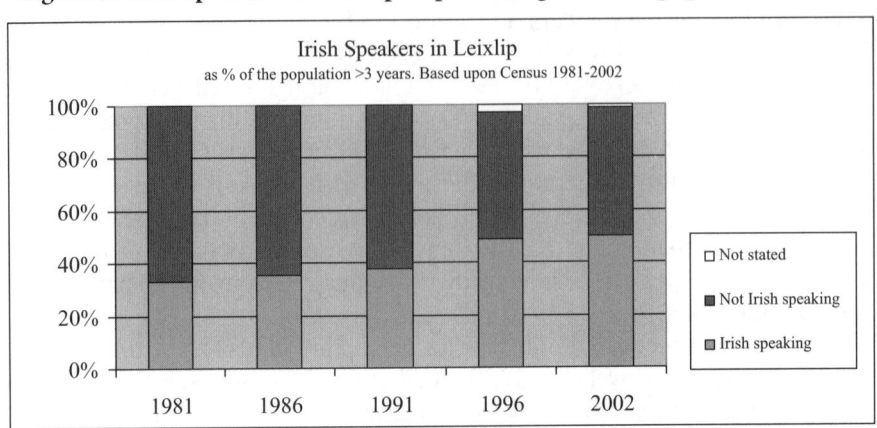

RK–"Yes. The schools are growing bigger, there are more children attending. I think the people want their children to go to Gaelic schools." (Respondent K–Leixlip resident. Mother of three children)

The Census data on Irish-speaking have only been available since 1981. Thus even when the last two decades show a growth of Irish speakers, it is still possible that the current percentage of almost half of the people indicating an ability to speak Irish reflects effectively a decline compared to the past. As older systematic statistics of Irish speakers are lacking, I ask an older, native respondent what language was spoken in Leixlip's past. He recalls his memories, set in the fifties of the last century.

> "Leixlip back then was a small hamlet... We were all English speaking... there were very few people who spoke Irish... you see North Kildare was over the centuries regarded as part of the Pale and Leixlip was deemed to be inside the Pale. There were a lot of estate houses here, they gave a lot of local employment... servants... agricultural... to cut their turf... harvest their crops... it was really a small rural society..." (Respondent D–Leixlip resident)

As a part of the Pale[28], the English-ruled area around Dublin, Leixlip has never been Irish speaking. Maybe it was Irish speaking in an ancient past? Leixlip as a town was founded in the early tenth century. According to *The Annals of the Four Masters* the Leinstermen were defeated in 915 by Norse invaders in Confey, and that is when the village of Leixlip is established as the "most westerly point of the Scandinavian Kingdom of Dublin, which extended from Skerries on the north to Arklow in County Wicklow in the south" (Nelson 1990: 1). Leixlip's name is of Viking origin (Nelson 1990). We can therefore

Figure 2. Irish speakers in Leixlip and Ireland as percentage of total population

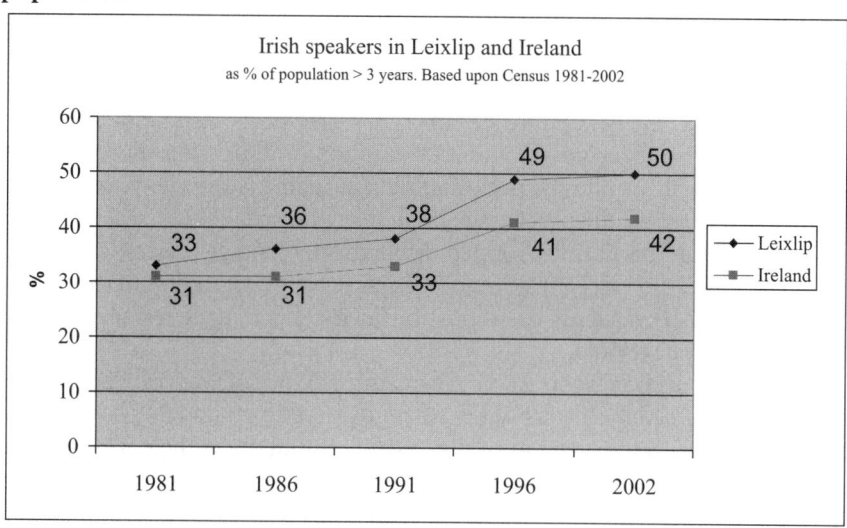

speculate that the proportion of Irish speakers in Leixlip is at the moment at a historical peak.

Bilingualism: now it is easier to pick up other languages

However, the above-mentioned homogeneity hypothesis is based on a uni-polar language approach, assuming that the growth of one language will inevitably lead to the decline and possible vanishing of another language. It does not take into account a development towards a world culture based upon a bipolar language system, whereby people will be increasingly bilingual. This bilingualism can take the shape of a language constellation where both (and possibly even more languages) fulfil different functions, used in different discourses. Huntington argues against the homogenization thesis not only because English speakers as percentage of the total world population have declined since 1958; he also refers to the limitations of the use of English as a lingua franca as an indicator for the emergence of a universal culture. "The use of English in this way, however, is *intercultural* communication; it presupposes the existence of separate cultures" (Huntington 1996: 61).

Yet in the case of Ireland, English can hardly qualify as a lingua franca and instrument of intercultural communication–apart from the use of English amongst Ireland's immigrant population. Whereas in some places English might replace Irish as a first language, supporting the homogeneity thesis, in other places English is not being replaced. Rather a previous monolingual population is made bi-lingual, a process of diversity rather than of homogeneity.

Whereas a bilingualism consisting of a lingua franca and a native home-spoken language might occur in other countries, in Ireland English is not the lingua franca and Irish is not the language spoken at home. In fact, it is very rarely spoken, as the next figure shows.

In 1996 the Census added an extra question,[29] addressing the frequency of the use of Irish. While the period of data available is too short to give any indication of a trend, the percentage of people who speak Irish in Leixlip on a daily basis has in this period dropped, while the percentage of people who can speak Irish but who rarely or never do has increased. Only a fifth of the inhabitants speak Irish on a daily basis, possibly a large percentage of them visiting an Irish speaking school.

In 1979 the primary school *Glór Na nGael* or "Voice of the Irish People" was established in Leixlip. The school is currently mostly funded by the National Government, with five percent of the budget coming from the parents.[30] The school was founded by people who immigrated into Leixlip from elsewhere in Ireland, wishing to educate their children in Irish. One of the people involved in the setting up of the school explains her motives as follows:

> "No, Irish is not my first language, but I came to it when I was twelve year of age. My father would have been very interested in it and wanted me to be educated in it and I agreed... so I was educated at secondary level through Irish and it kept up a love and an interest ever since. So I was delighted when I came to Leixlip and the Irish school was being talked about. So I came involved then when they set it up and circled the board of management and was manager of the school for sometime..." (Respondent H–Leixlip Resident)

Whereas the school seems not to have been initiated by people who were all native speakers, but mostly by people who were bilingual, the children who attend the school now are mostly neither from native Irish-speaking parents nor from the *Gaeltacht* (Irish-speaking areas).

> "... some would be generations Leixlip, five.. six.. generations Leixlip, some would be from Dublin.... Eh... quite a lot. Dublin would have been again...for several, as many generations back as they could go. But a lot would be originally from.... not necessarily from Gaeltacht areas.... but from outside Dublin, from the countryside" (Respondent G–Teacher Irish school).

The establishment of an Irish culture in English speaking Leixlip is therefore partly the product of *intra-national migration*. From that perspective the local

Figure 3. Use of Irish as percentage of Irish speakers in Leixlip

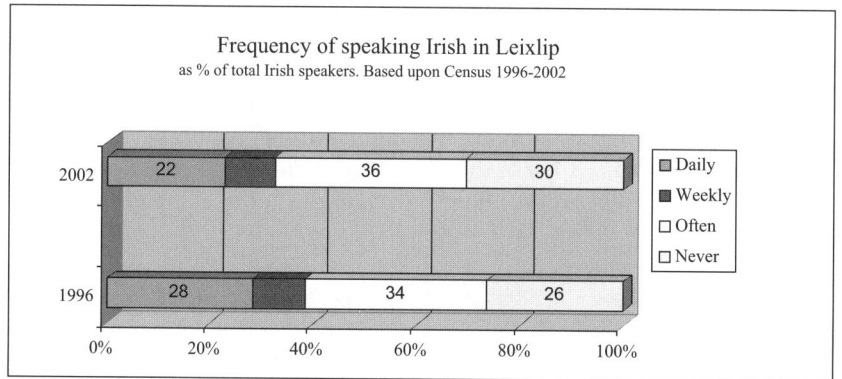

culture of Irish language in Leixlip is effectively an (intra-national) immigrant culture.

The increase in the number of people who can speak Irish coincides with the decline in the amount of people who actually do so on a daily basis. This might be related to the change in the age-structure of the population. The percentage of people under 19 dropped from 41% to 32% between 1996 and 2002 (CSO 1981-2002). With the daily speakers of Irish being mostly school-going children who will not continue to use the language on a daily basis after they have left school, speaking Irish seems to have a *symbolic* rather than a *communicative* purpose.

On an individual level the desire for distinction might be stronger when an individual's innate uniqueness or distinctiveness is felt under threat. Equally on the level of the group, a need for social distinction in order to establish or strengthen social cohesion will manifest itself more strongly when it is felt that this cohesion is under threat. To what extent is the emergence of bilingualism the product of a defensive strategy? To whom has it to be made clear that, in the wording of one of the local historians: "Leixlip is not an ordinary village, but a village with a past?" As a member of the Resident Association tells:

> "Sometimes they are just going too far. One of the estates was built for the Intel/ HP-people, approximately 1000 houses and they want to call it 'Cyberplain'.... much to our annoyance. So then we made them change it. It is now called Rinawade and it was recently sold under that name." (Respondent J.–member, Resident Association)

Beside "Leixlip residents" there are "Intel/ HP people" as well, as the previous quote shows. While the latter may execute power in the *economic* domain, they might go too far when executing dominance in the *symbolic* domain: the possession of language, local symbols, and heritage.

The question of naming occurs again when recently the adjacent Rinawade House, a two storey traditional country farmhouse that once stood as an isolated farmhouse in a rural area west of Leixlip's Main Street, was planned to be demolished and replaced with 351 "residential units." A number of residents have opposed the plans. One of the objections includes the wish for bilingual street-names. In its reaction *An Bord Pleanála*, the national Planning Appeals Board, writes:

> "*Bilingual Street Names:* Representations on this matter would best be made to the Local Authority whose function lies in sanction of streetname proposals. The Board should therefore not concern itself with *such detail.*"[31] (second emphasis added)

A detail? On the national level the bilingual street names might occur as a detail. Yet on the local level, battling with the global, language as an instrument of symbolic power becomes of great importance.

If a bi-polar cultural variety can be observed in Leixlip, with an expansive identity on one hand versus an explanatory identity on the other hand, then do we find polarization instead of homogenization? Polarization tends to refer to an antagonistic situation, possibly culminating in a clash, as indeed in Huntington's *Clash of Civilizations*. If we do find a bi-polar variety yet not an overt clash, then the question arises how this clash is prevented. For while the fear of "losing it all" fuels the need for a local identity amongst the local residents, the same fear of "losing it all" drives the global players to pay for the local identity in an effort to prevent polarization, as is discussed in the next paragraph.

Economic globalization funds the local cultural identity

Involvement in the local community is an explicit part of Intel's policy. In the Department of Community Affairs four people and their manager work full-time on the relationship with the local community. Besides that, Intel has established what is called *Community Advisory Panel* (CAP), consisting of representative members of the local community.[32]

> "They come in here, every second month and they meet with Intel and tell Intel what we should be working on... so there is really a two-way communication..." (Respondent B–spokesperson Intel)

In the following quote of a former vice-president of Intel, the implicit power the community has over the multi-national is revealed, as much as the awareness of that power amongst the Intel management. For you only need one...

> I–"How are the people selected on the CAP?"
> RQ–"Well, that is interesting... because we try to get them involved in that... you know... I think we had a period of three years... and then we would get new people aboard... and we would get their advice on getting new people aboard... so that was extremely important... for if we did not have the community *with* us.... they can stop you.... They can stop you."
> I–"How can they stop you?"
> RQ–"They can stop you...by objecting you to move on to the next development."
> I–"Really? They still have the power..."
> RQ–"Oh yes! Absolutely! Under the Irish constitution, all you need is one."
> I–"One?"
> RQ–"One!"
> I–"One... person..."
> RQ–"That's correct! And they can pull it off for three to six months... construction... that would hold up the whole thing...(*disturbed*) you might be never be able to do it again...! (*Recalling*) Or you go somewhere else in the world..." (Respondent Q– former Vice-President Intel Ireland)

While the local community recreates its own identity driven by a fear of "losing it all" (the language, the local history, ultimately possibly the local autonomy), similarly the global company, fuelled by a comparable fear of "losing it all" (the progress, the expansion, the construction, the success, ultimately possibly the local power) is more than willing to support the creation of the new local identity.

As part of Intel's policy of local involvement, it supports many local projects that contribute to the reinforcement of the local identity. *The Walking Tour of Leixlip* (Kelly 2001) features a description of the town crest, a picture of the bilingual street names, a visit to William Roantree's House ("Leixlip's Famous Fenian"), and a page-large advertisement for Intel Ireland stating: "Intel Ireland are delighted to support the *Walking Tour of Leixlip Village*. We aim to earn the support of our local communities through being responsible, concerned and involved" (Kelly 2001: 50). Not only this: Intel also supports the annual Leixlip Festival that "pays tribute to our Viking and Gaelic past." In a picture of the festival a banner crosses the street: "*Intel is delighted to support the Leixlip Festival.*"

While the coming of processes of economic globalization not only creates the need for the construction of a local identity–seemingly as a defence against what is felt as the intrusion of a global culture–it also makes the very construction economically possible. In the process the local community reclaims its power over the creation of its own identity.

This mechanism is shown in the following example of the civil actions of the principal teacher of the primary Irish school in Leixlip. She is not just a teacher, but a fervent defender of the Irish language. And she is the gatekeeper to a significant consumer market as well: of over four hundred pupils. Whether she receives promotional material from Irish business or from global companies like Nestle, if the material is only in English she will return it.

> "We don't distribute materials in English only, they have to be either bilingual or monolingual in Irish. Some posters are in English only… so we will send them back to them *(laughs)*. I won't distribute them… No, I won't. *(firmly)* I won't put up the posters." (Respondent P–Teacher Irish School)

However, the Irish teacher does not just fight with national and global companies over the use of the Irish language, but with the Irish government as well.

> "We receive this all the time. Look here, this is from Irish Post. A project on Irish Stamps…*(she shows the brochure, titled: "All about Irish Stamps")* All the material is in English. Look this. This is a poster for Irish Roads Safety Awareness poster… in English. Is not produced in Irish. They come daily. I have a standard letter. And if I have time… I send them off." (Respondent P–Teacher Irish School)

While there is apparently no national policy to provide all promotional material bilingually, this case suggests a stronger awareness of the importance of the national language and indeed the national identity on the local level than on a national level. The local, confronted with processes of globalization, searches for an identity through the re-implementation of the national language that locally maybe never existed and that nationally is deemed less relevant. However, at the same time the one who might be the implicit source of a diffuse felt threat obediently facilitates the need for distinction.

> I–"Have you ever received anything from Intel in English, to distribute in the school?"
> RP–"Oh they know… I have… but they know now…. that I won't…ehm… distribute that. So they prepare them especially…while often they fax me something to check or to approve it first. They will issue certificates in Irish… they do. All the competitions and the literature they produce is in Irish. … because we asked them. Also they don't want to…. well they are not going to leave us out, to exclude us from any of their education activities, just for the sake of not putting themselves into the trouble of not making out things in Irish… because we are big…" (emphasis added) (Respondent P– Teacher Irish School)

Suddenly the global company is no longer the big company and no longer is the school an ordinary school: "We are big," the principal teacher explains, implying that they can exert power over the global company through the use of the indigenous language, not as much as an instrument for communication but as a symbolic possession–almost as a weapon. For you only need one.

Conclusions: the resilience of cultural diversity

Just as the cultural logic of the emerging world society might not follow the logic of traditional societies as embedded within the boundaries of the nation-state, the cultural logic of global civil society might intrinsically differ from a civil society with "realms outside the power of the state" (Hann 1996: 5). Paradoxically, as I argue, within a global context local civil society reinvents the nation-state as a buffer against what is felt as a global penetration of the local community. Cultural homogeneity then is not intrinsic to globalization, just as globalization is not identical to the global expansion of American-based multi-nationals. On the contrary, rather than following a singular, in many ways deterministic, logic associated with global capitalism, globalization refers to the complexity of all those processes and actions incorporating the peoples of the world into one world society.

While examining the hypothesis that processes of economic globalization will lead to homogeneity in the cultural field, this research did not find such evidence. If sameness is a prerequisite for predictability and distinction a source for surprise, the surprising finding of this empirical research is that no evidence was found indicating an erosion of diversity sacrificed on the altar of homogeneity. Instead local cultural diversity[33] emerges, as the case-study of Leixlip in Co. Kildare shows, the town with one of the highest proportions of per capita foreign direct investment, located in the nation state with one of the most globalized economies in the world: the Republic of Ireland.

Huntington argues when rejecting the homogeneity thesis that the end of the Soviet empire and of the Cold War promoted the proliferation and rejuvenation of languages which had been suppressed or forgotten (Huntington 1996: 64), such as Estonian, Latvian, Lithuanian, Ukrainian, Georgian and Armenian, now the national languages of independent states. These language revivals occured shortly after or simultaneously with the nation-states. Yet the Irish nation-state is not recently established, albeit the Irish language revival can be placed within a history of oppression by the British Empire.

Just as homogeneity cannot be attributed solely to the global market players, diversity is not exclusively the product of the local civil society. Rather the emerging local identity is a multi-layered, triangular *Gesamt* creation of social agents within local civil society, the global multi-nationals and the (national) government, in processes characterized by mutual dependency.

The *global cultural assemblage* is created on the micro-level, quintessentially fuelled by the fear of "losing it all." Yet the newly created local identity quickly becomes the domain of the global. Through the channels of globalization, the local identity is distributed in an unprecedented mechanism of globalized local diversity world-wide.

The local historians sell their history books via the Internet to people throughout the world who somehow have a connection with Leixlip. Similarly, Intel disperses the locally generated expertise globally. The concept of a *Community Advisory Panel*, having started in Intel Ireland in 1992, is now implemented in nine Intels worldwide: Arizona, Oregon, Colorado, Ireland, Israel, Malaysia, Massachusetts, New Mexico and the Philippines.[34]

And what is Intel's latest trade-mark slogan? "Intel. Leap Ahead." Indeed, that reminds us of the motto of Leixlip's Town Crest that was shortly formulated after Intel's arrival in Leixlip: Léim ar Aghaidh, or Irish for "Leap Forward!" The local defines its own identity, feeling threatened by the global. More than fifteen years later, the global company uses the local identity that it has provoked to define itself in the global field. In the domain of the global the local comes alive, confirming the resilience of cultural diversity and the deep-felt intrinsic human need for uniqueness. Maybe globalization's biggest challenge is to bring forth unity in diversity, after all. Maybe that is the leap forward.

Notes

[1] This research would not have been possible without the support of the Royal Irish Academy Third Sector Research Program and of the Prince Bernhard Foundation, in Amsterdam. I am grateful to the Institute for International Integration Studies, Trinity College for the research facilities. I want to thank Prof Dr. R.J. Holton, head of Department of Sociology, Trinity College Dublin for his valuable comments on earlier drafts. I want to thank Prof Dr. Frances Ruane, former director Institute for International Integrations Studies of Trinity College Dublin and currently Director of the Economic and Social Research Institute in Dublin for her valuable help with the empirical research. I also want to thank the World Society Foundation in Zurich for all their ongoing support. I want to especially thank Dr. Mark Herkenrath for valuable comments on earlier drafts of this article and for the good teamwork.

[2] The literature tends to call multinationals "transnationals." I do not agree with that qualification as it suggests a footlessness that is often not justified. There is no doubt that both Intel and Hewlett-Packard are American-based multinationals and not just rootless transnational companies without conflicting loyalties between country and corporation. Conflicting loyalties between corporation, country, and indeed family are expressed in the words of Intel CEO Craig Barrett when he states in an interview with the Times of India "Intel will go where it will find talent. But I worry for the United States and I worry for my grandchildren." Source: Times of India, Sunday March 6th 2005. http://www1.timesofindia.indiatimes.com/articleshow/1042610.cms / 26 February 2006.

³ With the Dialectic Globalization Framework I propose to distinguish three main dialectics within theories on globalization: firstly I see a discrepancy between those who approach globalization-as-a-condition and a feature of modern reality versus those who visualize globalization-as-a-process. Secondly, I make a distinction between those who approach globalization-as-futurology and those who study globalization-as-reality. The third dialectic is seen as between a one-dimensional and a multi-dimensional approach to globalization (Van Der Bly 2005).
⁴ Too often globalization is portrayed as a mythical force, a Deus ex Machina to some and the invisible torturing poltergeist to others. Or, as what Hirst and Thompson (1996) have called a "contemporary myth" to allay fears for economic forces, as ancient myths were a way of masking and compensating for humanity's helplessness in the face of power of nature. Progress of science has contributed to the loss of some of our helplessness in the face of nature's powers. How can we now allow ourselves helplessness when faced with human forces seemingly spiraling out of control? The myth of globalization can only be demystified through explicitly investigating individual agency.
⁵ The other main processes of economic globalization that can be distinguished are the movement of people (migration and tourism) and of knowledge (e.g. Internet).
⁶ As Harré (1976) argues the risk of intensive research includes a total failure of the conceptual framework to be conceivable, while extensive research can always report some results. However, a choice for theoretical sampling minimizes that risk. The disadvantage of theoretical sampling is that the research population is explicitly *not* representative for the larger population. Yet one might wonder, how could any sample be representative for processes on a world scale, where the population includes the world population? This research did not aim to extrapolate results from a sample to a larger population. With intensive research I aimed to unravel the social mechanisms of globalization within the situation in which the researched persons act. The aim of generalisation is then to investigate to what extent these social mechanisms can be extrapolated to other situations in which processes of globalization occur similarly.
⁷ I.e. the research area is selected based upon the hypothetical model and presents results accordingly.
⁸ The *Globalization Index (2001-2004)* ranked for three successive years the Republic of Ireland on the first place (A.T/ Kearney / Foreign Policy Magazine 2001-2004).
⁹ Between 2002 and 2005.
¹⁰ Further in this research referred to as "Ireland".
¹¹ Between 8 October 2003 and 31 October 2005 and including participant observation, over twenty in-depth interviews with key-representatives in the area, thirty-five short interviews, visual analysis, document-analysis, and secondary analysis of census-material
¹² But was lost after the building of a dam in 1947 (Nelson 1990).
¹³ From 2,424 in 1971 to 11,938 in 1986. In 2002 15,016. (CSO 1981-2002).
¹⁴ http://www.intel.com/ireland/about/thesite/index.htm. 22 October 2005.
¹⁵ Information provided by Head Government and Public Affairs Officer Hewlett-Packard Ireland, d.d. 22-3-2004.
¹⁶ Brady, Shipman, Martin (2002: 1) "Leixlip Town Center Study. Prepared for Kildare County Council." Final report November 2002.
¹⁷ Op. cit. p 2.
¹⁸ "Firms considering opening production facilities in other countries, to a considerably greater extent than those remaining ate home, face uncertainties about how well the operations will actually run. (...) In these circumstances firms have a strong incentive to observe each others' decisions. (...) And this mutual observation can cause a tendency for investment to concentrate in few destinations, over and above the usual external economy arguments" (Krugman 1997: 49).
¹⁹ Albeit of a banal variety (Billig 1995).

[20] But by Diageo, a London based multinational. "Diageo is a global company, trading in over 180 markets around the world. The company is listed on both the London Stock Exchange (DGE) and the New York Stock Exchange (DEO). (...) Diageo was formed in 1997, following the merger of Guinness and GrandMet and is headquartered in London. The word Diageo comes from the Latin for day (dia) and the Greek for world (geo). We take this to mean every day, everywhere, people celebrate with our brands." http://www.diageo.com, 26 February 2006.

[21] However, the flagging of "banal localism" cannot be separated from nationalism, as the national history has shaped the local history and according to the inhabitants the local has increasingly defined the national history, as shown through the example of Guinness.

[22] http://www.kildare.ie/Leixlip. 26 February 2006.

[23] In 1990 the *Irish Countrywomen's Association* published *Leixlip: a local history* (1990), and Gerard Nelson's *A History of Leixlip, Co. Kildare* (Nelson 1990). In 2001 local historian Seamus Kelly produced a *Walking Tour of Leixlip*, supported by Intel Ireland. In 2005 John Colgan, who lives in the former Toll House opposite the Salmon Leap Inn, published an ambitious study on the local history, also sponsored by Intel (Colgan 2005). The website of the town publishes a large section on the local history http://kildare.ie/leixlip, written by John Wigle.

[24] Kelly (2002: 32).

[25] William Roantree lived from 1829-1918 (Kelly 2002: 32).

[26] The first time that the question was included in the Census was in 1981.

[27] During the period in which this research was carried out.

[28] What is remarkable is the wording the respondent chooses when describing that Leixlip was part of the Pale: it was *deemed* to be in the Pale, by some whim of fate. This reflects a negative perception of what it means to be part of the Pale: not something to be proud of. Some of the reasons why this respondent has a negative perception of being part of the Pale are given in this quote as well. For albeit "they" (the English) provided local employment, it was the kind of employment meant to serve them: "to cut their turf.... Harvest their crops...servants." "We" carried out the work, but "they" owned the land. Ireland's colonial past is still very much alive in the contemporary discourse of respondents, even when that past seems dead and buried in Ireland contemporary prosperity.

[29] "Question: IF 'Yes'. Do you speak Irish 'Daily, Weekly, Often, Never?' (CSO, 1981-2002).

[30] According to information provided by the principal teacher, 17 March 2004.

[31] Inspector's Report An Bord Pleanála "Demolish existing house and construct 351 residential units, at Leixlip, County Kildare," August 2004.

[32] Intel Public Affairs *"CAP Handbook"* (2004) Compiled from worldwide input by the CRC CAP Subteam. Feb 2004. Internal report.

[33] Manifestations of cultural homogeneity referring to mass media are not included in this research.

[34] Intel Public Affairs *"CAP Handbook"* (2004) Compiled from worldwide input by the CRC CAP Subteam. Feb 2004. Internal report.

References

Albrow, Martin and King, Elizabeth (eds). 1990. *Globalization, Knowledge and Society*. London, UK: Sage.

Billig, Michael. 1995. *Banal Nationalism*. London, UK: Sage.

Central Statistics Office Ireland. 1981-2002. *Small Area Population Statistics (SAPS) 1981-2002*, Dublin, Ireland: CSO.

Colgan, John. 2005. *Leixlip, County Kildare. Vol. 1*. Leixlip, Ireland: Tyrconnell Press.
Connor, Walker. 1993. "Beyond Reason: the Nature of the Ethno-national Bond." *Ethnic and Racial Studies* 16: 373-89.
Friedman, Thomas L. 2000. *The Lexus and the Olive Tree*. New York, NY: Anchor Books.
Hann, Chris and Elizabeth Dunn (eds.) 1996. *Civil Society. Challenging Western Models*. London, UK: Routledge.
Harré, Romano and Paul F. Secord. 1976. *The Explanation of Social Behaviour*. Oxford, UK: Blackwell.
Hertz, Noreena. 2001. *The Silent Take Over. Global Capitalism and the Death of Democracy*. London, UK: Heinemann.
Hirst, Paul Q. and Grahame Thompson. 1996. *Globalization in Question: the International Economy and the Possibilities of Governance*. Houndmills, UK: Palgrave Macmillian.
Huntington, Samuel P. 1997. *The Clash of Civilizations and the Remaking of World Order*. London, UK: Simon & Schuster.
Kearny, Andrew T. / Foreign Policy. 2002. "Globalization Index 2002." *Foreign Policy*, Jan-Feb 2002: 2-15.
Kearny, Andrew. T. / Foreign Policy. 2003. "Globalization Index 2003." *Foreign Policy*, Jan-Feb 2003: 60-72.
Kearny, Andrew T. / Foreign Policy. 2004. "Globalization Index 2004." *Foreign Policy*, March-April 2004: 54-69.
Kelly, Samuel. 2001. *A Walking Tour of Leixlip*. Leixlip, Ireland: Samuel Kelly.
Krugman, Paul R. 1997. "Good News from Ireland. A Geographical Perspective. *International Perspectives on the Irish economy*. Alan W. Gray (ed). Dublin, Ireland, Indecon Economic Consultants: 38-53.
McLuhan, Marshall. 1968. *War and Peace in the Global Village*. New York, NY, London, UK: Bantan.
Nelson, Gerald. 1990. *A History of Leixlip, Co. Kildare*. Leixlip, Ireland: Kildare County Library.
Ritzer, George.1995. *The McDonaldization of Society*. Thousand Oaks, CA and London, UK: Pine Forge Press.
Sloterdijk, Peter. 2005. *Im Weltinnenraum des Kapitals*. Frankfurt Am Main, Germany: Suhrkamp Verlag.
Smith, Anthony D. 1986. *The Ethnic Origins of Nations*. Oxford, UK: Basil Blackwell.
Van Der Bly, Martha C.E. 2005. "Globalization: A Triumph of Ambiguity." *Current Sociology* 53 (6): 875-893.
Wallerstein, Immanuel. 1979. *The Capitalist World Economy; Essays*. Cambridge, UK: Cambridge University Press.

Contributors

Xiangming Chen
Center of Urban and Global Studies,
Trinity College at Hartford

Yves Aléxandre Chouala
International Relations Institute of
Cameroon & Group of Administrative,
Political and Social Research,
University of Yaoundé II-Soa

John Gulick
Deptartment of Sociology,
University of Tennessee-Knoxville

Mark Herkenrath
Sociological Institute,
University of Zurich
& World Society Foundation, Zurich

Rafael Reuveny
School of Public and
Environmental Affairs,
Indiana University

Amir Sheikhzadegan
Sociological Institute,
University of Zurich

Jackie Smith
Department of Sociology,
University of Notre Dame

William R. Thompson
Department of Political Science,
Indiana University

Martha C.E. Van Der Bly
Centre for the Study of Global
Governance, London School
of Economics and Political
Science

Dawn Wiest
Department of Sociology,
University of Notre Dame

Patrick Ziltener
Sociological Institute,
University of Zurich